"Caught up in the frenzy of just being there, we have all been c[illegible] the possibilities the Net offers in a one-to-one world of idea and transactional commerce. Many have planted expensive seeds on the Net with the hope that they will germinate into something of value. Greenspun has thoroughly captured the logic of what can win from the viewpoint of both the creator, who may be, and the viewer, who is, king. Information and ideas can serve lofty purposes but without organization, tools to easily mine and find, and an audience to share and view, there is no purpose."

—Mark Miller
Executive Vice President & General Manager, Hearst Magazines

"Philip Greenspun interfaced our 60 GB Oracle medical record database to the Web in 1994. It took him three weeks and all it cost me was a 4 GB hard disk and some SIMMs for his Macintosh. Since then, Greenspun has become too rich and famous to write Perl anymore. I'm going to use this book to train some high school kids to replace him."

—Isaac S. Kohane, M.D., Ph.D.
Director, Children's Hospital Informatics Program

"Smart companies are using the Web to support collaboration. Smarter companies will be using the Web to support computer-to-computer transactions. Philip Greenspun has written the first book that explains how to do both elegantly."

—Mort Myerson, Chairman of Perot Systems Corporation

"IBM has been working for 20 years to build high performance relational database management systems. This book gives you field-tested ideas and techniques to unlock the data and deliver it to users across the Internet."

—John Patrick
Vice President of Internet Technology, IBM

"Greenspun's prize-winning and colorful Web publishing experience is as old as the Web and a must for all aspiring Web publishers.

—Michael L. Dertouzos
Director MIT Laboratory for Computer Science
Author of *What Will Be*

"There are a lot of books that will tell you how to design a web site that looks like something else—a computer game, or a print magazine—which would be great if web pages *were* computer games or print magazines. They aren't. Read this book to find out what they are"

—Robert S. Thau, Ph.D., author of the Apache httpd server

"This is the first book on RDBMS-backed Web sites that an intelligent programmer can enjoy."

—Doug McKee, Manager, Web Server Development, America OnLine

Database Backed Web Sites:

The Thinking Person's Guide to Web Publishing

DATABASE BACKED WEB SITES:

THE THINKING PERSON'S GUIDE TO WEB PUBLISHING

Philip Greenspun

Ziff-Davis Press
An imprint of Macmillan Computer Publishing USA
Emeryville, California

Publisher	Stacy Hiquet
Associate Publisher	Steven Sayre
Acquisitions Editor	Simon Hayes
Development Editor	Paula Hardin
Copy Editor	Kim Haglund
Technical Reviewer	Jin Choi
Proofreader	Jeff Barash
Cover Illustration and Design	Megan Gandt
Book Design	Bruce Lundquist
Page Layout	Janet Piercy
Indexer	Christine Spina

Ziff-Davis Press, ZD Press, and the Ziff-Davis Press logo are trademarks or registered trademarks of, and are licensed to Macmillan Computer Publishing USA by Ziff-Davis Publishing Company, New York, New York.

Ziff-Davis Press imprint books are produced on a Macintosh computer system with the following applications: FrameMaker®, Microsoft® Word, QuarkXPress®, Adobe Illustrator®, Adobe Photoshop®, Adobe Streamline™, MacLink®*Plus*, Aldus® FreeHand™, Collage Plus™.

Ziff-Davis Press, an imprint of
Macmillan Computer Publishing USA
5903 Christie Avenue
Emeryville, CA 94608

ISBN 1-56276-530-2

Manufactured in the United States of America
10 9 8 7 6 5 4 3 2 1

CONTENTS AT A GLANCE

1	Envisioning a Site That Won't Be Featured in suck.com	1
2	So You Want to Join the World's Grubbiest Club: Internet Entrepreneurs	12
3	Learn to Program HTML in 21 Minutes	32
4	Adding Images to Your Site	44
5	Publicizing Your Site (Without Irritating Everyone on the Net)	66
6	So You Want to Run Your Own Server	80
7	Learning from Server Logs	110
8	Java and Shockwave—The <BLINK> Tag Writ Large	132
9	Sites That Are Really Programs	148
10	When Is a Site Really a Database?	168
11	Relational Databases	180
12	Interfacing a Relational Database to the Web	214
13	Case Studies	252
14	Sites That Don't Work (And How to Fix Them)	308
15	A Future So Bright You'll Need to Wear Sunglasses	332
	Index	354

Table of Contents

Chapter 1 Envisioning a Site That Won't Be Featured in suck.com 1

You Can't Say "Web Publishing" without the Word "Publishing" 1

Example 1: Personal Home Page 2

Example 2: Camera Manufacturer 3

Example 3: Software Company 3

How Do You Know When You Are Done? 4

Become Illiterate (That Is, Present Multiple Views) 4

Think of the Web as Primary 7

Summary 11

Chapter 2 So You Want to Join the World's Grubbiest Club: Internet Entrepreneurs 12

The Steam Engine and the Railroad 14

Four Ways to Make Money from Your Site 15

Travel Example 22

Real Estate Example 23

Medical Example 23

We Lose Money on Every Hit But Make It Up on Volume 24

A Final Plea 27

Chapter 3 Learn to Program HTML in 21 Minutes 32

"One of Our Local Webmasters" 33

You May Already Have Won $1 Million 34

Document Structure 35

Now That You Know How to Write HTML, Don't 38

It's Hard to Mess Up a Simple Page 39

Why Graphic Designers Just Don't Get It 41

Summary 42

Chapter 4 Adding Images to Your Site 44

Are Net Users Really That Shallow? 45

Images on the Web Can Look Better Than on a Magazine Page 46

Start By Thinking about Building an Image Library 47

Using Kodak PhotoCD to Manage Your Image Library 47

Delivering Your Library to the Web 49

If It Worked You Wouldn't Want It 49

In Any Case, It Doesn't Work 49

Maybe You Want Flashpix 50

Choosing between GIF and JPEG 53

Creating GIF and JPEG from PhotoCD Image Pacs 53

Using Photoshop 53

Using Unix Tools 56

Organizing JPEGs on Your Web Server 61

Adding Images to Your Web Pages 62

Summary 63

Chapter 5 Publicizing Your Site (Without Irritating Everyone on the Net) 66

Search Engines 67

How Search Engines Look to the User 67

How Search Engines Work 68

Component 1: The Crawler (or "How to Get Listed by a Search Engine") 68

Component 2: The Full-Text Indexer 70

Component 3:User Query Processor 71

How to Stand Tall in the Search Engines 71

How Many Users Are You Getting from Search Engines? 72

Improving Your Pages' Chances Honestly (and Dishonestly) 74

And Now the Dishonest Part 75
Hiding Your Content from Search Engines (Intentionally) 75
Hiding Your Content from Search Engines (By Mistake) 76
Web Directories 77
Final Tip 78
Summary 78
Chapter 6 So You Want to Run Your Own Server 80
My Personal Choice 82
Choosing a Computer 84
Unix 85
Which Brand of Unix Box? 88
Windows NT 89
Unix versus NT 91
Final Hardware Selection Note 93
Server Software 93
API 93
RDBMS Connectivity 95
Support and Source Code Availability 95
Availability of Shrink-wrapped Plug-ins 96
Speed 97
AOLserver (a.k.a. GNNserver, NaviServer) 97
Apache 99
Netscape Enterprise/FastTrack 99
Oracle WebServer 2.0 103
Connectivity 104
ISDN 104
Your First T1 106
Cable Modems and ADSL 107
The Big Picture 108

Chapter 7 Learning from Server Logs 110

Case Studies 112

"I Want to Know How Many Users Requested Non-existent Files and Where They Got the Bad File Names." 112

"I Want to Know How Many People Are Looking at Chapter 3 of http://webtravel.org/samantha/." 113

"I Want to Know How Long the Average Reader of Chapter 3 Spends before Moving on to Chapter 4." 115

"I Sold a Banner Ad to Sally's Sad Saab Shop. I Want to Know How Many People Clicked on the Banner and Went Over to Her Site." 116

"I Want to Know the Age, Sex, and Zip Code of Every Person Who Visited My Site So That I Can Prepare a Brochure for Advertisers." 121

Case Studies Conclusions 125

Let's Back Up for a Minute 125

Enter the Log Analyzer 126

wwwstat 127

WebReporter 128

Relational Database-backed Tools 128

Summary 130

Chapter 8 Java and Shockwave—The <BLINK> Tag Writ Large 132

What Java Is 133

What It Is (Also) 136

What It Is (New Techno Stuff) 138

Too Bad It Doesn't Work 139

The 1970s 139

The 1980s 139

The 1990s 140

The Future So Bright You'll Need to Wear Sunglasses 140

You Need These Things 140

Encouragement 141
Using Java Applets on the Web 141
Animation Can Be Useful 142
When Java Makes Sense 142
Richer User Interface 143
Real-time Response 143
Real-time Updates 143
An Inspiring Example 144
Finally . . . Don't Get Too Excited by the Rich User Interface 146

Chapter 9 Sites That Are Really Programs 148

CGI Scripting 150
A Very Simple Perl CGI Script 151
My Unix Box Does Not Like to Fork 500,000 Times a Day 151
My RDBMS Does Not Like to Be Opened and Closed 500,000 Times a Day 152
Server APIs 152
AOLserver Example: Redirect 153
AOLserver Example: Bill Gates Personal Wealth Clock 155
The Right Way—Extending HTML 161
Server-parsed HTML 162
HTML as a Programming Language 163
Summary 166

Chapter 10 When Is a Site Really a Database? 168

The Hard Part 171

Step 1: The Data Model 171

Step 2: Legal Transactions 171

Step 3: Mapping Transactions onto Web Forms 171

The Easy Part 172

Prototyping the Site, My Theory 172

Prototyping the Site, the Reality 173

Do I Need a College Education to Understand Your System? 173

Why Don't Customers Wise Up? 174

Is There a Better Way? 176

Just Say No to Middleware 177

Summary 178

Chapter 11 Relational Databases 180

What's Wrong with a File System (and Also What's Right) 181

What Do You Need for Transaction Processing? 183

Finding Your Data (and Fast) 184

Enter the Relational Database 185

How Does This RDBMS Thing Work? 187

SQL the Hard Way 193

Brave New World 197

Braver New World 201

Choosing an RDBMS Vendor 202

Paying an RDBMS Vendor 203

Performance 204

Don't Forget to Back Up 206

Reliability 208

If You Hire an ISP, Buy the Right Service 210

What I Did for Myself 210

Summary 213

Chapter 12 Interfacing a Relational Database to the Web 214

How Does an RDBMS Talk to the Rest of the World? 215
How to Make Really Fast RDBMS-Backed Web Sites 219
CORBA: MiddleWare Meets VaporWare 222
Complexity (or "It Probably Won't Work") 223
What If It Did Work? 223
Aren't Objects the Way to Go? 224
Security 225
What Does This Stuff Look Like? 228
Server-side Web/RDBMS Products 233
Oracle WebServer 2.0 233
Informix Web DataBlade 236
Every Page a Transaction 239
Web Blade Workaround 1: EXEC Perl 239
Web Blade Workaround 2: Convert to AOL server 239
Web Blade Workaround 3: Convert to Meta-HTML 240
Web Blade Bottom Line 240
Netscape LiveWire 241
Meta-HTML 241
WebObjects, Microsoft IIS, and Others 242
AOLserver 243
Choosing 244
Bring in Da Noise, Bring in Da Junk 245
Canned Web Server Admin Pages 248
Spreadsheet-like Access 248
Forms Builders 248
Connecting 249
ODBC 250
Summary 251

Chapter 13 Case Studies **252**

Case 1: The Mailing List 254

Step 1: The Data Model 254

Step 2: Legal Transactions 254

Step 3: Mapping Transactions onto Web Forms 255

Step 4: Writing Code to Process the Forms 256

Case 2: The Mailing List 261

Case 3: The Birthday Reminder System 264

Step 1: The Data Model 265

Step 2: Legal Transactions 267

Step 3: Mapping Transactions onto Web Forms 269

Step 4: Writing Code to Process the Forms 269

Step 5: Step 5? 275

Case 4: The Bulletin Board 279

Can 30 Million Usenet Users Really Be Wrong? 281

Step 1: The Data Model 282

Step 2: Legal Transactions 283

Step 3: Mapping Transactions onto Web Forms 284

Step 4: Writing Code to Process the Forms 288

Case 5: The Bulletin Board (Again) 288

Step 1: The Data Model 288

Step 2: Legal Transactions 291

Step 3: Mapping Transactions onto Web Forms 291

Step 4: Writing Code to Process the Forms 292

Case 6: The Bulletin Board (Full-text Indexed) 294

Case 7: Classified Ads 295

Classifieds Idea: Categorize 297

Classifieds Idea: Automatic Management 298

Classifieds Idea: E-mail Alerts 298

Classifieds Idea: Show Off New Ads 298

Classifieds Idea: Auction 298

Steps 1–4 298

The Cover Page 300
The Auction System 306
Summary 307

Chapter 14 Sites That Don't Work (And How to Fix Them) 308

User Feedback 309
Category 1: How to Scan? 316
Category 2: General Photography Questions 316
Category 3: How to Make My Life As Cool As Yours? 319
But What about Comments? (Loquacious, Version 1.0) 319
Loquacious, Version 2.0 321
Loquacious, Version 3.0 325
Related Links 325
No Dead Links 327
Instant Updates 327
Spam Resistance 327
Distributed Management 328
How Does It Work? 328
General Lessons 329

Chapter 15 A Future So Bright You'll Need to Wear Sunglasses 332

Should Software Really Be Sold Like Tables and Chairs? 335
The Nub 335
Johnny the User 336
Amanda the User Interface Programmer 336
Joey the Image Editor Programmer 336
Adobe the Software Publisher 337
Choices Summary 337
A Better Way 337
Johnny the User 337

Amanda the User Interface Programmer 337
Joey the Image Editor Programmer 338
Adobe the Software Publisher 338
New World Order 338
A Less Radical Approach 339
Privacy 339
We Have a Network; We Can Do Better 339
Your User's Browser: a GE Range 340
Product Engineering: Theory versus Reality 340
What Kinds of Things Can Happen in a Networked House? 341
What Does This Mean to Me As a Web Publisher? 341
Personalization 342
Reader Ratings: A Big Mistake? 344
Client-side Personalization 346
What Does This Mean to Me As a Web Publisher? 347
Collaboratively Exchanged Data Models 348
Collaboratively Evolved Data Models 351
Grand Conclusion 352
Index **354**

Acknowledgments

Common courtesy demands that I thank all of the people who've generously given their time over the years to educate me about the Web and RDBMS. However, as deadly boring as the average computer book may be, the acknowledgments are inevitably far more boring. I have only ever seen one acknowledgments page with a scintilla of literary value, that for the Scheme Shell Reference Manual. I reprint it here in hopes of starting a refreshing trend toward all computer book authors reprinting this acknowledgment rather than thanking their families, dogs, editors, and so on.

> Who should I thank? My so-called "colleagues," who laugh at me behind my back, all the while becoming famous on my work? My worthless graduate students, whose computer skills appear to be limited to downloading bitmaps off of netnews? My parents, who are still waiting for me to quit "fooling around with computers," go to med school, and become a radiologist? My department chairman, a manager who gives one new insight into and sympathy for disgruntled postal workers?
>
> My God, no one could blame me—no one!—if I went off the edge and just lost it completely one day. I couldn't get through the day as it is without the Prozac and Jack Daniels I keep on the shelf, behind my Tops-20 JSYS manuals. I start getting the shakes real bad around 10 A.M., right before my advisor meetings. A 10 oz. Jack 'n Zac helps me get through the meetings without one of my students winding up with his severed head in a bowling-ball bag. They look at me funny; they think I twitch a lot. I'm not twitching. I'm controlling my impulse to snag my 9 mm Sig-Sauer out from my day-pack and make a few strong points about the quality of undergraduate education in Amerika.
>
> If I thought anyone cared, if I thought anyone would even be reading this, I'd probably make an effort to keep up appearances until the last possible moment. But no one does, and no one will. So I can pretty much say exactly what I think.
>
> Oh yes, the acknowledgments. I think not. I did it. I did it all, by myself.
>
> — Olin Shivers
>
> Cambridge, September 4, 1994

Well, I guess Olin thought it was easier than explaining why he had written a program to let people drive a 23-year-old operating system (UNIX) in a 35-year-old computer language (Lisp) ....

Envisioning a Site That Won't Be Featured in suck.com

You Can't Say "Web Publishing" without the Word "Publishing"

Become Illiterate (That Is, Present Multiple Views)

Think of the Web as Primary

Chapter 1

This is a book about how to be a nerd. A book about how to make a Web server on a cheap computer serve a million hits every day. About how to write clever programs that collect data from Web users and stuff them into a relational database. About how to add thousands of images to your Web site in a few minutes. About how to get serious about user interface design for Web sites.

Before ascending into Nerd Heaven, though, I thought it was worth two chapters to step back and ask, "Why did the world buy 10 million expensive computers and connect them together?" Was it really so that a kid in Botswana could look at a flashing GIF 89a logo from a Honda repair shop in Sunnyvale, California? And, if we don't think that is true, how should we design sites?

An alternative formulation of this question is "How can I design a site that won't be featured at http://suck.com?"

You Can't Say "Web Publishing" without the Word "Publishing"

When you put up a Web site, you are publishing. Virtually all of the important decisions that you must make are publishing decisions. Eventually you will have to select technology to support those decisions, but that is a detail.

Start by putting yourself in your users' shoes. Why are they coming to your site? If you look at most Web sites, you'd presume that the answer is "User is extremely bored and wishes to stare at a blank screen for several minutes while a flashing icon loads, then stare at the flashing icon for a few more minutes."

Academic computer scientists refer to this process of fitting software systems to people as "user modeling."

Slightly more content-rich sites are based on the user model of "User wants to look at product brochures" or "User wants to look at fancy graphics." After pulling the server logs for the sites that reflect these user models, though, it is tough to have much faith in them.

Think about it for a minute: If a user wanted a flashing computer screen and confusing user interface, he could stuff a CD-ROM into the drive. He could get an even more enticing show without the crummy user interface by picking up his television remote control and flipping channels. If a user wanted product brochures, he could get them by calling manufacturers or visiting shops. If a user wanted fancy graphics, he could flip through dozens of pages' worth in a print magazine in the amount of time it would take to load a single corporate Web page.

Users come to Web sites because they have questions. They are not bored losers. You are not doing them a favor by putting a product brochure online or showing them some huge logo GIF. They are doing you a favor by visiting your Web site. They are paying to visit your Web site, if not exactly with money then at least with their time. You have to give them something of value or they will never come back. Ever.

If you can anticipate user questions and make sure that your site answers them, then you will be a successful Web publisher.

EXAMPLE 1: PERSONAL HOME PAGE

Suppose that you are building a humble personal home page. Why would a user come to your page? Someone might be trying to contact you or send you a package. So you obviously need to include your phone number, mailing address, and, perhaps, fax number. Perhaps you've invited some people to your house for a party and they don't know how to get there; they can't call you because you're out shopping for bagels. So you should have a map to your house (I just made my home address a hyperlink to the Yahoo map server).

Imagine that a friend of yours is at a party talking to Dale, a beautiful member of whatever sex you happen to fancy. Your friend is describing your charity, great humanity, and kindness to animals. Dale, however, won't agree to meet you without seeing a photo first. So you'd better hope that there is a portrait of you somewhere on your home page before Dale and your friend stroll over to the WebTV.

Or imagine that you've given an interview to a reporter on deadline. It is 2 a.m. when the reporter realizes he forgot to ask you for some background biographical information. You'll be getting a wake-up call unless you remembered to put a copy of your resume online.

At this point, some people might object that this information is too, well, *personal* for a personal home page. The Internet frightens them. Sure, their phone number is listed, and the price they paid for their house is public information. And their credit record is open to almost anyone who cares. But they think that if their name is known to an Internet search engine, suddenly all of the privacy that they supposedly formerly had will evaporate. Well, my home phone number has been available via the Internet for 20 years, and my Web site gets about 500,000 hits a day. I include a picture of myself naked with my old dog George and maps to my house and office on my site. And just as I typed that last period, sitting in what I thought was the privacy of my own home, someone I didn't know called me up. At 8:20 p.m. on a Monday. Would I make a donation to the March of Dimes?

Probably about 1 percent of my unsolicited phone calls are from readers of my Web site. Surprisingly enough, people who find me on the Internet seem to send e-mail instead. Go figure.

EXAMPLE 2: CAMERA MANUFACTURER

Suppose instead that you make cameras for consumers. Why would a user come to your page? Possibly to look at brochures, so it might be nice to have some advertising literature on your site. But the most important users are existing customers, such as someone who is traveling with a fancy Nikon single-lens reflex and has forgotten how to work the flash. Caught without the owner's manual, this customer has surfed in from an Internet café hoping to find the full text online.

Someone with a broken camera will want to know how to get it fixed and how much it will cost. So you'll want to put up maps to your service centers, warranty details, and prices for out-of-warranty repairs. Your site is a natural focal point for customers to meet, interact, and share their experiences with each other. So you should have moderated Q&A forums, bulletin boards, and classified ads where your customers can contribute.

EXAMPLE 3: SOFTWARE COMPANY

Everything that I said about the camera manufacturer goes for the software company as well. However, the camera maker is under no obligation to demonstrate an understanding of the Internet. But if you are in the computer business, you can't afford to have your customers say "My 10-year-old built a better Web site than that last week."

All of your documentation must be online and current. Demonstration programs, ideally running on the server or as Java applets, should be available.

Customers ought to be able to purchase and download everything that you sell. If you can't use the Internet effectively, then why would anyone believe that you are capable of doing anything with computers effectively?

HOW DO YOU KNOW WHEN YOU ARE DONE?

You can objectively measure how well your site meets user needs. Are you getting a lot of e-mail questions? As soon as two users ask the same question, you should beef up your site to answer it unattended: Build a page, fix the navigation model, or tune your search engine.

Since you are a competent webmaster, you are running a full-text search engine on your site. Why not hack the CGI scripts so that the search engine sends you e-mail when a query results in zero matches. Given information about which user queries are failing, you can add content or keywords as appropriate.

At this point you can relax. You aren't a loser with a big budget, a lot of ugly graphics, and no traffic. Users are not leaving your site in frustration, shaking their heads, and saying "They just don't get it." Now that you are safe from the wags at suck.com, what can you do to make your site site fulfill its potential?

BECOME ILLITERATE (THAT IS, PRESENT MULTIPLE VIEWS)

Look up "Bomarzo" in the Michelin Green Guide to Italy: "Extending below the town is the park of the 16th-century Villa Orsini (Parco dei Mostri) which is a Mannerist creation with a series of fantastically shaped sculptures." Compare that description to the photos in Plates B and C (in the color plate section of this book), showing just a tiny portion of the Parco dei Mostri ("Park of Monsters"). Do these not suggest a somewhat richer place than the sentence in the Michelin guide? Yet the sight of tourists slavishly following the Michelin guide is a commonplace. Something really fascinating and unexpected is happening in front of them, but they have their noses buried in the guide, trying to figure out what the next official point of interest is. Such a tourist is *literate.* Not literate in the "I read classics at Oxford" sense, but literate in the "knowledge is closed" sense. Everything about Italy can fit into a book. Perhaps the 350 pages of the Green Guide aren't enough, but some quantity of writers and pages would suffice to encapsulate everything worth knowing about Italy.

Oral cultures do not share this belief. Knowledge is open-ended. People may hold differing opinions without one person being wrong. There is not necessarily one truth; there may be many truths. Though he didn't grow up in an oral culture, Shakespeare knew this. Watch *Troilus and Cressida* and its five perspectives on the nature of a woman's love. Try to figure out which perspective Shakespeare thinks is correct.

Feminists, chauvinists, warmongers, pacifists, Jew-haters, inclusivists, cautious people, heedless people, misers, doctors, medical malpractice lawyers, atheists, and the pious are all able to quote Shakespeare in support of their beliefs. That's because Shakespeare uses the multiple characters in each of his plays to show his culture's multiple truths.

In the 400 years since Shakespeare we've become much more literate. There is usually one dominant truth. Sometimes this is because we've truly figured something out. It is kind of tough to argue that a physics textbook on Newtonian mechanics should be an open-ended discussion. Yet even in the natural sciences, one can find many examples where the culture of literacy distorts discourse.

If you were able to stay awake long enough to read through an academic journal for taxonomic botanists, you'd learn that not all botanists agree on whether Specimen 947 collected from a particular field in Montana is a member of species X or species Y. But you'd see quite clearly that everyone publishing in the journal agreed on the taxonomy, or how to build a categorization tree for the various species.

Note: **I learned all of this interesting stuff about taxonomic botanists from Peter Nürnberg; see his paper at ftp://bush.cs.tamu.edu/pub/publications/papers/96.webnet/96.webnet.html.**

However, if you were able to stay awake long enough to get through a cocktail party in a university's department of botany, you'd discover that even this agreement is illusory. There is widespread disagreement on what is the correct taxonomy. Hardly anyone believes that the taxonomy used in journals is correct but they have to stick with it for publication because otherwise older journal articles would be rendered incomprehensible. Taxonomic botany based on an oral culture or a computer system capable of showing multiple views would look completely different.

Open today's *New York Times*. A Republican politician is arguing for relaxed regulations on widgets. A Democrat is quoted arguing in favor of tightened regulations. There is a vote; widget regulations are tightened. On the surface, it looks like multiple perspectives. Yet at a cocktail party, your friend Sue might argue that the government shouldn't be regulating widgets at all. Joe would probably interrupt her to say that widget regulation is a canard; we really ought to talk about flag burning. Dana would bring up the *Simpsons* episode where Bart went on a school field trip to the widget factory. Alan would tell his grandfather's widget factory stories from World War II. Elizabeth would talk about how she was surprised to see that they had no widgets in New Zealand and apparently did not miss them. Compared to the texture of the cocktail party, the *New York Times* article sounds like two rich old white guys saying more or less the same thing.

Some people like a one-truth world. If you have a huge advertising and PR budget, then you can control your public image very effectively in a literate world. Ford Motor Company has enough money to remind you 2,000 times a year that "Quality is Job One;" unless you lost a friend in a Pinto gas tank explosion, you probably will eventually come to agree. Microsoft via the genius of Bill Gates invented the mouse-windows user interface, reliable operating systems, affordable computing, and the Internet; if you don't think all that is true, ask someone who has never used a computer and whose only exposure to the industry is through mass media.

Perhaps it is because I'm a few billion dollars short of the necessary funds to create a one-truth world of my own, but I think the greatest artistic achievements hold the mirror up to a multiple-truth life. The Internet and computers, used competently and creatively, make it much easier and cheaper to collect and present multiple truths than in the old world of print, telephone, and snail mail. Multiple-truth Web sites are much more interesting than single-truth Web sites and therefore will get a lot more traffic. For example, the car manufacturers' sites are mostly collections of product brochures tarted up with flashing graphics. They get minimal traffic compared to the plain text rec.auto.* newsgroups, which present the real experience of car owners from around the world. The newsgroups don't have pictures, animation, sound, or video clips. But they have multiple truths.

OK, enough philosophy and Shakespeare. This is the point in the infomercial where the guy wearing the CAT Diesel cap asks, "Do I need a college education to build one of these here multiple-truth Web sites?" The answer is no.

- *Step 1: Put up some magnet content.* Your distribution cost is now zero. So take every document that you've ever distributed to anyone and put it on your site. In my case, I'll write a 50-page story about Costa Rica and illustrate it with 200 pictures (see Plate D) before inviting people to contribute their wisdom.

  General Electric (http://www.ge.com) is a rare good example of a corporate site that takes the Web as distribution medium seriously. They have brochures, yes, but also owner's manuals and installation guides for every GE product. If you moved into an apartment with a GE appliance but the previous tenants did not leave you the instructions, you can grab a PDF file from the GE site and print it.

- *Step 2: Develop technical means for collaboration.* Your Web server should indeed be barfing out your content at a steady clip, but in a way its most important role is to slurp up content from users. My photography subsite (http://photo.net/photo) pumps out 400,000 files every day with my photographs and writing. More interesting to me, though, are the comments collected by my Loquacious system for each page and my indexed categorized question-and-answer forum, shown in Figure 1.1. Users are helping me build a great repository of photography knowledge. I'm pretty diligent about responding to questions in the forum, but my happiest hours are spent watching users answer each others' questions.

  You don't have to be a traditional publisher per se to benefit from collaboration tools. Manufacturers can collect and redistribute consumer comments about dealers who carry their products. Academic researchers can collect comments, ideas, and questions sparked by their writings. An example of such responses can be seen in Figure 1.2.

- *Step 3: Be prepared to interact with users.* This means that if you have a question-and-answer forum, spend the time to answer the questions. It also means moderating the forum to delete uninteresting threads. It means killing idiotic comments on the comment server but keeping the relevant ones, even those that savagely disagree with your point of view.

Does this sound like too much work? If your site is commercial and you claim to be a smart businessperson, then you ought to be able to figure out a way to interact with users more cheaply over the Internet than via 800 numbers. If you are a writer or a photographer who has built a non-commercial site, then disintermediating the publisher means total artistic freedom. User feedback might be annoying at times, but if you want to be insulated from your readers, why publish on the Web at all?

Think of the Web as Primary

A site that exists primarily to tease people off the Internet into buying something will almost always cry out to be ignored. Web sites should stand alone.

Joe Greedy puts up a site showing the cover of his book and a headline: "Buy me for $17." You'd think that this would be the lamest possible Web site. But Mr. Greedy manages to earn extra suck points by making sure that the only ordering option is by telephone. That way the modem crowd will be forced to write down the number on a Post-It and then disconnect before they can order their pile of processed tree carcass.

photo.net

a question and answer forum associated with photo.net.

[Ask a Question | Search | Unanswered Questions | New Answers]

New Questions

- Selection of a focusing segment under partial metering for Elan 2E.
- Kodalux Mailers
- pentax spotmatic info
- USM upgrade
- Focusing rails?
- Canon EOS A2 is only $100 more than Elan IIe; which is better?
- Experiences with Olympus Mju-II?
- Bronica C, anyone knowledgeable?
- Recommended tests for a used camera and lens?
- The "best" choice for a wide angle lens
- Long exposure times (dusk/dawn/night)
- Where can I get an "international" model Canon A2?
- Photographing Pewter Sculptures
- Sigma Wide angle zoom?
- Nikon N70 (28-80) vs. Elan II/IIe (28-105)
- How to check used lenses
- Canon replacing the A2e (EOS-5) body? (not until August)
- Canon 28-105 USM v. 24-85 USM
- Exposure latitude revisited
- Pixilation

Art

- Is Hiro your hero?

Figure 1.1: The question-and-answer forum in http://photo.net/photo, which contains more than 1,500 archived messages. Answers are e-mailed automatically to the user who posted the question, even months later. Users can choose to be notified by e-mail of new messages instantly, daily, or weekly. (Note: If you'd like to run a similar forum on your own site, just visit http://webtools.com/wtr/ and fill out a form. The software is free and you can even use one of my Web/RDBMS servers for free.)

Jane Clever puts the full text of her book online. With several hundred pages of text instead of one, her content will be several hundred times more likely to attract users of search engines. By enabling online ordering for those dead-tree huggers, Ms. Clever will sell far more copies of her book than Mr. Greedy. Also, with 100,000 hits per day, Ms. Clever can sell ads on her site and links to other Web publishers.

Another kind of site that almost always disappoints is the adjunct to the physical event. Pathfinder did a companion to a traveling museum show by

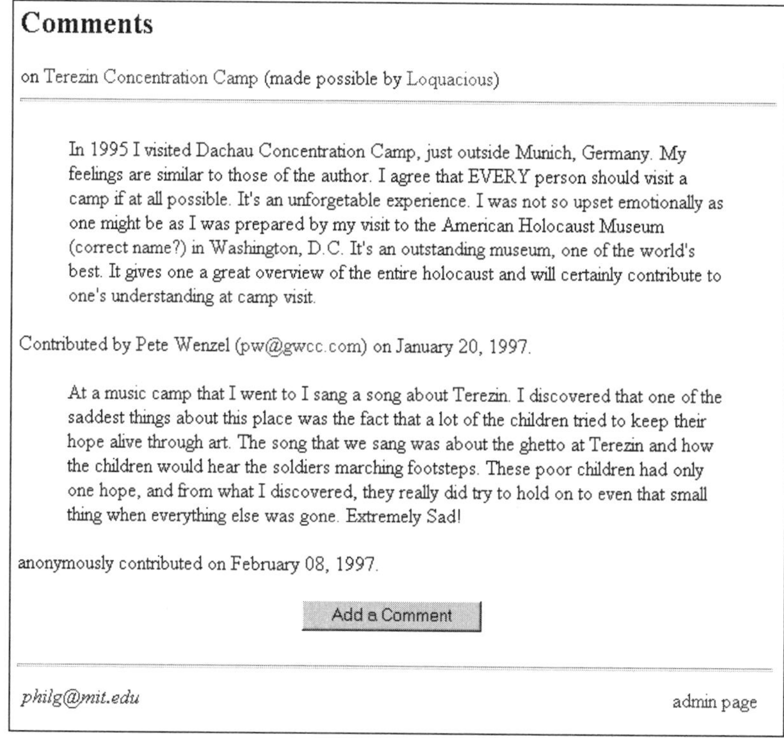

Comments

on Terezin Concentration Camp (made possible by Loquacious)

> In 1995 I visited Dachau Concentration Camp, just outside Munich, Germany. My feelings are similar to those of the author. I agree that EVERY person should visit a camp if at all possible. It's an unforgetable experience. I was not so upset emotionally as one might be as I was prepared by my visit to the American Holocaust Museum (correct name?) in Washington, D.C. It's an outstanding museum, one of the world's best. It gives one a great overview of the entire holocaust and will certainly contribute to one's understanding at camp visit.

Contributed by Pete Wenzel (pw@gwcc.com) on January 20, 1997.

> At a music camp that I went to I sang a song about Terezin. I discovered that one of the saddest things about this place was the fact that a lot of the children tried to keep their hope alive through art. The song that we sang was about the ghetto at Terezin and how the children would hear the soldiers marching footsteps. These poor children had only one hope, and from what I discovered, they really did try to hold on to even that small thing when everything else was gone. Extremely Sad!

anonymously contributed on February 08, 1997.

Add a Comment

philg@mit.edu admin page

Figure 1.2: The Loquacious comment server collecting reader responses to my Berlin/Prague story (http://webtravel.org/bp/). The original 30-page story and 80 photographs attracted a reader-contributed story about the Terezin concentration camp. That story in turn attracted the comments that you see here (http://db.photo.net/com/philg/bp/terezin.html). If you'd like to use the Loquacious system for your own Web site, just visit http://webtools.com/wtr/. It is free.

well-known photographers such as Annie Liebowitz. The biggest available pictures on the Web site were tiny, occupying about 1/100th of my 20-inch screen. The editor of the site asked me to add a link from photo.net to the Pathfinder site. I refused, saying that my readers were accustomed to filling their screens with the 500x750 pixel and 1000x1500 pixel images on my site. They would just get frustrated squinting at the tiny Pathfinder images. He replied that the museum show photographers were concerned about copyright infringement. I said "Well, maybe they shouldn't be on the Net. They are getting plenty of promotion in bookstores, museums, magazines. Why don't you find some less known photographers for whom the Web is primary?"

In October 1995, the MIT Media Lab threw itself a tenth anniversary party. I skipped it so that I could take snapshots of colored trees in Vermont, but my friends said that the physical event was fabulous: little gifts for everyone, cleverly packaged; a Photomosaic poster by Rob Silvers; women in plastic pants. As an adjunct to the physical event, the Media Lab was going to create the best Web site ever. They got NYNEX to bring in a 45-Mbps T3 network connection; you wouldn't want millions of users to get slowed down working their way through MIT's 100-Mbps backbone. They got Hewlett-Packard to donate a huge pile of multiprocessor machines with disk arrays. They hired expert consultants to plug all the computers in and hook them up to the network. They hired professionals to do graphic design and site layout.

After getting back from foliage country, I visited http://www.1010.org with high hopes. There wasn't any magnet content. Nobody had bothered to write stories or take pictures. Every day a Media Lab editor posed a question and then sat back to watch a Usenet-style discussion evolve. There were only a handful of postings in each area. One user had contributed a smiley face. Colon dash right-paren. That was his entire message. This didn't really shock me until I noticed that on a scale from 1 to 7, this post had been rated 4.3 by other users. Yes, several other users had taken the trouble to rate this three-character posting. When the ten-day Web event was over, the massive disk arrays held almost enough user-contributed data to fill two 3.5 inch floppies.

How could so much money and hardware have resulted in a site that an elementary school would have been embarrassed to make public? The Web site wasn't primary. The party was the important thing. The Media Lab, one of the last groups at MIT to put up a Web site, had no real Internet culture. They wanted to reach corporate managers and bring them into the physical space of the Lab. Since corporate managers didn't tend to have a TCP/IP connection on their desktop, it wasn't obvious how the Internet would be useful in attaining the Media Lab's goals.

Note: Don't try to visit http://www.1010.org. The Media Lab eventually got Web-savvy enough to realize the embarrassment value of such a site and pulled the plug on the server.

Money is nice. Bandwidth is nice. Graphic design is occasionally nice. But your Web site will suck if you see it as a pimple on the butt of something much larger.

Summary

The stuff in this chapter isn't meant to be true. I'm not a great writer like Shakespeare (yes, I know that I could write this observation up for *Duh* magazine; you don't have to send e-mail). I'm unable to transcend the medium of the printed page and present multiple truths. My hope is that I have provoked you into doing the following:

- Putting yourself into your user's shoes before planning your site's content. Why would they come to your site and what can you do to make sure that their visit is rewarded?
- Thinking seriously about the Web's potential as a medium for collaboration. In intelligent, thoughtful hands, the Internet is more powerful than the printed page.

This chapter was about people talking to computers and people talking to each other with a computer mediator. In the next chapter, we'll talk about how computers talking to each other could finally deliver all of the benefits that the Computer Age was supposed to have conferred on us (and, if you insist, how you can make a buck off of it).

So You Want to Join the World's Grubbiest Club: Internet Entrepreneurs

THE STEAM ENGINE AND THE RAILROAD

FOUR WAYS TO MAKE MONEY FROM YOUR SITE

WE LOSE MONEY ON EVERY HIT BUT MAKE IT UP ON VOLUME

A FINAL PLEA

Chapter 2

"The guy with the Web site." That's how my friends introduce me at parties. I guess that says something about what a rich, multifaceted, textured personality I've developed by spending 15 out of my 33 years at MIT. Yeah. Anyway, the response from my new acquaintances is invariably the same: "How are you going to make money off your Web site?"

If they'd been told I'd spent $20 on a subscription to *Playboy*, they wouldn't ask how I intended to make money off that. If they knew I'd splurged for a $5,000 Viking stove, they wouldn't ask if I was going to start charging my brunch guests $5 each. If I told them I dropped $20,000 on a Dodge Caravan, they wouldn't ask if I was going to charge my dog $10 for every trip.

Web site hosting can cost less than any of these things; why does everyone assume that it has to make money? I did not set up my site to make money. I set up my site so that my friend Michael at Stanford could see the slides I took while driving from Boston to Alaska and back. It turns out that my site has not made money. Yet I do not consider my site a failure. My friend Michael at Stanford can look at my slides anytime he wants to by typing "http://webtravel.org/samantha/".

I'm not saying that this should be everyone's goal. After all, you might not know my friend Michael at Stanford. Or, if you do know him, you might not like him. But keep in mind that if you are destined to lose money on your site, it is much less humiliating if you can say that making money wasn't the idea.

If you can't remember that greed is one of the seven deadly sins, then I suppose it is worth thinking about how to make money on the Internet. First, ask yourself the question, "Why do we think that there *is* money to be made off the Internet?" Karl Taylor Compton, former president of MIT, said it best in 1938: "In recent times, modern science has developed to give mankind, for the first time in the history of the human race, a way of securing a more abundant life which does not simply consist in taking away from someone else."

I believe that *computers* will secure a more abundant life for the human race. Mine would not have been a controversial statement in 1960, when IBM was just beginning to saturate corporate America with mainframes. It was obvious to everyone in 1960 that computers were going to usher in a new Age of Leisure. In 1997, my statement seems absurd. Computers have been around for fifty years now without doing much for the average person. In fact, it is a commonplace among economists that computers have reduced the productivity of American business.

Computers by themselves are a liability. Getting information into and out of them is so expensive that using paper and file cabinets is probably less trouble. Sure, in 1997 we don't see too many people manually writing payroll checks or calculating artillery shell trajectories. But most people get through most parts of their day without relying on a computer. Why don't I think that will be true in another 50 years? Because of the network.

The Steam Engine and the Railroad

James Watt's 1765 steam engine didn't change your life unless you were pumping water out of coal mines. A steam-powered factory could have produced enough goods to supply an entire nation, but since there was no way to distribute that output there wasn't much point in building such a factory. With the railroad came the ability to serve a national market with one factory. Factories grew enormous and pulled people out of the countryside to work inside the Satanic Mills. It was the mounting of the steam engine on rails and the spreading of railroads across nations that transformed society, not the steam engine *per se*. The computer is the steam engine of today; the network is the railroad.

With a ubiquitous network, all of the information that you consume will arrive in a machine-readable form. If the information is structured appropriately, as with standards like Electronic Document Interchange (EDI), it will arrive in a form that is immediately applicable to your internal databases without human intervention. Your computer will truly be able to handle routine transactions on your behalf.

When the network infrastructure is powerful enough that most houses enjoy video-rate bandwidth, the computer will be able to support your collaboration with other people. If you had TV-quality video and audio links to your collaborators and a shared workspace, you wouldn't have to commute to work or fly around from city to city so much. Though I don't like to predict the demise of a 3,000-year-old trend toward urbanization, it indeed seems possible that collaboration tools might enable some people to move out to the country yet still keep their urban jobs.

The Internet will change society. Some people will get rich off that change. I guess you might as well be one of them. Probably your safest bet is to figure out where all those telecommuters are going to end up living and open a little mall there with a McDonalds, MicroCenter, and Trader Joe's. But this is a book about building publicly accessible Web sites, so here are my ideas.

Four Ways to Make Money from Your Site

I think that all consumer-oriented Web services fall into at least one of the four categories below. If you are starting a new site for the purpose of making money, it is worth considering which categories your planned services fall into and how hard it is to make money in those categories.

Here are the categories:

1. *Sites that provide traditional information.* This type of site, shown in Figure 2.1, requires the least imagination but also the most capital investment. Find bodies of information that consumers in the 1980s bought offline and sell them online. This includes movies/videos/television, newspapers, magazines, weather reports, and stock market information. A classical example is an online magazine or newspaper. Revenue comes from advertising, links to sites that do retail transactions and give you a kickback, and occasionally subscriptions. Putting up a Category 1 site requires almost no imagination, technology, or investment, but it will cost you a fortune in the long run as you keep buying content to keep it fresh.
2. *Sites that provide collaboratively created information.* This is information that was virtually impossible to collect before the Internet. A dead-trees example would be the *Consumer Reports* annual survey of automobile reliability. They collect information from their readers via mail-in forms, collate the results, and publish them once a year. The Internet makes this kind of activity less costly for the provider and provides much more immediate and deeper information for the user. For example, each user can tell you how frequently his car has broken down and you end up with a valuable database of car reliability statistics to give back to users collectively. Revenue comes from the same sources as in Category 1 but production expenses are lower. It costs money to establish your server as a forum for users to exchange data. You have to buy some magnet content

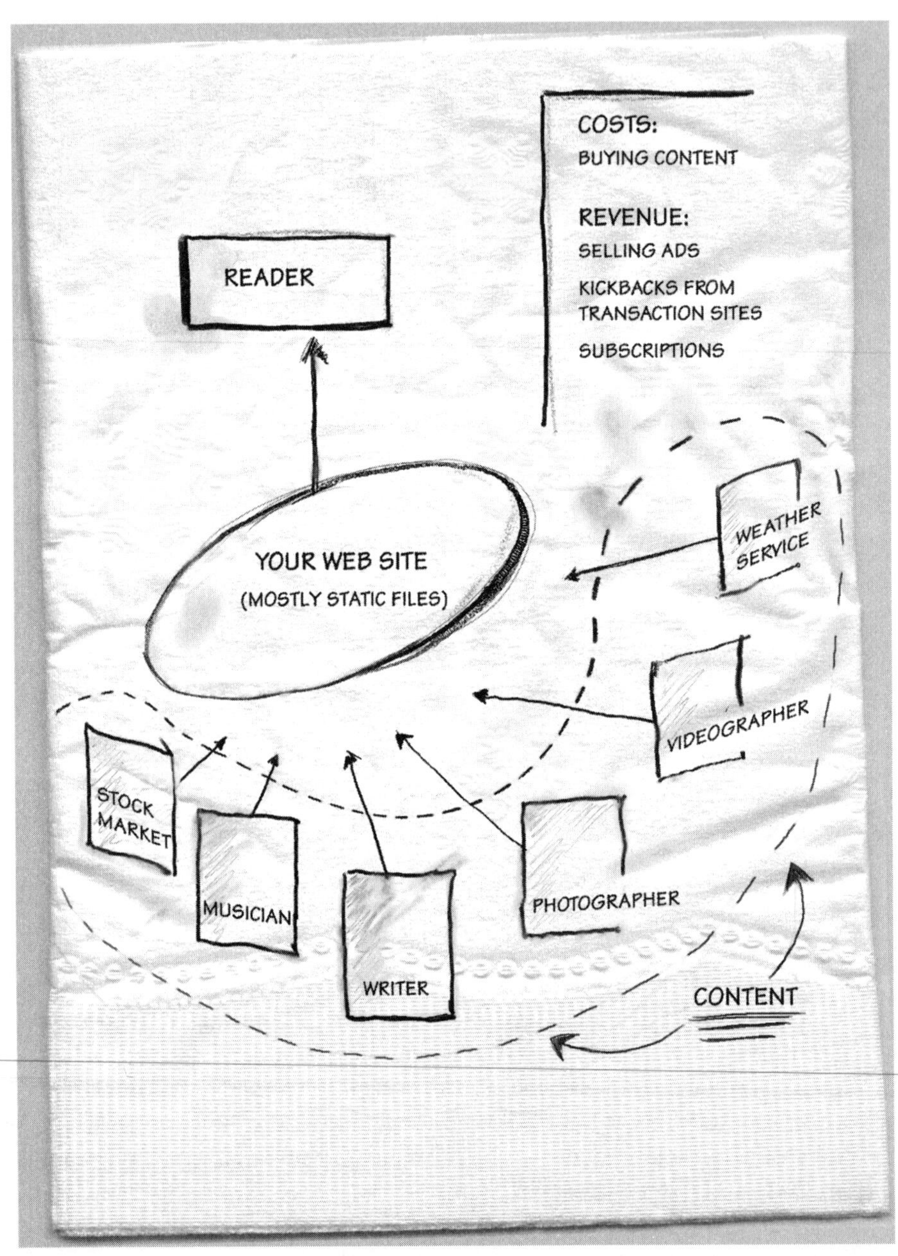

Figure 2.1: A Category 1 site simply provides bodies of information that consumers in the 1980s obtained offline

and write some programs. But once established, the site can grow in popularity with very little additional investment on your part. See Figure 2.2 for an example of a Category 2 site.

3 *Sites that provide a service via a server-side program.* An example of this would be providing a wedding planning program. The user tells you how much he or she wants to spend, when and where the wedding is, who is invited, and so on. Your program then figures a detailed budget, develops an invitation list, and maintains gift and thank-you lists. You are then in a position to sell an ad to the Four Seasons hotel that will be delivered to couples getting married on June 25, who live less than 100 miles away, with fewer than 80 guests, who have budgeted more than $17,000. Or, suppose that you can convince people to use your server to fill out their income tax return. Why should they go to the trouble of installing a program on their computer that they are only going to use once. Your Web site is so much more convenient! Meanwhile, as they are filling out their taxes, you are building up a database of information that they would ordinarily be reluctant to give you, such as how much money they made last year. Armed with this information, you can sell very expensive and highly targeted advertising. Did the user make more than $350,000 last year? Rolls-Royce might pay you $10 to show the user an ad for the Corniche IV. Did the user cheat on his return? VARIG would probably pay you $25 to run a page with Brazil's extradition laws and fares to Rio.

An example of a Category 3 site is shown in Figure 2.3.

4 *Sites that define a standard that enables a consumer to seamlessly query multiple databases.* For example, car dealers have computers managing their inventory, but that data is imprisoned on the dealers' computers and is unavailable to consumers in a convenient manner. Suppose you define a standard that allows the inventory computers inside car dealerships to download their current selection of cars, colors, and prices. You get the car dealers to agree to provide their information to you. Then your site becomes a place where a consumer can say "I want a new dark green Dodge Grand Caravan with air conditioning and antilock brakes that's for sale within 60 miles of zip code 02176." From your query to the dealers' multiple databases, your user can get a list of all the cars available that match their criteria, and can jump right to the relevant dealer's Web site. For another example, note that just about every bank has a computer database of the interest rate they will pay on a certificate of deposit. But this data is not in any standard form. You engineer a standard that lets bank computers tell your Web server what CDs are available and at what rate. Then, when a

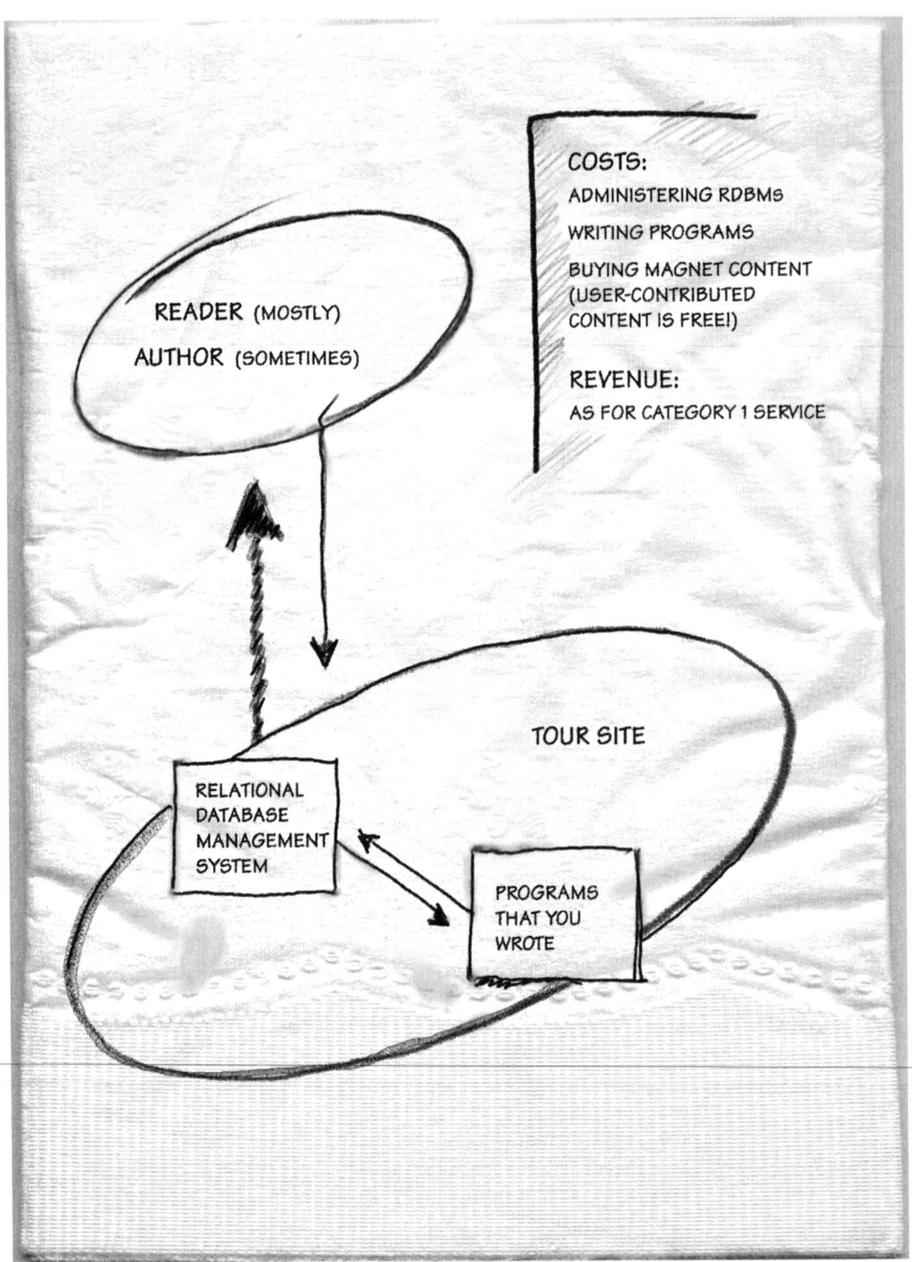

Figure 2.2: A Category 2 site provides collaboratively created information. Even a humble classified ad system falls into this category

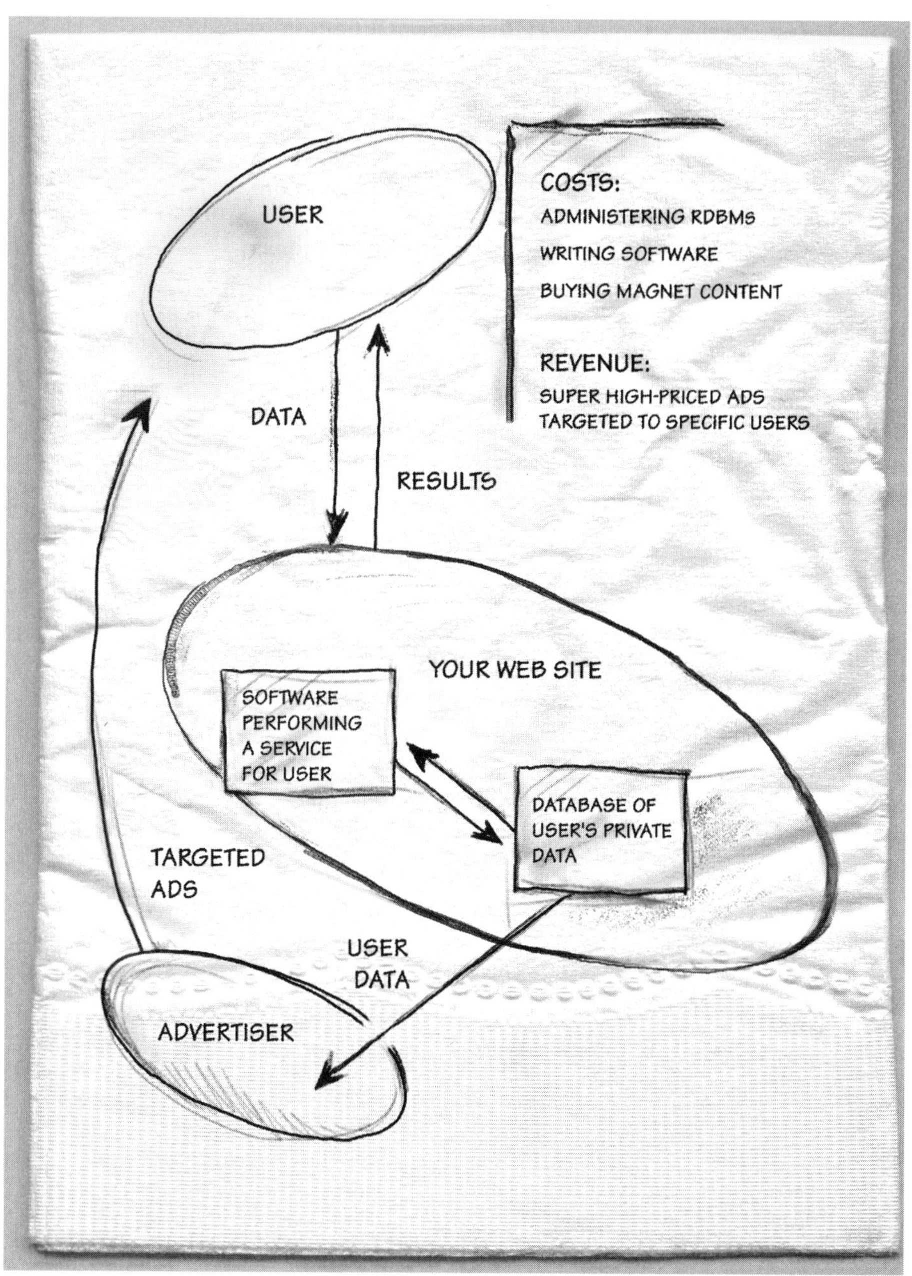

Figure 2.3: Category 3 sites provide a service to the user via a server-side program.

consumer visits your site and indicates an interest in six-month CDs, your server can display a list of the banks, ordered by interest rate offered. If the consumer clicks through to a bank and buys a CD, you collect a commission. See Figure 2.4 for an example of how a Category 4 site might be set up.

In terms of bang per dollar invested, the most expensive type of site is Category 1. To create a site like this, you have to hire writers, pay photographers and editors, and scrupulously maintain your site. If you stop updating for one day, people may turn away to a competitor's site.

A Category 2 site is very cheap to start up. You spend a little bit of money for programming, a data model, and "anchor content." Thereafter the site expands itself. Category 3 sites require much more investment and effort, particularly in selling ads and working with advertisers, but they have potentially much higher payoffs since you know so much more about your users. An advertiser won't pay too much for an ad on the Netscape home page, perhaps a few cents per impression. All that anyone knows about the readers is that they haven't changed their browser's default first page. An advertiser will pay a lot more for an ad on a search engine's site, if it is delivered only to those people who've entered query words relevant to the product advertised. For example, Century 21 would pay a lot to have their ad delivered to people who included "real estate" in their query string. If you learn enough about your reader, you might be able to charge an advertiser several dollars just to display one banner ad to that reader.

Category 4 is probably the most lucrative because it harnesses the full power of the Internet. Entering this area requires having the right connections and making the proper business arrangements. It is the Category 4 sites that will change the way the computer is seen. In a Category 3 car site, you might offer users a new car planning service. You know what kinds of car they need, their budgets, and where they live. You can charge car manufacturers and local dealerships quite a bit to serve banner ads that might tempt particular users. But in a Category 4 site, you know which user is about to drive to which dealer to buy which car with which options. You can demand a commission from the selling dealer. You can charge $50 to a competing dealership to run an ad that says "Just wait two days and Joe Foobar Toyota will have that same color sedan in stock. The price will be $75 lower and Joe Foobar Toyota is ten miles closer to your house than the dealer you're planning to buy from."

Let's consider how we'd use these categories to build services for a variety of fields.

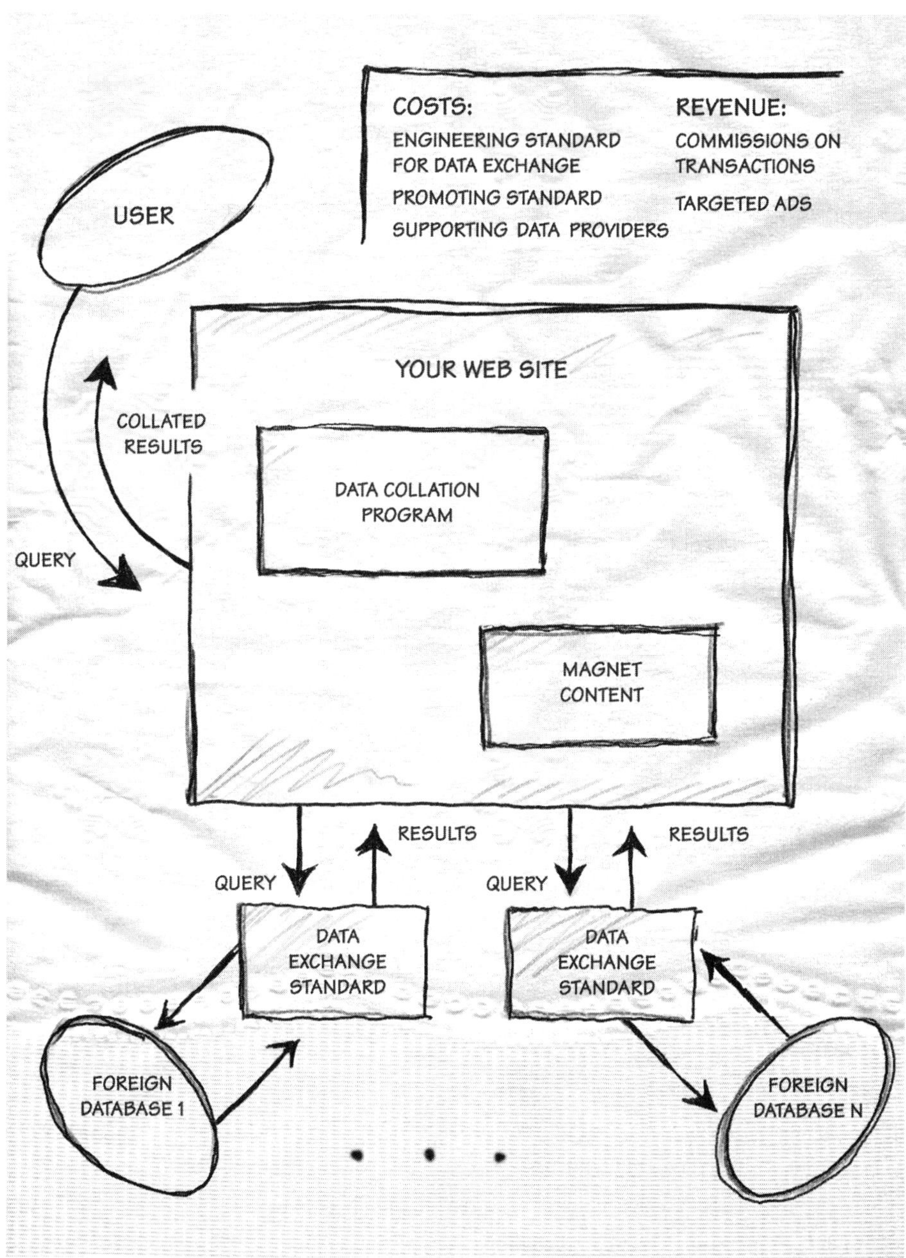

Figure 2.4: Category 4 sites define a standard for cooperation among databases and then let users seamlessly query them all.

TRAVEL EXAMPLE

A lot of money dangles from the travel tree. Vendors and consumers are separated by vast distances and numerous intermediaries. Each intermediary extracts a commission. It is the sum total of those commissions that is potentially available to Web travel sites.

Traditional publishers do their best to capture these commissions with guidebooks, magazines, advertising supplements, and plain old brochures. Despite the vast forests that are chopped down in this valiant attempt, dead-trees publishers aren't satisfying travelers. A subscriber opens a travel magazine and finds all of the articles either much too long, because he or she isn't planning to visit the city described, or much too short, because he or she has a definite trip planned and is hungry for detail. Travel books are better, though they generally suffer from the "one voice" problem and the best written books usually don't have any pictures because of the expense of color printing can't be justified when there aren't any ads.

Traditional travel publishers don't even try to give consumers the most critical information, such as how well the last 100 people who went there liked it. An Internet travel site starts off with a huge relevance advantage. Search engines consistently deliver travel URLs to people who are about to book a trip or leave for a destination. No other advertising-carrying medium comes close, except perhaps the airplane and hotel magazines that consumers get after they've started their trip.

The most important Category 1 service for a travel site is magnet content that will attract people to Category 2, 3, and 4 services. You can organize all kinds of Category 2 services around magnet content. For example, suppose that your magnet content in an Italian site says, "I went into the cathedral at Assisi to reload my camera; there were some pictures on the walls. I think somebody next to me said they were painted by a guy named 'Joe.'" Somewhere out there on the Net there is a guy who did his art history Ph.D. on those frescoes by Giotto. Your magnet content's function is to draw that expert into surfing your site and contributing a few paragraphs via your comment server.

You will also want to have classified ads for vacation homes and tour packages, Q&A forums, and a quality rating system for tour operators and hotels. What makes this all more useful than rec.travel.europe is that the magnet content gives structure to the user-contributed thoughts.

Note: Check out http://webtravel.org/webtravel/ for a glimpse at my idea of what a Category 1 and 2 travel Web site should be like.

The obvious Category 3 service for a travel site is a trip planning system. Your database will know where the consumer intends to be at every hour of every day of the trip. With that kind of information about your readers, if you can't sell high-priced ads for delivery to specific people, it won't be my fault!

The obvious Category 4 application is a hotel room booking system. Your server queries all the hotel reservation computers and the consumer can query you: "Show me the available hotel rooms in Paris for September 15–20, sorted by distance from the Louvre and then by price. Oh, and convert the prices to American dollars, please."

REAL ESTATE EXAMPLE

Real estate agents in the United States collect a 6 percent commission every time they connect buyer and seller. This leads to musings like "Why does New York have so much garbage and Los Angeles so many real estate agents?" (Standard answer: "Because New York had first choice.") This kind of humor would hurt real estate agents' feelings if they weren't raking in $142 billion each year (according to the 1992 Census).

Realtors are precisely the sorts of intermediaries that Internet technology is supposed to eliminate. If you were trying to capture a share of this $142 billion, you'd want to start in Category 1 with articles about moving or character sketches for neighborhoods. This content would attract search engine users. Moving into Category 2, you'd run a commission-based classified ad system to connect renters with landlords and buyers with sellers. For a Category 3 service, perhaps you could create a moving planner. You'd get the old address, the new address, and the moving date from the user. You could use that data to help the user disconnect and hook up utilities, compute cost-of-living differences, and arrange travel. Meanwhile, you are bombarding the person with ads from competing communications, furniture, and appliance vendors in the new locale. For a Category 4 application you'd cut deals with other real estate sites to query their databases. If a user makes a transaction on that foreign site, you split the commissions.

MEDICAL EXAMPLE

Joe Schmoe is treated at five different hospitals over a three-year period. Each hospital has a sophisticated computer medical record system. When Mr. Schmoe visits Hospital Number 6, they create a record for him on *their* big database. But even though Joe's entire medical record is available in electronic form, the new hospital has no way to import it from the previous five hospitals. So they don't realize that Joe is allergic to an obscure drug. Joe dies.

You could have saved Joe's life. You could have built a Web site where Joe can store and control his own medical record. When he goes to a new hospital, he can authorize them to retrieve portions of his record and to store their findings back on his personal server. Then when he goes to a new hospital, they can download his record and find out just which drugs will provoke a life-threatening allergic reaction.

This is a Category 4 site with a vengeance. All of the challenge is in figuring out to make disparate databases talk to each other. The data models on the hospital systems can be radically different. Even trivial differences, such as different abbreviations for the same disease, can prevent databases from understanding each other. You have to find a way to get these databases to cooperate even though they were never designed to do that.

Big companies do this all the time, of course. They'll decide that, starting July 1, everyone is moving to the big new central database system and everyone will use the same part number for a #8 machine screw. They have the money, resources, and authority to make this happen. On the Internet, there are many more organizations who could benefit from data exchange, but there is much less trust, less money, and no central authority.

There is a huge technical challenge in figuring out a cheap automated or semi-automated method of integrating databases. In fact, this is my primary research focus at MIT. Though my partners and I have done some interesting things in the medical domain, I won't say that we've got any kind of general solution. As soon as we do, we'll have a killer Web site.

That's a whirlwind tour of the four ways to break down consumer Web services. Assuming you run with one of my ideas or come up with a great one of your own, you'll be on your way to achieving the Holy Grail of the Web: traffic.

We Lose Money on Every Hit But Make It Up on Volume

If nobody ever visits your site, then you won't make any money. Advertisers don't like to place ads where nobody will see them. You can't sell stuff to nobody. Collecting a middleman's commission on no transactions is not very attractive. If you have visitors then you at least have a chance to make money, even if you didn't have a specific plan when you set up the site.

Internet commerce is the most obvious method of making money from a popular site, but it may not be the best. Internet commerce appeals to a particularly male fantasy. Guys like the idea that after a short initial period of programming, a computer will tirelessly slave away for them, making them money 24 hours a day. Set up the site, walk away, and watch the money pile up in your bank account.

You can feed this fantasy by reading articles in the business press about http://amazon.com, the perennial poster children for Internet commerce.

They set up what is essentially a front-end to a wholesale book distributor's database, and now they are selling books every few seconds. It sounds like they are rolling in money.

Well, it turns out that I know some people who work at amazon.com. The customers don't always fill out the forms exactly right. The books aren't always in stock like they should be. The customers send e-mail asking when their books are going to be shipped. So instead of one Unix box and a big vault for the cash, the company has 200 employees sucking all the money out of it. And remember, this is the best that anyone has really done: high expenses and high sales. More typical is an Internet store with high expenses and low or no sales.

If amazon.com offers a cautionary lesson to those who would make their fortune processing transactions, it offers an encouraging lesson to those who would publish deep content. They have an "associated bookstore" program. You become an associated bookstore by adding an encoded link from your pages to amazon. This doesn't mean you have to uglify your site with sales promotions. In my case, I just went through http://photo.net/photo and replaced

```
You should check the Kodak Professional Photoguide
```

with

```
You should check the
<a href="http://www.amazon.com/exec/obidos/ISBN=0879857595/photonetA/">
Kodak Professional Photoguide
</a>
```

When users click on the link, they are presented with an order form from amazon.com. Should the order be completed, amazon will kick back to me 8 percent of the price of the book. I got some e-mail from a travel agent offering a similar arrangement. If I linked to them from my travel pages, they'd kick back to me half of their travel agent's commission (about 12 percent) on any sales that resulted from the link.

It occurred to me that, in a perfectly competitive environment, referral arrangements like this would eventually result in almost all of the profit being paid to the owner of the content. Transaction processors will earn a normal return on their investment, but nothing extra. Why? I'm currently linking to amazon.com for an 8 percent blandishment. If Barnes & Noble offers me 12 percent, I can write a perl script to grind over my 1,000 .html pages and replace references to amazon.com with references to Barnes & Noble. If I were linked to a travel agent offering me 50 percent of their commission, a travel agent late to the Internet booking market might offer me 100 percent of their commission in hopes of capturing my users as repeat customers. Another five minutes with perl and all of my static .html pages are pointing to a new travel agent.

Word to the wise: Be sure to carefully check out the conditions under which you get paid. All of the revenue from my site is donated to Angell Memorial Animal Hospital here in Boston. With 5,000 readers on my Web site every day, I figured all that money flowing from amazon.com would buy the dogs filet mignon in gold-plated bowls. But it turns out that special orders are excluded from my take. And a lot of the books that I recommend are special order only. And if the user buys ten books in the session, I only get paid for the one title that I recommended. This was beginning to seem unfair. After all, suppose I refer Joe User to amazon for a special order book that I think he should read. While he is there, he swells amazon's coffers by picking up ten more books. I get nothing. Nada. Zip.

The worst was yet to come. Amazon only pays a referral fee if the user you refer buys the book that you recommend and does so from the very first amazon page he or she is shown. Suppose I refer Jane Clever to amazon.com to buy *The Practical SQL Handbook.* She looks at the amazon page and is happy with the book, price, and so on. But she decides to browse around a bit before ordering. She ultimately ends up buying *The Practical SQL Handbook* and $500 of other database books. I get nothing. Nada. Zip.

The amazon folks say that they don't expect too many people to go browsing before purchasing. This, of course, is common sense: When you go to a store knowing that you need something, you always walk right up the register and buy it before turning your head to the left or right and looking to see if there is anything else you need. Yeah. And just in case the user isn't predisposed to browse, amazon provides about 25 internal links on the page that they serve for their associated bookstores (see Figures 2.5 and 2.6). If the user clicks the order button then the associated bookstore will get a referral fee. If the user clicks any of the other 25 links, such as "books on SQL," "books on relational databases," "browse," "books by the same author," or "search," then amazon has gotten itself a new customer without having to pay anything.

How does this work in practice? Listing 2.1 shows a weekly report from amazon.com to me.

I sent people to the amazon site 2,651 times. Only four of those people ignored the 25 extra links and bought books off the very first page. One of them bought a special order book for which the dogs at Angell got nothing. Bottom line: The standard Internet price for a click-through is 10 cents; it would have cost amazon.com $265 per week to get these users by purchasing ads on other folks' sites; amazon got them from me for $3.95.

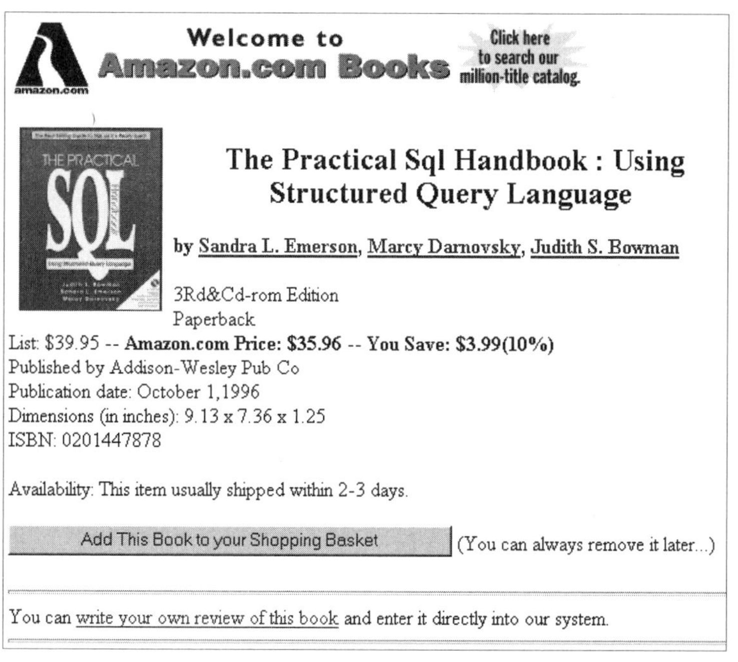

Figure 2.5: The first page a user sees when referred to amazon.com from an amazon.com "associated bookstore." The referring site will get an 8 percent commission, but only if the user orders immediately without being tempted by the 25 other links on the page.

A Final Plea

I suppose that it is possible to make money with a Web site. But before you build your site, take a moment to think about the things that you went into because you thought you could make money. How many of them proved satisfying in the long run? How many actually made money?

You could start your Web site by asking, "What can I get from this right now?" Alternatively, you could start out by asking, "What can I give people?" I expect that in the long run, you'd be about equally likely to make money with either approach. I started with the latter.

I gave away my pictures. I gave away my stories. I gave away to "competitors" my advice and software. The Web gave me back a large and growing audience

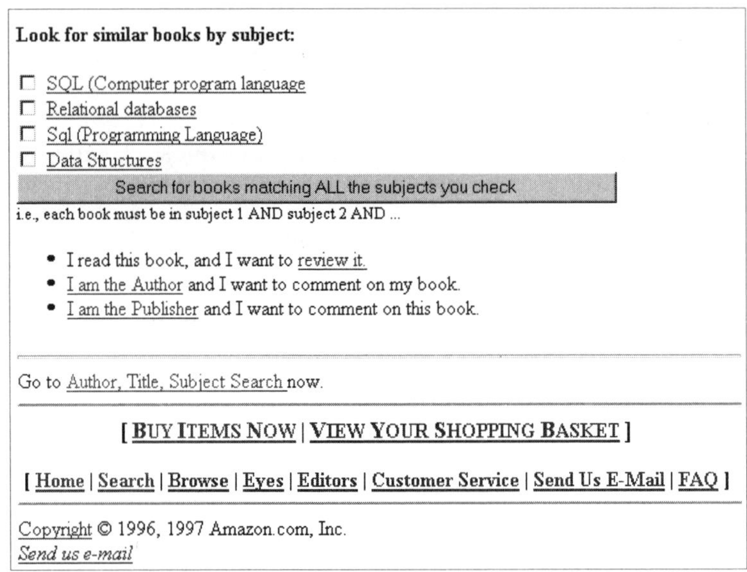

Figure 2.6: The bottom of the same amazon.com page. Note the profusion of links; clicking on any one of which will result in the referring site getting no commission.

for my work. The Web gave me back some money, to be sure. But I actually do place a higher value on some of the e-mail that I've gotten:

> "Thanks for getting me thru some sloooow weekends at work. . . . I have been working all the holiday weekends here at Directory Assistance & I wouldn't have made it out alive without your book. Thanks for sharing."
>
> —*Mary in Wisconsin*

> "I love your book for two reasons. First, it's great, the story is fresh and honest. The second is of course that it is the kind of thing that this technology has been building for—it somehow makes all those millions of dollars spent on computers, on the Net, on decades of development seem like there might have been a reason for it all. Thanks for the warm glow."
>
> —*Jonathan in New Zealand*

Listing 2.1: Weekly report on my commission from amazon.com

```
Click-throughs and sales by individual book
For the week of 15-Dec-96 through 21-Dec-96
Store ID photonet

                           YOUR
   ISBN      HITS ORDERED   FEE  TITLE
----------- ---- ------- ------ ---------------------------------------
0028604881     5      0    0.00 Baedeker Prague (Baedeker Guides)
0028609034     3      0    0.00 Frommer's Prague and the Best of the Cz
006091985X     1      0    0.00 Modern Baptists
0062771590     1      0    0.00 Access Cape Cod Martha's Vineyard & Nan
0070074178     1      0    0.00 **2** Principles of Corporate Finance (
014012991X     4      0    0.00 Tales of a Shaman's Apprentice : An Eth
0201447878     3      0    0.00 The Practical Sql Handbook : Using Stru
0201622165    10      0    0.00 MacIntosh Human Interface Guidelines
0240800265     9      1    0.00 **2** Basic Photographic Materials and
                      1         sold at  0% off list price of   44.95
024080158X    11      0    0.00 **2** View Camera Technique
0240802519    28      0    0.00 **2** The Hasselblad Manual : A Compreh
0393315290     4      0    0.00 A Random Walk Down Wall Street : Includ
0679025723    15      0    0.00 Fodor's : The Czech Republic & Slovakia
0679733485     1      0    0.00 The Marriage of Cadmus and Harmony
0679765425     2      0    0.00 **1** The New Yorker Book of Dog Cartoo
0684830426     1      0    0.00 **1** The Great Gatsby (Scribner Classi
0810960885     1      0    0.00 *** This item no longer in our catalog
0811807622   726      0    0.00 The Body : Photographs of the Human For
0821223321     2      0    0.00 America in Passing
0823049752    56      0    0.00 Photography
082306459X  1152      0    0.00 Graphis Nudes
0855339438   135      0    0.00 **2** The Workbook of Nudes and Glamour
0864422458     2      0    0.00 Lonely Planet Czech and Slovak Republic
0871062380     4      0    0.00 Berlin (Cadogan City Guides)
0879857595     7      0    0.00 Kodak Professional Photoguide
0893815322   329      0    0.00 Edward Weston : Nudes
089526529X     2      0    0.00 Hill Rat : Blowing the Lid Off Congress
0899330169     5      0    0.00 Vermont Atlas & Gazetteer
0899332501     2      0    0.00 Maine Atlas and Gazetteer
0899332544     5      0    0.00 New Hampshire Atlas and Gazetteer
0911515003     2      0    0.00 **2** The Permanence and Care of Color
0918373883     2      0    0.00 **2** New Zealand Handbook
0936262389    30      0    0.00 Infrared Photography Handbook
1558603239     2      0    0.00 **2** Joe Celko's Sql for Smarties : Ad
1560986220     5      0    0.00 Pinhole Photographs : Photographs (Phot
1564400069     1      0    0.00 **2** New York (Cadogan City Guides)
```

Listing 2.1: Weekly report on my commission from amazon.com (Continued)

```
1564581845     1     0     0.00 New York (Eyewitness Travel Guides)
1564585034     9     0     0.00 Prague (Eyewitness Travel Guides)
1566910153    22     1     1.08 New Mexico Handbook
                     1          sold at 10% off list price of   14.95
1566910358     8     2     2.87 Costa Rica Handbook (2nd Ed)
                     2          sold at 10% off list price of   19.95
1568842031     2     0     0.00 The Unix-Haters Handbook/Book and Barf
1858281210    10     0     0.00 The Czech & Slovak Republics : The Roug
1860110150    11     0     0.00 Prague : Cadogan City Guides (3rd Ed)
1880559234     1     0     0.00 Mastering Black-And-White Photography :
188332338X     1     0     0.00 Czech and Slovak Republics Guide
1885492022     1     0     0.00 The New York Dog Owner's Guide : Everyt
1885559003     2     0     0.00 Passage to Vietnam : Through the Eyes o
188555902X     2     0     0.00 Passage to Vietnam/Cd-Rom
2061569072    11     0     0.00 Michelin Green Guide : New England (7th
6301973259     1     0     0.00 **2** Marty
----------- ---- ------- ------ ---------------------------------------
    Totals: 2651     4     3.95
```

Learn to Program HTML in 21 Minutes

"One of Our Local Webmasters"

Now That You Know How to Write HTML, Don't

It's Hard to Mess Up a Simple Page

Why Graphic Designers Just Don't Get It

Chapter 3

H*ardcopy* featured a 10-year-old boy one night. His psychotic mother wouldn't take her meds and was beating him up. He wanted to live with his father but the judge wouldn't change his custody arrangement. So the 10-year-old kid built a Web site to encourage Internetters to contact the judge in support of a change in custody.

I tell this story to my friends who ask me for help in building their static HTML Web sites: "The abused 10-year-old got his site to work; I think you can, too."

If they persist, I tell them to find a page that they like, choose Save As in Netscape, then edit the text with the editor of their choice. I've never known anyone who couldn't throw together a simple page in under 21 minutes.

"One of Our Local Webmasters"

Having said all of that, now I'm going to explain how to write HTML. Why? It all started the day that Jim Clark, chairman of Netscape, came to MIT to give a Laboratory for Computer Science Distinguished Lecture. In previous years, the lecturers had been grizzled researchers who'd toiled anonymously for decades at places like Bell Labs and Stanford. In 1996, we had two billionaires: Bill Gates and Jim Clark. Before the lecture, Michael Dertouzos, the director of our lab, was touring Clark around the CS building. Clark stopped in the hallway outside my office to ask some questions about a framed photograph. The official hosts came into my office and dragged me away from my terminal to tell Jim Clark how I'd taken a picture of a waterfall in New Hampshire.

This was my big moment; I was being introduced to the one man in the world with enough power to fix everything wrong with the Web standards. I was sure that Dertouzos would tell him about what a computer science genius I was. He was going to talk about my old idea to add semantic tags to HTML documents, about the work I'd done to make medical record databases talk to each other to support Internet-wide epidemiology, about all the collaboration systems I'd built that hundreds of Web sites around the world were using.

"This is Philip Greenspun," the lab director began, "one of our local webmasters."

Yeah.

Anyway, part of a real webmaster's job is to assist new users in getting their pages together. So in that spirit, here is my five-minute HTML tutorial.

YOU MAY ALREADY HAVE WON $1 MILLION

Then again, maybe not. But at least you already know how to write legal HTML:

```
My Samoyed is really hairy.
```

That is a perfectly acceptable HTML document. Type it up in a text editor, save it as index.html, and put it on your Web server. A Web server can serve it. A user with Netscape Navigator can view it. A search engine can index it.

Suppose you want something more expressive. You want the word *really* to be in italic type:

```
My Samoyed is <I>really</I> hairy.
```

HTML stands for Hypertext Markup Language. The <I> is markup. It tells the browser to start rendering words in italics. The </I> closes the <I> element and stops the italics. If you want to be more tasteful, you can tell the browser to emphasize the word *really:*

```
My Samoyed is <EM>really</EM> hairy.
```

Most browsers use italics to emphasize, but some use boldface and browsers for ancient ASCII terminals (Lynx, for example) have to ignore this tag or come up with a clever rendering method. A picky user with the right browser program can even customize the rendering of particular tags.

There are a few dozen more tags in HTML. You can learn them by choosing View Source from Netscape Navigator when visiting sites whose formatting you admire. This is usually how I learn markup. You can learn them by visiting Web Tools Review (http://webtools.com/wtr), shown in Figure 3.1, and clicking through to one of the comprehensive online HTML guides. Or you can buy *HTML: The Definitive Guide* (Musciano and Kennedy, O'Reilly, 1996).

The Web Tools Review

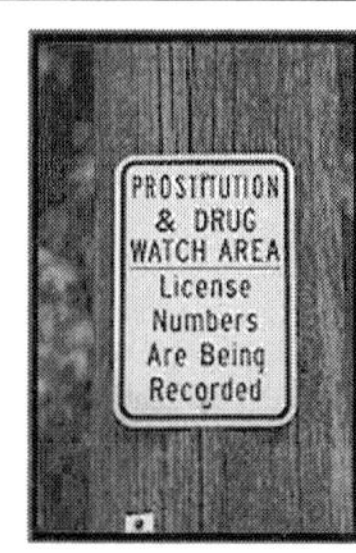

An on-line journal for developers of World Wide Web sites. Lessons learned the hard way by webmasters at sites like Travels with Samantha, with over 3500 users/day and 2 GB of traffic.

Dis' ain't yo' mama's guide to building "home pages."

New! Read my new book on how to think about your Web publishing philosophy, make money (shudder), and build RDBMS-backed Web sites. Then...

Add Collaboration to Your Web Site Right Now

Free services to make your Web site collaborative **right now**. You don't need to install a relational database management system or a new Web server. You just fill out some forms on my site...

First, let users add themselves to a private mailing list that only you can send email to with my SPAM mailing list service. Then allow users to contribute related links to your pages with my BooHoo link manager. Users can contribute comments on any of your pages once you tell my Loquacious comment server about your site.

If you want your readers to start talking to each other more directly, then set up LUSENET to run a Question-and-Answer forum or a threaded discussion for your site.

If you want something more than this, you'd better look for some programming assistance in the Web Tools Review Help Wanted Ads.

All of these services are free.

Figure 3.1: Web Tools Review (http://webtools.com/wtr/), my personal favorite source for pointers to HTML authoring resources

DOCUMENT STRUCTURE

Armed with a big pile of tags, you can start strewing them among your words more or less at random. Though browsers are extremely forgiving of technically illegal markup, it is useful to know that an HTML document officially consists of two pieces: the *head* and the *body*. The head contains information about the document as a whole, such as the title. The body contains information to be displayed by the user's browser.

Another structure issue is that you should try to make sure that you close every element that you open. So if your document has a <BODY> then it should have a </BODY> at the end. If you start an HTML table with a <TABLE> and don't have a </TABLE>, Netscape Navigator may display nothing. Tags can overlap, but you should close the most recently opened before the rest. For example, for something both boldface and italic, you would type the following:

```
My Samoyed is <B><I>really</I></B> hairy.
```

Something that confuses a lot of new users is that the <P> element used to surround a paragraph has an optional closing tag </P>. Browsers by convention assume that an open <P> element is implicitly closed by the next <P> element. This leads a lot of publishers (including lazy old me) to use <P> elements as paragraph separators. Figure 3.2 shows the code and Netscape appearance for a basic HTML document.

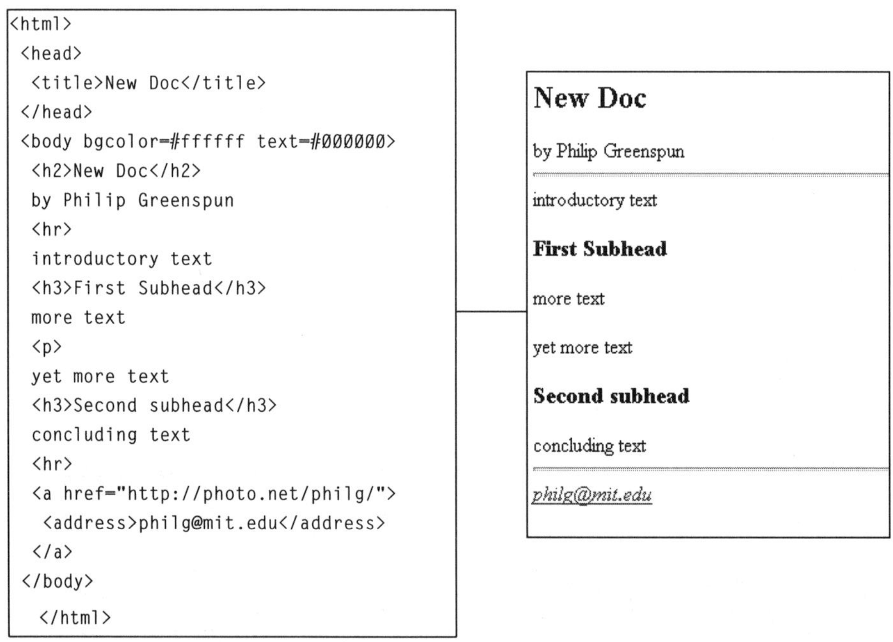
<html>
<head>
<title>New Doc</title>
</head>
<body bgcolor=#ffffff text=#000000>
<h2>New Doc</h2>
by Philip Greenspun
<hr>
introductory text
<h3>First Subhead</h3>
more text
<p>
yet more text
<h3>Second subhead</h3>
concluding text
<hr>
<a href="http://photo.net/philg/">
<address>philg@mit.edu</address>
</a>
</body>
</html>
New Doc
by Philip Greenspun
introductory text
First Subhead
more text
yet more text
Second subhead
concluding text
philg@mit.edu

Figure 3.2: A basic HTML document in my personal style, source code and Netscape's rendering

Figure 3.2 shows the source code which I will usually use to start out a Web document. Though saving this code in a file named "something.html" will cause my Web server program to tell browsers that this is an HTML document, the <HTML> element at the top provides insurance. Note that this tag is closed at the end of the document.

I put in a <HEAD> element mostly so that I can legally use the <TITLE> element to give this document a name. Whatever text I place between <TITLE> and </TITLE> will appear at the top of the user's Netscape window, on his Go menu, and in his bookmarks menu should he bookmark this page. After closing the head with a </HEAD>, I open the body of the document with a <BODY> element to which I've added some parameters to manually set the background to white and the text to black. Some Web browsers default to a gray background, and the resulting lack of contrast between background and text offends me so much that I abandon most of my principles and change the colors manually.

Just below the body, I have a headline, size 2, wrapped in an <H2> element. This will be displayed to the user at the top of the page. I probably should use <H1> but browsers typically render that in a font too huge even for my bloated ego. Underneath the headline, I'll often put "by Philip Greenspun" or something else indicating authorship, perhaps with a link to the full work. After that comes a horizontal rule tag: <HR>. The one really good piece of advice I've gotten from a graphic designer was Dave Siegel's admonition against overuse of horizontal rules. I use <H3> headlines in the text to separate sections and only put an <HR> at the very bottom of the document.

Underneath the last <HR>, I sign my document with "philg@mit.edu" (my e-mail address, unchanged since 1976). The <ADDRESS> element usually results in an italics rendering. The <A HREF= says "This is a hyperlink." If the reader clicks anywhere from here up until the </A> then the browser should send him to http://photo.net/philg/. I think that all documents on the Web should have a signature like this. Readers expect that they can scroll to the bottom of a browser window and find out who is responsible for what they've just read.

Note: **I could make this an <a href="mailto:philg@mit.edu"> so that the reader's browser would pop up a new e-mail message window. I did it that way for a few years but then I realized that a lot of users were asking, "Where can I find x on your site?" So I instead direct them to my home page which functions as a sort of table of contents for my site and which also has a link to my full-text search engine. I guess I should probably change my signature to read "Philip Greenspun" instead of "philg@mit.edu" but I haven't.**

NOW THAT YOU KNOW HOW TO WRITE HTML, DON'T

> **"Owing to the neglect of our defences and the mishandling of the German problem in the last five years, we seem to be very near the bleak choice between War and Shame. My feeling is that we shall choose Shame, and then have War thrown in a little later, on even more adverse terms than at present."**
>
> **—Winston Churchill in a letter to Lord Moyne, 1938 [Gilbert, 1991]**

HTML represents the worst of two worlds. We could have taken a formatting language and added hypertext anchors so that users had beautifully designed documents on their desktops. We could have developed a powerful document structure language so that browsers could automatically do intelligent things with Web documents. What we actually *have* with HTML is a hybrid: ugly documents without formatting *or* structural information.

Eventually the Web will work like a naïve user would expect it to. You ask your computer to find you the cheapest pair of blue jeans being hawked on the World Wide Web and ten seconds later you're staring at a photo of the product and being asked to confirm the purchase. You see an announcement for a concert and click a button on your Web browser to add the date to your calendar; the information gets transferred automatically. More powerful formatting isn't far off, either. Eventually there will be browser-independent ways to render the average novel readably.

Note: See my paper "We Have Chosen Shame and Will Get War" at http://photo.net/philg/research/shame-and-war.html for more on the subject of semantic tags.

None of this will happen without radical changes to HTML, however. We'll need *semantic tags* so that publishers can say, in a way that a computer can understand, "this page sells blue jeans," and "the price of these jeans is $25 U.S." Whether we need them or not, we are sure to get new formatting tags with every new generation of browser. (Personally I can't wait to be able to caption photographs and figures, an idea that was new in word processing programs of the 1960s.)

If the information that you are publishing is at all structured, it doesn't make sense to store it in HTML files. You are throwing all of that structure away. When HTML version 7.3 comes out, you'll have to manually edit 1,000 files to take advantage of the new features.

What you need is a database. You don't need a scary huge relational database management system like I discuss later in the book. If you aren't updating your data in real-time, an ordinary text file is fine. You just don't want it to be formatted in HTML.

For example, suppose that you are putting a company phone directory on the Web. You can define a structured format like this:

```
first name|last name|department|office number|home number|location
```

There is one line for each person in the directory. Fields are separated by vertical bars. So a file at MIT might look like this:

```
Philip|Greenspun|eecs|253-8574|864-6832|ne43-609
Rajeev|Surati|athletics|253-8581|555-1212|dupont gym
```

and so on. From this one file, a 20-line Perl or Tcl script can generate

- A public Web page showing names and office phone numbers
- A public Web page for each department showing names and office phone numbers
- A private Web page for each department showing names and home phone numbers

If you decide to start using a new HTML feature, you don't have to edit all these pages manually. You just need to change a few lines in the Perl or Tcl script and then rerun it to regenerate the HTML pages.

The high level message here is that you should think about the structure of the information you are publishing first. Then think about the best way to build an investment in that structure and preserve it. Finally, devote a bit of time to the formatting of the final HTML that you generate.

It's Hard to Mess Up a Simple Page

People with limited time, money, and experience usually build fairly usable Web sites. However, there is no publishing concept so simple that money, knowledge of HTML arcana, and graphic design can't make slow, confusing, and painful for users. After you've tarted up your site with frames, graphics, and color, check the server log to see how much traffic has fallen. Then ask yourself whether you shouldn't have thought about user interface stability.

CD-ROMs are faster, cheaper, more reliable, and a more engaging audio/visual experience than the Web. Why then do they sit on the shelf while users greedily surf the slow, unreliable, expensive Web? Stability of user interface.

There are many things wrong with HTML. It is primitive as a formatting language and it is almost worthless for defining document structure. Nonetheless, the original Web/HTML model has one big advantage: All Web pages look and work more or less the same. You see something black, you read it. You see something gray, that's the background. You see something blue (or underlined), you click on it.

When you use a set of traditional Web sites, you don't have to learn anything new. Every CD-ROM, on the other hand, has a sui generis user interface. Somebody thought it would be cute to put a little navigation cube at the bottom right of the screen. Somebody else thought it would be neat if you clicked on the righthand page of an open book to take you to the next page. Meanwhile, you sit there for 15 seconds feeling frustrated, with no clue that you are supposed to do anything with that book graphic on the screen. The CD-ROM goes back on the shelf.

The beauty of Netscape 2.0 and more recent browsers is that they allow the graphic designers behind Web sites to make their sites just as opaque and hard to use as CD-ROMs. Graphic designers are not user interface designers. If you read a book like the *Macintosh Human Interface Guidelines* (Apple Computer, Inc.; Addison-Wesley, 1993), you will appreciate what kind of thought goes into a well-designed user interface. Most of it has nothing to do with graphics and appearance. Pull-down menus are not better than pop-up menus because they look prettier; they are better because you always know exactly where to find the Print command.

Some of the bad things a graphic designer can do with a page were possible even way back in the days of Netscape 1.1. A graphic designer might note that most of the text on a page was hyperlinks and decide to just make all the text black (text=#000000, link=#000000, vlink=#000000). Alternatively, he or she may choose a funky color for a background and then three more funky colors for text, links, and visited links. Either way, users have no way of knowing what is a hyperlink and what isn't. Often designers get bored and change these colors even for different pages on the same site.

Frames are probably the worst Netscape innovation yet. The graphic designer, who has no idea what size or shape screen you have, is blithely chopping it up. Screen space is any user's most precious resource and frames give the publisher the tools to waste most of with ads, navigation "aids," and other items extraneous to the document that the user clicked on. What's worse, with Netscape Navigator 2.0, when the user clicked on the Back button to undo his last mouse click, Navigator would undo hundreds of mouse clicks and pop him out of the framed site altogether. Newer Web browsers handle frames a little more gracefully, but none of them handle scrolling as well as NCSA Mosaic did in 1993. In the old days, any Web site that brought up scroll bars could be scrolled down with a press of the space bar. With frames, even if there is only one scroll bar on screen, the space key does nothing until you click the mouse in the subwindow that owns the scroll bar.

I'm not saying that there isn't a place in this world for pretty Web sites. Nor even that frames cannot sometimes be useful. However, the prettiness and utility of frames must be weighed against the cold shock of unfamiliar user interface that will greet the user. This comparison is very seldom done and that's a shame.

Why Graphic Designers Just Don't Get It

Graphic designers get interfaces so wrong because they never figured out that they aren't building CD-ROMs. With a CD-ROM, you can control the user's access to the content. Borrow a copy of David Siegel's *Creating Killer Web Sites* and note that he urges you to have an "entry tunnel" of three pages with useless slow-to-load GIFs on them. Then there should be an "exit tunnel" with three more full-page GIFs. In between, there are a handful of "content" pages that constitute the site *per se.*

Siegel is making some implicit assumptions: that there are no users with text-only browsers; that users have a fast enough Net connection that they won't have to wait 45 seconds before getting to the content of a site; that there are no users who've turned off auto image loading; that there is some obvious place to put these tunnels on a site with thousands of pages. Even if all of those things are true, if the internal pages do indeed contain any content, AltaVista will roar through and wreck everything. People aren't going to enter the site by typing in "http://www.greedy.com" and then let themselves be led around by the nose *by you.* They will find the site using a search engine by typing a query string that is of interest *to them.* The search engine will cough up a list of URLs that it thinks are of interest *to them.* AltaVista does not think a Dave Siegel "entry tunnel" is "killer." In fact, it might not even bother to index a page that is just one GIF.

AltaVista is going to send a user directly to the URL on your server that has the text closest to the user's query string. AltaVista doesn't care that your $125-an-hour graphic designer thought this URL should be one-third of a frame. AltaVista doesn't care that the links to your home page and related articles are in another subwindow.

So, if you intend to get radical by putting actual content on your Web server, then it is probably a good idea to make each URL stand on its own. Throw in a link to the page author, the service home page, and the next page in a sequence if the URL is part of a linear work. Remember, the Web is not there so that you can impose what you think is cool on readers. Each reader will have his own view of the Web. Maybe that view was barfed up by a search engine. Maybe that view is links from his friend's home page. Maybe that view is a link from a personalization service that sweeps the Internet every night to find links and stories that fit your interest profile. Your task as a Web publisher is to produce works that will fit seamlessly not into the Web as you see it, but into the many Webs that your readers see.

SUMMARY

Here's what you should have learned in this chapter:

- Learning basic HTML shouldn't take more than a few minutes.
- The more HTML you know, the uglier and harder to use your site is likely to be.
- HTML is not powerful enough to express the most interesting structural characteristics of your documents; consider using a database of some kind instead and generating your HTML pages programmatically.

In the next chapter we'll discuss building and presenting libraries of photographs.

Adding Images to Your Site

Are Net Users Really That Shallow?

Images on the Web Can Look Better Than on a Magazine Page

Start By Thinking about Building an Image Library

Using Kodak PhotoCD to Manage Your Image Library

Maybe You Want Flashpix

Choosing between GIF and JPEG

Creating GIF and JPEG from PhotoCD Image Pacs

Organizing JPEGs on Your Web Server

Adding Images to Your Web Pages

Chapter 4

At this point you might be thinking that I've developed a multiple personality disorder. "Didn't he just recommend flushing all the graphics?" Well, I did. Hey, "Consistency is the hobgoblin of little minds" (Emerson; slightly out of context). Seriously, though, I'm not being inconsistent, as you'll see after looking at the following equations:

Web graphics = hard-to-understand bloated substitutes for text

pictures = content

A typical Web graphic is a GIF containing pixels that form themselves into the words *Next Page.* This communicates nothing extra to the user over the 9-byte ASCII string "Next Page." On the other hand, a sentence that says "Unix is generally preferred by big smelly hackers who seldom bathe" can be made much more powerful if it appears next to a photograph of a shirtless long-haired guy with a distended stomach, poking away at some C code.

Are Net Users Really That Shallow?

I think I'm a pretty average Net user. And at one time I was impressed by a beautiful poem, a compelling argument, a well-turned phrase. Then I watched my 73,425th hour of network television. Now what I'd really like to see in my Netscape window is a full-length episode of *The Simpsons.* However, the Internet isn't really designed to transmit audio and video in real-time. But plain text doesn't always grab me if I'm just surfing and not searching for something specific. So how is a Web publisher to capture readers like me? Images. A lot of Web readers will come for pictures and stay if the writing is good.

I've gotten literally hundreds of e-mail messages from *Travels with Samantha* readers who say things like "I bookmarked this site (http://www.webtravel.org/samantha/) a year ago because of the pictures. Over the last three days I came back and read all 19 chapters."

IMAGES ON THE WEB CAN LOOK BETTER THAN ON A MAGAZINE PAGE

Computer monitors don't have the resolution of photographic prints but they can display a wide range of tones. If you take care with your images, you may be able to present the user with the jewel-like experience of viewing a photographic slide.

High-quality black-and-white photographic prints have a contrast range of about 100 to 1. That is, the most reflective portion of a print (whitest highlight) reflects 100 times more light than the darkest portion (blackest shadow). The ideal surface for reflecting a lot of light would be extremely glossy and smooth. The ideal surface for reflecting very little light would be something like felt.

It is not currently possible to make one sheet of paper that has amazingly reflective areas and amazingly absorptive areas. Magazine pages are generally much worse than photographic paper in this regard. Highlights are not very white and shadows are not very black, resulting in a contrast ratio of about 20:1.

Slides have several times the contrast range of a print. That's because they work by blocking the transmission of light. If the slide is very clear, the light source comes through almost undimmed. In portions of the slide that are nearly black, the light source is obscured. Photographers always suffer heartbreak when they print their slides onto paper because it seems that so much shadow and highlight detail is lost. Ansel Adams devoted his whole career to refining the *Zone System,* a careful way of mapping the brightness range in a natural scene (as much as 10,000:1) into the 100:1 brightness range available in photographic paper.

Computer monitors are closer to slides than prints in their ability to represent contrast. Shadows correspond to portions of the monitor where the phosphors are turned off. Consequently, any light that comes from these areas is just room light reflected off the glass face of the monitor. You would think that the contrast ratio from a computer monitor would be 256:1 since display cards present 256 levels of intensity to the software. However, monitors don't respond linearly to increased voltage. Contrast ratios of something like 100:1 to 170:1 are therefore more typical.

Most Web publishers never take advantage of the monitor's ability to represent a wide range of tones. Rather than starting with the original slide or negative, they slap a photo down on a flatbed scanner. A photographic negative can only hold a tiny portion of the tonal range present in the original scene. A proof print from that negative has even less tonal range. So it is unsurprising that the JPEG resulting from this scanned print is flat and uninspiring.

Start By Thinking about Building an Image Library

As a publisher, you must think about building a digital image library. A successful image library has the following properties:

- You obtain high-quality digital representations of each image.
- Once scanned, you never have to go back to the original negative or slide.
- You can quickly find an image.

Obtaining a high-quality scan isn't so difficult. You must go back to whatever was in the camera—that is, the original negative or slide. You should not scan from a dupe slide. You should not scan from a print. The scan should be made in a dust-free room or you will spend the rest of your life retouching in PhotoShop. Though resolution is the most often mentioned scanner specification, it is not nearly as important as the maximum density that can be scanned. You want a scanner that can see deep into shadows, especially with slides.

Never going back to the original slide or negative again means never. If a print magazine requests a high-resolution image to promote your site, you should be able to deliver a 2,000x3,000 pixel scan without having to dig up the slide again. If there is a fire at your facility and all of your slides burn up, you should have a digital backup somewhere sufficient for all your future needs.

Quick retrieval means that if a user says, "I like the picture of the tiger in *Heather Has Two Mommies* (http://photo.net/zoo)," you can quickly find the high-resolution digital file.

Using Kodak PhotoCD to Manage Your Image Library

Kodak PhotoCD is a scanning standard that kills three birds with one, er, CD. Every image on a CD is available in five resolutions, the highest of which is 2,000x3,000. Kodak will tell you that you can make photographic-quality prints up to 20x30 inches in size from the scans. Scans are made from original negatives or slides in dust-controlled environments inside photo labs. The newest generation (1996) of PhotoCD scanners can read *reasonably* deep into slide film shadows. If you want more shadow detail and an additional 4,000x6,000 scan, you can get a Pro PhotoCD made.

Rather than taking up 5MB of hard disk space, which you might be tempted to scavenge when you think a Web project has been completed, a PhotoCD scan permanently resides on a CD-ROM. That means you will always have the scan available if an unanticipated need arises. If a book publisher decides that they must have an image, you can make the full .pcd file available on your Web server.

Quickly locating an image on PhotoCD is facilitated by Kodak's provision of index prints. You can work through a few hundred images per minute by looking over the index prints attached to each CD-ROM. What does all of this cost? From $1 to $3 for a standard scan from a 35mm original; about $15 for a Pro scan from a medium format or 4x5-inch original. When you consider that you are getting 500MB of media with each PhotoCD, the scanning *per se* is free (in other words, it is cheaper to have a PhotoCD made than to buy a hard disk capable of storing that much data).

My Favorite PhotoCD Vendors

Kodak sells turn-key Picture Imaging Workstations (PIWs) to photo labs who wish to make PhotoCDs. They cost about $100,000 plus another $80,000 for the high-resolution scanner that can handle larger-than-35mm originals and make ProPhotoCDs.

Like everything else in the photo lab world, you get what you pay for with PhotoCD scanning. Better labs have better dust control and are more careful handling your originals. I like Advanced Digital Imaging in Colorado (1-800-888-3686), Boston Photo Imaging in Massachusetts (617-267-4086), and ZZYZX in Los Angeles (1-800-995-1025).

The easiest to find PhotoCD scanning service is that provided by Kodalux, the processing lab owned by Kodak. Their scans tend to be dirty, requiring hours of touch-up work in PhotoShop. Furthermore, they lost or ruined my last three orders and then didn't return phone calls inquiring after my originals. Nor do I like the New York labs that I've tried, especially Duggal. Their prices are high and their dust control is poor.

My favorite professional photo lab is Portland Photographics (1-800-622-4227) but they hadn't bought a PIW as of February 1997. Check my recommended photo labs page, http://photo.net/photo/labs.html for my latest thoughts on this subject.

DELIVERING YOUR LIBRARY TO THE WEB

Users are not going to thank you if you present a 5MB .pcd Image Pac file straight from the PhotoCD. For starters, it would take 12 minutes to download with a 56-kbps modem. And then when they were all done, they wouldn't be able to view the file because most Web browsers don't understand Kodak PhotoCD format.

The official Kodak line is that you should use their PhotoCD on the Web CGI scripts and Java applets. You store the 5MB Image Pacs on your server and reference them like this:

```
<img src="/cgi-bin/pcd/naked-nerd-and-dog.pcd">
```

When the user requests an HTML page with this in-line reference, his browser will then invoke the Kodak-provided CGI script named "pcd" on your server. The program will extract the default resolution image out of the Image Pac file naked-nerd-and-dog.pcd and then deliver it to the user. You can add extra incantations to the reference and get other sizes. You can make the image "interactive" by referencing a Java applet instead:

```
<applet code=PcdApplet.class width=192 height=153>
<param name=src value="/cgi-bin/pcd/naked-nerd-and-dog.pcd">
</applet>
```

Now the user can zoom and scroll with a little toolbar that comes up on the bottom of the photo.

If It Worked You Wouldn't Want It There are so many problems with this official Kodak solution that it is tough to know where to begin. The first problem is one of publishing philosophy/user modeling. Do your readers want a toolbar at the bottom of each image? Do they want to have to learn to use the pcd applet just so that they can surf your site? Would not the pleasant activity of Web browsing then become a little too much like the hard work of using Adobe PhotoShop?

Most sites have a very simple user interface as regards pictures. They show you a small one. If you want a bigger view, you click on it. If you have a slow connection and a passionate interest in only one section of an image, I guess you would long for the user interface that Kodak presents, but I'm not sure it is worth the extra mental burden for other surfers.

In Any Case, It Doesn't Work Well, at least it doesn't work for me. I have 4,000 images online. At 5MB per image for the full Image Pac, that would require 20GB of hard disk space. I'm storing JPEGs at three resolutions (up to 1,000x1,500) for those same images for about 200K per image (less than 1GB total). Even if I had enough disk space, my antique HP Unix box could not possibly handle forking a CGI process for every IMG request. The machine gets perhaps ten requests for in-line images every second during peak hours. Right now these requests are handled by threads in an already-running AOLserver process, which can comfortably handle 500,000 hits per day on an old 50 MIPS machine like mine. I'd be lucky to get 50,000 hits per day out of it were I to switch to a CGI-based image server.

Kodak never really bothered to support PhotoCD on the Web. They distributed raw C code that they somehow expected people to edit and compile. There wasn't even a make file as you'd expect to get from a 16-year-old kid who wanted to distribute a C program. I'm writing this a year after Kodak introduced PhotoCD on the Web and have never yet encountered the technology in use on any Web site.

Maybe You Want Flashpix

Kodak, Hewlett-Packard, and Microsoft got together to turn Live Picture's hierarchical image format into a multivendor standard. Live Picture is a program similar to Adobe PhotoShop. PhotoShop uses the *wrong* stuff: If you have 100MB of image data but your monitor can only display 3MB, PhotoShop insists on manipulating those 100MB of data with every mouse movement you make. This makes PhotoShop interactive only in a theoretical sense if you are working with prepress images. Live Picture uses the *right* stuff: You work on a monitor-sized proxy for the final image. Every command executes instantly because you are only working with a few megabytes of image data. The 100MB full-sized image remains untouched on the disk until you've fin-

Alternatives to PhotoCD

Kodak PhotoCD is not always the best scanning solution. If you have slide film and need to see all the detail in the shadows, then you'll want to spring for a drum scan. These cost $25 to $75 each at service bureaus. Drum scanners use photomultiplier tubes that can read much higher densities than the CCD scanners used by Kodak for the Picture Imaging Workstation.

If you want to get to the Web very quickly, then it might be best to start with a digital camera. Personally, I'm not very fond of any of the lower-priced ones, but the $10,000-plus Kodak/Nikon and Kodak/Canon SLRs work well. In five years I'm sure that $1,000 digital cameras will deliver fairly high quality. Still, I'll probably still be using a film-based camera if only so that I can have a high-resolution image suitable for wall-size enlargements.

ished your edits. Then, at night, after you've gone home, Live Picture applies all of the edits you made to the proxy to the full-sized image. It might take hours, but you're home sleeping so you don't get frustrated.

It turns out that Adobe's implementation of the wrong idea was better than Live Picture's implementation of the right idea. Hence PhotoShop dominates the market. Enter the Web, however, and Live Picture's right idea looks even righter.

One hundred megabytes of data still takes a long time for your CPU to crunch. But before your CPU can even think about crunching it, the data has to be transmitted to your machine. That could take hours. So the publisher has to decide in advance exactly which sizes of images users are likely to need, with what quality, and with what cropping. Then he or she has to make them all available on the server and provide some kind of user interface to let the user know what is available. This is the same problem that Kodak thought it was solving with PhotoCD on the Web (see above). However, Flashpix solves it a bit more generally. Images can be any size or aspect ratio. They don't have to originate from a PhotoCD scan.

Much more interesting, though, is how Flashpix deals with the problem of "it looked great on my Macintosh monitor but it looks crummy on all those PCs out there." Current popular Web image formats such as GIF and JPEG files cannot provide any hints to client programs about how the image is supposed to look. Your graphic designer might have worked really hard using PhotoShop to get a particular shade of yellow into a graphic but there is no way for PhotoShop to encode in a GIF or JPEG file what shade of yellow the designer was actually seeing on the monitor. Depending on the final viewer's monitor and display card, the shade of yellow might be much darker or lighter.

Flashpix supports multiple color spaces. The first one, likely to be of most interest to Web publishers, is a calibrated RGB color space, NIFRGB, that was designed specifically for Flashpix. Another color space option is Photo YCC, which is what the Kodak PhotoCD Image Pac files already use. When a Flashpix image in one of these color spaces arrives on a computer using any kind of color management software, the image can be viewed and printed as intended by the designer.

Compression is handled rather elegantly by Flashpix, merging the best of GIF and JPEG. For line art with broad areas of the same color, Flashpix allows "single color compression." For photographs, Flashpix provides the option of JPEG compression.

A Flashpix file can contain data about the image such as a description to facilitate indexing and retrieval, the name of the photographer, camera settings, the type of film originally used, the method of scanning, and so on. More interestingly, the Flashpix file can contain virtual versions of the image by storing editing commands. In other words, you can have three different croppings and color corrections available from the same file merely by recording a few bytes of editing commands. When a user requests Version 2, the Flashpix reader pulls the raw bits from the file, re-executes the editing commands, and presents the final image on screen.

Currently, any of the PhotoCD vendors mentioned above can make you a CD-ROM with Flashpix-format scans instead of PhotoCD scans. Unfortunately, a Kodak marketing genius decided that the Flashpix format disks should only go to up to 4 Base resolution (1,024x1,536). That makes it impossible to build a digital image library from Flashpix CDs because you'll have to track down the original slide or negative and get a high-resolution scan when an image is requested for print use. Also, you're paying the same price from the PhotoCD lab for one-quarter of the bits. I guess it all makes sense if you have an MBA.

What else is bad about Flashpix? Some of the same things that are bad about PhotoCD on the Web. You need a lot of disk space to keep high-resolution images around. The people pushing the standard are all excited about giving users a Java applet that looks like PhotoShop Lite when all the users really want is to click and get a bigger picture. Your server might have to work much, much harder to deliver the same quantity of images to your users.

The worst thing about Flashpix, though, is that not too many readers have gone to http://image.hp.com and downloaded the Netscape plug-in. That means you'll have to maintain two parallel sites, one with Flashpix and one with standard JPEGs. Ugh. In the pre-Netscape days, this would have been a good time for content negotiation between the browser and server. The idea was that the browser would tell the server what kinds of data formats it could accept and then the server would pick the best kind of data to deliver. For example, if a browser asked for a file named "foobar" and said it could accept GIF or JPEG, the server would deliver the file "foobar.jpg". Netscape more or less trashed this system by producing a popular browser that wouldn't say what kind of data formats it could accept and then producing a family of server programs that couldn't negotiate with other brands of browsers.

I guess I will start thinking seriously about publishing in Flashpix when 50 percent of my users have a browser that shipped with native support for Flashpix. The idea of forcing people to go and load a plug-in just so that they can view my content is anathema to me. When 85 percent of users are Flashpix-capable then I suppose I would do a Flashpix-only site. Until then, I'll stick with formats that Netscape understands: GIF and JPEG.

CHOOSING BETWEEN GIF AND JPEG

For line art, use GIF. For photographs, use JPEG. It is as simple as that. The compression algorithm for GIF works extremely well if you have large areas that are the same color. The compression algorithm for JPEG is optimized for photographic images and hence produces files about one-third the size of a similar quality GIF. GIFs are limited to 256 colors; JPEGs can contain the full 24-bit color palette.

I personally don't like interlaced GIFs (Netscape 1.0 and higher) or progressive JPEGs (Netscape 2.0 and higher). The theory behind these formats is that the user can at least look at a fuzzy full-sized proxy for the image while all the bits are loading. In practice, the user is *forced* to look at a fuzzy full-sized proxy for the image while all the bits are loading. Is it done? Well, it looks kind of fuzzy. Oh wait, the top of the image seems to be getting a little more detail. Maybe it is done now. It is still kind of fuzzy, though. Maybe Greenspun wasn't using a tripod. Oh wait, it seems to be clearing up now...

A standard GIF or JPEG is generally swept into its frame as the bits load. The user can ignore the whole image until it has loaded in its final form, then take a good close look. He never has to wonder whether more bits are yet to come.

For some examples and discussion of the effect of image format on file size, see Plates E through I in the color plate section.

CREATING GIF AND JPEG FROM PHOTOCD IMAGE PACS

USING PHOTOSHOP

If you have a lot of time and/or money and/or not too many images, the best way to convert PhotoCD Image Pacs to GIF or JPEG is with Adobe PhotoShop. Here's the procedure that I think results in the best conversion:

1 Make sure that your computer has enough video RAM to provide 24 bits per pixel ("millions of colors" on the Macintosh, "True Color" on Windows). Everyone deserves to have a Trinitron monitor, 17 inches or larger. You will need at least 32MB of RAM to work with medium-sized images; 64MB would be better. Unless you are unusually patient, you will want a computer that can do fast floating point arithmetic: that is, a Power Mac or a Pentium Pro. If you're on a Macintosh, use the Knoll Gamma Corrector that comes with PhotoShop and set it to 2.2, thus degrading your machine's beautifully designed graphics system to the point

that it is closer to the typical Unix or PC-compatible box. If you are running PhotoShop under Windows, then you probably have a machine that is fairly close to the average Internet user's. Just calibrate PhotoShop (File > Color Settings > Monitor Setup) until a JPEG brought into PhotoShop looks about the same as a JPEG in an adjacent Netscape window.

2. Open the IMG00n.PCD files on the PhotoCD from Adobe PhotoShop using the Kodak Color Management System (included with PhotoShop), transforming from Photo YCC space to Adobe RGB. *If you are on a Macintosh, do not use the PICT pseudo-files created by the operating system; they aren't optimally converted.*
3. Remove the "PhotoCD haze." Start with the Levels command to see a histogram of the intensities in the image. Note that there is probably nothing at either the full white or full black ends of the spectrum. Try pushing the Auto Levels button. If the results are too radical, undo it and manually slide the white point a bit to the left and the black point a bit to the right.
4. Edit and crop as desired. A WACOM drawing tablet makes it much easier to do fine touch-up work or realize artistic ambitions with PhotoShop. If you can't afford the desk space for a tablet, then at least get a 3M Precise Mousing Surface (the only perfect computer product I've ever purchased).
5. If you want to add a black border, change the background color to black and use the Canvas Size command to increase the canvas to 102 percent in width and height. I like black borders.
6. When you are satisfied with your image, save it as a PhotoShop native format file using the Save As command.
7. Use the Unsharp Mask filter once with the settings given in Table 4.1.

Table 4.1: Unsharp Mask Filter Settings

Image	Resolution	Amount	Radius	Threshold
Base/16	128x192	100	0.25	2
Base/4	256x384	100	0.5	2
Base	512x768	100	1.0	2
4 Base	1,024x1,536	100	2.0	2
16 Base	2,048x3,072	100	4.0	2

Be prepared to undo and change the settings if the result isn't what you want. Unsharp Mask finds edges between areas of color and increases the contrast along the edge. The Amount setting controls the strength of the filter. I usually stick to numbers between 60 percent and 140 percent. Radius controls how many pixels in from the color edge are affected (so you need higher numbers for bigger images). Threshold controls how different the colors on opposing sides of an edge have to be before the filter goes to work. You need a higher threshold for noisy images or ones with subtle color shifts that you want left unsharpened.

8. Use the Save a Copy command to write your image out as JPEG, medium quality. I usually pick a descriptive file name, add the image number from the PhotoCD, and then explicitly add a ".jpg" because I know that I'll be FTPing this file to a Unix server; for example, "hairy-dog-37.jpg".
9. Use the Revert command to reload the unsharpened PhotoShop format file from disk.
10. Use the Image Size command to shrink the picture, then use Unsharp Mask again.
11. Save the small image as JPEG, low or medium quality. I use the same file name as in Step 8, but with an extra "-sm" before the extension: "hairy-dog-37-sm.jpg". This lets a little Perl script on my Unix box find the corresponding files and generate HTML IMGs for the small JPEGs that are anchors for hyperlinks to the larger JPEGs.

One of the rationales behind this approach is that you never sharpen twice and that sharpening is always the very last image-processing step. That's why an intermediate PhotoShop native format file is necessary.

If you have many images and can't afford to edit each one individually, then you have a variety of alternatives. One is to use Action Lists in Adobe PhotoShop 4.0. These allow you to record a series of PhotoShop commands and then play them back on an image or play them back on a batch of images in a directory. Action Lists are easy to use but are, regrettably, difficult to share because they can only be saved or loaded en masse. Meaning I cannot give you two of my favorite actions for you to add to your PhotoShop; I can only give you my entire Action List file which you must replace your entire Action List file with.

There are a variety of PhotoShop plug-ins that simultaneously do something akin to Auto Levels plus Unsharp Mask. I've had pretty good luck with Intellihance by Extensis (http://www.extensis.com). The most powerful tool for batch-processing images on a Mac or PC is Debabelizer from Equilibrium.

Note: The Debabelizer Web site is http://www.equilibrium.com, and it is a beautiful example of how not to be a Web publisher. If you search for "debabelizer" in AltaVista or Infoseek, you probably won't find their site. That's because they fell in love with the GIFs that their program can produce. Search engines can't read GIFs. So a nearly text-free site like Equilibrium's is doomed to obscurity.

USING UNIX TOOLS

If you are an experienced Unix user, you'll probably find it more convenient to do your batch processing in Unix where all the familiar scripting languages are available. My favorite Unix tool is ImageMagick. ImageMagick is one of the most powerful image-processing systems available. It is free, runs on Unix and Win 95/NT, and is distributed with source code. Listing 4.1 shows the summary of its capabilities that you get when you type "convert -h" (Note: the Unix man and Web documentation is much more extensive). You can find precompiled binaries for most Unix variants and also Windows 95/NT at http://www.wizards.dupont.com/cristy/ImageMagick.html.

Listing 4.1: Summary of ImageMagick's Capabilities

```
Version: @(#)ImageMagick 3.8.0 97/01/15 cristy@dupont.com

Usage: imconvert [options ...] input_file output_file

Where options include:
  -adjoin             join images into a single multi-image file
  -average            average a set of images
  -blur factor        apply a filter to blur the image
  -border geometry    surround image with a border of color
  -box color          color for annotation bounding box
  -charcoal factor    simulate a charcoal drawing
  -colors value       preferred number of colors in the image
  -colorspace type    GRAY, OHTA, RGB, XYZ, YCbCr, YIQ, YPbPr, or YUV
  -comment string     annotate image with comment
  -compress type      RunlengthEncoded or Zip
  -contrast           enhance or reduce the image contrast
  -crop geometry      preferred size and location of the cropped image
  -cycle amount       cycle the image colormap
  -delay value        display the next image after pausing
  -density geometry   vertical and horizontal density of the image
  -despeckle          reduce the speckles within an image
  -display server     obtain image or font from this X server
  -dispose method     GIF disposal method
  -dither             apply Floyd/Steinberg error diffusion to image
```

Listing 4.1: Summary of ImageMagick's Capabilities (Continued)

```
-draw string          annotate the image with a graphic primitive
-edge factor          apply a filter to detect edges in the image
-emboss               emboss an image
-enhance              apply a digital filter to enhance a noisy image
-equalize             perform histogram equalization to an image
-flip                 flip image in the vertical direction
-flop                 flop image in the horizontal direction
-font name            X11 font for displaying text
-frame geometry       surround image with an ornamental border
-gamma value          level of gamma correction
-geometry geometry    preferred size or location of the image
-implode amount       implode image pixels about the center
-interlace type       None, Line, Plane, or Partition
-label name           assign a label to an image
-loop iterations      add Netscape loop extension to your GIF animation
-map filename         transform image colors to match this set of colors
-matte                store matte channel if the image has one
-modulate value       vary the brightness, saturation, and hue
-monochrome           transform image to black and white
-negate               apply color inversion to image
-noise                add or reduce noise in an image
-normalize            transform image to span the full range of colors
-opaque color         change this color to the pen color
-page geometry        size and location of the Postscript page
-paint radius         simulate an oil painting
-pen color            color for annotating or changing opaque color
-pointsize value      pointsize of Postscript font
-quality value        JPEG quality setting
-raise value          lighten/darken image edges to create a 3-D effect
-region geometry      apply options to a portion of the image
-roll geometry        roll an image vertically or horizontally
-rotate degrees       apply Paeth rotation to the image
-sample geometry      scale image with pixel sampling
-scene value          image scene number
-segment values       segment an image
-shade degrees        shade the image using a distant light source
-sharpen factor       apply a filter to sharpen the image
-shear geometry       slide one edge of the image along the X or Y axis
-size geometry        width and height of image
-solarize thresold    negate all pixels above the threshold level
-spread amount        displace image pixels by a random amount
-swirl degrees        swirl image pixels about the center
-texture filename     name of texture to tile onto the image background
-transparent color    make this color transparent within the image
-treedepth value      depth of the color classification tree
```

Listing 4.1: Summary of ImageMagick's Capabilities (Continued)

```
  -undercolor geometry control undercolor removal and black generation
  -verbose             print detailed information about the image

Change '-' to '+' in any option above to reverse its effect.  For
example,  specify +matte to store the image without an matte channel.

By default, the image format of `file' is determined by its magic
number.  To specify a particular image format, precede the filename
with an image format name and a colon (i.e. ps:image) or specify the
image type as the filename suffix (i.e. image.ps).  Specify 'file' as
'-' for standard input or output.

The following image formats are recognized:

  Tag   Description
  ------------------------------------------------------------
  AVS   AVS X image file.
  BMP   Microsoft Windows bitmap image file.
  CMYK  Raw cyan, magenta, yellow, and black bytes.
  DCX   ZSoft IBM PC multi-page Paintbrush file
  DIB   Microsoft Windows bitmap image file.
  EPS   Adobe Encapsulated PostScript file.
  EPS2  Adobe Level II Encapsulated PostScript file.
  EPSF  Adobe Encapsulated PostScript file.
  EPSI  Adobe Encapsulated PostScript Interchange format.
  FAX   Group 3.
  FITS  Flexible Image Transport System.
  GIF   CompuServe graphics interchange format; 8-bit color.
  GIF87 CompuServe graphics interchange format; 8-bit color (version 87a).
  GRADATION gradual passing from one shade to another.
  GRAY  Raw gray bytes.
  HDF   Hierarchical Data Format.
  HISTOGRAM
  HTML  Hypertext Markup Language with a client-side image map
  JBIG  Joint Bi-level Image experts Group file interchange format.
  JPEG  Joint Photographic Experts Group JFIF format; compressed 24-bit color.
  MAP   Colormap intensities and indices.
  MATTE Raw matte bytes.
  MIFF  Magick image file format.
  MONO  Bi-level bitmap in least-significant-byte (LSB) first order.
  MPEG  Motion Picture Experts Group file interchange format.
  MTV   MTV Raytracing image format.
  Netscape
        Netscape 216 color cube.
  NULL  NULL image.
```

Listing 4.1: Summary of ImageMagick's Capabilities (Continued)

```
PBM   Portable bitmap format (black and white).
PCD   Photo CD.
PCX   ZSoft IBM PC Paintbrush file.
PDF   Portable Document Format.
PGM   Portable graymap format (gray scale).
PICT  Apple Macintosh QuickDraw/PICT file.
PNG   Portable Network Graphics.
PNM   Portable anymap.
PPM   Portable pixmap format (color).
PREVIEW
PS    Adobe PostScript file.
PS2   Adobe Level II PostScript file.
RAD   Radiance image file.
RGB   Raw red, green, and blue bytes.
RGBA  Raw red, green, blue, and matte bytes.
RLA   Alias/Wavefront image file; read only.
RLE   Utah Run length encoded image file; read only.
SGI   Irix RGB image file.
SUN   SUN Rasterfile.
TEXT  Raw text file; read only.
TGA   Truevision Targa image file.
TIFF  Tagged Image File Format.
UYVY  16bit/pixel interleaved YUV.
TILE  tile image with a texture.
VICAR Read only.
VID   Visual Image Directory.
VIFF  Khoros Visualization image file.
X     Select image from X server screen.
XC    Constant image of X server color.
XBM   X Windows system bitmap, black and white only.
XPM   X Windows system pixmap file (color).
XWD   X Windows system window dump file (color).
YUV   CCIR 601 1:1:1 file.
```

Once you have installed ImageMagick, you can simply type "convert *from-file name to-file name*" at the Unix shell prompt and the ImageMagick program figures out what to do. There are also a lot of powerful options. Here's how I make a thumbnail JPEG:

```
convert -interlace NONE -sharpen 50 -border 2x2 \
-comment 'copyright Philip Greenspun' \ '/cdrom/PHOTO_CD/IMAGES/IMG0013.PCD;1[1]'
bear-salmon-13-sm.jpg
```

Note that this is all a single shell command. I've used a bunch of optional image-processing flags before the from-file name. Because I don't like progressive

JPEGs (see above), the default from ImageMagick, I invoke "-interlace NONE". Any kind of scanning introduces some fuzziness into the image so I ask ImageMagick to sharpen a bit with "-sharpen 50". I want a two-pixel border all around, so I use "border 2x2". I could choose the color but the default will be black. Finally, ImageMagick lets me add a comment to the JPEG file. Anyone who opens the JPEG with a standard text editor like Emacs will be able to see that it is "copyright Philip Greenspun" (conceivably other programs might display this information, but PhotoShop doesn't seem to, either on the Macintosh or Windows).

The from-file name, "/cdrom/PHOTO_CD/IMAGES/IMG0013.PCD;1[1]," is mostly dictated by the directory structure on a PhotoCD. However, the final "[1]" tells ImageMagick to grab the 128x192 pixel thumbnail out of the Image Pac ("Base/16" size in Kodak parlance). The to-file name, "bear-salmon-13-sm.jpg," is cunningly chosen. I try to include some kind of picture description in the file name but also make sure to include the image number on the original PhotoCD so as to make retrieval of the entire Image Pac easier. Finally, I make sure that all of my thumbnail images end in a "-sm."

For the medium-sized JPEG, the following ImageMagick command suffices:

```
convert -interlace NONE -sharpen 50 -border 5x10 -comment 'copyright
Philip Greenspun' -font 6x9 -pen white -draw 'text 600,520 "copyright
1993 philg@mit.edu"' '/cdrom/PHOTO_CD/IMAGES/IMG0013.PCD;1[3]' bear-
salmon-13.jpg
```

Note that here I've added an additional few commands to set the text font size, set the text color to white, and draw a bit of text in the ten-pixel border: "copyright 1993 philg@mit.edu". I'm not sure that this will discourage piracy, but it is fairly unobtrusive and doesn't take any extra time to include. Note that the from-file name now is suffixed with "[3]" indicating the "Base" resolution, 512x768. Note also that the to-file name has been stripped of its "-sm" suffix, since I am storing the larger file this time.

Finally, I like to publish a really good-sized 4 Base image. That's 1,024x1,536 pixels, enough to almost fill a modern computer's 1,200x1,600 screen. Users who paid the big bucks for a 21-inch monitor are going to be frustrated if you don't publish your best images in this size. The conversion command is almost the same but I ask for size "[4]" off the PhotoCD and add a "-big" suffix to the to-file name.

```
convert -interlace NONE -sharpen 50  -border 5x10 \
-comment 'copyright Philip Greenspun' -font 6x9 -pen white \
-draw 'text 1370,1029 "copyright 1995 philg@mit.edu"' \
'/cdrom/PHOTO_CD/IMAGES/IMG0013.PCD;1[4]' bear-salmon-13-big.jpg
```

Most Unix boxes already have the NetPBM utilities installed, in which case you just need to find a copy of Hadmut Danisch's HPCDTOPPM program (freeware, available from ftp://ftp.ise.fhg.de/pub/graphics/ and also bundled as part of LINUX). Here is a Unix pipeline that shows the program in use:

```
hpcdtoppm -3 /cdrom/PHOTO_CD/IMAGES/IMG0013.PCD | \
cjpeg -quality 75 -o  > bear-salmon-13.jpg
```

HPCDTOPPM writes a PPM format file to standard output which the CJPEG program reads from standard input. The "-3" option in the invocation of HPCDTOPPM asks for the base resolution (512x768) image.

The "-quality 75" in CJPEG delivers an image which is one-third the size of a "quality 95" image and looks equally good to me on a 24-bit monitor.

My current practice is to write a small description file for each of my PhotoCDs. It contains one line for each image on the disk specifying image number, file name, which resolutions to convert, caption, and so on. I then use a Perl script to loop through these description lines. It calls ImageMagick to add borders, a copyright notice, and some sharpening. The script also writes out .html index files with in-line thumbnails, each hyperlinked to larger JPEGs.

Using this method, I've been able to add about 4,000 images to my Web server with only a few minutes of hand-labor. The quality isn't as good as I would have gotten by using PhotoShop, but, should automated tools improve, I can rerun my scripts in a matter of minutes. Not having spent hundreds of hours in PhotoShop gives me time and energy to write stories to accompany the photos.

No matter what means you use to produce the JPEGs, you should be careful how you organize them in your Web server's file system.

Note: If you would like to use the same Perl scripts, which should run under Unix and Windows NT/95, just download them from http://photo.net/philg/how-to-scan-photos.html.

ORGANIZING JPEGS ON YOUR WEB SERVER

When I got my first PhotoCDs back, for *Travels with Samantha*, I dumped all of the GIFs and JPEGs into the same directory as the .html files. That was stupid.

A few months after my site went up, magazines started asking for high-resolution digital files corresponding to, say, "http://webtravel.org/samantha/bear-fight.jpg." I wanted to send them the original .pcd file from the PhotoCD, but the URL told me nothing about which of my dozens of PhotoCDs held the Image Pac. When I'd use an image from *Travels with Samantha* in another service, such as http://photo.net/photo, I'd have to use a cross reference. After a couple years of this, I hit upon the following system:

- Keep a separate directory for each PhotoCD with a name like "pcd1253", where the "1253" corresponds to the last four digits of the Kodak serial number, printed prominently on the index print that comes with the disk and less prominently around the CD-ROM's spindle hole.

- If you manipulate images from this disk, put them in a subdirectory like "pcd1253/manipulated-images".
- Make all of your references from HTML files absolute paths to the server root; for example,

```
<IMG SRC="/photo/pcd1253/pink-lady-and-dogs-8-sm.jpg">
```

I like to keep an index page for each PCD that contains absolute links to each image, each one ready to be cut and pasted into another HTML file and work properly.

Adding Images to Your Web Pages

An image-rich HTML document need not take any longer to load than an image-free document. In 1994, Netscape extended the HTML element IMG with WIDTH and HEIGHT attributes. If set, they tell modern browsers how big an image will be once loaded. That way the browser is able to lay out the complete text of an HTML document before *any* of the images have loaded. Here's an example for a thumbnail:

```
<IMG SRC="/photo/pcd1253/pink-lady-and-dogs-8-sm.jpg"
WIDTH=192 HEIGHT=128>
```

If the image isn't exactly 128x192, the browser will resize it to fit. Netscape Navigator isn't going to lovingly resize your image the way that PhotoShop would, so make sure that you get these numbers right. I never trust myself to type these tags correctly. I run WWWis (originally "wwwimagesize"), a Perl program that grinds over an .html file, grabs all of the GIF and JPEG files to see how big they are, then writes out a new copy of the .html file with WIDTH and HEIGHT attributes for each IMG. With a one-line shell command on my Unix server, WWWis managed to update about 1,000 .html files in a few minutes. The program is free and available from http://www.tardis.ed.ac.uk/~ark/wwwis/.

Nowadays, as soon as I finish converting a PhotoCD to JPEG format, I run WWWis over the index file for that PhotoCD. Then, when I cut and paste the IMG elements into my content pages, the WIDTH and HEIGHT attributes are already there.

Other attributes potentially worth adding to your HTML tags are the following:

- "hspace=5 vspace=5" These will tell the browser to leave five pixels of white space around the image.

- "border=0" If the IMG is a hyperlink to a larger JPEG, it will be surrounded by a blue border. If you think this blue border is ugly, then you can set border=0 to turn it off. Personally, I leave the border because it serves as a user interface cue.
- "align=left" This lets text flow around the right edge of the IMG.

At this point, you can put your PhotoCD in the filing cabinet and go home.

Summary

Here is what you should have learned in this chapter:

- Photographs are valuable content, as distinct from graphics which are generally a waste of your money and the user's downloading time.
- Always scan from an original negative or slide, never from a print.
- Think seriously about the fact that you are building an image library and whether the Kodak PhotoCD system can help you.
- Build a structured database of information about your images that you can use for automatic conversion to JPEG format, file naming, and captioned HTML code generation.
- Use WIDTH and HEIGHT tags in your IMGs so that the text on pages with in-line images doesn't take longer to load.

A Note about Copyright

For my first couple of years publishing on the Web, I got very huffy about copyright infringement. I entertained dark thoughts of litigation when I saw one of my photos, without credit or payment, filling the space between ads in *Forbes* or *Interactive Week* (published by "the other Ziff-Davis"). I didn't spend days behind a tripod waiting for the perfect moment so that people could use my work to promote their ugly commercial ventures.

But, realistically, litigation in the United States isn't for middle-class people. I couldn't afford to hire a team of lawyers to chase down the miscreants and I didn't want to spend my life filing lawsuits myself. I decided to focus my energy on creating new works and not lose sleep over piracy of the old ones.

Then, one of my readers e-mailed me a Web page with an uncredited usage of one of my bear photographs from *Travels with Samantha:* "Yes, the IRS does try to intimidate and bully you. And, they publicly crucify some public figure each year (Willie Nelson, Leona Helmsley, Darryl Strawberry, Pete Rose, etc.) who has been caught with allegedly 'fudged' returns. But, as you will learn, there is NO LAW, anywhere, that mandates you file a tax return! " For $88-$1,000, you could purchase assistance in "How to STOP Paying Federal Income Tax—LEGALLY!"

This wasn't exactly what I had in mind when I set up my site, so I sent the company some e-mail requesting that they remove the picture. The response was frustrating but I was open-mouthed in admiration of its creativity:

```
Our programmer says that he has never seen your book, and that the picture
came from a site that listed lots of pix (both gif & jpg) which were
presented as available for download by anyone!

At this point we are not interested in getting into a tussle with you, but
the question is now open whether the picture is original with you or you
took the picture from the same source.

We'll need some coroberation to verify your claim to the picture before we
go any farther.

Dana Ewell, CEO
!SOLUTIONS! Group
```

(Continued)

(Continued from previous page)

I still didn't have enough money to hire a team of lawyers to put the genie back in the bottle but I thought I could use my assets: (1) My site is more interesting than average; (2) My site is more stable and, because it is so old, better-indexed than average. Every time another publisher used one of my 4,000 online images with a hyperlinked credit, I might earn a new reader. Did their site suck? So much the better. The user wouldn't be likely to press the Back button once he or she arrived at my site through the "photo courtesy Philip Greenspun" link. Of course, my site is non-commercial so extra readers don't bring me any cash, but I do like the idea that my work is broadly exposed to people who might not find it otherwise. That took care of the good-faith users. Could I use my site's stability and presence in Web indices to deal with the bad-faith users?

It hit me all at once. An online Hall of Shame. I'd send non-crediting users a single e-mail message. If they didn't mend their ways, I'd put their names in my Hall of Shame for their grandchildren to find. I figure that anyone reduced to stealing pictures is probably not creative enough to build a high Net profile. So a search for their name won't result in too many documents, one of which will surely be my Hall of Shame. What if the infringer were to retaliate by putting up a page saying "Philip Greenspun beats his Samoyed"? Nobody would ever find it because an AltaVista search for "Philip Greenspun" returns too many documents. Try it right now, then try "Shawn Bonnough" for comparison, making sure to include the string quotes in both queries.

A practical-minded person might argue that my system doesn't get me any cash or stop any infringement. A technology futurist might argue that one of the micropayment schemes from the 1960s is going to be set up Real Soon Now. Both of these people are right, I guess, but I won't be sorry if what seems to be the evolving custom on the Internet solidifies into law: Send e-mail asking for permission to republish, be scrupulous about crediting authors, and prepare to be vilified if you flout these rules.

Would that be the best possible system? Maybe not, but it has to be much more efficient for society than a bunch of corporations hiring lawyers to sling mud at each other in court. Under my system, we can enjoy seeing our work (with credit) on other folks' sites, vent our spleens at midnight by adding to a Web page of transgressors, and then move on to new productive activities.

Publicizing Your Site (Without Irritating Everyone on the Net)

Search Engines

Web Directories

Final Tip

Chapter 5

A good way to publicize your site is to buy a 60-second commercial during the Super Bowl. A black screen with your URL in white should get the message out. Your users will scribble down the URL on the cover of *Parade* magazine and then check it later. Suppose, however, that a six-pack of Budweiser should be spilled on that copy of *Parade*. Your URL is lost to the user unless he roots around in the Web directories and search engines. Web directories are manually maintained listings of sites, organized by category. If your Super Bowl spot was clear that you are selling beads, then the user might find http://www.yahoo.com/Business_and_Economy/Companies/Hobbies/Beading/ and follow a link from there to your server. More likely, though, a user will just go into a search engine and type "beads." This chapter is about making sure that your site is at the top of the list computed by the search engine.

Search Engines

So if a Web directory is a manually maintained listing of sites, then a search engine is fully automated, right? So what's to know? Plenty, as it turns out. If you know the guts of how search engines operate, you can make them work for you.

HOW SEARCH ENGINES LOOK TO THE USER

The search engine's job is to produce a private view of the World Wide Web where links are sorted by relevance to the user's current interest. So if the user types "history of Soho London," a page of links to pages detailing the history of this neighborhood is expected. The search engine user will bypass "entry tunnels" and bloated cover page GIFs and go right to the most relevant content anywhere on your Web server. That's the theory anyway.

HOW SEARCH ENGINES WORK

All the search engines have three components (see Figure 5.1). Component 1 grabs all the Web pages that it can find. Component 2 builds a huge full-text index of those grabbed pages. Component 3 waits for user queries and serves lists of pages that match those queries. Your Web server deals with Component 1 of the public search engines. When you are surfing http://altavista.digital.com or http://www.webcrawler.com, you are talking to Component 3 of those search engines.

Component 1: The Crawler (or "How to Get Listed by a Search Engine")

Each search engine's crawler has a database of URLs it knows about. When time comes to rebuild the index, the crawler grabs every URL in this database to see if there are any changes or new links. It follows the new links, indexes the documents retrieved, and will eventually recursively follow links from those new documents.

If your site is linked from an indexed site, you do not have to take any action to get indexed. For example, Brian Pinkerton's original WebCrawler knew about the MIT Artificial Intelligence Laboratory home page (http://www.ai.mit.edu), grabbed a list of Lab employees linked from the page, then followed a link from there to my personal home page (http://photo.net/philg). As soon as I finished *Travels with Samantha* (http://webtravel.org/samantha), I linked to it from my home page. WebCrawler eventually discovered the new link, followed it, and then followed the links to individual chapters. The full text of my book was indexed without my ever being aware of WebCrawler's action.

This Web is getting larger and the search engine crawlers have a tough time keeping up. It might be six months before a crawler revisits your page to see if anything has changed, though the more aggressive ones try to do it once every six weeks. If you are impatient to get your site indexed and/or you recently changed a lot of content and/or nobody is linking to you, it is worth using the "add my URL" forms on the search engine sites. The specific URLs that you enter will be available to querying users within a few days (AltaVista) or weeks (WebCrawler).

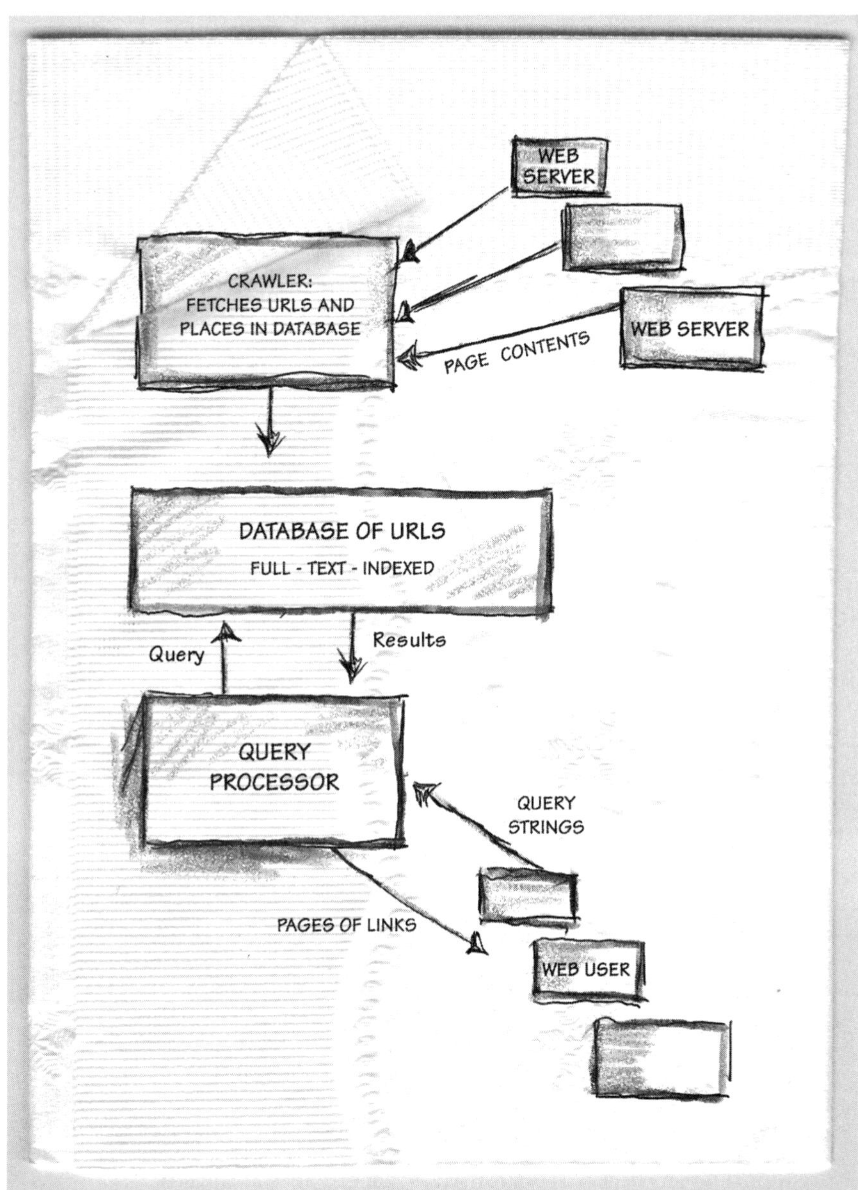

Figure 5.1: A generic Web search engine. Note that these are logical components and might all be running on one physical computer

Component 2: The Full-Text Indexer Table 5.1 shows the word-frequency histogram for the first sentence of *Anna Karenina.*

Table 5.1: Example of Word Frequency Histogram

Word	Frequency
all	1
another	1
but	1
each	1
families	1
family	1
happy	1
in	1
is	1
its	1
one	1
own	1
resemble	1
unhappy	2
way	1

You might think that this sentence makes better literature as "All happy families resemble one another, but each unhappy family is unhappy in its own way," but the computer finds it more useful in this form.

After the crude histogram is made, it is typically adjusted for the prevalence of words in standard English. So, for example, the appearance of *resemble* is more interesting to the engine than *happy* because *resemble* occurs less frequently in standard English. Words that are very common, such as *is,* are thrown away altogether.

Component 3: User Query Processor The query processor is the public face of a search engine. When the query machine gets a search string, such as "platinum mines in New Zealand," the *in* and probably the *New* are thrown away. The engine delivers articles that have the most occurrences of *platinum* and *Zealand*. Suppose that *Zealand* is a rarer word than *platinum*. Then a Web page with one occurrence of Zealand is favored over one with one occurrence of platinum. A Web page with one occurrence of each word is preferred to an article where only one of those words shows up. This is a standard text retrieval algorithm in use since the early 1980s.

For relatively stupid indexer/query processor pairs, this is where the sorting stops. Smarter engines, however, use some further knowledge about the Web. For example, they know that

- Whatever is wrapped in the <TITLE> element is the most interesting part of the document.
- Pages with the requested query words plus *home* or *homepage* are the very best matches of all. So, in response to a "Travels with Samantha" query, smart engines will list the *Travels with Samantha* home page above any of the 17 chapters.
- An initial headline (enclosed in an <h1> tag or similar) is more important than the rest of the document. So a Web page where the query words appear in a headline is preferred over one where they appear in the footer.

How to Stand Tall in the Search Engines A good way to measure the thoroughness of the corruption of the Internet is to type a query like "most reliable car" into the search engines (see Figure 5.2). Then look at the banner ads in the results pages. Do you think it is a coincidence that the banner ad above the search results is always for a car-related Web site? People are buying words. Yes, words. For thousands of dollars per month. Publishers pay the big bucks and every time a user queries for "car" or "home" or "money", a relevant banner ad is served up.

If you can't afford to buy words then you will just have to earn exposure in the search engines the honest way: content. If you craft your page carefully, then your URL will appear in plain text, if not at the very top of the page, then at least just below some richer publisher's banner ad.

Search engines take an even dimmer view of graphics than I do. You might have paid $25,000 for a flashing GIF or a Java animation; AltaVista does not care. It won't even download the ugly thing. You might have thought that lots of little GIFs with pretty text were better than plain old ASCII, but AltaVista

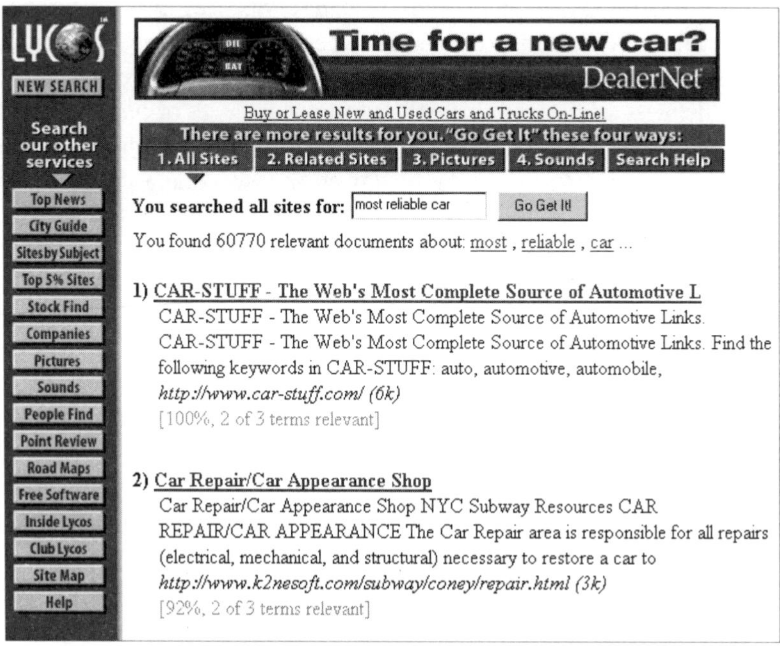

Figure 5.2: Result of typing "most reliable car" into http://www.lycos.com. Note the banner ad on top for DealerNet.

doesn't think so. Search engines don't try to do OCR on GIFs to figure out what words are formed by the pixels. So if you've invested a sufficient amount in graphic design, your page won't be indexed at all.

What you want is text, text, text.

The more text on your site, the more words and therefore the greater chance that you'll have a combination of words for which users are searching. If you want readers to find you in the search engines, it's much better to spend $20,000 licensing the full text of a bunch of out-of-print books than on a graphical makeover of your site.

HOW MANY USERS ARE YOU GETTING FROM SEARCH ENGINES?

Often the user's browser will tell your Web server the URL from which the user clicked to your site. If you have a reasonably modern Web server program, it can log this *referer header* (yes, "referer" is misspelled in the HTTP standard).

Sometimes the referer URL will contain the query string. You can use this information to see what people are trying to find on your site. Someone I know runs a computer answer service, and regularly scans the logs for the "gooseggs"—

queries that didn't find any matches in the database. The answers to many of these questions are then added to the database, except not query strings like these:

```
http://sckb.ucssc.indiana.edu/kb/cgi-bin/WebQuery?searchText=how
  +to+decide+sex+of+baby&maxhits=50
http://sckb.ucssc.indiana.edu/kb/cgi-bin/WebQuery?searchText=please
  +somebody+mail+me+from+anywhere&maxhits=50
http://sckb.ucssc.indiana.edu/kb/cgi-bin/WebQuery?searchText=Kermit
  +the+Frog's+underwear+size?&maxhits=50
http://sckb.ucssc.indiana.edu/kb/cgi-bin/WebQuery?searchText=should
  +I+use+ice+or+heat+for+a+sore+back&maxhits=50
```

Sometimes a user talks to the search engine via HTTP POST instead of GET. That makes the referer header much less interesting.

```
www-aa0.proxy.aol.com - - [01/Jan/1997:18:57:21 -0500]
"GET /photo/nudes.html HTTP/1.0" 304 0
http://webcrawler.com/cgi-bin/WebQuery
"Mozilla/2.0 (Compatible; AOL-IWENG 3.0; Win16)"
```

We know that this user is an AOL Achiever because he is coming to my site from an AOL proxy server. We know that he is at least mildly naughty because his WebCrawler search has come up with http://photo.net/photo/nudes.html as an interesting URL for him. And the user-agent header at the end supposedly tells us that he is using Netscape Navigator (Mozilla) 2.0, though the "compatible" indicates in fact that perhaps he is using Microsoft Internet Explorer.

Advertising

Does advertising on the Web work? If what you're advertising is another Web site, the answer seems to be yes. Buying words on the search engines seems to be good value. At a cost of about $5,000 a week, one of my consulting clients pumped their site up very quickly from 100,000 to 300,000 hits per day by buying words.

How much does advertising cost? Web publishers seem to be able to charge between one and four cents per impression (showing of a banner ad to a user) and five to ten cents per click-through (a user actually clicking on the banner).

I get about 5,000 visitors a day on my personal site. If I wanted an extra 5,000, it would cost me about $400 a day to pull them in from other sites by buying banner ads. On the other hand, if you look at Chapter 2, you'll see that amazon.com managed to acquire 2,641 click-throughs from me for $3.95. That's only $0.0015 for each click-through. So if I had some kind of transaction system on my site and promised other Web publishers a kickback, I could apparently pull in those extra 5,000 readers for only $7.50 a day.

Hmmm, I guess I should stop writing now and get to work on a transaction system and associates program...

Here's an AltaVista user:

```
modem22.truman.edu - - [01/Jan/1997:23:41:08 -0500]
"GET /photo/body-paint.html HTTP/1.0" 200 7667
http://www.altavista.digital.com/cgi-
bin/query?pg=q&what=web&fmt=.&q=body+painting+-auto+-automobile+-repair
"Mozilla/3.01 (Win95; I; 16bit)"
```

This user is more advanced. He's not using AOL. He's making a direct connection from his machine at Truman State University (Missouri). At first glance, it appears that he's had a problem with his car because he is searching for "body painting auto automobile repair." Won't he be surprised that AltaVista sent him to the rather naughty http://photo.net/photo/body-paint.html? Actually he won't be. I showed this to my friend Jin and he said "look at the little minuses in front of *auto*, *automobile*, and *repair*. He was looking for documents that contained *body* and *painting* but *not* any of the auto repair words."

Sometimes the Web really does work as it should...

```
245.st-louis-011.mo.dial-access.att.net - - [01/Jan/1997:20:50:31 -0500]
"GET /cr/maps/ HTTP/1.0" 302 361
http://www-att.lycos.com/cgi-bin/pursuit?
cat=lycos&query=Costa+Rica%2Bmap&matchmode=or
"Mozilla/2.02E (Win95; U)"
```

This fellow, apparently an ATT Worldnet user, wanted a map of Costa Rica and found it at http://webtravel.org/cr/maps/.

The bottom line is that, if you have a content-rich site, you should be getting approximately 50 percent of your users from search engines.

IMPROVING YOUR PAGES' CHANCES HONESTLY (AND DISHONESTLY)

If you want to take the time to add META elements to the head section of your HTML documents, then most search engines will try to learn from them. If you have some extra keywords that you think describe your content, but that don't fit into the article or don't get enough prominence in the user-visible text, just add

```
<META name="keywords" content="making money fast greed">
```

to your page (remember that it is only legal within the <HEAD> of the document). People who do this tend to repeat the words over and over:

```
<META name="keywords" content="making money fast greed money
money money money money money money fast fast fast greed">
```

which presumably does increase relevance—and therefore prominence—on badly programmed search engines. Eventually the search engine programmers are going to get tired of seeing the sleaziest sites given the most prominence, though, and only index each keyword once (AltaVista currently records 0, 1, and "2 or more" occurrences of a word, so "money money" and "money money money" are indistinguishable).

Keep in mind also that, though information in META elements is never displayed on a page, all of your users will have to wait for these META tags to download. So you don't really want to put 50,000 bytes of text in the keywords tag (AltaVista in any case will only index the first 1,024 bytes).

A potentially more useful META tag is "description":

```
<META  name="description" content="Journal for sophisticated
Web publishers, specializing in RDBMS-backed sites.">
```

Normally a search engine will condense the textual content of your site into something resembling a description. Perhaps it takes the first 25 words and serves that up along with the title. This becomes especially problematic if you have a graphics-heavy site with no content at all. If the first few sentences of a page aren't what you'd like people to see when a search engine offers it up as an option, then include a description META tag on that page.

And Now the Dishonest Part That's how it is all supposed to work. Of course, immediately people started to subvert the system by adding keyword tags like "nude photos of supermodels" to their boring computer science research papers and sleazy get-rich-quick schemes.

A more clever approach to getting extra hits is reprogramming your Web server. The server first determines if a request is being made by a robot by looking at the user-agent header and/or matching the hostname against *.webcrawler.com, *.altavista.digital.com, *.lycos.com, and so on. If the client is a robot, then the server delivers content calculated to match queries, such as "making money fast on the Internet by taking photos of nude supermodels." Otherwise, on the assumption that the request is coming from a real person, the server redirects the client to a page of your choice.

You've made the Web a less user-friendly place, but you've got more hits. If every publisher did this then people would stop using search engines, but of course not every publisher is going to do this.

HIDING YOUR CONTENT FROM SEARCH ENGINES (INTENTIONALLY)

Sometimes you don't want search engines to find your stuff. Here are some possible scenarios:

- You have a mirror of http://webtravel.org/samantha at http://euro .webtravel.org/samantha, a computer in Finland. You don't want people searching in Infoseek to find the Finland mirror.
- You have a draft version of a document whose URL you've distributed to a few friends. Some of them have linked to it from their home pages despite your instructions to keep the URL private. Their home pages are known to the search engines so the search engines will find your document before it is ready.
- You have an area where users can click to request standardized searches through a changing database. Each search requires 20 minutes of crunching by your server. You don't want robots initiating searches.

WebCrawler was the first robot on the Web. The folks who've taken it over from Brian Pinkerton maintain a Robots page that gives information about how Web robots work at http://info.webcrawler.com/mak/projects/robots/robots.html. This page links to the Standard for Web Exclusion, which is a protocol for communication between Web publishers and Web crawlers. You the publisher put a file on your site, accessible at /robots.txt, with instructions for robots. Here's an example that addresses my mirror site problem given above. I created a file at http://euro.webtravel.org/robots.txt containing the following:

```
User-agent: *
Disallow: /samantha
Disallow: /philg
Disallow: /cr
Disallow: /nz
Disallow: /webtravel
Disallow: /bp
Disallow: /~philg
Disallow: /zoo
Disallow: /photo
Disallow: /summer94
```

The "User-agent" line specifies for which robots the injunctions are intended. Each "Disallow" asks a robot not to look in a particular directory. Nothing requires a robot to observe these injunctions but the standard seems to have been adopted by all the major indices nonetheless.

HIDING YOUR CONTENT FROM SEARCH ENGINES (BY MISTAKE)

If you hire an MBA to "proactively leverage your Web publishing paradigm into the next generation model" then you can be pretty sure he will come up with the following brilliant idea: Require registration. As soon as you require users to register, you can give much more detailed information about them to your advertisers.

Unfortunately, if half of your readers have been coming from search engines, you'll only have half as many readers. AltaVista is not going to log into your site. Lycos is not going to fill out your demographics form. WebCrawler does not know what its username and password are supposed to be on www.greedy.com.

I don't have an MBA but I managed to hide a tremendous amount of my content from the search engines by stupidity in a different direction. I built a question and answer forum for http://photo.net/photo. Because I'm not completely stupid, all the postings were stored in a relational database. I used the AOLserver with its brilliant TCL API to get the data out of the database and onto the Web. The cleanest way to develop software in this API is to create files named foobar.tcl among one's document tree. The URLs end up looking like "http://db.photo.net/bboard/fetch-msg.tcl?msg_id=000037."

So far so good.

AltaVista comes along and says, "Look at that question mark. Look at the strange .tcl extension. This looks like a CGI script to me. I'm going to be nice and not follow this link even though there is no robots.txt file to discourage me."

Then WebCrawler says the same thing.

Then Lycos.

I achieved oblivion.

Then I had a notion that I developed into a concept and finally programmed into an idea: Write another AOLserver TCL program that presents all the messages from URLs that look like static files, such as "/fetch-msg-000037.html", and point the search engines to a huge page of links like that. The text of the Q&A forum postings will get indexed out of these pseudo-static files and yet I can retain the user pages with their *.tcl URLs. I could convert the user pages to *.html URLs but then it would be more tedious to make changes to the software (see my discussion of why the AOLserver *.tcl URLs are so good in the next chapter).

Web Directories

It was easy in the old days. In 1994 there was just Yahoo. Yahoo was the original Web directory, reasonably well-built and well-maintained by David Filo and Jerry Yang, electrical engineering graduate students at Stanford. You'd submit your site to Yahoo and NCSA What's New and wait for traffic and links to develop organically.

By 1995 there was Yahoo and a bunch of pathetic wannabe imitation directories. There were too many entries in NCSA What's New for anyone to bother reading them so NCSA shut down the page.

By 1997 some of the pathetic wannabes had become so bloated with money and staff that they actually had pretty reasonable directories. In this competition they were aided by Yahoo's apparent inability to write a Perl script to grind over their database and flush all the obsolete links.

If you are unwilling to figure out who is running all of the directories these days, then it is probably worthwhile to use a service that submits your site information to the directories for you. Here are a few:

- Submit-it! (http://www.submit-it.com/)
- Pointers-to-Pointers (http://www.homecom.com/global/pointers.html)
- Postmaster (http://www.netcreations.com/postmaster/)

Don't obsess over getting listed in every possible directory. In the long run the search engines will be much more important sources of users than the directories. Furthermore, it is much easier as a publisher to work with the search engines. They visit your site periodically and notice if things have changed.

Final Tip

Reorganize your file system after you're listed in all the Web directories and search engines. That way users will be sure to get "404 Not Found" messages after finding your site in Yahoo or WebCrawler.

Summary

Here's what you should have learned in this chapter:

- About half of your users will come from search engines.
- The more text you have on your site, the more likely users are to find your site.
- Users who come from search engines will arrive at arbitrary interior pages, so it is important that you always have links back to the top levels of your documents.
- Web directories and search engines will contain all kinds of links to your interior pages, so think carefully before changing any file names on your server.

If you are smart about managing your profile in the search engines and Web directories, you'll have so much traffic that your server will melt unless you carefully read the next chapter on how to choose server hardware and software.

So You Want to Run Your Own Server

My Personal Choice

Choosing a Computer

Server Software

Connectivity

Chapter 6

There are three levels at which you can take responsibility for your Web site:

- You are a user of a remote machine.
- You are the owner/administrator of a machine inside someone else's network.
- You are the owner/administrator of a machine inside your own network.

If your Web site is simply on a remote machine that someone else administers, then your only responsibility is periodically transferring your static files there, and perhaps some CGI scripts. As soon as the remote server is behaving the way you want, you can walk away until it is time to update your site. You can go away on vacation for two months at a stretch. If you need expensive software, such as a relational database, you can simply shop for a site-hosting service that includes use of that software as part of a package.

The downside of using someone else's Web server is that you are entirely at the mercy of the system administrators of the remote machine. If e-mail for your domain isn't being forwarded, you can't get your own consultant or go digging around yourself—you have to wait for people who might not have the same priorities that you do. If you are building a sophisticated relational database-backed site, you might not have convenient access to your data. Competent providers will usually manage a domain-level site for $100 to $200 per month.

If you are the owner of a Web-serving computer inside someone else's network, then you have total freedom to make changes to your configuration and software. You'll have root password and shell access and therefore can use the machine for software development or other experiments. Whoever is hosting your box is responsible for network connectivity. If packets aren't getting to your machine, they'll probably notice and do something about it. You don't have to pay the $2,500 per month cost of a T1 line yourself.

The downside to running your own box is that you have to carefully watch over your computer and Web server program. Nobody else will care about whether your computer is serving pages. You'll have to carry a pager and sign up for a service like Uptime (http://webtools.com/wtr/) that will e-mail you and beep you when your server is unreachable. You won't be able to go on vacation unless you find someone who understands your computer and Web server configuration to watch it for you. Unless you are using free software, you may have to pay shockingly high licensing fees. Internet service providers charge between $250 and $2,000 a month for physical hosting, depending on who supplies the hardware, how much system administration the ISP performs, and how much bandwidth your site consumes.

If you are the owner of a machine inside your own network, then you can sit right down at the console of your Web server and do software development or poke through the database. This can be a substantial convenience if you are running an RDBMS-backed Web site and there is no obvious way to have development and production sites. If you are already paying to have a high-speed network connection to your desktop, then the marginal cost of hosting a server this way may be zero (a fact that was not lost on university students throughout the early years of the Web). The downside is that you have all of the responsibilities and hassles of owning a server physically inside someone else's network, plus all of the responsibilities and hassles of keeping the network up.

My Personal Choice

Which hosting option did I choose for my personal Web site? The last one, of course. At MIT we don't let random commercial losers host our Web sites. We've had a hardwired network since the 1960s, so of course we always do things at the highest level of professionalism. In fact, during the "papal visit" (when Bill Gates came to speak), the director of our lab took particular care to note that MIT was "the home of the Web."

He probably hadn't read this problem report that I had sent to some folks with whom I share a Web server:

```
1) Saturday, 6:30 am: we had a 2-second power glitch
2) we do not have an uninterruptible power supply for Martigny [HP Unix file
   server for a cluster of user machines] so it crashed
3) we don't have an uninterruptible power supply for Swissnet [swissnet.ai.mit.edu,
   our Web server, an antique HP Unix workstation] so it crashed
4) there is something we never figured out about Swissnet so that it doesn't boot
   properly after a power interruption
5) Saturday, 4 pm: I went down to the 3rd floor and manually instructed Swissnet
   to boot from its root disk, thus ending almost 10 hours of off-the-Web time
6) Somewhere along the line, Tobler [one of the user machines managed from
   Martigny] tried to reboot.  Because it couldn't get to Martigny, it booted
   from a locally attached disk. This disk was the old Swissnet root disk [we'd
   hooked it up to Tobler after upgrading from HP-UX 9.x to 10.10 because we
   thought we might need some files from it].  Tobler consequently advertised
   itself as "18.23.0.16" [Swissnet's IP address].
7) Saturday, 10:30 pm: Radole [the main router for the MIT Laboratory for
   Computer Science] saw that there were two computers advertising themselves as
   18.23.0.16 and apparently decided to stop routing to the physical Swissnet on
   the 3rd floor
8) Sunday, 4 pm: I arrive at work to a phone message from Brian: "Swissnet's
   routing is hosed".  I reboot the machine. No improvement.  I page George
   Rabatin [LCS network administrator and the Radole guru].
9) Sunday, 5 pm: George figures out that the problem is Tobler's false
   advertising.  We turn Tobler off.
10) Sunday, 9 pm: George has manually purged all the caches on Radole and I've
   rebooted Swissnet but still no routing.
11) Sunday, 11 pm: George Rabatin declares a "network emergency" with the main
   MIT Net administrators so that they can probe the Building 24 FDDI router
   [FDDI is the 100 Mbit/second token ring that serves the entire MIT campus.]
12) Sunday, midnight: One of the MIT guys manually flushed the ARP cache on the
   FDDI router and Swissnet instantly came back into existence.  Given that
   Tobler wasn't on the same subnet and that Radole supposedly stopped doing
   proxy ARP around seven months ago, it is a mystery to me how this router
   could have had an ARP entry (mapping IP address to hysical Ethernet hardware
   address) for Faux Swissnet. But it apparently did. So we're back on the Web.

Good news: We saved $500 by not buying two uninterruptible power supplies. We
found out that George Rabatin is a hero.

Bad news: We probably denied services to about 5000 users over 34 hours. We
burned up about 20 person-hours of various folks' time on a Sunday trying to fix
a problem that we created.
```

That's how professionals do things.

Choosing a Computer

Computers are the tools of the devil. It is as simple as that. There is no faith strong enough that it cannot be shaken by Unix or any Microsoft product. The devil is real. He lives inside C programs.

Hardware engineers have done such a brilliant job over the last 40 years that nobody notices that, in the world of commercial software, the clocks all stopped in 1957. Society can build a processor for $50 capable of executing 200 million instructions per second. Marvelous. With computers this powerful, the amazing thing is that anyone still has to go into work at all. Perhaps part of the explanation for this apparent contradiction is that, during its short life, the $50 chip will consume $10,000 of system administration time.

Everything that I've learned about computers at MIT I have boiled down into three principles:

- Unix: You think it won't work, but if you find the right guru, you can make it work.
- Macintosh: You think it will work, but it won't.
- PC/Windows: You think it won't work, and it won't.

In theory, a Macintosh or Windows 95 machine could function as a low-volume Web server for static files. However, since those operating systems lack multiprocessing and memory protection, you'd have to dedicate an entire machine to this task. Finally, you'd never be able to do anything interesting with a Mac- or Windows 95-hosted site because relational database management systems such as Oracle require a multitasking operating system.

Note: The NeXT operating system is based on Mach, a reimplementation of Unix created in the mid-1980s at Carnegie-Mellon University. So if (when?) Apple ships a Macintosh running the NeXT operating system, it will basically be a Unix box (see below) for the purposes of Web service.

Most people buying a server computer make a choice between Unix and Windows NT. These operating systems offer important 1960s innovations like multiprocessing and protection among processes. Certainly the first thing to do is to figure out which operating system supports the Web server and database management software that you want to use (see the rest of this chapter and book for more on that topic). If the software that appeals to you runs on both operating systems, then make your selection based on which computer you, your friends, and your coworkers know how to administer. If that doesn't result in a conclusion, then read the rest of this section.

UNIX

Buying a Unix machine guarantees you a descent into Hell. It starts when you plug the computer in and it won't boot. Yes, they really did sell you a $10,000 computer with an unformatted disk drive. There is only one operating system in the world that will run on your new computer, but the vendor didn't bother to install it. That's how you are going to spend your next couple of nights. You'll be asked dozens of questions about disk partitioning and file system journaling that you couldn't possibly answer. Don't worry, though, because Unix vendors have huge documentation departments to help you. Unfortunately, your computer shipped without any documentation. And, although the marketing department has been talking about how this vendor is God's gift to the Internet, the rest of the company still hasn't jacked into this World Wide Internet thing. So you won't find the documentation on the Web.

So you decide to save some trees and order a documentation CD-ROM. You plug it into your nearest Macintosh or PC and . . . nothing happens. That's right, the documentation CD-ROM isn't usable unless you have a completely working Unix computer made by the same company.

A week later, you've gotten the machine to boot and you call over to your Web developer: "Set up the Web server." But it turns out that your developer can't use the machine. Everything in Unix is configured by editing obscure incantations in text files. Virtually all competent Unix users edit text in a program called Emacs, probably the best text editor ever built. It is so good that the author, Richard Stallman, won a MacArthur genius fellowship. It is also free. But that doesn't mean that it meets the standards of Unix vendors. No, the week-long installation process has left you only with VI, an editor that hardly anyone worth hiring knows how to use.

So you download the Emacs source code over the Internet and try to compile it. Good luck. Your computer didn't come with a compiler. The most popular C compiler for Unix is GCC, another free program from Richard Stallman. But it would have been too much trouble for the vendor to burn that onto their software CD-ROM, so you don't have it.

At this point you are in serious enough trouble that you have to hire a $175-per-hour consultant just to make your computer function. Two days and $4,000 later, your computer is finally set up the way a naïve person would assume that it would have shipped from the factory.

That's what setting up a Unix box is like. If it sounds horribly painful, rest assured that it is. The reason that anyone buys these computers is that usually they are administered in clusters of 100 machines. The time to administer 1,000 Unix boxes is about the same as the time to administer one and therefore the administration cost per machine isn't ruinous. This will be cold comfort to you if you only have the one Web server, though.

There is an upside to all of this. The operating system configuration resides in hundreds of strangely formatted text files. During the week you spent setting up Unix, you cursed this feature. But once your system is working, it will

Why Not Solaris?

Solaris has always been a problem child. The first three versions were so bad that many Sun customers still use SunOS, an operating system that Sun abandoned some years ago. My friends who develop Web server programs are always having to add patches to work around bugs in the Solaris 2.5 implementation of the basic Internet protocols (TCP/IP). Another friend nearly lost a $200,000 database-backed Web site development contract because the client thought the server was unresponsive. The client had a slow Internet connection but he was getting much faster downloads from other sites. In June 1996, Sun discovered a number of bugs in their implementation of TCP that resulted in modem users getting as little as one-hundredth of the throughput that they should have gotten. Solaris-backed Web sites had been effectively shutting out modem users for months. Sun developers and sophisticated Web site developers hadn't noticed because they were all on fast networks.

Sun didn't spend too much time or energy fixing all these TCP bugs because they were so pleased with their "We are the Internet" ad campaigns. Many of these ads highlighted Sun's involvement with the *24 Hours in Cyberspace* Web site. Somehow they didn't mention this anecdote, which appeared in the May 1996 issue of *Byte* magazine (page 27):

> "Sun lent 60 of its latest UltraSparc workstations, two SS-1000 database servers (each with eight CPUs, 1GB of RAM, and an 84-GB RAID-5 disk array), and three Netra servers for FTP and e-mail ...
>
> "Amazingly, when the big day arrived, everything worked. Well, almost. The technicians never did trace the source of that 175-MB-per-hour memory leak. The network slowed to a crawl when the server dwindled to about 300MB of RAM. However, they recovered the memory by rebooting the server every four hours, a solution good enough for a short-term project."
>
> **Note: A memory leak occurs when a C program allocates some memory for temporary use but then, due to a programmer error, forgets to free it.**

(Continued)

continue working forever. As long as you don't go into Emacs and edit any of those configuration files, there is no reason to believe that your Unix server won't function correctly. It isn't like the Macintosh or Windows worlds where things get silently corrupted and the computer stops working.

(Continued from previous page)

This is a common problem with the 1950s programming language technology on which current commercial software is based. Programming languages developed in the 1960s, such as Lisp, manage storage automatically so that programmers can't make these sorts of mistakes. However, the ascendance of microcomputers has pushed these more modern languages into academia. Java is the first time in recent memory that the common technologies of the 1960s are again available to industrial programmers.

If you'd shelled out $250,000 for a SPARCserver 1000 that was leaking 1,000 bytes of memory every time it served a Web page or graphic, you'd probably want someone to fix the problem. Unfortunately Sun has fragmented itself into multiple corporations. If you call the people to whom you wrote the check, they will be happy to give you a 30-minute explanation of the new Sun corporate structure and how it ensures that you get the best possible service. They won't fix your computer, though. Surely you want someone at the software company or the service company. The software people will say, "It sounds like a hardware problem. We've contracted out hardware maintenance in your area to the phone company. Call them."

Yes, the phone company. So a guy from the phone company who has never logged into a Unix box in his life comes over and starts swapping boards. This is especially fun when they swap CPU boards and forget to pull the ID proms so none of the per-CPU licensed software works after "the fix." I also enjoyed the time that one of these phone company guys replaced an 85MHz motherboard with a 70MHz motherboard. It didn't fix the problem we were having but it did slow the computer down by about 20 percent. Sun refused to believe that the computer had ever been an 85MHz machine until we dug up the original invoice.

Everybody I know who has tried using Sun for something important has either switched to HP, switched to SPARC clones from Tatung, or bought themselves a big pile of spares and a full-time crew of in-house wizards.

Which Brand of Unix Box? Hewlett-Packard makes the fastest and most reliable Unix computers. You would think that Unix would be impossible to support because different sites have completely different configurations. Nonetheless, I've found that the HP support people can usually telnet into my machines and fix problems over the network themselves. If you call them at 1 a.m., you'll be working with an engineer in Australia. If you call at 4 a.m., you'll be working with their staff in England.

Silicon Graphics seems to be a popular choice among my friends who run huge multiprocessor servers. Digital ALPHA servers are very popular with those who have big relational database management systems.

The main problem with all of these kinds of Unix is that the latest and greatest Web server software either won't be available for your computer or it won't really have been tested. Unix is not a standard. A program that works on HP's Unix will not work on Silicon Graphics's Unix. If you want to pull programs off the Net and have them just work, the best kind of Unix to have is SPARC/Solaris from Sun.

Truly sophisticated Unix people seem to run Unix on standard PC hardware. The most popular Unix for PCs is Linux, an entirely free operating system. You can download it off the Net for nothing. Or you can pay $50 to a company like Red Hat (www.redhat.com) for a CD-ROM. After making a few mouse clicks in the installer, your PC will be running

- Unix
- Emacs, Perl, Tcl, gcc, the X Window System, ImageMagick, and all the other software that you would have paid a consultant $50,000 to install on your Digital, HP, or Sun box
- The Apache Web server
- An NFS server to deliver files to other Unix machines
- A Windows-protocol file server to deliver files to Windows machines
- An AppleShare file and print server to deliver files to Macintoshes

And all of this will be running out of several CPUs simultaneously if you recompile the kernel to do symmetric multiprocessing.

Running a free Unix on a PC entails a different philosophy from buying hardware and software from the same company. You are abandoning the fantasy that there is a company out there who will support you if only you give them enough money. You or someone you hire will take a little more responsibility for fixing bugs. You have the source code, after all. If you want support, you have to make an intelligent decision about who can best provide it.

PC hardware is so much cheaper than workstation hardware that for the price of one regular Unix workstation you will probably be able to buy two complete PC systems, one of which you can use as a hot backup. Keep in mind that 99 percent of PC hardware is garbage. A friend of mine is a small-time Internet service provider. He runs BSDI on a bunch of PC clones. A hard disk was generating errors. He reloaded from backup tape. He still got errors. It turned out that his SCSI controller had gone bad some weeks before. It had corrupted both the hard disk and the backup tapes. He lost all of his data. He lost all of his clients' data.

- *Lesson 1:* You are less likely to lose with an SCSI controller designed by a real engineer at Hewlett-Packard than you are with one thrown in on a $49 sound card.
- *Lesson 2:* Mirrored disks on separate SCSI chains. Period.

What stops me from running Linux is not fear of unreliable hardware or divided responsibility for software and hardware bugs. It is that big software companies don't trust this model or market. You can't get Adobe PhotoShop for Linux. You can't buy the Netscape Web servers for Linux. Free software often works better than commercial solutions, but not always. I have more software options with my HP-UX and SPARC/Solaris machines even if they are much harder to set up.

I'll leave you with an anecdote about my desktop Hewlett-Packard 715/80 Unix workstation. Let's see how long it has been up:

```
orchid.lcs.mit.edu 33: uptime
 11:30pm  up 53 days, 10:28,  5 users,  load average: 0.10, 0.07, 0.06
```

Yes, that's 53 days, 10 hours, 28 minutes. It is running a relational database management system. It is serving ten hits per second to the Web from an AOLserver process listening on four different IP addresses. It is running the X Window System so that I can use it from my home computer just as easily as if I were on campus at MIT. Yet though this is an old computer, not nearly as powerful as a Pro that a child might find under a Christmas tree, it is doing all of this while working only about one-tenth of the time. That's what a load average of 0.10 means.

WINDOWS NT

When I was a kid I didn't like the taste of Coca-Cola. After I'd been exposed to 100,000 TV commercials and billboards for Coke, I decided that it was the best drink in the world. Just opening a can made me feel young, good-looking, athletic, surrounded by gorgeous blondes.

Windows NT is sort of like that. At first glance it looks like a copy of Unix (which in turn was a copy of operating systems from the 1960s) with a copy of the Macintosh user interface (which in turn was based on systems developed at Xerox PARC in the 1970s). I didn't think much more about it.

Eventually the Microsoft PR mill convinced me that Windows NT was the greatest computer innovation ever. Bill Gates had not only invented window systems and easy to use computers, but also multitasking, protection among processes, and networking. It would be like Unix without the obscurity.

I told all of my friends how they were losers for running Unix. They should switch to NT. It was the future. That was more or less my constant refrain until one pivotal event changed my life: I actually tried to use NT.

Having once watched three MIT wizards each spend ten hours installing a sound card in a PC, I was in no mood to play with clones. I got myself an Intel Inside and Intel Outside genuine Intel-brand PC. I reformatted the hard drive with NT File System (NTFS) and installed WinNT Server. The machine booted smoothly but running any program triggered Macintosh emulation mode: You move the mouse but nothing happens on the screen.

I spent two weeks trying to figure out why the user interface was crashing, reinstalling NT several times. I enlisted the help of a professional NT administrator. He tried eight different combinations of file systems but none of them worked.

What I learned: Do not buy a computer that isn't "NT certified." In fact, don't buy one unless the vendor has already installed the version of NT that you intend to use. Personally I'd buy a Hewlett-Packard system.

I started over with a Pentium Pro 200 and NT 4.0 Server. The operating system installed flawlessly, but my MIT undergrad PC wizard never could get the machine to execute a CGI script from either the Netscape FastTrack Server or the included Microsoft Web server. It took several weeks and three MIT wizards to get the machine to talk to the HP Laserjet down the hall.

NT Success Story 1: I downloaded some fax software from Microsoft. It was never able to talk to my modem or send a fax, but it did consume 20 percent of the machine's CPU and grew to 30MB in size. The standard system-monitoring tools that come with NT make it almost impossible to figure out what is killing one's machine.

NT Success Story 2: I bought an HP Laserjet 5M printer for my house that I might be the first one on my block with a duplexing printer. It took me 5 seconds to get my Macintosh to print to it. It took me 5 minutes to get all of the Unix boxes at MIT to print to it. It took me 5 hours to get my Windows NT computer to recognize this printer, even though both were on the same Ethernet wire. As part of my 5-hour saga, I had to download a 4MB program from the HP Web site. Four megabytes. That's larger than any operating system for any computer sold in the 1970s. Mainframes in the 1970s could run entire airlines with less than 4MB of code.

UNIX VERSUS NT

Below is a summary chart of the differences between Unix and NT Web servers.

	Unix	**NT**
Easy to maintain remotely	Yes	No
Consultants	Cheap and smart	Expensive and stupid
Price of software	Free or expensive	Cheap
Reliability	High	Medium
Support	Depends on vendor; sometimes excellent	Microsoft
Price of hardware	Cheap with Linuxes; expensive with other Unices	Cheap

Most of the people I know who are facile with both NT and Unix have eventually taken down their NT Web servers and gone back to Unix. The WebCrawler's comprehensive statistics, gathered as it indexes the Web, confirm my anecdotal evidence: As of January 1997, Unix sits behind 84 percent of the world's Web sites; NT sits behind 7 percent.

It turns out that, once you get to a certain level of traffic, you want your Web server in a closet right up against the routers that carry bits out of your building. You might think that the user interface of Unix sucks. But, thanks to X, it doesn't get any worse if you stay in your comfortable office or cozy house and drive your Web server remotely. Any program that you can run on the console, you can run from halfway around the world. Most sysadmins don't even go up to the physical machine to reboot their Unix boxes.

Unless you are a lot smarter than anyone I know, you will need consultants. You're buying into a user community when you buy into an operating system. A big part of the Unix user community consists of the smartest and poorest-paid people in the world: science and engineering graduate students. Moreover, these people are used to helping each other over the Net, usually for no money. When I'm running a Unix program at a commercial site and want an enhancement, I send the author e-mail asking if he'll make the changes for $200 or so. Since most such requests come from users at universities who can't offer any money, this kind of proposal is invariably greeted with delight. When I'm confronted with a useless Unix box that doesn't have Emacs on it, I get the client to hire a friend of mine in Texas to install it. He telnets in and lets the compiler run while he's answering his e-mail in another window.

By contrast, anyone who has learned to install Microsoft Word on a Windows NT machine is suddenly a $150-an-hour consultant. Unless you count nerdy high school kids, there is no pool of cheap expertise for NT. And because NT boxes are tough to drive remotely, a wizard at another location can't help you out without disturbing his daily routine.

There is no technical reason why it couldn't have been the other way around, but it isn't. A true Windows NT wizard is making $175,000 a year maintaining a financial firm's servers; he isn't going to want to bother with your Web server.

Software licensing can be much more expensive with Unix. True, much of the best and most critical software is free. But many software firms have figured out that if you were stupid enough to pay $10,000 for a Sun SPARCstation 5 that is slower than your next-door neighbor's 7-year-old's Pentium 166 then you are probably stupid enough to pay three times as much for the same software. If you intend to purchase a lot of commercial software for your Web server, it is probably worth checking vendor price lists first to make sure that you couldn't pay for the entire NT machine with the Unix/NT license fee spread.

Note: Web server software and relational database management systems seem to be two areas where NT and Unix pricing are often the same.

Unix wizards love to tell horror stories about Unix in general and Solaris in particular. That's usually because the best of them were accustomed to the superior operating systems of the 1960s and '70s that Unix replaced. But the fact remains that Windows NT is less reliable than Unix and has more memory leaks. In the Microsoft culture it is amazing when a computer stays up and running for more than one day, so nobody complains if it takes them two months to make Oracle work or if the NT server has to be rebooted once a week.

Support can be much better with Unix. The whole idea of the Apple and Microsoft support 800 number doesn't make any sense in an Internet age. Why are you talking into a telephone telling someone what text is appearing on your screen? Your computers are both on the Internet and capable of exchanging data at perhaps 500,000 bps. I'm not so sure about the other Unix vendors, but I know from personal experience that Hewlett-Packard has figured this out. Plus you actually get better support when you dial in at 4 a.m. because the kind of people willing to take a tech support job in England are much more able than the kind of people willing to take a tech support job in California. Keep in mind that support does not *have* to be much better with Unix. I've personally never gotten any useful assistance from the official Sun support apparatus.

That's about as much as I can say. I don't think that there is a universal truth for making the NT/Unix choice other than my original one: Computers are tools of the devil. I learned that from a tenured professor in computer science at MIT. I think he is still trying to get his Macintosh to stop crashing.

FINAL HARDWARE SELECTION NOTE

Whatever server computer you buy, make sure that you get an uninterruptible power supply and mirrored disks. You should not go offline because of a power glitch. You should not go offline because of a disk failure. If you do decide to take the Unix plunge, lay in a big stock of books from O'Reilly (http://www.ora.com).

Server Software

Once you have bought a Web server *computer*, you need to pick a Web server *program*. The server program listens for network connections and then delivers files in response to users' requests. These are the most important factors in choosing a program:

- Quality of application programming interface (API)
- Tools for connecting to relational database management systems (RDBMS)
- Support and source code availability
- Availability of shrink-wrapped plug-in software packages
- Speed

Each of these factors needs to be elaborated.

API

Unless your publishing ambition is limited to serving static files, you will eventually need to write some programs for your Web site. It is quite possible that you'll need to have a little bit of custom software executing every time a user requests any file. Any Web server program can invoke a common-gateway interface (CGI) script. However, CGI scripts impose a tremendous load on the server computer. Furthermore, an all-CGI site is less straightforward for authors to maintain and for search engines to search than a collection of HTML files.

A Web server API makes it possible for you to customize the behavior of a Web server program without having to write a Web server program from scratch. In the early days of the Web, all the server programs were free. You would get the source code. If you wanted the program to work differently, you'd edit the source code and recompile the server. Assuming you were adept at reading other people's source code, this worked great until the next version of the server came along. Suppose the authors of NCSA HTTPD 1.4 decided to organize the program differently than the authors of NCSA HTTPD 1.3. If you wanted to take advantage of the features of the new version, you'd have to find a way to edit the source code of the new version to add your customizations.

An API is an abstraction barrier between your code and the core Web server program. The authors of the Web server program are saying, "Here are a bunch of hooks into our code. We guarantee and document that they will work a certain way. We reserve the right to change the core program but we will endeavor to preserve the behavior of the API call. If we can't, then we'll tell you in the release notes that we broke an old API call."

An API is especially critical for commercial Web server programs where they don't release the source code at all. Here are some typical API calls from the AOLserver documentation (http://www.aolserver.com):

ns_user exists *user* returns 1 (one) if the specified *user* exists and 0 (zero) if it does not.

ns_sendmail *to from subject body* sends a mail message

The authors of AOLserver aren't going to give you their source code and they aren't going to tell you how they implement the user/password database for URL access control. But they give you a bunch of functions like "ns_user exists" that let you query the database. If they redo the implementation of the user/password database in the next release of the software, then they will redo their implementation of ns_user so that you won't have to change your code. The ns_sendmail API call not only shields you from changes by AOLserver programmers, it also allows you to not think about how sending e-mail works on various computers. Whether you are running AOLserver on Windows NT, HP Unix, or Linux, your extensions will send e-mail after a user submits a form or requests a particular page.

Aside from having a rich set of functions, a good API has a rapid development environment and a safe language. The most common API is for the C programming language. Unfortunately, C is probably the least suitable tool for Web development. Web sites are by their very nature experimental and must evolve. C programs like Microsoft Word remain unreliable despite hundreds of person-years of development and thousands of person-years of testing. A small error in a C subroutine that you might write to serve a single Web page could corrupt memory critical to the operation of the entire Web server and crash all of your site's Web services. On operating systems without interprocess protection, such as Windows 95 or the Macintosh, the same error could crash the entire computer.

Even if you were some kind of circus freak programmer and were able to consistently write bug-free code, C would still be the wrong language because it has to be compiled. Making a small change in a Web page might involve dragging out the C compiler and then restarting the Web server program so that it would load the newly compiled version of your API extension.

By the time a Web server gets to version 2.0 or 3.0, the authors have usually figured that C doesn't make sense and have compiled in an interpreter for Tcl, Java byte codes, or JavaScript.

RDBMS CONNECTIVITY

You've chosen to publish on the Web because you want to support collaboration among users and customize content based on each individual user's preferences and history. You see your Web site as a lattice of dazzling little rubies of information. The Unix or Windows NT file system, though, only understands burlap sacks full of sod. As you'll find out when you read my chapters on building database-backed Web sites, there aren't too many interesting things that you can implement competently on top of a standard file system. Sooner or later you'll break down and install a relational database management system (RDBMS).

You'll want a Web server that can talk to this RDBMS. All Web servers can invoke CGI scripts that in turn can open connections to an RDBMS, execute a query, and return the results formatted as an HTML page. However, some Web servers offer built-in RDBMS connectivity. The same project can be accomplished with much cleaner and simpler programs and with a tenth of the server resources.

SUPPORT AND SOURCE CODE AVAILABILITY

Most computer programs that you can buy in the 1990s are copies of systems developed in the 1960s. Consider the development of a WYSIWYG word processor. A designer could sit down in 1985 and look at ten existing what-you-see-is-what-you-get word processors: Xerox PARC experiments from 1975, Mac Write, workstation-based systems for documentation professionals (such as Interleaf). The designer would not only have access to the running programs but also to user feedback. By 1986 the designer hands off the list of required features to some programmers. By 1987, the new word processor ships. If enough of the users demand more sophisticated features, the designers and programmers can go back to Interleaf or Frame and see how those features were implemented. Support consists of users saying, "It crashes when I do *x*," and the vendor writing this information down and replying, "Then don't do *x*."

By 1989, the next release of the word processor is ready. The "new" features lifted from Interleaf are in place and "doing *x*" no longer crashes the program.

Does this same development cycle work well for Web server programs? Although the basic activity of transporting bits around the Internet has been going on for three decades, there was no Web at Xerox PARC in 1975. There is no one designer who can anticipate even a fraction of user needs. Web publishers cannot wait years for new features or bug fixes.

An important feature for a Web server is source code availability. If worst comes to worst, you can always get a wizard programmer to extend the server or fix a bug. Vendor indifference cannot shut down your Web site. That doesn't mean you should ignore commercial servers that are only available as binaries. They may offer features that let you build a sophisticated site in a fraction of the time it would take with a more basic public-domain server.

If you can't get source code then you must carefully consider the quality of the support. What is the culture of the vendor like? Do they think, "We know a lot more than our users and every couple of years we'll hand them our latest brilliant innovation," or "We have a lot to learn from our users and will humbly work to meet their needs"? A good vendor knows that even a whole company full of Web wizards can't come up with all the good ideas. They expect to get most of their good ideas from working with ambitious customers. They expect to deliver patched binaries to customers who find bugs. They expect to make a customer problem their own and keep working until the customer is online with his publishing idea.

AVAILABILITY OF SHRINK-WRAPPED PLUG-INS

Are your ideas banal? Is your Web site like everyone else's? If so, you're a good candidate for shrink-wrapped software. In a field changing as rapidly as Web publishing, packaged software usually doesn't make anyone's life easier. Sometimes a $500 program is helpful but the grand $50,000 package ends up being a straitjacket because the authors didn't anticipate the sorts of sites that you'd want to build.

Still, as the Web matures, enough commonality among Web sites will be discovered by software vendors to make shrink-wrapped software useful. An example of a common need is "I just got a credit card from a consumer and I want to bill it before returning a confirmation page to him." Often these packages can be implemented as CGI scripts suitable for use with any Web server. Sometimes, however, it is necessary to add software to the API of your Web server. If you are using a Web server that is popular among people publishing similar sites, then you are more likely to be able to buy shrink-wrapped software that fits into your API.

SPEED

It is so easy now to get a high-efficiency server program that I initially thought this point wasn't worth mentioning. In ancient times, the Web server forked a new process every time a user requested a page, graphic, or other file. The second generation of Web servers pre-forked a big pool of processes—say, 64 of them—and let each one handle a user. The server computer's operating system ensured that each process got a fair share of the computer's resources. A computer running a pre-forking server could handle at least three times the load. The latest generation of Web server programs uses a single process with internal threads. This has resulted in another tripling of performance.

It is possible to throw away 90 percent of your computer's resources by choosing the wrong Web server program. Traffic is so low at most sites and computer hardware so cheap that this doesn't become a problem until the big day when the site gets listed on the Netscape site's What's New page. In the summer of 1996 that was good for several extra users every second at the Bill Gates Personal Wealth Clock (http://www.webho.com/WealthClock). I'm glad now that I had been thinking about efficiency in the back of my mind.

Given these criteria, let's evaluate some of the more intelligent choices in Web server programs.

AOLSERVER (A.K.A. GNNSERVER, NAVISERVER)

America Online doesn't run Internet Protocol among their millions of subscribers. They have a strictly 1960s-style time-sharing model with their own proprietary protocols and software. Yet AOL decided to keep one corporate foot in the 1980s by buying up the best Internet technology companies it could find. One of them was NaviSoft, a Santa Barbara company that made by far the most interesting Web server of 1995: NaviServer. Despite having been subjected to a humiliating series of name changes, AOLserver remains a strong product.

AOLserver has a rich and comprehensive set of API calls. Some of the more interesting ones are the following:

- ns_sendmail (sends e-mail)
- ns_geturl (grabs a Web page from another server)
- ns_schedule_daily (specifies a procedure to be run once a day)

These kinds of API calls let you write sophisticated Web/e-mail/database systems that are completely portable among different versions of Unix and Windows NT.

These are accessible from C and, more interestingly, from the Tcl interpreter that they've compiled into the server. I have written thousands of Tcl procedures to extend the AOLserver and have never managed to crash the server from Tcl. There are several ways of developing Tcl software for the AOLserver but the one with the quickest development cycle is to use *.tcl URLs.

A file with a .tcl extension anywhere among the .html pages will be sourced by the Tcl interpreter. So you have URLs like "/bboard/fetch-msg.tcl". If asking for the page results in an error, you know exactly where in the Unix file system to look for the program. After editing the program and saving it in the file system, the next time a browser asks for /bboard/fetch-msg.tcl the new version is sourced. You get all of the software maintenance advantages of interpreted CGI scripts without the CGI overhead. A future version of AOLserver will probably include a Java API as well.

Though AOLserver shines in the API department, its longest suit is its RDBMS connectivity. The server can hold open pools of connections to multiple relational database management systems. Your C or Tcl API program can ask for an already-open connection to an RDBMS. If none is available, the thread will wait until one is, then the AOLserver hands your program the requested connection, into which you can pipe SQL. This architecture improves Web/RDBMS throughput by at least a factor of ten over the standard CGI approach.

Support and source code availability are weak points for AOLserver. Though free, AOLserver is a commercial product and AOL won't give out the source code. The documentation and the API are superb, so you really shouldn't ever need the source code if everything works as advertised. However, AOLserver is a C program, and, though the developers of AOLserver are probably the best C programmers I've met, no C program ever works as advertised. This is particularly true when the C program is built on the shaky foundation of modern operating systems.

When AOLserver was a $5,000 product, support was amazing. I would complain about a bug and three hours later receive a patched binary. After the AOL buyout and a reorganization or two, support really suffered. If you were running on SGI Unix, you were golden because that's what Primehost, AOL's commercial Web site hosting arm, runs. Otherwise, good luck to you. They were short-staffed at NaviSoft and didn't feel like writing workarounds for Solaris bugs. Check http://www.aolserver.com/ for the current support situation.

Availability of shrink-wrapped software for the AOLserver is nil. AOLserver has a very small market share and most of the people who run it are capable of writing their own back-end systems. They aren't going to pay $50,000 for a program to serve advertising banners when they could write a few pages of Tcl code to do the same thing more reliably. Of course, AOLserver can run packages of CGI scripts as well as any other Web server, so you can still install important packages like the Excite search engine for Web servers.

AOLserver 1.0 was the first of the threaded Web server programs and is therefore right up there with the fastest products on the market. A typical Unix box can serve about 800,000 static hits a day with AOLserver 2.1.

One final note about AOLserver: If you want to exploit its Tcl API and RDBMS connectivity without any sysadmin or dbadmin hassles, then you can pay about $200 a month for a virtual server in someone else's cluster. You get your own domain name, your own database, and redundant T1 or T3 connectivity. ISPs providing this service include Primehost (http://www.primehost.com), AM Computers (http://am.net), and a German outfit (http://www.carpe.net).

APACHE

Proceeding alphabetically, we arrive at the most popular Web server, Apache. WebCrawler credits Apache with a 35 percent share of the Web server program market. Apache seems to be used at the very simplest and the very most complex Web sites. The simple users just want a free server for static files. The complex users basically need a custom Web server but don't want to start programming from scratch.

The Apache API reflects this dimorphism. The simple users aren't expected to touch it. The complex users are expected to be C programming wizards. So the API is flexible but doesn't present a very high-level substrate on which to build.

Support for Apache is as good as your wallet is deep. You download the software free from http://www.apache.org and then buy support separately from the person or company of your choice. Because the source code is freely available, there are thousands of people worldwide who are at least somewhat familiar with Apache's innards.

Big companies that like to spend big dollars on shrink-wrapped software don't generally trust free software. Hence, I haven't seen too many packages for the Apache API.

Apache is a pre-forking server and is therefore reasonably fast. Bottom line: 80 percent of Web sites have decided that a source code–available server is the right one for them; Apache is the best and most popular of the source code–available server programs.

NETSCAPE ENTERPRISE/FASTTRACK

About 12 percent of the Internet's sites run various versions of the Netscape servers. That's not a lot better than the ancient CERN server. However, this market share is misleading because it isn't adjusted for the number of hits served. Many of the most heavily accessed and funded sites use the Netscape servers.

The Netscape 2.0 servers have a variety of APIs. They carry over their dangerous C API from their 1.x server programs. There is also a Java API and a

JavaScript API (LiveWire). For my taste, any C API is too dangerous. Java is a safe language, but it requires compilation and then installation of the compiler output into the server. You can build a Web site this way but it is a bit like digging a flower bed with a backhoe. The Netscape tool that shows the most promise is LiveWire, which attempts to cover some of the same ground as AOLserver's Tcl API, including efficient RDBMS connectivity.

Let's start by considering the development cycle. Suppose that three graphic designers have been working on a Web site for two months. They've built a directory on their Web server of 30 .html files. Then they call in a programmer to add a dynamic page or two, perhaps one that talks to the database. These pages must be wrapped up into a LiveWire application. A programmer can add JavaScript inside <SERVER> tags to any of the .html files. However, these aren't parsed by the Enterprise Server on the fly. The LiveWire application has to be compiled into a .web file. Then the programmer has to go into the application manager (an administration Web page) and load the application into the Enterprise Server.

Suppose now that a typo is discovered in a dynamic page. The graphic designer edits the file as always and reloads the page. Nothing is changed. That's because the .html file was distilled into a .web compiled object.

So the graphic designer asks the programmer to recompile the application from the Unix shell and/or figure out the Site Manager program and recompile the application. Upon reload, the page is . . . unchanged!

The Enterprise Server is a running C program. It has loaded the byte-code compiled .web file into its memory and will not reexamine the .web file ever. So someone has to go into the application manager and say, "Restart this particular application."

A change that with AOLserver would require a few keystrokes in Emacs or Netscape Gold requires three steps with Enterprise/LiveWire:

1. Edit the .html file.
2. Recompile the .web file.
3. Restart the LiveWire app from the appmgr.

Not so great, eh? Well, suppose you can get past the painful development cycle. What about the API per se?

You can't call a function to send e-mail. You can't call a function that will go out on the Net and grab a Web page from another server. Thus, even the simplest AOLserver sites that I've built would not be feasible in LiveWire. However, Netscape is supposedly going to rectify some of these deficiencies in the 3.0 version of the server.

One nice feature about LiveWire is that there is a lot of infrastructure for maintaining per-client state. Netscape has developed a fairly clean hierarchy of what they call *objects* (really just data structures). There is a request object that contains data from the form that the user just submitted and other information that might vary per request. There is a client object that contains data intended to persist for a client's session. There is a project object that persists for as long as the application is running and a server object that persists for as long as the server is running.

These objects provide a natural and simple way to maintain state. For example, if an application has to compute something with a very expensive database query, it could cache the result in the project object. Setting information for a client session is very straightforward as well. You can just say, "client.session_id = 37;" and the server will remember.

The semantics of client objects are good, but Netscape's implementation of them in LiveWire 1.01 is abysmal. You have several choices for maintaining these objects. What you'd think would be the best way to do this is to hold them on the server and then reference them via a unique key stored either in a magic cookie or encoded in the URL.

Netscape provides this method, but they provide it in an incompetent fashion. The documentation refers to a server-side "database" of these objects but it isn't a real database management system like Oracle. When a page wants to get client object information, LiveWire "checks out" the entire object and subsequently denies even read access to these objects to other pages. This avoids bugs due to lack of concurrency control, but it means that the client object is unusable for many applications. Two subframes of the same frame, for example, cannot both get client object info. Or if the user, deciding that one database-backed page is too slow, opens another browser window and uses that to connect to another portion of the same LiveWire app, then the second connection won't be able to get to the client object data it expects. This will probably result in a server-side error.

If you want stuff to work, you probably have to set LiveWire to ship all the data back and forth to the client with every page access. This approach has several disadvantages, the first of which is speed. You are gratuitously transporting potentially many kilobytes of data back and forth across the network.

The second drawback is flexibility. Browsers aren't required to store more than 20 cookies for a particular path, so you can't have more than 20 client object variables. I don't think the programmer even gets a warning when this number has been exceeded and information is being lost.

One of the most serious objections is that confidential information may have to be sent back to the user. Netscape's examples include scenarios where the RDBMS username and password are stored in a client object. One certainly wouldn't want these residing in a random user's Netscape .cookie file. Or even private information that the user has supplied, like a credit card number—a side effect of using a Web site shouldn't be that the user's credit card number ends up stored back on the client computer (which might, for example, be a machine in a public library's reading room).

Database connections are handled more efficiently from LiveWire than with CGI, but less efficiently than with the AOLserver. AOLserver allows you to set up a reasonable number of simultaneous connections for the database—eight, for example—and then all the users share those connections. The operating system sees a stable configuration because the number of processes remains constant. Netscape's basic model is: one user of a LiveWire application equals one database connection. This means that the server is forking fairly frequently as users come and go on the site. You might even have two or three database connections for a single user if you don't want your whole site to be one monolithic LiveWire app.

Database vendors like Oracle are still living in the 1980s when it comes to their C libraries, which aren't "thread-safe." Unfortunately, the modern way to build Web servers is not with Unix multiprocessing but with threads. NaviSoft dealt with this rather elegantly by adding some locks to the Illustra C library and then writing external driver processes for other RDBMS vendors. Netscape deals with this by saying, "One Enterprise Server process will only have one connection to the RDBMS." So that means you have to carefully set up your Enterprise Server to have lots of processes and very few threads per process. In the end, if you have 100 users interacting with your server, you'll have 100 Netscape Enterprise processes spawned plus 100 RDBMS server processes spawned. Your CPU and memory vendors will be very pleased indeed with this server load requirement. You'd probably be able to handle the same number of users with AOLserver on a quarter or one-eighth the server horsepower.

Depending on your licensing arrangement with the RDBMS vendor, you might find that it costs a lot of extra money to have hundreds of simultaneous connections rather than a handful.

Note: If you are running Windows NT, the situation is a bit different. Enterprise Server runs as only one process on NT and relies on database vendors producing thread-safe libraries. Unfortunately, Informix (the database bundled with LiveWire PRO) didn't get with the program. Their library is not thread-safe. Hence each LiveWire application can only keep one connection to the database open at once.

Big companies like to buy Netscape server programs because they think they will get support. Netscape support can be useful if you have done something wrong in configuring the server. If you are a paid-up customer, you can e-mail them your .conf files and they will figure out what the correct incantations should be. However, if your problem is due to a bug in their code, then the support staff is at sea. They will try to help you find a workaround, but I've never really seen them persist. Nor have I ever seen them deliver a patched binary to fix a problem identified by a customer.

The problems that I've personally encountered with Netscape Enterprise include:

- Installer dumped core on HP-UX. (E-mail never answered.)
- Server periodically hangs on Solaris, that is, it stops serving pages though the process does not die. (Installed a Unix cron job to kill and restart unresponsive Enterprise servers.)
- Server did not properly observe redirects on HP-UX. (Netscape support came up with a couple of half-baked workaround attempts but solving the problem required ripping out Enterprise and installing AOLserver.)

Source code is not available for Netscape servers; if you don't like the support that you get from the company, then you are stuck.

The best reason for running the Netscape servers is the availability of shrink-wrapped software packages for their C API. People with big money run the Netscape servers, so Web technology companies always port their CGI scripts into the Netscape API first.

Like all threaded servers, Enterprise and FastTrack are very fast.

ORACLE WEBSERVER 2.0

If you've ever tried to use http://www.oracle.com (one of the slowest and least reliable sites on the Internet), then you probably won't be in the market for this server program. Nonetheless, you'd expect it to be quite adept at connecting to relational databases, or at least the Oracle relational database.

WebServer 2.0 includes Java and PL/SQL APIs. Both are rather underpowered by AOLserver standards. For example, if you want your PL/SQL-backed page to send e-mail, you have to install (literally) another 100MB of Oracle software. You can connect to the Oracle RDBMS through either Java or PL/SQL, but both approaches are extremely slow. Server throughput and responsiveness are about one order of magnitude worse than with AOLserver. Probably Perl CGI scripts running behind a conventional Web server like Apache would be just as fast as WebServer 2.0.

No source code is available for Oracle WebServer and support is illusory at best. In their released version of WebServer 2.0, there was only one way for a PL/SQL-backed page to issue an HTTP redirect. This crashed the entire Web server. It took a week of plowing through the Oracle support organization to figure out that this was a known bug. This is the kind of thing that the AOLserver folks would have fixed in a few hours. Netscape would have rushed a patch release out the door if anyone had found a bug like this. It took Oracle six months to fix the bug.

My theory of why Oracle is unable to support a Web server is that they are so steeped in the RDBMS, a technology that has changed very gradually since its inception in 1970. The art of collaborating with customers to find the best solution is natural to a lot of Web software vendors but not to RDBMS vendors.

The kinds of companies that would be likely to take Oracle's word for it and install WebServer 2.0 are also the kinds of companies that would be likely to purchase shrink-wrapped software. However, I've never seen anyone offering shrink-wrapped software for Oracle WebServer 2.0, perhaps because, as of January 1997, the NetCraft folks could only find 310 sites worldwide that were running it (versus 87,000 Netscape-backed sites).

I never figured out how fast Oracle WebServer 2.0 was at serving static files and Oracle has never posted any benchmarks on their site. It is a threaded server so presumably the answer is "fast enough."

CONNECTIVITY

Having an eight-headed DEC Alpha with 1GB of RAM in your living room is an impressive personal Web server, but not if it has to talk to the rest of the Internet through a 28.8 modem. You need some kind of high-speed Internet connection.

ISDN

Integrated Services Digital Network (ISDN) is a 128-kbps point-to-point connection from the phone company. It is the bare minimum bandwidth that you need to run any kind of Web server, though most publishers would be far better off co-locating a Unix box in a T1-connected network somewhere and remotely maintaining it.

If you decide to take the ISDN plunge for your home or business in order to manage that co-located Web server, try to get one vendor to take responsibility for the entire connection. Otherwise, your position will be the following: You want packets to go from the back of your Macintosh into the Net. If the packets are getting stalled, it could be a malfunctioning or misconfigured BitSURFR, in which case you need to call Motorola tech support (yeah, right). It could be the line, in which case you should call your local telephone company. It could be your Internet service provider, in which case you should pray.

With three organizations pointing fingers at each other and saying it's the other guys' fault, it is amazing to me that anyone has ever gotten ISDN to work. I finally got mine to work by scrapping the Motorola BitSURFR and getting an Ascend Pipeline 50 router, the product recommended by my ISP (an in-house MIT organization). They wanted me to get an Ascend 50 so that they could configure it properly and I would just have to take it home and it would work.

It didn't.

I called Ascend tech support and waited two minutes on hold before being connected to Jerome. He dialed into one of my ISDN channels and poked around inside the Pipeline 50. Then he said, "Your subnet mask is wrong for the range of IP addresses that they've given you. I fixed it." I noted that my Macintosh was complaining that another computer on the same wire was claiming that same IP address. "Oh, you've got Proxy ARP turned on," Jerome said. "I've turned it off. Everything should work now."

It didn't.

It turns out that MIT bought its big ISDN concentrator from Ascend as well. So I had Jerome connect into that and poke around. "They've set the subnet mask incorrectly for you there as well."

The only thing that could have darkened my day at this point was the bill. ISDN was designed in the 1970s to provide efficient, reasonably low-cost point-to-point digital communication across the continent. You really cared to whom you were connected and would be willing to pay a big price for that service.

Now people just want to use ISDN for Internet access. They don't really care to whom they are connected. In fact, having to choose an ISP is an annoyance and they would probably much rather the phone company took the bits and routed them into the Net. However, due to regulatory restrictions and corporate inertia, the Regional Bell Operating Companies (RBOCs) haven't all caught up to this.

Most of the RBOCs charge you per minute if you are using your ISDN line to call across town with a data connection. An example of a forward-thinking RBOC is Pacific Bell. They will provide you a complete package: ISP service, modem, and line. For this you pay $75 per month. If you use the line between 8 a.m. and 5 p.m. Monday through Friday, you pay 1 cent per minute. So if you left your line connected continuously you'd pay an extra $120 per month. By contrast, assuming you could ever get three vendors in Massachusetts to work together, the same pattern of usage would cost you 1.6 cents a minute times 24 hours times 60 minutes times 30 days equals . . . about $700 a month!

If you want to call a little farther or, God forbid, your line is billed at business rates, you could be paying a lot more. One guy in my lab at MIT got a bill from NYNEX for $2,700 one month. NYNEX will be naming their next building after him, I guess.

A more common approach is to defraud the phone company by programming your equipment to originate all calls with a voice header. It looks to the phone company like you've made a voice call to another ISDN telephone and are chatting away. But your ISP has in fact programmed their "modem bank" to answer all calls whether they have voice or data headers. You end up getting 56K instead of 64K per channel but you only pay the voice tariff, for which there is usually a flat monthly rate.

The reaction to this common practice varies among the RBOCs. The good ones say, "We really ought to provide flat-rate ISDN data for customers. In fact, we really ought to just give them Internet service before they all desert us for the cable TV companies." A more common attitude is, "We're never going to do flat-rate ISDN because the customers are tying up our switches and capacity and it is costing us and we'd really like to disallow flat-rate voice, too, so that the analog modem crowd doesn't clutter our switches."

YOUR FIRST T1

If you want to join the club of Real Internet Studs, then at a minimum you need a T1 line. This is typically a 1.5-Mbps dedicated connection to somebody's backbone network. You generally get the physical wire from the local telephone monopoly and they hook it up to the Internet service provider of your choice. The cost varies by region. In the San Francisco Bay Area, you can get a whole package from PacBell including the wire plus the Internet packet routing for $800. More typical is a $2,000-a-month package from a vendor like ANS, BBN, MCI, or Sprint (the four leading backbone operators).

I think it is risky to rely on anyone other than these four companies for T1 service. It is especially risky to route your T1 through a local ISP who in turn has T1 service from a backbone operator. Your local ISP may not manage their network competently. They may sell T1 service to 50 other companies and funnel you all up to Sprint through one T1 line.

You'll have to be serving about 500,000 hits a day before you max out a T1 line (or be serving 50 simultaneous real-time audio streams). When that happy day arrives, you can always get a 45-Mbps T3 line for about $50,000 a month.

CABLE MODEMS AND ADSL

The cable network is almost ideal topologically for providing cheap Internet. There is one wire serving 100 or 200 houses. Upstream from this there is a tree of wires and video amplifiers. The cable company can say, "We declare the wire going to your house to be a Class C subnet." Then they put a cable modem in your house that takes Ethernet packets from the back of your computer and broadcasts them into an unused cable channel. Finally, the cable company just needs to put an Internet router upstream at every point where there is a video amp. These routers will pull the Internet packets out of the unused cable channels and send them into one of the usual Internet Backbones.

If all of the folks on your block started running pornographic Web servers on their NT boxes, then you'd have a bit of a bandwidth crunch because you are sharing a 10-Mbps channel with 100 other houses. But there is no reason the cable company couldn't split off some fraction of those houses onto another Ethernet in another unused video channel.

My friend Pete lives in Newton, Massachusetts, and he was one of the original Continental Cablevision beta testers. I asked him how long it took him to hook up his Macintosh to the network. "Thirty-seven seconds." Though Continental only promises 1.5 Mbps in and 300 kbps out, he says that it is faster than being inside MIT Net. The price is $60 a month for unlimited access and that includes some traditional ISP services like POP mail and a News server. If you don't trust your cable company, don't give up on your local phone company. In their more candid moments and incarnations, the phone companies more or less concede that ISDN sucks. Their attempt to keep you from pulling the plug on them and letting your cable monopoly supply all of your communications needs is Asymmetrical Digital Subscriber Line (ADSL).

Telephony uses 1 percent of the bandwidth available in the twisted copper pair that runs from the central phone office to your house ("the local loop"). ISDN uses about 10 percent of that bandwidth. With technology similar to that in a 28.8 modem, ADSL uses 100 percent of the local loop bandwidth, enough to deliver 6 Mbps to your home or business. There are only a handful of Web sites on today's Internet capable of maxing out an ADSL line. The price will certainly be very low because the service was primarily designed to deliver video streams to consumers, in competition with video rental stores and pay-per-view cable.

As a Web publisher, your main question about ADSL will be what happens to the packets. There is no reason the phone company couldn't build a traditional hierarchical data network to sit in their central offices next to their point-to-point network. Then they could sell you low-cost one-vendor Internet access and their cost would be comparable to that of the cable companies.

Some of the RBOCs, however, are afflicted with the brain-damaged notion that people want to choose their router hardware and their ISP. So you'll have to buy an ADSL line from your RBOC and then also cut a deal with ANS, BBN, MCI, or Sprint to carry your packets into the Net.

THE BIG PICTURE

Processing power per dollar has been growing exponentially since the 1950s. In 1980, your home computer was lucky to execute 50,000 instructions per second and a fast modem was 2,400 bps. In 1997, your home computer can do 200 million instructions per second but it communicates through a 28,800-bps modem. You've gotten a 4,000-fold improvement in processing power but only a tenfold improvement in communication speed.

The price of bandwidth is going to start falling at an exponential rate. Your challenge as a Web publisher is to figure out ways to use up all that bandwidth.

Learning from Server Logs

Case Studies

Let's Back Up for a Minute

More on OpenMarket

Chapter 7

What do you want to know? Figure that out and then affirmatively devise a logging strategy. If your goal is to fill up your hard disk, then any Web server program will do that quite nicely with its default logs. However, this information might not be what you want or need.

Here are some examples of starting points:

- "I want to know how many users requested non-existent files and where they got the bad file names."
- "I want to know how many people are looking at Chapter 3 of http://webtravel.org/samantha/."
- "I want to know how long the average reader of Chapter 3 spends before moving on to Chapter 4."
- "I sold a banner ad to Sally's Sad Saab Shop. I want to know how many people clicked on the banner and went over to her site."
- •"I want to know the age, sex, and zip code of every person who visited my site so that I can prepare a brochure for advertisers."

Let's take these one at a time.

CASE STUDIES

"I WANT TO KNOW HOW MANY USERS REQUESTED NON-EXISTENT FILES AND WHERE THEY GOT THE BAD FILE NAMES."

You can configure your Web server program to log every access by writing a line into a Unix file system file (I've broken it up here into multiple lines for readability, but it is actually written with no new lines):

```
ip248.providence.ri.pub-ip.psi.net - - [28/Jan/1997:12:35:54 -0500]
"GET /sammantha/travels-withsammantha.html HTTP/1.0"
404 170
-
"Mozilla/3.0 (Macintosh; I; 68K)"
```

The first field is the name of the client machine. It looks like someone who connects via PSI in Providence, Rhode Island. My AOLserver has written the date and time of the connection and then the request line that the user's browser sent: "GET /sammantha/travels-withsammantha.html HTTP/1.0". This says "get me the file named /sammantha/travels-withsammantha.html and return it to me via the HTTP/1.0 protocol." This is close to /samantha/travels-with-samantha.html but not close enough for the Unix file system, which tells the AOLserver that it can't find the file. The AOLserver returns a 404 File Not Found message to the user. We see the 404 status code in the log file and then the number of bytes sent (170). The dash after the 170 normally contains the value of the "referer header" (yes, it is misspelled in the standard). In this case that field is empty, meaning either that the user has typed in the URL directly from "Open Location" or that the user's browser did not supply a referer header indicating the page from which the user clicked. I instructed my AOLserver to log the user-agent header so I know that this person is using Netscape (Mozilla) 3.0 on the Macintosh. Netscape 3.0 definitely does supply the referer header. So unless I can drive down to Providence and teach this user how to spell, we're both out of luck.

Moving on to the next 404 . . .

```
hd07-097.compuserve.com - - [28/Jan/1997:12:42:53 -0500]
"GET /philg/photo/canon-70-200.html HTTP/1.0" 404 170
http://www.cmpsolv.com/photozone/easy.htm
"Mozilla/2.0 (compatible; MSIE 2.1;  Windows 3.1)"
```

Here's a user from CompuServe. This person is asking for my review of the Canon EOS 70-200/2.8L lens (a delicious $1,500 piece of glass) and gets the same 404 and 170 bytes. But this user's referer header was "http://www.cmpsolv.com/photozone/easy.htm". There is a link from this page to a non-existent file on my server. Does that mean the photozone folks at cmpsolv.com are losers? No, it means I'm a loser.

I didn't think carefully enough about my file system organization. The file used to be at /philg/photo/canon-70-200.html but then I created a canon subdirectory and moved this review into it. So now a correct request would be for /philg/photo/canon/canon-70-200.html.

What should I do about this? I could try to find the maintainers of photozone and send them an e-mail message asking them to update their link to me. Creating extra work for them because of my incompetence—that seems like a nice way to pay them back for doing me a favor by linking to me in the first place. Alternatively, I could reconfigure my AOLserver to redirect requests for the old file name to the new file. I have already installed quite a few of these redirects, a testament to my inability to learn from experience. Finally, I could be relatively user-unfriendly and put an HTML file at the old location saying "Please click to the new location." That's not really any less trouble than installing the redirect, though, so there wouldn't much point to doing it unless I was using someone else's Web server where I wasn't able to install redirects.

> **Note:** An interesting side note about this server log entry is the user-agent header: "Mozilla/2.0 (compatible; MSIE 2.1; Windows 3.1)". The first part says "I'm Netscape 2.0." The second part says "I'm Microsoft Internet Explorer 2.1." A couple of years ago, Web publishers with too much time and money to spend programmed their services to deliver a frames-based site to Netscape 2.0 Achievers and a non-frames site to other browsers. The CGI or API scripts made the decision of which site to display based on whether the user-agent header contained the string "Mozilla/2.0." Microsoft, anxious that its users not be denied the wondrous user interface experience of frames, programmed Internet Explorer to pretend to be Netscape 2.0 so that publishers wouldn't have to rewrite their code.

"I WANT TO KNOW HOW MANY PEOPLE ARE LOOKING AT CHAPTER 3 OF HTTP://WEBTRAVEL.ORG/SAMANTHA/."

My answer here could be adapted from an article in *Duh* magazine: Search the server log for "GET /samantha/samantha-III.html". Here's a typical log entry:

```
ld20-147.compuserve.com - - [30/Jan/1997:18:28:50 -0500]
"GET /samantha/samantha-III.html HTTP/1.0" 200 17298
http://www-swiss.ai.mit.edu/samantha/samantha-II.html
"Mozilla/2.01E-CIS (Win16; I)"
```

The host name tells us that this person is a CompuServe user. The document requested was Chapter 3 and it was successfully delivered (status code of 200; 17,298 bytes served). The referer header is "samantha-II.html", meaning that this reader was reading Chapter 2 and then clicked on "next chapter." Finally, we learn that the reader is running Netscape 2.01 on a Windows 3.1 box.

What are the subtleties here? First, the user might be coming through a caching proxy server. America Online, for example, doesn't let most of its users talk directly to your Web server. Why not? For starters, AOL doesn't use Internet protocols so their users don't have software that understands TCP/IP or HTTP. Even if their users had Internet software, AOL only has a limited connection to the rest of the world. When 100 of their users request the same page, say, http://www.playboy.com, at around the same time, AOL would rather that only one copy of the page be dragged through their Internet pipe. So all of their users talk first to the proxy server. If the proxy has downloaded the page from the Internet recently, the cached copy is delivered to the AOL user. If there is no copy in the cache, the proxy server requests the page from your Web server and finally passes it on to the AOL customer.

A lot of companies require proxy connections for reasons of security. This was already an issue in pre-Java days but Java provides the simplest illustration of the security problem. A badly implemented Java-enhanced browser will permit an applet to read files on a user's computer and surreptitiously upload them to a foreign Web server. At most companies, the user's computer has the authority to read files from all over the internal company network. So one downloaded Java applet could potentially export all of a company's private data. On the other hand, if the company uses a firewall to force proxy connections, it can enforce a "no Java applet" policy. Computers with access to private information are never talking directly to foreign computers. Internal computers talk to the proxy server and the proxy server talks to foreign computers. If the foreign computer manages to attack the proxy server, that may interfere with Web browsing for employees but it won't compromise any internal data since the proxy server is outside of the company's private network.

Company security proxies distort Web server stats just as badly as AOL's private protocol-Internet bridge proxies. In my server's early days, there was one computer at Digital that downloaded about 250 .html files a day. I thought, "Wow, this guy at DEC must be my biggest fan; I really must find out whose machine this is." I eventually did find out. The computer was not sitting on a bored engineer's desktop; it was the proxy server for the entire corporation.

If proxy servers result in statistical understatements of traffic, user behavior can result in overstatements. Suppose a user with a flaky connection is trying to read Chapter 3 of *Travels with Samantha* and two of the 18 in-line images don't load properly. The user clicks "reload" in hopes of getting a fully illustrated page, adding 19 spurious hits to the server log (one for the .html file and 18 for the in-lines).

These statistical inaccuracies troubled me until I realized, "Hey, I'm not launching the Space Shuttle here." On average, more downloads equals more readers. The number of people reading Chapter 3 is pretty well correlated with the number of "GET /samantha/samantha-III.html" requests. I'll just collect that number and be happy.

Suppose you aren't as easy-going as I; what can you do to get more accurate data? See the next section.

"I WANT TO KNOW HOW LONG THE AVERAGE READER OF CHAPTER 3 SPENDS BEFORE MOVING ON TO CHAPTER 4."

I remember when my Web site was new, back in the winter of 1993-94. Every day or two I'd load the whole HTTPD access log into Emacs and lovingly read through the latest lines, inferring from the host name which of my friends it was, tracing users' paths through *Travels with Samantha,* seeing where they gave up for the day.

Lately, my server gets 25 hits a second during peak hours. Emacs is happy to display a 25MB log file so there is no reason why volume per se should keep me from doing "visual thread analysis." A big problem, though, is that these hits are coming from dozens of simultaneous users whose threads are intertwined. Worse yet, I don't see the readable host names that I've printed in this book. A Web server only gets IP addresses which are 32-bit integers. You have to explicitly do a "reverse Domain Name System (DNS)" lookup to turn an IP address into a readable name; for example, "129.34.139.30" turns into "ibm.com". Reverse DNS consumes network and CPU resources and can lead to the server process hanging. My physical server is a pathetic old Unix box so I turned it off. My even more pathetic and older brain is then completely unable to untangle the threads and figure out which users are getting which files in which sequence.

One approach to tracking an individual reader's surfing is to reprogram your Web server to issue a magic cookie to every user of your site. Every time a user requests a page, your server will check to see if a cookie header has been sent by his browser. If not, your server program will generate a unique ID and return the requested page with a Set-Cookie header. The next time the user's browser requests a page from your server, it will set the cookie header so that your server program can log "user with browser ID #478132 requested /samantha/samantha-III.html."

This gives you a very accurate count of the number of users on your Web site and it is easy to write a program to grind over the server log and print out actual user click streams.

Problems with this approach? Not all browsers support the Netscape Magic Cookie protocol (introduced with Netscape 1.0; see http://webtools.com/wtr/ for a link to the spec). AOL's proprietary browser has been the perennial exception. And some users set their browsers to warn them before setting cookies. If they reject the cookie that you try to set, their browser will never give it back to your server program. So you keep issuing cookies to users unable or unwilling to accept them. If such a user requests 50 documents from your server, casually implemented reporting software will see him as 50 distinct users requesting one document each.

"I SOLD A BANNER AD TO SALLY'S SAD SAAB SHOP. I WANT TO KNOW HOW MANY PEOPLE CLICKED ON THE BANNER AND WENT OVER TO HER SITE."

The number of click-throughs is information that is contained only in Sally's server log. She can grind through her server log and look for people who requested "/index.html" with a referer header of "http://yoursite.com/page-with-banner-ad.html". Suppose your arrangement with Sally is that she pays you ten cents per click-through. And further suppose that she has been hanging around with Internet Entrepreneurs and has absorbed their philosophy. Here's how your monthly conversation would go:

You: How many click-throughs last month, Sally?

Sally: Seven.

You: Are you sure? I had 28,000 hits on the page with the banner ad.

Sally: I'm sure. We're sending you a check for 70 cents.

You: Can I see your server logs?

Sally: Those are proprietary!

You: I think something may be wrong with your reporting software; I'd like to check.

Sally [*sotto voce* to her sysadmin]: "How long would it take to write a Perl script to strip out all but seven of the referrals from this loser's site? An hour? OK."

Sally [to you]: "I'll put the log on my anonymous FTP site in about an hour."

Of course, Sally doesn't have to be evil-minded to deny you this information or deliver it in a corrupted form. Her ISP may be running an ancient Web server program that doesn't log referer headers. Some of your readers may be using browsers that don't supply referer headers. Sally may lack the competence to analyze her server log in any way.

What you need to do is stop linking directly to Sally. Link instead to a "click-through server" that will immediately redirect the user to Sally's site but keep a thread alive to log the click-through. If you have a low-tech site, your click-through script could dump an entry to a Unix file. Alternatively, have the thread establish a connection to a relational database and record the click-through there.

What if you have a really low-tech site? You are hosted by an ISP that doesn't know how to spell "relational database." Fill out a form on my click-through server and establish a realm for your site. My server will log click-throughs and prepare reports for you. See Figure 7.1 for the architecture of this system.

In addition to being the author of the click-through server software, I also use the software to collect statistics on my personal site. Here's a portion of one of my report pages:

```
http://harmoniamundi.com/ (from materialism/stereo.html) : 1
http://nz.com/webnz/flying_kiwi/ (from nz/nz-mtn-bike.html) : 10
http://nz.com/webnz/flying_kiwi/ (from nz/iwannago.html) : 2
http://www.acura.com/ (from philg/cars/nsx.html) : 50
http://www.adiweb.com/ (from photo/credits.html) : 1
http://www.adiweb.com/ (from webtravel/vietnam/) : 3
http://www.adiweb.com/ (from photo/speed-graphic.html) : 8
http://www.adiweb.com/ (from photo/labs.html) : 27
http://www.alanet.com/ (from summer94/french-quarter.html) : 5
http://www.alanet.com/ (from summer94/new-orleans-zoo.html) : 13
http://www.architext.com/ (from photo/credits.html) : 2
http://www.audioadvisor.com/ (from materialism/stereo.html) : 1
http://www.bhphotovideo.com/ (from photo/edscott/spectsel.htm) : 5
http://www.bhphotovideo.com/ (from photo/where-to-buy.html) : 386
http://www.bhphotovideo.com/ (from photo/labs.html) : 5
http://www.bostonphoto.com/ (from photo/labs.html) : 40
http://www.bostonphoto.com/ (from photo/travel/foliage.html) : 16
http://www.bostonphoto.com/ (from photo/credits.html) : 1
http://www.calphalon.com/ (from materialism/kitchen.html) : 2
http://www.canon.com/ (from photo/canon/canon-reviews.html) : 47
http://www.chesky.com/chesky/ (from materialism/stereo.html) : 2
http://www.cool.co.cr/crexped.html (from cr/central-valley.html) : 29
http://www.cool.co.cr/crexped.html (from cr/tour-operators.html) : 37
http://www.cool.co.cr/crexped.html (from cr/baru.html) : 5
http://www.cool.co.cr/crexped.html (from cr/tortuga-lodge.html) : 9
http://www.cool.co.cr/toping/tur/faq.html (from cr/index.html) : 13
http://www.cris.com/~tnv2001/ (from materialism/stereo.html) : 3
http://www.cuisinart.com/ (from materialism/kitchen.html) : 2
http://www.dacorappl.com/ (from materialism/kitchen.html) : 3
http://www.goodnet.com/~rmnsx (from philg/cars/nsx.html) : 45
```

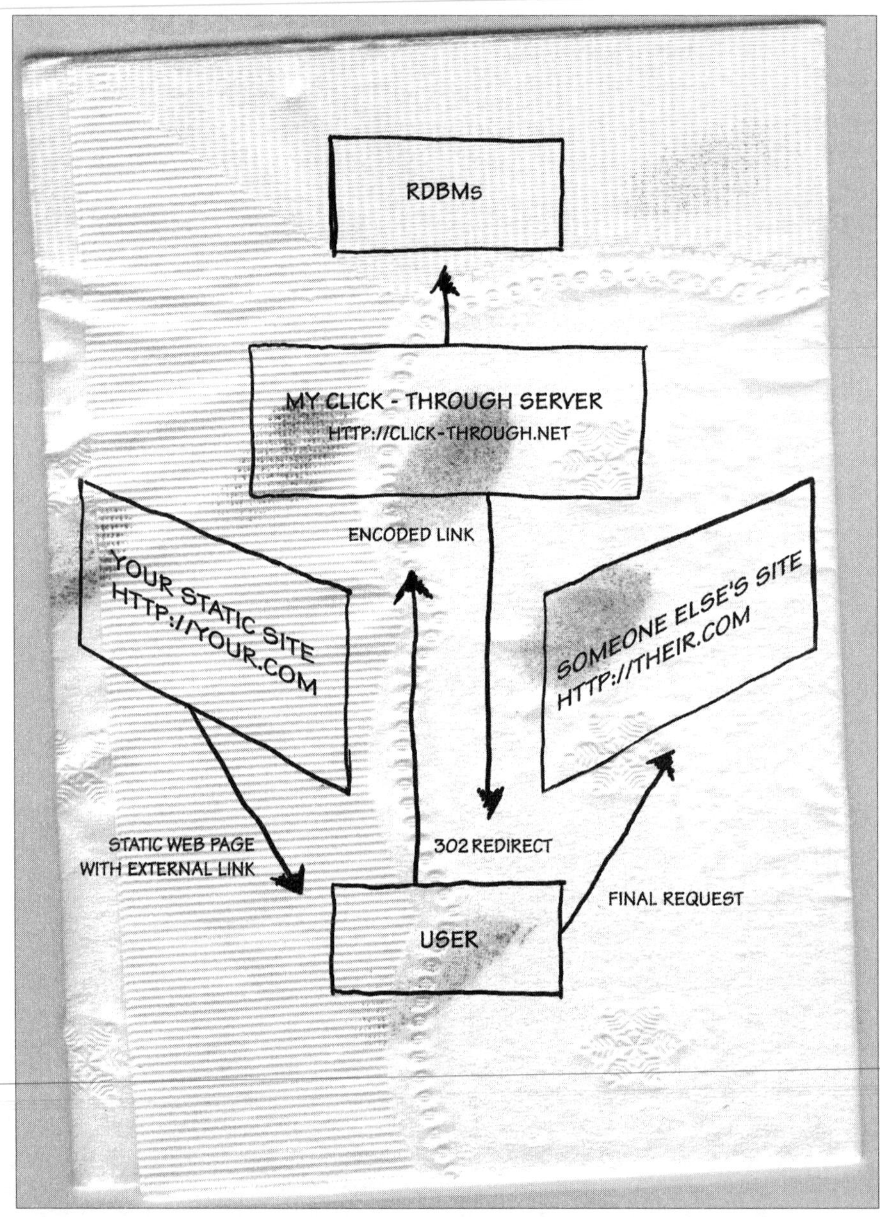

Figure 7.1: My click-through monitoring service, available at http://webtools.com/wtr/, allows low-tech Web publishers to measure traffic going from their site to foreign sites.

```
http://www.hasselblad.com/ (from photo/rollei-6008.html) : 11
http://www.hearstnewmedia.com/ (from photo/credits.html) : 2
http://www.hp.com/ (from photo/credits.html) : 1
http://www.intel.com/ (from photo/credits.html) : 1
http://www.keh.com/ (from photo/credits.html) : 3
http://www.keh.com/ (from photo/alex.html) : 7
http://www.keh.com/ (from photo/where-to-buy.html) : 137
http://www.klt.co.jp/nikon/ (from photo/nikon/nikon-reviews.html) : 67
http://www.kodak.com:80/ciHome/APS/APS.shtml (from photo/aps.html) : 22
http://www.kyocera.com/kai/input.html (from materialism/kitchen.html) :3
http://www.lcs.mit.edu/ (from photo/credits.html) : 1
http://www.lightroom.com/ (from photo/labs.html) : 11
http://www.lightroom.com/masking.html (from photo/labs.html) : 9
http://www.monstercable.com/ (from materialism/stereo.html) : 1
http://www.moon.com/ (from cr/moon/index.html) : 27
http://www.mpex.com/ (from photo/where-to-buy.html) : 59
http://www.novanet.co.cr/milvia/index.html (from cr/milvia.html) : 10
http://www.p-c-d.com/ (from materialism/kitchen.html) : 4
http://www.portphoto.com (from samantha/gift-shop.html) : 11
http://www.portphoto.com (from photo/labs.html) : 23
http://www.portphoto.com/ (from photo/labs.html) : 1
http://www.sheffieldlab.com/ (from materialism/stereo.html) : 2
http://www.theabsolutesound.com/ (from materialism/stereo.html) : 1
http://www.thermador.com/ (from materialism/kitchen.html) : 2
http://www.vanguard.com/ (from materialism/money.html) : 3
http://www.wweb.com/cayman (from webtravel/cayman.html) : 50
http://www.zzyzxworld.com/ (from photo/credits.html) : 1
http://www.zzyzxworld.com/ (from photo/labs.html) : 11
```

Take a look at the second line. It shows that ten people clicked from my New Zealand mountain biking story to http://nz.com/webnz/flying_kiwi/ (a tour company's home page). About 15 lines down, we see that 386 people were referred to http://www.bhphotovideo.com/ from my photo.net magazine's "where to buy" page. Hmm . . . That's getting to be an interesting number. What if we click on it?

```
February 03, 1997 : 34
February 02, 1997 : 41
February 01, 1997 : 45
January 31, 1997 : 44
January 30, 1997 : 42
January 29, 1997 : 54
January 28, 1997 : 60
January 27, 1997 : 66
```

Hmmm . . . 45 people a day, people who were reading my reviews of cameras in http://photo.net/photo, then decided to click on "where to buy," and then decided to click on my link to B&H Photo's home page. I've always liked B&H Photo, but my evil twin wonders how much another camera shop would pay us to make just a few changes to the text of http://photo.net/photo/where-to-buy.html.

Anyway, not to bore you too thoroughly by walking you statically through a dynamic site, but it seems like a good time to show off the advantages of using an RDMBS for this. The click-through server can slice and dice the reports in all kinds of interesting ways. Suppose I want to lump together all referrals from my personal site to B&H Photo regardless of which page they are from. Click:

```
February 03, 1997 : 38
February 02, 1997 : 42
February 01, 1997 : 49
January 31, 1997 : 48
January 30, 1997 : 45
January 29, 1997 : 55
January 28, 1997 : 61
January 27, 1997 : 68
```

What about that day when there were 48 click-throughs? Where did they come from? Oh, "48" seems to be a hyperlink. Let me click on it:

```
from photo/edscott/spectsel.htm : 1
from photo/labs.html : 1
from photo/nature/atkins-primer.html : 2
from photo/where-to-buy.html : 45
```

Hmmm . . . This "where to buy" page seems to be crushing the competition as far as links out. Can I see a report of all the click-throughs from this page to others?

```
February 03, 1997 : 60
February 02, 1997 : 71
February 01, 1997 : 94
January 31, 1997 : 81
January 30, 1997 : 76
January 29, 1997 : 100
January 28, 1997 : 101
January 27, 1997 : 111
```

What about February 1? Where did those 94 click-throughs go?

```
to http://www.bhphotovideo.com/ : 45
to http://www.keh.com/ : 22
to http://www.mpex.com/ : 12
to http://www.pricehunter.com/interpro/index.html : 15
```

Oooh! I'm in RDBMS heaven now. And all I had to do was:

1 Fill out a Web form to establish a realm on the click-through server.

2 Replace things like "http://www.bhphotovideo.com" with things like "http://clickthrough.photo.net/ct/philg/photo/where-to-buy.html?send_to=http://www.bhphotovideo.com/" in my static .html files.

If you want to get these reports for your own Web site, just visit http://webtools.com/wtr to get started.

"I WANT TO KNOW THE AGE, SEX, AND ZIP CODE OF EVERY PERSON WHO VISITED MY SITE SO THAT I CAN PREPARE A BROCHURE FOR ADVERTISERS."

The traditional answer to this request is "all you can get is IP address; HTTP is an anonymous peer-to-peer protocol." Then Netscape came out with the Magic Cookie protocol in 1994. It looked pretty innocent to me. The server gives me a cookie. My browser gives it back to the server. Now I can have a shopping basket. My friends all said, "This is the end of privacy on the Internet, Greenspun, and you're a pinhead if you can't figure out why."

So I thought about it for a while. Then I started adding some code to my click-through server.

Suppose I add an invisible GIF to my photo.net page:

```
<img width=1 height=1 border=0
src="http://clickthrough.photo.net/blank/philg/photo/index.html">
```

This is a coded reference to my click-through server. The first part of the URL, "blank", tells the click-through server to deliver a 1-pixel blank GIF. The second part, "philg", says "this is for the philg realm, whose base URL is http://photo.net/." The last part is a URL stub that specifies where on the philg server this blank GIF is appearing.

Suppose that http://photo.net/photo/index.html is the first page that Joe User has ever requested with one of these GIFs from clickthrough.photo.net. In that case, his browser won't offer a cookie to clickthrough.photo.net. My program sees the cookie-less request and says, "Ah, new user, let's issue him a new browser_id and log this request with his IP address and user-agent header." Suppose Joe is the sixth user that clickthrough.photo.net has ever seen. My program then issues a

```
Set-Cookie:  ClickthroughNet=6; path=/;
expires=Fri, 01-Jan-2010 01:00:00 GMT
```

This code tells Joe's browser to return the string "ClickthroughNet=6" in the cookie header every time it requests any URL from clickthrough.photo.net (that's the "path=/" part). This cookie would normally expire when Joe terminated his browser session. However, I'd really like to track Joe for a while so I explicitly set the expiration date to January 1, 2010. I could have made it last longer, but I figured that by 2010 Joe ought to have abandoned all of his quaint notions about privacy and will be submitting his name, address, home phone number, and VISA card number with every HTTP GET.

Every time Joe comes back to http://photo.net/photo, his browser will see the IMG reference to the click-through server again. Normally, his browser would say, "Oh, that's a GIF that I cached two days ago so I won't bother to rerequest it." However, I wrote my program to include a "Pragma: no-cache" header before the blank GIF. This instructs proxy servers and browser programs not to cache the reference. They aren't required to obey this instruction, but most do.

So Joe's browser will request the blank GIF again. This time, though, his browser will include a cookie header with his browser ID so my click-through server can just return the blank GIF and then keep a thread alive to log the access.

Now I can ask questions like "What are all the times that the Netscape with browser_id 6 requested tagged pages from my server?" and "What percentage of users return to http://photo.net/photo more than twice a week?"

To make life a little more interesting, suppose I add a little bit of code to http://www.webho.com/WealthClock (Bill Gates Personal Wealth Clock):

```
<img width=1 height=1 border=0
src="http://clickthrough.photo.net/blank/webho/WealthClock">
```

Note that www.webho.com is a different server from photo.net. If photo.net had issued Joe User's browser a cookie, his browser would not offer that cookie up to www.webho.com. But photo.net did not issue Joe a cookie; *clickthrough*.photo.net did. And that is the same server being referenced by the in-line IMG on the Wealth Clock. So my click-through server will be apprised of the access.

Here's how it would work and why you should surrender any lingering hope you might have of maintaining privacy on the Web (see Figure 7.2). Suppose that three publishers cooperate and agree to serve all of their banner ads from http://noprivacy.com. When Joe User visits search-engine.com and types in "acne cream", the page comes back with an IMG referencing noprivacy.com. Joe's browser will automatically visit noprivacy.com and ask for "the GIF for SE9734." If this is Joe's first time using any of these three cooperating services, noprivacy.com will issue a Set-Cookie header to Joe's browser. Meanwhile, search-engine.com sends a message to noprivacy.com saying "SE9734 was a request for acne cream pages." The "acne cream" string gets stored in noprivacy.com's database

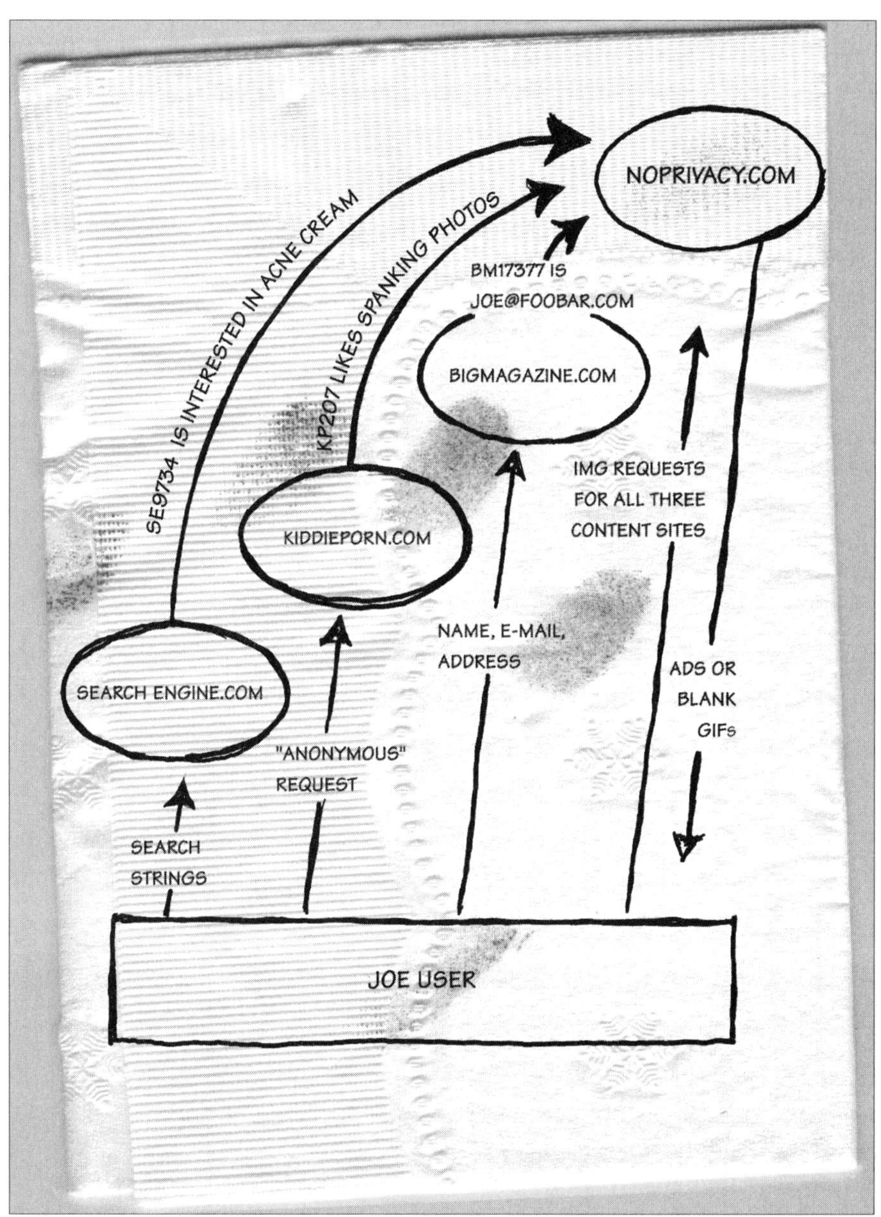

Figure 7.2: Magic cookies mean the end of privacy on the Internet.

along with "browser_id 7586." When Joe visits bigmagazine.com, he is forced to register and give his name, e-mail address, snail mail address, and credit card number. There are no ads in bigmagazine.com. They have too much integrity for that. So they include in their pages an IMG referencing a blank GIF at noprivacy.com. Joe's browser requests "the blank GIF for BM17377" and, because it is talking to noprivacy.com, the site that issued the Set-Cookie header, includes a cookie header saying "I'm browser_id 7586." When all is said and done, the noprivacy.com folks know Joe User's name, his interests, and the fact that he has downloaded six spanking JPEGs from kiddieporn.com.

Finally, I added an extra few lines of code to my click-through stats collector. IF there was a browser_id AND detailed logging was enabled, THEN also write a log entry for the click-through.

After all of this evil work is done, what do we get?

```
Realm where originally logged: philg
original IP address: 18.23.10.101
browser used initially: Mozilla/3.01 (WinNT; I)
email address:

CLICK STREAM

1997-01-30 01:44:36 Page View: philg/photo/index.html
1997-01-30 01:46:11 Page View: philg/photo/where-to-buy.html
1997-01-30 01:46:17 Clickthrough from text ref: philg/photo/where-to-buy.html
   to http://www.bhphotovideo.com/
1997-01-30 02:30:46 Page View: webho/WealthClock
1997-01-31 13:13:17 Page View: webho/WealthClock
1997-02-01 08:04:15 Page View: philg/photo/index.html
1997-02-01 18:33:17 Page View: philg/photo/index.html
1997-02-03 12:46:18 Page View: philg/photo/where-to-buy.html
1997-02-03 14:53:56 Page View: webho/WealthClock
```

We know that this guy was originally logged at 18.23.10.101 (my home computer) and that he is using Netscape 3.01 on Windows NT. We don't yet know his e-mail address, but only because he hasn't yet visited a guestbook page served by clickthrough.photo.net.

Then there is the click stream. We know that he downloaded the photo.net home page at 1:44 a.m. on January 30, 1997. Two minutes later, he downloaded the "where to buy" page. Six seconds later, he clicked through to B&H Photo. Forty-five minutes later, he showed up on another server (the webho realm) viewing the Wealth Clock. The next day at 1:30 p.m., this guy checks the Wealth Clock again. On February 1, 1997, he visits photo.net at 8:04 a.m. and then again at 6:33 p.m. He's back on the "where to buy" page on February 3. Two hours after that, he's checking the Wealth Clock once more.

If I get enough Web sites to cooperate in using one click-through server and even one of those sites requires registration, offers a contest, or does anything else where users type in names and e-mail addresses, it is only a matter of time before I can associate browser_id 6 with "philg@mit.edu; Philip Greenspun; 5 Irving Terrace, Cambridge, MA 02138."

Of course, I don't have to use this information for evil. I can use it to offer users a page of "new documents since your last visit." Suppose someone comes to the photo.net home page for the fourth time. I find that he has looked at my travel page but not read *Travels with Samantha.* I probably ought to serve him a banner that says "You might like *Travels with Samantha;* click here to read it."

Does this all sound too futuristic and sinister to be really happening? Have a look at your browser's cookies file. With Netscape Navigator, you'll find this as "cookies.txt" in the directory where you installed it. With Internet Explorer, you can find one file per cookie by doing View > Options > Advanced > View (Temporary) Files. See if there is an entry that looks like this:

```
ad.doubleclick.net    FALSE   /    FALSE   942191940    IAF   248bf21
```

Then go to http://www.doubleclick.net/ and see the long list of companies (including AltaVista) that are sharing this ad server so that your activity can be tracked. Of course, Double Click assures everyone that your privacy is assured.

CASE STUDIES CONCLUSIONS

Here are the conclusions that we can draw from these case studies:

- Your readers have no privacy and haven't had any ever since late 1994 when the Netscape Magic Cookie protocol came out.
- Vital information for most Web publishers, such as number of click-throughs, is unobtainable from standard server logs and traditional linking practices.
- With a little bit of RDBMS programming or a visit to http://webtools.com/wtr/, you're on your way to collecting the information that you need.

LET'S BACK UP FOR A MINUTE

Suppose that the preceding talk about click-throughs and cookies has overloaded your brain. You don't want to spend the rest of your life programming Tcl and SQL. You don't even want to come to http://webtools.com/wtr and fill out a form. You just want to analyze the server logs that you've already got.

Is that worth doing?

Well, sure. As discussed in the first case above, you certainly want to find out which of your URLs are coughing up errors. If you have hundreds of thousands of hits per day, casual inspection of your logs isn't going to reveal the 404 File Not Found errors that make users miserable. This is especially true if your Web server program logs errors and successful hits into the same file.

You can also use the logs to refine content. My very first log summary revealed that half of my visitors were just looking at the slide show for *Travels with Samantha.* Did that mean they thought my writing sucked? Well, maybe, but it actually looked like my talents as a hypertext designer were lame. The slide show was the very first link on the page. Users had to scroll way down past a bunch of photos to get to the Chapter 1 link. I reshuffled the links and traffic on the slide show fell to 10 percent.

You can also discover "hidden sites." You might have read Dave Siegel's book and spent $20,000 designing http://yourdomain.com/entry-tunnel.html. But somehow the rest of the world has discovered http://yourdomain.com/old-text-site.html and is linking directly to that. You're getting 300 requests a day for the old page, whose information is badly organized and out of date. That makes it a hidden site. You'd ceased spending any time or money maintaining it because you thought there weren't any users. You probably want to either bring the site up to date or add a redirect to your server to bounce these guys to the new URL.

Finally, once your site gets sufficiently popular, you will probably turn off host name lookup. As mentioned above, Unix named is slow and sometimes causes odd server hangs. Anyway, after you turn lookup off, your log will be filled up with just plain IP addresses. You can use a separate machine to do the nslookups offline and at least figure out whether your users are foreign, domestic, internal, or what.

ENTER THE LOG ANALYZER

The first piece of Web "technology" that publishers acquire is the Web server program. The second piece is often a log analyzer program. Venture capitalists demonstrated their keen grasp of technology futures by funding at least a dozen companies to write and sell commercial log analyzer programs. This might have been a great strategy if the information of importance to Web publishers were present in the server log to begin with. Or if there weren't a bunch of more reliable freeware programs available. Or if companies like Netscape hadn't bundled log analyzers into their Web server programs.

Anyway, be thankful that you don't have money invested in any of these venture funds and that you have plenty of log analyzer programs from which to choose. These programs can be categorized along two dimensions:

- Source code availability
- Stand-alone or substrate-based

Whether or not the source code is available is extremely important in a new field like Web publishing. As with Web server programs, software authors can't anticipate your needs or the evolution of Web standards. If you don't have the source code, you are probably going to be screwed in the long run. Generally the free public domain packages come with source code and the commercial packages don't.

A substrate-based log analyzer makes use of a well-known and proven system to do storage management and sometimes more. Examples of popular substrates for log analyzers are Perl and relational databases. A stand-alone log analyzer is one that tries to do everything by itself. Usually these programs are written in primitive programming languages like C and do storage management in an ad hoc manner. This leads to complex source code that you might not want to tangle with and ultimately core dumps on logs of moderate size.

Here's my experience with a few programs . . .

wwwstat This is an ancient public-domain Perl script, available for download and editing from http://www.ics.uci.edu/WebSoft/wwwstat/. I found that it doesn't work very well on my sites for the following reasons:

- There are at least three URLs to get to many of my pages: http://webtravel.org/~philg/samantha/travels-with-samantha.html was what I used initially. Then I discovered the "index.html" religion so http://webtravel.org/~philg/samantha/ is another gateway to the same page. Then I got a little symlink-happy and made http://webtravel.org/samantha/ work. But I also made http://webtravel.org/philg/samantha/ work, too. So there are six URLs for the same file. They are all reported separately by wwwstat and there was no easy way to group them together. I think the latest version is beginning to have grouping capabilities.
- wwwstat doesn't count "distinct hosts" like a lot of other tools. In the era of proxy servers, counting distinct hosts is a mighty crude way to gauge number of users, but it is better than nothing.
- wwwstat doesn't understand the extra information that modern Web servers log, such as browser and referer. These extra items don't interfere with wwwstat, but you don't get a "90 percent using Netscape" report, either.

- wwwstat formerly had no built-in facility for doing host name lookup, though it now does.

I've fed wwwstat 50MB and larger log files without once seeing it fail. There is a companion tool called gwstat that makes pretty graphs from the wwwstat output. It is free but you have to be something of a Unix wizard to make it work.

There are a lot of public domain tools newer than wwwstat listed in http://www.yahoo.com/Computers_and_Internet/Software/Internet/World_Wide_Web/Servers/Log_Analysis_Tools/. A lot of wizards seem to like analog (referenced from Yahoo), but I haven't tried it.

WebReporter This is a stand-alone commercial product, written in C and sold for $500 by OpenMarket. It took me two solid days of reading the manual and playing around with the tail of a log file to figure out how to tell WebReporter 1.0 what I wanted. For a brief time, I was in love with the program. It would let me lump certain URLs together and print nice reports saying "Travels with Samantha cover page." I fell out of love when I realized that

- If you want cumulative reports, you have to freeze your groups when you start accumulating data. That makes WebReporter a great tool for sites where files are never added, subtracted, or moved. Yeah.
- It dumped core trying to show ASCII histograms of activity from a puny little log file (just an hour or two's worth of data for a popular site).

When I complained about the core dumps, they said, "Oh yes, we might have a fix for that in the next release. Just wait four months." So I waited and let some friends at a commercial site beta test the new release. How do you like it? I asked. They responded quickly: "It dumps core."

My experience with WebReporter has made me wary of stand-alone commercial products in general. Cumulative log data may actually be important to you. Why do you want to store it in a proprietary format accessible only to a C program for which you do not have source code? What guarantee do you have that the people who made the program will keep it up to date? Or even stay in business?

Relational Database-backed Tools What are the characteristics of our problem anyway? Here are some obvious ones:

- We need to maintain a data set over many years.
- We can't know now what kinds of queries we're going to do into this data set.
- We may end up with many gigabytes of data.

- We don't trust one vendor to serve all of our needs. We can't afford to lose access to our data if an application code vendor folds.

Do these sound like the problems that IBM thought they were solving in the early 1970s with the relational model? Call me an Oracle whore but it seems apparent that the correct tool is a relational database management system.

So brilliant and original was my thinking on this subject that the net.Genesis guys (http://www.netgenesis.com/) apparently had the idea a long time ago. They make a product called net.Analysis that purports to stuff server logs into a (bundled) Informix RDBMS in real time.

Probably this is the best of all possible worlds. You do not surrender control of your data. With a database-backed system, the data model is exposed. If you want to do a custom query or the monolithic program dumps core, you don't have to wait four months for the new version. Just go into SQL*PLUS and type your query. Any of these little Web companies might fold and/or decide that they've got better things to do than write log analyzers, but Oracle, Informix, and Sybase will be around. Furthermore, SQL is standard enough that you can always dump your data out of Brand O into Brand I or vice versa.

More importantly, if you decide to get a little more ambitious and start logging click-throughs and/or sessions, you can use the same RDBMS installation

More on OpenMarket

An interesting aside to this experience with the software was an opportunity to see how OpenMarket is making Internet commerce a reality:

- Their demo site for the new version was down. So I couldn't try the software on their machines.
- When I asked for a new copy of the software to fix the core dumping problem, they said I'd have to pay for it. There was apparently no warranty on the broken version I'd bought a couple of months earlier.
- Several e-mail messages asking how much the new copy would cost went unanswered. Finally, I was told to telephone (yes, *telephone*) a particular saleswoman for a quote.
- I managed to get the saleswoman's e-mail address and sent her mail. She never answered.

That's when it occurred to me that I'd managed to serve several billion hits with software from Netscape and NaviSoft (AOLserver) without ever having to telephone either company.

and do SQL JOINs on the vanilla server log tables and the tables from your more sophisticated logs.

Caveats? Maintaining a relational database is not such a thrill, though using it for batch inserts isn't too stressful. If you don't want the responsibility of keeping the RDBMS up 7x24 then you can have your Web server log to a file as usual and insert the data into your RDBMS in batches. If you do decide to go for real-time logging, be a little bit thoughtful about how many inserts per second your RDBMS can handle. I maintain some RDBMS benchmarks at http://webtools .com/wtr but the bottom line is that you should start to worry if you need to log more than ten hits per second on a standard Unix box with one disk.

SUMMARY

Here's what you should have learned from reading this chapter:

- You can collect a metric buttload of data about user activity on your site without too much effort.
- You have to think and work if you want to collect data that is truly more interesting than what a ten-year-old could get from his home Web server and a freeware stats package.
- You can use free software and services from http://webtools.com/wtr to do a lot of the fancy tricks that well-funded Web publishers use.

What do I do with my server logs? My server is programmed to delete them every few hours. The logs are about 50MB a day on a machine with only 4GB of disk space. I got tired of struggling with WebReporter. I realized that I didn't have any advertisers who cared. Collecting gigabytes of useless information is probably good preparation for a career in Fortune 500 middle management but I don't really want a job where I couldn't take my dog to work.

It would be nice to get a rough idea of who is reading what on my site, but not if maintaining a complicated program is going to keep me from writing more content.

Java and Shockwave—The <BLINK> Tag Writ Large

What Java Is

What It Is (Also)

What It Is (New Techno Stuff)

Too Bad It Doesn't Work

You Need These Things

Encouragement

Using Java Applets on the Web

When Java Makes Sense

An Inspiring Example

Finally . . . Don't Get Too Excited by the Rich User Interface

Chapter

8

I'm hoping that you didn't buy this book because you thought it would teach you Java. But on the off chance that you did, I'm going to start this chapter by writing down everything that I know about Java. If you already know Java, then you'll probably want to skip over this section.

What Java Is

Java is a computer language. To understand whether it is a good or bad computer language, you have to ask, "Why do I need a computer language?" After all, if you were to buy a bare Pentium processor chip from Intel, it would come with a book listing valid instructions for the Pentium, such as "add two numbers together," "subtract 34 from the number in Register %eax," or "jump to address #457 if the result of the last subtraction was 0." It is a bit tough to see how adding up several million of these instructions would turn into a program like Netscape Navigator, Adobe PhotoShop, or the Oracle relational database management system.

Computer languages used by programmers are designed to be readable by humans, but it is inefficient to build computer hardware that understands human-readable instructions. A hardware processor understands simple machine codes such as "load memory location #4576 into Register %eax." The Pentium processor used in the example in Figure 8.1 understands i386 machine code. A computer program called a *compiler* translates human-readable languages such as C and Java into i386 machine code. This method of getting programs to run has two principal drawbacks. Drawback 1: Every time the

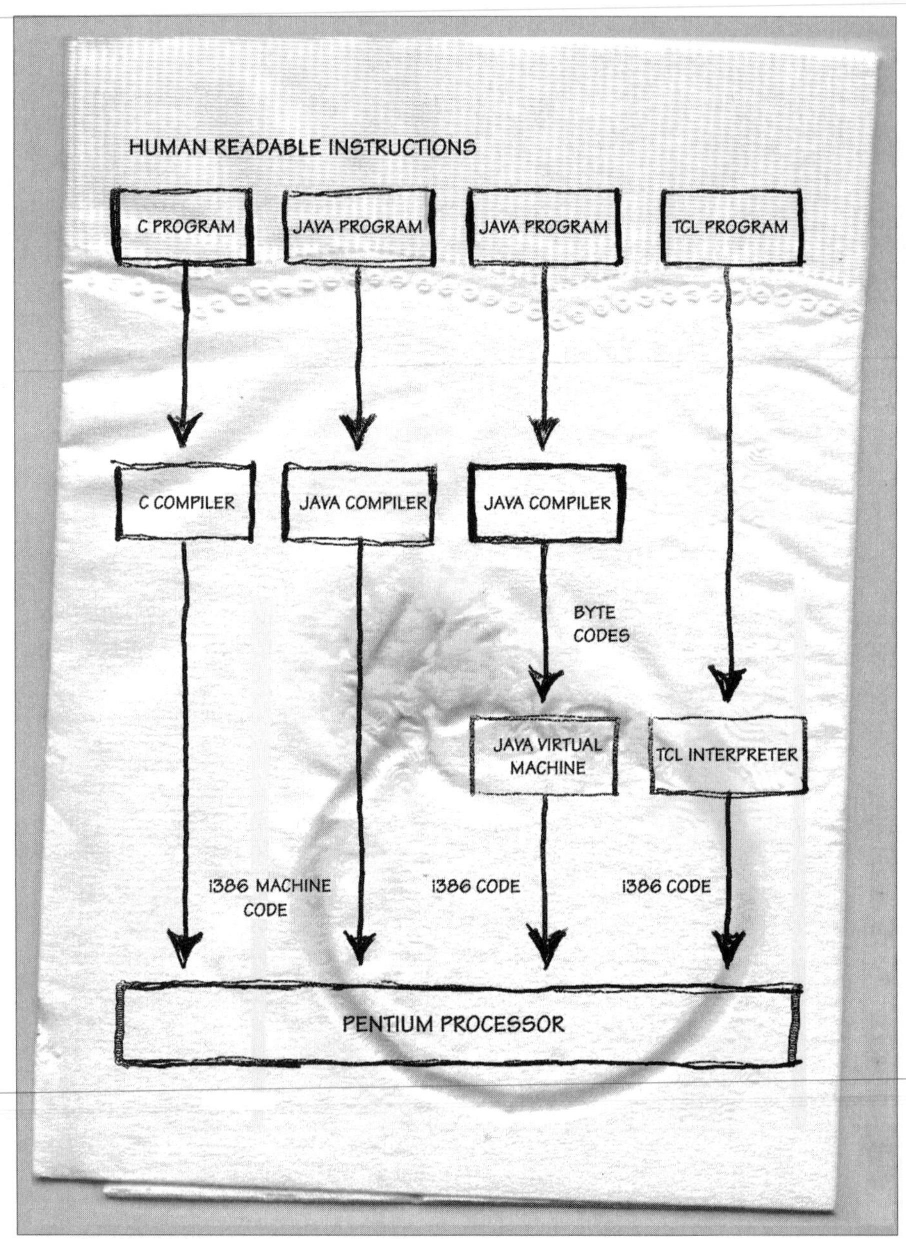

Figure 8.1: Compiled and interpreted languages

programmer wants to test a change, he or she has to rerun the compiler. This slows down software development. Drawback 2: The output of the compiler is not typically portable. It will only run on a Pentium. It may only run on a Pentium with Windows NT 4.0. Every time you run a program in an interpreted language such as Tcl, you send the human-readable code to an interpreter. This works around both drawbacks but results in rather sluggish execution. Java "the system" allows the programmer to compile to Java interpreter byte code. Testing changes still requires a tedious recompilation, so we haven't escaped Drawback 1. However, the output of the compiler is portable to any computer running the Java virtual machine.

John Locke was apparently having this same difficulty back in 1690 when he wrote "An Essay Concerning Human Understanding":

> "The acts of the mind, where it exerts its power over simple ideas, are chiefly these three: 1. Combining several simple ideas into one compound one, and thus all complex ideas are made. 2. The second is bringing two ideas, whether simple or complex, together, and setting them by one another so as to take a view of them at once, without uniting them into one, by which it gets all its ideas of relations. 3. The third is separating them from all other ideas that accompany them in their real existence: this is called abstraction, and thus all its general ideas are made."

Note: Before you congratulate me on my literacy, let me admit that I stole this quote from the only good book on computer programming that I've ever read, *Structure and Interpretation of Computer Programs* (Abelson and Sussman; MIT Press, 1996).

One does not program in i386 machine code because it lacks powerful *means of combination*, by which compound expressions are built from simpler ones, and *means of abstraction*, by which compound objects can be named and manipulated as units. Without means of combination and means of abstraction, a big computer program would never be understandable to a human.

Over the past four decades, many high-level computer languages have been developed. The most powerful of these languages is Lisp, invented at MIT in 1959 and today used only by people who are either trying to solve extremely difficult problems—the best layout for a big integrated circuit ("micro chip"), for example—and paradoxically by people who don't think of themselves as programmers at all (draftsmen who are adding shortcuts to AutoCAD).

One of Lisp's best features is that it allows the programmer to think of the computer as having infinite memory. Interactive programs have to create and destroy objects all of the time; for example, a word processor has to store a new paragraph typed by the user but then delete it if the user changes his mind. Lisp provides functions to create data structures but none to delete them. This would work great if you could go down to the computer store and bring home a physical machine with infinite memory. Since you can't, Lisp incorporates a garbage collection system that tracks down data structures that are no longer being used. This space is then scavenged and made available so that the running program can continue to behave as though the memory were infinite.

The most popular computer language of the early 1990s was C. A C programmer is supposed to track every object he has created and explicitly identify which ones are no longer needed. If 20 programmers are working together on a big system, they all have to coordinate with each other on the storage allocation scheme. If one of the 20 programmers makes a mistake, the same memory location ends up being used by two subroutines and the program begins to return erroneous results. Usually the program will crash eventually, bringing down the entire machine in the case of Macintosh and non-NT Windows operating systems.

The "perennially crashing C program problem" was attacked in different ways. Big corporations attacked it by moving their critical programs into safe languages, notably SQL, the declarative language of their relational database management systems. Users attacked it by saving their work every five minutes. Computer language nerds attacked it by inventing new computer languages.

Java is one of those new languages. As a language per se, it doesn't look like much of a revolution. Java has some of the most important features of Lisp, like automatic storage management and an object system. But so do dozens of these other new computer languages. And so, for that matter, did Lisp implementations of the 1970s. If people wanted to write software and compile it into machine code, they'd be a lot better off writing Common Lisp. So there must be more to Java.

WHAT IT IS (ALSO)

Java is an interpreter. Lisp could run as an interpreted language back in 1959 so there must be something else.

Java is an interpreter installed on almost every Internet user's desktop. You can write a Java program, compile it to Java interpreter byte code, and then it will run on any computer with a standard Web browser installed (see Figure 8.2). This is the most interesting thing about Java. MS/DOS was not an innovative system. Yet it was worth programming for because it was so widely installed. Java will be a lot more widely installed than MS/DOS.

Note: Java is not truly an interpreted language. You cannot make a change to a Java program with a text editor and immediately see the results the next time you run the program. Before testing your change, you must run a compiler to translate Java source code into either Java byte code or

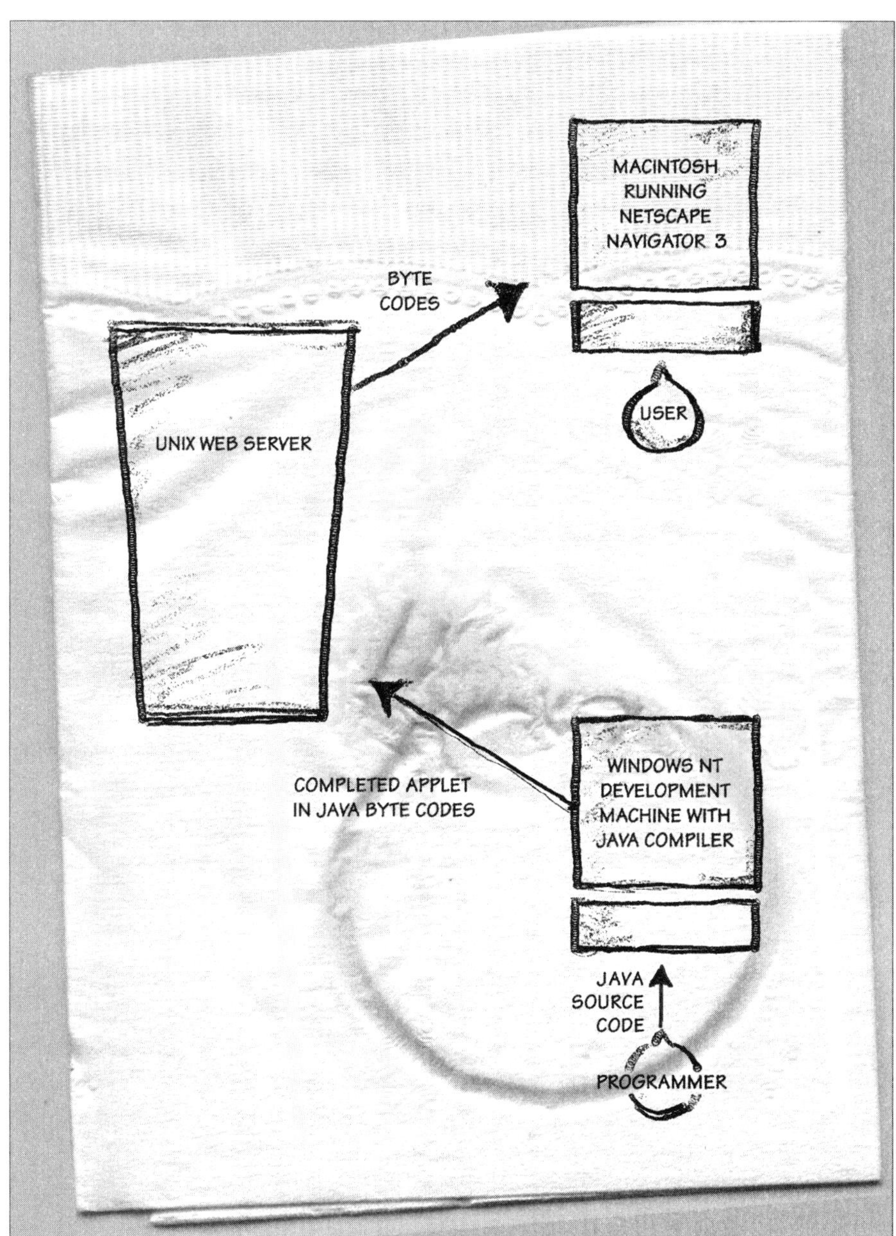

Figure 8.2: Users loading Web pages from a server will be able to run Java applets as long as their browser incorporates a Java virtual machine. The programmer need never be aware of the user's choice of computer or operating system.

native machine code for the particular processor inside your computer. It may be much more convenient to use a purely interpreted language such as Tcl or JavaScript or a language such as Lisp that gives you the option of interpretation or compilation.

WHAT IT IS (NEW TECHNO STUFF)

It is true that most of the hyped techno-advantages of Java were available to thoughtful programmers in 1960. However, Java contains a few genuinely new ideas. The most important of these is the byte code interpreter's security system. The Java team really thought about the implications of grabbing code off an untrusted network and running it alongside trusted software with access to private information.

There are three components to Java virtual machine security:

- Verifier
- Class Loader
- Security Manager

The Verifier looks through the downloaded instructions to make sure that they can't do anything illegal. Most of this checking is *type inference:* Look at the input data types, look at the operations performed on that data, and make sure that the results are of legal types.

The Class Loader is responsible for grabbing Java binary classes from the network and managing their interaction. It is possible to implement a Class Loader that partitions interactions among Java code. For example, if you were building a Web browser, you might want to prevent classes loaded from different sites from interacting with each other.

The Security Manager handles requests by Java byte code for system resources such as local files, network ports, and input/output hardware. If you were using a Java interpreter to run a company network with company software, you'd probably want a Security Manager with very loose policies. Java code ought to be able to read and write to the local disk, talk to any other computer on the company network, and display output to the user. If you were writing a Web browser to run Java code downloaded from foreign sites, you'd want a very unforthcoming Security Manager. Access to local files would be forbidden. Access to the network, except to talk to the IP address from which the applet was downloaded, would be forbidden.

How well does all this security stuff work? Not so well that Java security holes don't periodically make the front page of the *New York Times.* These aren't holes in the fundamental scheme, though. They are problems with Sun's implementation of the Verifier or Netscape's implementation of the Class Loader and Security Manager. Unlike half-baked systems like Microsoft's ActiveX, Java security is fundamentally sound.

Another new feature in Java is multithreading. There have been multi-threaded Lisps for decades. You can even exploit multithreading in AOLserver Tcl scripts thanks to Doug and Jim's featureful API. But Java puts multithreading into the language spec so your code is portable among implementations and operating systems. Virtually every Internet application requires multi-threading. One thread talks to the network, one thread listens for user input, one thread drives the sound card, one thread manages windows and menus.

Too Bad It Doesn't Work

Oh yes, there is one little problem with developing Java applets: They will inevitably crash the user's browser.

The Java PR literature explains on every third page how Java will finally save you from all those buggy C programs. Unlike C, Java doesn't let those cubicle-dwelling drones allocate storage and manipulate pointers. Unlike C, Java doesn't screw up arithmetic when you move a program from one computer to another. C sucks. Java rules.

And what language did these bold pioneers use to implement the Java virtual machine?

C.

Of course, there *are* moderately reliable C programs. The Unix operating system, for example. It has only taken 25 calendar years and several hundred thousand programmer-years to get most of the bugs out.

Here's my capsule history of software reliability . . .

THE 1970s

In the 1970s, programmers wrote safe programs on top of a reliable *high-level* substrate. They were using Lisp, a language that was produced by some of the best programmers in the world for their own use. Bad programmers often wrote reliable programs and great programmers pushed back the frontiers.

THE 1980s

In the 1980s, programmers wrote unsafe programs on top of a reliable *low-level* substrate. They were using C, a low-level language that doesn't have much of a run-time system. Assuming the CPU hardware was functioning correctly, a great C programmer could write a program that would not crash. Of course, most C programmers either weren't so great or were attempting to build complex systems. The programs crashed and sometimes took the user's whole computer with them (with a Macintosh or Windows, for example). Even the best programmers were unable to do more than write copies of systems that had been built in safe languages during the 60s and 70s.

THE 1990s

We're back to the 1970s and a safe language (Java) but this time we're using an *unreliable* high-level substrate (the Java virtual machine). Thus no matter how skilled the Java programmer, no Java program can ever run reliably. It is only a matter of time before the Java applet that you publish will crash the user's Web browser. Unless he is using Windows NT or Unix, there is a fair chance that your Java applet will crash his entire computer.

THE FUTURE SO BRIGHT YOU'LL NEED TO WEAR SUNGLASSES

There is enough money behind Java that I suppose someone will eventually write a reliable virtual machine and window system. Just don't hold your breath.

YOU NEED THESE THINGS

To write Java applets for your Web site, you need something to translate your Java source code, designed to be human-readable, into Java byte code that will be understandable by the interpreter running inside your users' browsers. In more humble times, you'd use a compiler. Now you really need a development environment. If there is a mistake in your program, the development environment will show you where it is in the source rather than barfing up a cryptic error message.

As of February 1997, the consensus among my Java nerd friends is that Symantec Café (http://www.symantec.com) is the best development environment. They also cautioned me against using any of the special Symantec classes, which are allegedly slow and buggy. Symantec also produces dbANYWHERE, the currently favored technique of getting Java on Windows machines to talk to a relational database.

As for documentation, there are plenty of Java books out there. Some of them hit the streets even before the applet classes were finalized. Unfortunately, it would seem that it takes a bit longer to write a clear language tutorial than it does to make an insta-book biography of Marcia Clark. My friend Sean tells everyone to buy *Teach Yourself Java in 21 Days* (Perkins and Lemay; Sams, 1996), but supposedly this is obsolete advice. Folks on the Net seem to like *The Java Tutorial*, available in hypertext at http://www.javasoft.com/nav/read/Tutorial/index.html or as an 831-page pile of dead trees (Campione and Walrath; Addison-Wesley, 1996). If you want technical information right from the horse's mouth, then you need *The Java Language Specification* (Gosling, Joy, and Steele; Addison-Wesley, 1997). Guy Steele was a driving force behind standardized Lisp back in the 1980s so he knows something about computer languages.

I like O'Reilly books. They don't have enough money to flood the world with advertising. They don't have enough MBAs to realize that time-to-market is more important than quality. I'd start with *Exploring Java* (Niemeyer and Peck; O'Reilly, 1996), a 400-page tutorial. Once you've read all of that, you can keep *Java Language Reference* (Grand; O'Reilly, 1997) next to your 3M Precise Mousing Surface (like a mouse pad, but good). If you heeded the rest of my advice in this chapter, you are probably using Java for a network application, in which case you'll want *Java Network Programming* (Harold; O'Reilly, 1997). If on the other hand, you've gone over to the dark side and just want to simultaneously tickle every multimedia device on your readers' machines, then you need *Java Threads* (Oaks & Wong; O'Reilly, 1997).

Encouragement

You *should* learn Java. I predict that it will gradually supplant C over the next ten years. Java is going to be big. You heard it here first.

Using Java Applets on the Web

> "Maybe if I make stuff flash I'll get more traffic. Well, it is easier than writing content anyway."

I talked to a glass blowing artist when he was planning his Web site. He wanted to hire the slickest Web design firm in Boston. "My work is visual. I have to have an amazingly good-looking Web page," Tony said.

How is anyone going to find your good-looking site? AltaVista doesn't recognize images and Java applets and graphic design. It only indexes text. For a lot less money, you could buy the online rights to an interesting book on glass blowing. Then anytime anyone typed the query "glass blowing" into a search engine, they'd get to your site and you could sell them glassware.

"But I want my site to be really cool," Tony responded.

ANIMATION CAN BE USEFUL

If you are trying to demonstrate the workings of a mechanism, show the steps of an algorithm, or just have some fun with a strip show, then animation can be useful. But try to be careful that you aren't just spending a lot of time and money turning your pages into visual irritations. Also remember that until Java implementations stabilize, you are always running the risk of crashing your users' browsers and, with Macintosh and non-NT Windows operating systems, their entire machines.

It is finally worth remembering what brought users to the Web in the first place: control and depth. Software like Java and Shockwave enables you to lead users around by the nose. Flash them a graphic here, play them a sound there, roll the credits, and so on. But is that really why they came to your site? If they want to be passive, how come they aren't watching TV or going to a lecture?

It seems like an obvious point, but I mention it because I've seen so many tools to convert PowerPoint presentations into Web sites. The whole point of a slide-based presentation is that you have a room full of people all of whose thoughts have to be herded in a common direction by the speaker. Ideas are condensed to the barest bones because there is such limited time and space available and because the speaker is going to embroider them. The whole point of the Web is that each reader finds his own path through a site. There is unlimited time and space for topics in which the reader has a burning interest.

When Java Makes Sense

Despite the flaws in today's Java implementations, the idea of moving programs around the network was great in the 1970s and is still great. If nothing else, it is a technology that promises to free us from a lot of system administration pain. You paid for a powerful processor on your desktop so you ought to be able to run lots of programs. Yet you don't really want to be responsible for installing all those programs, making sure that your operating system version is compatible, and upgrading to newer versions of the application.

Client-side Java can make a good site great in the following situations:

- You need a richer user interface than you can get with HTML forms.
- You need to respond to user input without network delays—mouse movements, for example.
- You need to give the user real-time updates.

RICHER USER INTERFACE

A richer user interface is always harder to learn. Your readers don't *want* to learn how to use new programs. They already learned how to use a Web browser and probably also word processing, spreadsheet, and drawing programs. However, it is possible that you can come up with a Java applet that delivers such a great benefits that people will invest in learning your user interface.

Suppose I'm doing a mundane camera ownership survey. If the user owns a point-and-shoot camera, it doesn't make sense to ask which accessory lenses and flashes he owns. However, if he says, "I have a Nikon 8008," then I'd like to present a list of Nikon flash model numbers as options. I can do this now by essentially asking one question per HTML form. The user says, "I own an SLR (Single Lens Reflex)," then submits that form; "I own a Nikon," then submits that form; "I own an 8008," then submits that form, and my server finally generates the appropriate accessory flash form.

With a Java applet, the user's choice on the P&S/SLR menu will affect the choices available on the camera brand menu which in turn will affect the choices available on the camera model menu. Is this better? It will take longer to download. Not only do you have to send the user Java byte code but also all the text that you have in your database of camera models, only a small portion of which will ever be presented. On the plus side, the user can work in another window while the applet is downloading and, once loaded, the applet is much more responsive than a succession of forms.

REAL-TIME RESPONSE

Some of the user-interface devices on a computer are just not well-suited to the stateless request-response HTTP protocol. Even a continuous network connection might not be good enough unless the Web server and Web client are physically close to each other. Examples of user-interface devices that require real-time response are the mouse, the tablet, and the joystick.

You would not want to use a drawing tool that needed to go out to the network to add a line. An HTML forms-based game might be fun for your brain but it probably won't have the visceral excitement of Doom. Anything remotely like a video game requires code executing on the user's local processor.

REAL-TIME UPDATES

Obvious candidates for Java include things like stock tickers and newsfeeds. The user can launch an applet that spends the whole day connected to a quote or headline server and then scrolls text around the screen. Though obvious, these are applications where Java isn't essential. The information provider could just as easily have written a "client-pull" HTML document by adding the following element to the HEAD:

```
<META HTTP-EQUIV=REFRESH CONTENT="60; URL=update.cgi">
```

The user's browser will fetch "update.cgi" 60 seconds after grabbing the page with this element.

The need for Java is a bit more pressing in a chat system. You want a new posting to be immediately transmitted to all the participants.

A chat system? A reimplementation of America Online? Is that really all we can do with Java?

An Inspiring Example

Medical records are fragmented. If a patient is treated in five hospitals, he will have five separate electronic medical records. That's understandable. What is unexpected is that even if a patient stays in one hospital, he will generally have several electronic medical records. Each department in a hospital generates and stores its own data to some extent. Whether and to what extent these departmental databases interoperate is determined by technology choices, the network infrastructure, and management politics.

Suppose that you are a programmer given the task of making all the data on one patient available to authorized personnel anywhere inside the hospital. This includes demographics data from the MIS shop, laboratory results, and real-time waveforms from machines in the intensive care unit. The traditional solution would be to design a monolithic computer system, presumably running some kind of relational database management software, into which all departments were required to contribute data. Then you'd budget to develop custom client software to run on all the different kinds of computer around the hospital.

A traditional solution of this form takes a long time to develop. Often it takes so long that the completed system does not fulfill the organization's goals, not because of bugs in the system, but because those goals have changed. Since a huge computer system is extremely expensive to develop, this leaves everyone with a bitter taste in their mouths and reluctant to start over on the next big system.

Anyone with an MBA these days can say "Let's build an intranet!" What would that mean in the hospital? First and most obviously, you abandon the idea of writing custom client software. The user interface to the system will be a Web browser, perhaps sprinkled with Java applets when standard HTML is inappropriate. Now the hospital does not have to worry about Mac/PC/Unix compatibility. Nor will there be any work associated with client computer operating system upgrades. If a department wants to change from Windows 3.1 to Windows NT 4.0 then they just need to get Netscape running; they don't need to ask you to recompile your client software.

Another aspect of intranets is that one doesn't build custom protocols. If you have data to offer, install a Web server and maybe a few API or CGI scripts to make the data available via Hypertext Transfer Protocol (HTTP). If a program needs data then it should get it by making an HTTP GET request from the appropriate server. AOLserver, Apache, NCSA, and Netscape are all better engineered general purpose servers than you are going to be able to write with your meager programming resources. Stick to worrying about the content that is transmitted in response to the GET.

In our hospital example, this means that the departments don't have to dump their data into a central Oracle database and then rely on that. Each department can continue to use their current system. This flexibility has enormous operational and political appeal. All each department need do is install a Web server to make its data available to other departments. In the case of the MIS department, this is very easy. They can just read the RDBMS-backed Web site chapters in this book and will be up and running a few days later. The intensive care unit, however, has to install a Windows NT or Unix machine next to all the monitoring instruments. This computer will run a Web server and some custom software to grab real-time data from the instruments and make it available via HTTP. A client that wants this data can just say "GET /heart-monitor-stream.tcl?monitor-id=icu2317 HTTP/1.0" and the server will deliver the waveforms as it receives them from the monitor.

Is there anything left for you to do? All the data in the hospital is now available by HTTP and all the client machines are running Netscape. A doctor anywhere in the hospital can walk over to a Netscape client machine and find out how Joe Schlebotnik's heart is doing. That is, assuming the first thing that comes to the doctor's mind when he thinks of Joe is "http://icuweb/heart-monitor-stream.tcl?monitor-id=icu2317". Oops. I guess you can't go home yet. You still have to build a patient-centered Web server somewhere. A doctor can query this server to ask, "What's the story with Joe?" and the patient-centered server queries all the hospital departments to put together a Joe Schlebotnik Web site on the fly.

Here again you want to use standard Web technology. It would be painful, tedious, and bug-prone to write a custom program to take the streaming data from the ICU and pass it into a Java applet running inside the doctor's Netscape Navigator. So instead you install a flexible Web server program on your conglomeration server and write a small Tcl or Java program to run inside its API. Figure 8.3 shows how the pieces fit together.

Is this practical today? Just barely. My friend Zak and I have been building medical Web/database systems like this at Boston's Children's Hospital and MIT since about 1994. Children's runs a 60GB Oracle installation which made it very easy to get interesting data. Even the first prototypes that we kludged together in Oraperl CGI scripts worked better than a lot of the custom Mac and Windows apps that medical information systems vendors were selling.

Zak's latest thinking in this area involves using the Netscape Enterprise Server as the conglomeration server. His group has added a thin layer of Java to the Enterprise Server for taking in real-time data streams and then serving them back out. In contrast to the unreliable client-side Java implementations with their bug-ridden window systems, server-side Java seems quite stable.

You can check out the system at http://w3health.com/.

Finally . . . Don't Get Too Excited by the Rich User Interface

My final comment is a cautionary one. Don't get too excited by the possibility of offering a rich custom user interface with Java. Adobe PhotoShop has a beautiful user interface but it took them hundreds of person-years to perfect. It takes them hundreds of person-years to test each new version. It costs them millions of dollars to write documentation and prepare tutorials. It takes users hours to learn how to use the program. You don't have a huge staff of programmers to concentrate on a single application. You don't have a full-time quality assurance staff. You don't have a budget for writing documentation and tutorials. Even if you did have all of those things, your users don't have extra hours to spend learning how to use the Web site that you build. Either they are experienced Web users and they want something that works like other sites or they are naïve users who will want their effort in learning to use Netscape and your site to pay off when they visit other sites.

Does that mean I'm suggesting that your Web site be 100 percent static? Au contraire! Read the next chapter to find out how to write server-side programs.

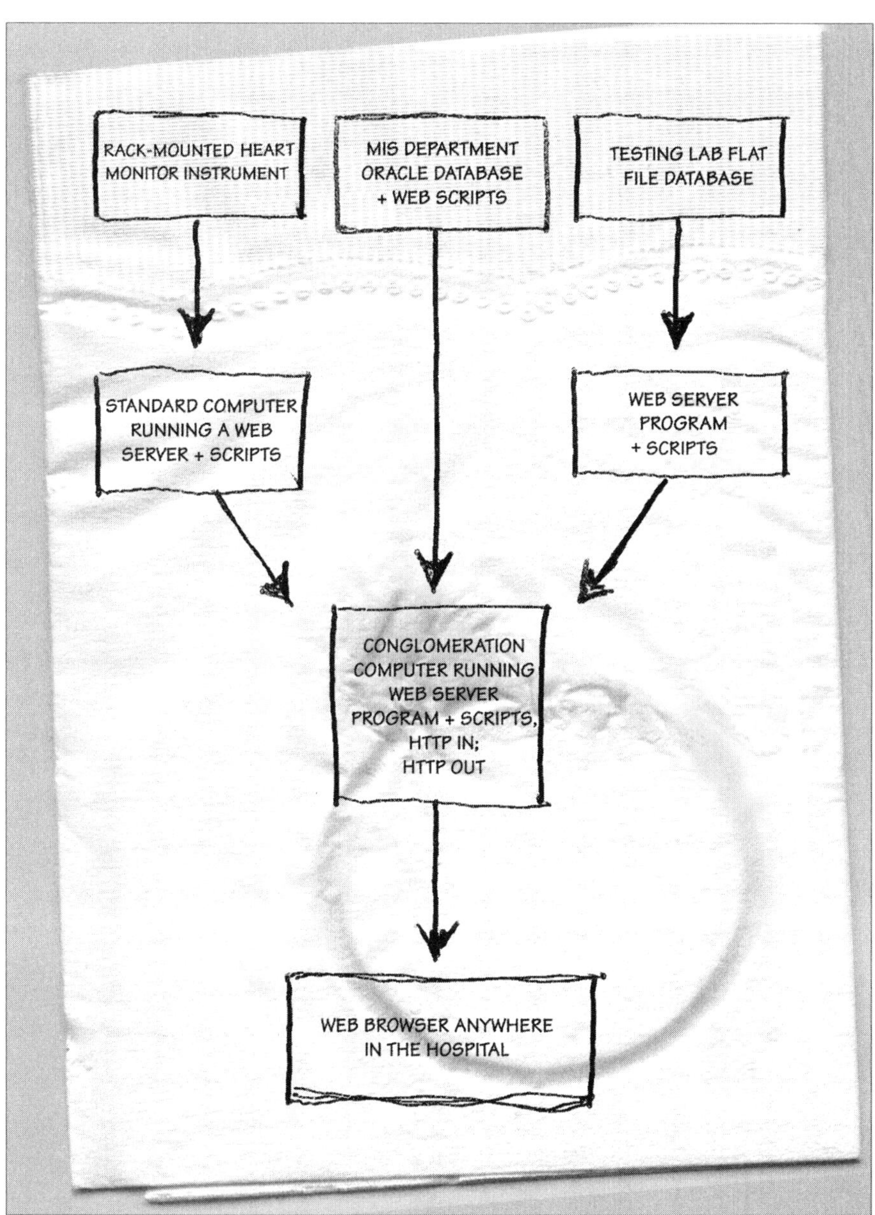

Figure 8.3: A hospital intranet using a conglomeration server

Sites That Are Really Programs

CGI Scripting

Server APIs

The Right Way—Extending HTML

Chapter 9

The classic (circa 1993) Web site comprises static .html files in a Unix file system. This kind of site is effective for one-way non-collaborative publishing of material that seldom changes.

You needn't turn your Web site into a program just because the body of material that you are publishing is changing. Sites like http://www.yahoo.com, for example, are sets of static files that are periodically generated by programs grinding through a dynamic database. With this sort of arrangement, the site inevitably lags behind the database but you can handle millions of hits a day without a major investment in computer hardware, custom software, or thought.

If you want to make a collaborative site, however, then at least some of your Web pages will have to be computer programs. Pages that process user submissions have to add user-supplied data to your Web server's disk. Pages that display user submissions have to look through a database on your server before delivering the relevant contributions.

Even if you want to publish completely static, non-collaborative material, at least one portion of your site will require server-side programming: the search engine. To provide full-text search over your material, your server must be able to take a query string from the user, compare it to the files on the disk, and then return a page of links to relevant documents.

This chapter discusses the options available to Web publishers who need to write program-backed pages.

CGI SCRIPTING

Every Web server program provides a facility known as the Common-Gateway Interface (CGI). The CGI standard is an abstraction barrier that dictates what a program should expect from the Web server (for example, user form input) and how the program must return data to the Web server program for it to eventually be written back to the Web user. If you write a program with the CGI standard in mind, it will work with any Web server program. You can move your site from NCSA HTTPD 1.3 to Netscape Communications 1.1 to AOLserver 2.1 and all of your CGI scripts will still work. You can give your programs away to other webmasters who aren't running the same server program. Of course, if you wrote your CGI program in C and compiled it for an HP Unix box, it isn't going to run so great on their Windows NT machine.

Oops.

Most CGI scripts are written in Perl, Tcl, or some other interpreted computer language. The systems administrator installs the Perl or Tcl interpreter once and then Web site builders on that machine can easily run any script that they write or download off the Net.

Another advantage of CGI and interpreted languages is that the software development cycle is very tight. A message shows up in the error log when a user accesses "http://yourserver.nerdu.edu/bboard/subject-lines.pl". If your Web server document root is at /web (my personal favorite location), then you know to edit the file /web/bboard/subject-lines.pl. After you've found the bug and written the file back to the disk, the next time the page is accessed the new version of the subject-lines Perl script will be interpreted. You don't have to spend time searching for the responsible piece of code. You don't have to recompile and relink any code. You don't have to restart your Web server to make it aware of the new version of the software.

This tight development cycle is essential for Web projects, which tend to be hastily thrown together by overworked programmers. It isn't worth producing a jewel-like system to sit behind a Web site because the whole service may be redesigned in six months.

Considering how straightforward this task is and what a nasty first computer language Perl is, the number of dead-trees books on how to write a CGI script is rather depressing. Among the best of them is *CGI Programming on the World Wide Web* (Gundavaram; O'Reilly, 1996).

If you don't want to read that book, or the numerous CGI tutorials available on the Web, or the comments in other folks' source code, then here is my basic summary of Unix CGI:

- The server stuffs a bunch of information into Unix "environment variables": the name of the host that made the request, for example.
- Form variable values get to the script via an environment variable (if a GET) or via `standard-in` (if a POST).
- The server binds `standard-out` effectively to "the client's screen" so that the CGI script thinks it is writing straight to the user.
- The first thing the CGI script must write is a `content-type` header that tells the client what sort of data to expect (HTML, plain text, a GIF, a JPEG, and so on).

A VERY SIMPLE PERL CGI SCRIPT

```
#!/usr/contrib/bin/perl

# the first line in a Unix shell script says where to find the
# interpreter. If you don't know where perl lives on your system, type
# "which perl", "type perl", or "whereis perl" at any shell
# and put the result after the #!

print "Content-type: text/html\n\n";

# now we have printed a header (plus two newlines) indicating that the
# document will be HTML; whatever else we write to standard output will
# show up on the user's screen

print "<h3>Hello World</h3>";
```

It is that easy to write Perl CGI scripts and get server independence, a tight software development cycle, and ease of distribution to other sites. With that in mind, you might ask how many of these wonderful things do I have on my Web server? One. It was written by Architext and it looks up user query strings in the site's local full-text index. Why don't I have more?

MY UNIX BOX DOES NOT LIKE TO FORK 500,000 TIMES A DAY

Every time a CGI script is run, the Web server computer has to start a new process (fork). Think about how long it takes to start a program on a Macintosh or Windows NT machine. It is a thousand times faster to indent a paragraph in an already-running word processor than it is to fire up that word processor to view even a one-paragraph document. I don't want my users to wait for this and I don't want to buy an eight-headed DEC ALPHAserver.

MY RDBMS DOES NOT LIKE TO BE OPENED AND CLOSED 500,000 TIMES A DAY

Any time that I add collaboration to my site, user data is going into and out of a relational database management system (RDBMS). The RDBMS is implemented as a server that waits for requests for connections from client programs (see Chapter 11). IBM, Oracle, Sybase, and Informix have been working for two decades to make the RDBMS fast once a connection is established. Until the Web came along, however, nobody cared too much about how long it took to open a connection. With the Web came the CGI script, a program that runs for only a fraction of a second. In its brief life, it must establish a connection to the RDBMS, get the results of a query, and then close the connection. Users would get their data in about one-tenth the time if their requests could be handled by an already-connected RDBMS client.

Server APIs

Enter the server application programming interface (API). As I discussed in Chapter 6 ("So You Want to Run Your Own Server"), most Web server programs allow you to supplement their behavior with extra software that you write. This software will run inside the Web server's process, saving the overhead of forking CGI scripts. Because the Web server program will generally run for at least 24 hours, it becomes the natural candidate to be the RDBMS client.

Each server program has a different API. This is immediately a problem. Suppose that you write a collection of C code to run inside the Netscape Commerce Web server's API. Then you are forced to convert to AOLserver because you need built-in RDBMS connectivity or to Apache because you need to use a server where the source code is available. Now the C code that you wrote for the Netscape API will have to be rewritten.

The problem could get a lot worse. Suppose that you wrote your scripts for Oracle WebServer's PL/SQL API or AOLserver's Tcl API or Netscape Enterprise's JavaScript API. Competing Web servers don't even have APIs for those languages.

Does that mean it is wise to program in C, the language for which an API is most commonly provided? I don't think so. A bug in your program could result in the entire Web server crashing. Despite the fact that I'll be locked into a particular server program, I prefer to choose a server carefully and then program in a safe language.

AOLSERVER EXAMPLE: REDIRECT

When my friend Brian and I were young and stupid, we installed the NCSA 1.3 Web server program on our research group's file server, martigny.ai.mit.edu. We didn't bother to make an alias for the machine like "www.brian-and-philip.org" so the URLs we distributed looked like "http://martigny.ai.mit.edu/samantha/".

Sometime in mid-1994 the people who depended on Martigny, whose load average had soared from 0.2 to 3.5, decided that a 100,000 hit per day Web site was something that might very nicely be hosted elsewhere. It was easy enough to find a neglected HP Unix box, which we called swissnet.ai.mit.edu. And we sort of learned our lesson and did not distribute this new name in the URL but rather aliases: "www-swiss.ai.mit.edu" for research publications of our group (known as "Switzerland" for obscure reasons); "webtravel.org" for my travel stuff; "photo.net" for my photo stuff; "pgp.ai.mit.edu" for Brian's public key server; "samantha.rules-the.net" for fun.

But what were we to do with all the hard-wired links out there to martigny.ai.mit.edu? We left NCSA 1.3 loaded on Martigny but changed the configuration files so that a request for "http://martigny.ai.mit.edu/foo/bar.html" would result in a 302 redirect being returned to the user's browser so that it would instead fetch http://www-swiss.ai.mit.edu/foo/bar.html.

Two years later, in August 1996, we upgraded Martigny from HP-UX 9 to HP-UX 10. Nobody bothered to install a Web server on the machine. People began to tell me, "I searched for you on the Web but your server has been down since last Thursday." Eventually I figured out that the search engines were still sending people to Martigny, a machine that was in no danger of ever responding to a Web request since it no longer ran any program listening to port 80.

Rather than try to dig up a copy of NCSA 1.3, I decided it was time to get some experience with Apache, the world's most popular Web server. I couldn't get the 1.2 beta sources to compile. So I said, "This free software stuff is for the birds; I need the heavy-duty iron." I installed the 80MB Netscape Enterprise Server and sat down with the frames- and JavaScript-heavy administration server. After fifteen minutes, I'd configured the port 80 server to redirect. There was only one problem: It didn't work.

So I spent a day going back and forth with Netscape tech support. "Yes, the Enterprise server definitely could do this. Probably it wasn't configured properly. Could you e-mail us the obj.conf file? Hmmm . . . it appears that your obj.conf file is correctly specifying the redirect. There seems to be a bug in the server program. You can work around this by defining custom error message .html files with Refresh: tags so that users will get popped over to the new server if they are running a Netscape browser."

I pointed out that this would redirect everyone to the swissnet server root, whereas I wanted "/foo/bar.html" on Martigny to redirect to "/foo/bar.html" on Swissnet.

"Oh."

They never got back to me.

So I finally installed AOLserver 2.1 which doesn't have a neat redirect facility, but I figured that the Tcl API was flexible enough that I could make the server do what I wanted.

First, I had to tell AOLserver to feed all requests to my Tcl procedure instead of going to look around in the file system:

```
ns_register_proc GET / martigny_redirect
```

This is a Tcl function call. The function being called is named ns_register_proc. Any function that begins with "ns_" is part of the NaviServer Tcl API (NaviServer was the name of the program before AOL bought NaviSoft in 1995). ns_register_proc takes three arguments: method, URL, and procname. In this case, I'm saying that HTTP GETs for the URL "/" (and below) are to be handled by the Tcl procedure martigny_redirect:

```
proc martigny_redirect {conn ignore} {

    append url_on_swissnet "http://www-swiss.ai.mit.edu" \
                           [ns_conn url $conn]

    ns_returnredirect $conn $url_on_swissnet

}
```

This is a Tcl procedure definition, which has the form "proc *procedure-name arguments body*". martigny_redirect is defined to take two arguments, conn (an AOLserver connection), and a second argument called ignore (the second argument is only useful when multiple URLs are registered to the same proc). When martigny_redirect is invoked, it first computes the full URL of the corresponding file on Swissnet. The meat of this computation is a call to the API procedure "ns_conn" asking for the URL that was part of the request line.

With the full URL computed, martigny_redirect's second body line calls the API procedure ns_returnredirect. This writes back to the connection a set of 302 redirect headers instructing the browser to rerequest the file, this time from "http://www-swiss.ai.mit.edu".

Here's what I learned from this experience:

- Hugely hyped popular commercial software may not be able to perform even the simplest task.
- Commercial software support is of little value in the Web business.
- You want to have the source code, and/or
- You want to have a flexible, safe, easy-to-use API.

AOLSERVER EXAMPLE: BILL GATES PERSONAL WEALTH CLOCK

Academic computer scientists are the smartest people in the world. There are an average of 800 applications for every job. And every one of those applicants has a Ph.D. Anyone who has triumphed over 799 Ph.D.s in a meritocratic selection process can be pretty sure that he or she is a genius. Publishing is the most important thing in academics. Distributing one's brilliant ideas to the adoring masses. The top computer science universities have all been connected by the Internet or ARPAnet since 1970. A researcher at MIT in 1975 could send a technical paper to all of his interested colleagues in a matter of minutes. With this kind of heritage, it is natural that the preferred publishing medium of 1990s computer science academics is . . . dead trees.

Yes, dead trees.

If you aren't in a refereed journal or conference, you aren't going to get tenure. You can't expect to achieve quality without peer review. And peer review isn't just a positive feedback mechanism to enshrine mediocrity. It keeps uninteresting papers from distracting serious thinkers at important conferences. For example, there was this guy in a physics lab in Switzerland, Tim Berners-Lee. And he wrote a paper about distributing hypertext documents over the Internet. Something he called the Web. Fortunately for the integrity of academia, this paper was rejected from conferences where people were discussing truly serious hypertext systems.

Anyway, with foresight like this, it is only natural that academics like to throw stones at successful unworthies in the commercial arena. IBM and their mainframe customers provided fat targets for many years. True, IBM research labs had made many fundamental advances in computer science, but it seemed to take at least ten years for these advances to filter into products. What kind of losers would sell and buy software technology that was a decade behind the state of the art?

Then Bill Gates came along with technology that was 30 years behind the state of the art. And even *more* people were buying it. IBM was a faceless impediment to progress but Bill Gates gave bloated monopoly a name, a face, and a smell. And he didn't have a research lab cranking out innovations. And every non-geek friend who opened a newspaper would ask, "If you are such a computer genius, why aren't you rich like this Gates fellow?" This question was particularly depressing for graduate students earning $1,300 a month. For them, I published *Career Guide for Engineers and Scientists* (http://photo.net/philg/careers.html).

I thought starving graduate students forgoing six years of income would be cheered to read the National Science Foundation report that "Median real earnings remained essentially flat for all major non-academic science and engineering occupations from 1979-1989. This trend was not mirrored among the overall work force where median income for all employed persons with a bachelor's degree or higher rose 27.5 percent from 1979-1989 (to a median salary of $28,000)."

I even did custom photography for the page (see Figure 9.1, below).

Achievement Gallery

Portraits of people who are putting their advanced training to good use.

Rachel, PhD Biology UCLA 1992, enjoys the wealth of material comforts that she has accumulated during 10 years of hard work in science.

(click on the photo for a 500x750 JPEG; click here for a 1000x1500 screen-filling image)

Figure 9.1: Achievement Gallery portion of http://photo.net/philg/careers.html

Naturally I maintained a substantial "Why Bill Gates is Richer than You" section on my site but it didn't come into its own until the day my friend Brian showed me that the U.S. Census Bureau had put up a real-time population clock at http://www.census.gov/cgi-bin/popclock. There had been stock quote servers on the Web almost since Day 1. How hard could it be to write a program that would reach out into the Web and grab the Microsoft stock price and the population, then do the math to come up with Figure 9.2.

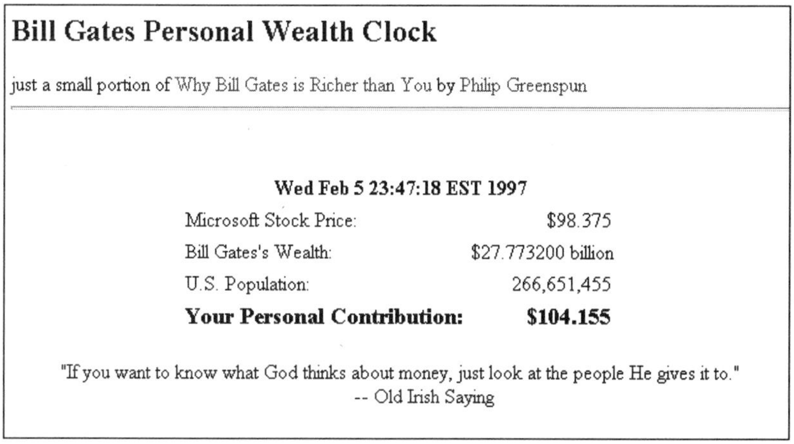

Bill Gates Personal Wealth Clock

just a small portion of Why Bill Gates is Richer than You by Philip Greenspun

Wed Feb 5 23:47:18 EST 1997

Microsoft Stock Price:	$98.375
Bill Gates's Wealth:	$27.773200 billion
U.S. Population:	266,651,455
Your Personal Contribution:	**$104.155**

"If you want to know what God thinks about money, just look at the people He gives it to."
-- Old Irish Saying

Figure 9.2: http://www.webho.com/WealthClock

This program was easy to write because the AOLserver Tcl API contains the ns_geturl procedure. Having my server grab a page from the Census Bureau is as easy as

```
ns_geturl "http://www.census.gov/cgi-bin/popclock"
```

Tcl the language made life easy because of its built-in regular expression matcher. The Census Bureau and the Security APL stock quote folks did not intend for their pages to be machine-parsable. Yet I don't need a long program to pull the numbers that I want out of a page designed for reading by humans.

Tcl the language made life hard because of its deficient arithmetic. Some computer languages—Pascal, for example—are strongly typed. You have to decide when you write the program whether a variable will be a floating-point number, a complex number, or a string. Lisp is weakly typed. You can write a mathematical algorithm with hundreds of variables and never specify their types. If the input is a bunch of integers, the output will be integers and rational numbers (ratios of integers). If the input is a complex double precision floating-point number, then the output will be complex double precision. The type is determined at run-time. I like to call Tcl "whimsically" typed. The type of a variable is never really determined. It could be a number or a string. It depends on the context. If you are looking for a pattern, "29" is a string. If you are adding it to another number, "29" is a decimal number. But "029" is an octal number, so trying to add it to another number results in an error.

Anyway, here is the code. Look at the comments.

```
# this program copyright 1996, 1997 Philip Greenspun (philg@mit.edu)
# redistribution and reuse permitted under
# the standard GNU license

# this function turns "99 1/8" into "99.125"
proc wealth_RawQuoteToDecimal {raw_quote} {
    if { [regexp {(.*) (.*)} $raw_quote match whole fraction] } {
       # there was a space
       if { [regexp {(.*)/(.*)} $fraction match num denom] } {
           # there was a "/"
           set extra [expr double($num) / $denom]
           return [expr $whole + $extra]
       }
       # we couldn't parse the fraction
       return $whole
    } else {
       # we couldn't find a space, assume integer
       return $raw_quote
    }
}

###
#   done defining helpers, here's the meat of the page
###

# grab the stock quote and stuff it into QUOTE_HTML
set quote_html \
    [ns_geturl "http://qs.secapl.com/cgi-bin/qs?ticks=MSFT"]

# regexp into the returned page to get the raw_quote out
regexp {Last Traded at</a></td><td align=right><strong>([^A-z]*)</strong>}
$quote_html match raw_quote

# convert whole number + fraction, e.g., "99 1/8" into decimal,
# e.g., "99.125"
set msft_stock_price [wealth_RawQuoteToDecimal $raw_quote]

set population_html [ns_geturl "http://www.census.gov/cgi-bin/popclock"]

# we have to find the population in the HTML and then split it up
# by taking out the commas
regexp {<H1>[^0-9]*([0-9]+),([0-9]+),([0-9]+).*</H1>} \
       $population_html match millions thousands units

# we have to trim the leading zeros because Tcl has such a
```

```
# brain damaged model of numbers and thinks "039" isn't a number
# this is when you kick yourself for not using Common Lisp
set trimmed_millions [string trimleft $millions 0]
set trimmed_thousands [string trimleft $thousands 0]
set trimmed_units [string trimleft $units 0]

# then we add them back together for computation
set population [expr ($trimmed_millions * 1000000) + \
                     ($trimmed_thousands * 1000) + \
                     $trimmed_units]

# and reassemble them in a string for display
set pretty_population "$millions,$thousands,$units"

# Tcl is NOT Lisp and therefore if the stock price and shares are
# both integers, you get silent overflow (because the result is too
# large to represent in a 32 bit integer) and Bill Gates comes out a
# pauper (< $1 billion). We hammer the problem by converting to double
# precision floating point right here.
#
# (Were we using Common Lisp, the result of multiplying two big 32-bit
# integers would be a "big num", an integer represented with multiple
# words of memory; Common Lisp programs perform arithmetic correctly.
# The time taken to compute a result may change when you move from a
# 32-bit to a 64-bit computer but the result itself won't change.)

set gates_shares_pre_split [expr double(141159990)]
set gates_shares [expr $gates_shares_pre_split * 2]

set gates_wealth [expr $gates_shares * $msft_stock_price]

set gates_wealth_billions \
    [string trim [format "%10.6f" [expr $gates_wealth / 1.0e9]]]

set personal_share [expr $gates_wealth / $population]

set pretty_date [exec /usr/local/bin/date]

ns_return $conn 200 text/html "<html>
<head>
<title>Bill Gates Personal Wealth Clock</title>
</head>
<body text=#000000 bgcolor=#ffffff>

<h2>Bill Gates Personal Wealth Clock</h2>

just a small portion of
<a href=\"http://www-swiss.ai.mit.edu/philg/humor/bill-gates.html\">
```

```
Why Bill Gates is Richer than You
</a>

by

<a href=\"http://www-swiss.ai.mit.edu/philg/\">Philip Greenspun</a>

<hr>

<center>
<br>
<br>

<table>

<tr><th colspan=2 align=center>$pretty_date</th></tr>

<tr><td>Microsoft Stock Price:
    <td align=right> \$$msft_stock_price

<tr><td>Bill Gates's Wealth:
    <td align=right> \$$gates_wealth_billions billion

<tr><td>U.S. Population:
    <td align=right> $pretty_population

<tr><td><font size=+1><b>Your Personal Contribution:</b></font>
    <td align=right>  <font size=+1><b>\$$personal_share</font></b>

</table>

<p>

<blockquote>

\"If you want to know what God thinks about money, just look at the
 people He gives it to.\" <br> -- Old Irish Saying

</blockquote>

</center>

<hr>

<a href=\"http://www-swiss.ai.mit.edu/philg/\">
<address>philg@mit.edu</address>
</a>

"
```

So is this the real code that sits behind http://www.webho.com/WealthClock?

Actually, no. You'll find the real source code linked from the above URL.

Why the differences? I was concerned that, if it became popular, the Wealth Clock might impose an unreasonable load on the subsidiary sites. It seemed like bad netiquette for me to write a program that would hammer the Census Bureau and Security APL several times a second for the same data. It always seemed to me that users shouldn't have to wait for the two subsidiary pages to be fetched if they didn't need up-to-the-minute data.

So I wrote a general purpose caching facility that can cache the results of any Tcl function call as a Tcl global variable. This means that the result is stored in the AOLserver's virtual memory space and can be accessed much faster even than a static file. Users who want a real-time answer can demand one with an extra mouse click. The calculation performed for them then updates the cache for casual users.

Does this sound like overengineering? It didn't seem that way when Netscape put the Wealth Clock on their What's New page for two weeks (summer 1996). The URL was getting two hits per second. Per *second.* And all of those users got an instant response. The extra load on my Web server was not noticeable. Meanwhile, all the other sites on Netscape's list were unusably slow. Popularity had killed them.

Here are the lessons that I learned from this example:

- Powerful APIs lead to innovative Web sites; I would probably have never gotten around to writing the Wealth Clock if it hadn't been for the ns_geturl call.
- Hard-core performance engineering pays off; Web sites can catch on fast—you heard it here first.
- You want to get your site linked from one of the Netscape Navigator buttons.

The Right Way—Extending HTML

Which of the technologies we've discussed is going to dominate server-side programming? Will it be CGI/Perl on super-fast machines? Tcl, Java, or C API code? Visual BASIC?!? I predict "none of the above."

What powerful language will sit behind the Web sites of the future?

HTML.

HTML? But didn't we spend all of Chapter 3 saying how deficient it was even as a formatting language? How can HTML function as a server-side programming language?

SERVER-PARSED HTML

In the beginning, there was server-parsed HTML. You added an HTML comment to a file, as, for example

```
<!--#include FILE="/web/author-info.txt" -->
```

and then reloaded the file in a browser.

Nothing changed. Anything surrounded by "<!--" and "-->" is an HTML comment. The browser ignores it.

Your intent, though, was to have the Web server notice this command and replace the comment with the contents of the file /web/author-info.txt. To do that, you have to change the file name of this URL to have an .shtml extension. Now the server knows that you are actually programming in an extended version of HTML.

The AOLserver takes this one step further. To the list of standard SHTML commands, they've added #nstcl:

```
<!--#nstcl script="ns_geturl http://cirrus.sprl.umich.edu/wxnet/fcst/boston.txt" -->
```

which lets a basically static HTML page use the ns_geturl Tcl API function to go out on the Internet, from the server, and grab http://cirrus.sprl.umich.edu/wxnet/fcst/boston.txt before returning the page to the user. The contents of http://cirrus.sprl.umich.edu/wxnet/fcst/boston.txt are included in place of the comment tag.

This is a great system because a big Web publisher can have its programmers develop a library of custom Tcl functions that its content authors simply call from server-parsed HTML files. That makes it easy to enforce style conventions company-wide. For example,

```
<!--#nstcl script="webco_captioned_photo samoyed.jpg \

{This is a Samoyed, probably the best looking dog you will ever see.}" -->
```

might turn into

```
<h3>
<img src="samoyed.jpg"
     alt="This is a Samoyed, probably the best looking dog
          you will ever see.">
This is a Samoyed, probably the best looking dog you will ever see.
</h3>
```

until the day that the Webco art director decides that HTML tables would be a better way to present these images. So a programmer redefines the procedure webco_captioned_photo, and the next time they are served, thousands of image references instead turn into

```
<table>
<tr>
  <td><img src="samoyed.jpg"
           alt="This is a Samoyed, probably the best looking dog
                you will ever see.">
  <td>This is a Samoyed, probably the best looking dog
      you will ever see.
</tr>
</table>
```

HTML AS A PROGRAMMING LANGUAGE

As long as we're programming our server, why not define a new language, "Webco HTML?" Any file with a .whtml extension will be interpreted as a Webco HTML program and the result, presumably standard HTML, will be served to the requesting users. Webco HTML has the same syntax as standard HTML, just more tags. Here's the captioned photo example:

```
<CAPTIONED-PHOTO "samoyed.jpg"
"This is a Samoyed, probably the best looking dog you will ever see.">
```

Just like the Tcl function, this Webco HTML function takes two arguments, an image file name and a caption string. And just like the Tcl function, it produces HTML tags that will be recognized by standard browsers. I think it is cleaner than the "include a Tcl function call" .shtml example because the content producers don't have to switch back and forth between HTML syntax and Tcl syntax.

How far can one go with this? Pretty far. The best of the enriched HTMLs is Meta-HTML (http://www.mhtml.com). Meta-HTML is fundamentally a macro expansion language. We'd define our captioned-photo tag thusly:

```
<define-tag captioned-photo image-url text>
  <h3>
    <img src="<get-var image-url>" alt="<get-var text>"> <br>
    <get-var text>
  </h3>
</define-tag>
```

Now that we are using a real programming language, though, we'd probably not stop there. Suppose that Webco has decided that it wants to be on the leading edge as far as image format goes. So it publishes images in three formats: GIF, JPEG, and progressive JPEG. Webco is an old company so every image is available as a GIF but only some are available as JPEG and even fewer as progressive JPEG. Here's what we'd really like captioned-photo to do:

1. Change the function to take just the file name as an argument, with no extension; for example, "foobar" instead of "foobar.jpg".
2. Look at the client's user-agent header.
3. If the user-agent is Mozilla 1, then look in the file system for foobar.jpg and reference it if it exists (otherwise reference foobar.gif).
4. If the user-agent is Mozilla 2, then look in the file system for foobar-prog.jpg (progressive JPEG) and reference it; otherwise look for foobar.jpg; otherwise reference foobar.gif.

This is straightforward in Meta-HTML:

```
<define-function captioned-photo stem caption>
  ;;; If the user-agent is Netscape, try using a JPEG format file
  <when <match <get-var env::http_user_agent> "Mozilla">>
    ;;; this is Netscape
    <when <match <get-var env::http_user_agent> "Mozilla/[2345]">>
      ;;; this is Netscape version 2, 3, 4, or 5(!)
      <if <get-file-properties
          <get-var mhtml::document-root>/<get-var stem>-prog.jpg>
           ;;; we found the progressive JPEG in the Unix file system
          <set-var file-to-reference = <get-var stem>-prog.jpg>>
    </when>

    ;;; If we haven't defined FILE-TO-REFERENCE yet,
    ;;; try the simpler JPEG format next.
    <when <not <get-var file-to-reference>>>
      <if <get-file-properties
            <get-var mhtml::document-root>/<get-var stem>.jpg>
          <set-var file-to-reference = <get-var stem>.jpg>>
    </when>
  </when>

  ;;; If FILE-TO-REFERENCE wasn't defined above, default to GIF file
  <when <not <get-var file-to-reference>>>
    <set-var file-to-reference <get-var stem>.gif>
  </when>

  ;;; here's the result of this function call, four lines of HTML
  <h3>
  <img src="<get-var file-to-reference>" alt="<get-var caption>">
  <br>
  <get-var caption>
  </h3>
</define-function>
```

This example only scratches the surface of Meta-HTML's capabilities. The language includes many of the powerful constructs such as session variables that you find in Netscape's LiveWire system. However, for my taste, Meta-HTML is much cleaner and better implemented than the LiveWire stuff. Universal Access offers a "pro" version of Meta-HTML compiled with the OpenLink ODBC libraries so that it can talk efficiently to any relational database (even from Linux!).

Is the whole world going to adopt this wonderful language? Meta-HTML does seem to have a lot going for it. The language and first implementation were developed by Brian Fox and Henry Minsky, two hard-core MIT computer science grads. Universal Access is giving away their source code (under a standard GNU-type license) for both a stand-alone Meta-HTML Web server and a CGI interpreter that you can use with any Web server. They distribute precompiled binaries for popular computers. They offer support contracts for $500 a year. If you don't like Universal Access support, you can hire the C programmer of your choice to maintain and extend their software. Minsky and Fox have put the language into the public domain. If you don't like any of the Universal Access stuff, you can write your own interpreter for Meta-HTML, using their source code as a model.

What then are savvy Web technologists doing?

Tripping over themselves to use crippled server-parsed HTML systems that you could implement with 100 lines of Meta-HTML code. A typical example of the genre is NetCloak from Maxum Development (http://www.maxum.com). Here's an excerpt from their user's manual:

```
<HIDE_DAY day1 day2 ...>

This command hides the HTML text on the specified day(s). The valid
days are MON, TUE, WED, THU, FRI, SAT, SUN. As always, multiple days
may be specified, as in this example, which would hide text during
the work week:

<HIDE_DAY MON TUE WED THU FRI>
```

That's about as powerful as NetCloak gets. They don't really have much respect for HTML syntax and spirit; the command to close a <HIDE_DAY> is not </HIDE_DAY> as you'd expect but rather <SHOW>. NetCloak costs money, only runs on the Macintosh, and the source code is not available. The lack of source code is probably annoying to people who are using the 2.1 version on the Macintosh; it apparently crashes the server when presented with a malformed URL.

Why am I picking on NetCloak? Because it came to my attention in an article about computer language copyright. It seems that people are fighting over the rights to implement this language and sell it. They could download Meta-HTML for free, write a NetCloak compatibility package in a few hours, and spend the rest of the day building an Oracle-backed collaborative Web site. But instead they spend their time with lawyers and dream of a world where a Web page could have a different look on weekends.

Summary

Server-side programming is straightforward and can be done in almost any computer language, including extended versions of HTML itself. However, making the wrong technology decisions can result in a site that requires ten times the computer hardware to support it. Bad programming can also result in a site that becomes unusable as soon as you've gotten precious publicity. Finally, the most expensive asset you are developing on your Web server is content. It is worth thinking about whether your server-side programming language helps you get the most out of your investment in content.

When Is a Site Really a Database?

THE HARD PART

THE EASY PART

PROTOTYPING THE SITE, MY THEORY

PROTOTYPING THE SITE, THE REALITY

DO I NEED A COLLEGE EDUCATION TO UNDERSTAND YOUR SYSTEM?

Chapter 10

The last few chapters have focused on technology. Technology for its own sake does not make for a popular Web site, though. Let's step back to thinking about the publishing model again. Technology should always serve the publishing model, not vice versa. In Chapter 2, I presented four ways of standing tall on the Web:

1. *Sites that provide traditional information.* This is the type of site that requires the least imagination but also the most capital investment. Find bodies of information that consumers in the 1980s bought offline and sell them online. This includes movies/videos/television, newspapers, magazines, weather reports, and stock market information. Revenue comes from advertising, links to sites that do retail transactions and give you a kickback, and occasionally subscriptions.
2. *Sites that provide collaboratively created information.* This is information that was virtually impossible to collect before the Internet. A dead-trees example would be the *Consumer Reports* annual survey of automobile reliability. They collect information from their readers via mail-in forms, collate the results, and publish them once a year. The Internet makes this kind of activity less costly for the provider and provides much more immediate and deeper information for the user. Revenue comes from the same sources as in Category 1 but production expenses are lower.
3. *Sites that provide a service via a server-side program.* An example of this would be providing a wedding planning program. The user tells you how much he or she wants to spend, when and where the wedding is, who is

invited, and so on. Your program then figures a detailed budget, develops an invitation list, and maintains gift and thank-you lists. You are then in a position to sell an ad to the Four Seasons hotel that will be delivered to couples getting married on June 25, who live less than 100 miles away, with fewer than 80 guests, who have budgeted more than $17,000.

4 *Sites that define a standard that enables a consumer to seamlessly query multiple databases.* For example, car dealers have computers managing their inventory, but that data is imprisoned on the dealers' computers and is unavailable to consumers in a convenient manner. Suppose you define a standard that allows the inventory computers inside car dealerships to download their current selection of cars, colors, and prices. You get the car dealers to agree to provide their information to you. Then your site becomes a place where a consumer can say, "I want a new dark green Dodge Grand Caravan with air conditioning and antilock brakes that's for sale within 60 miles of zip code 02176." From your query to the dealers' multiple databases, your user can get a list of all the cars available that match their criteria, and can jump right to the relevant dealer's Web site.

If you are trying to get rich and famous under Category 1, providing traditional information on the Web, then your site isn't really a database except in a degenerate way. On the other hand, unless you have Time-Warner's budget to keep it up to date, you probably won't be standing all that tall.

Categories 2 through 4 are really databases disguised as Web servers. Information is collected in small structured chunks from a variety of simultaneous sources. It is distributed in response to queries that cannot be anticipated when the data are stored. You might not be an Oracle Achiever. You might not know how to spell "SQL." But if your site falls into Categories 2 through 4 then you are running a database.

As long as you are running a database, you might as well do it right. Building a database-backed Web site requires a hard part that is heavy on the thinking and an easy part that is heavy on the implementation. Before you start building, though, you need a publishing idea. Let's suppose that you want to build a mailing list system for your site. You want users to be able to add and remove themselves. You need their e-mail addresses and you want their real names. You want to be the only one who can view the list and the only one who can send mail to the list.

The Hard Part

We have to take our publishing idea (the mailing list) and apply three standard steps:

1. Develop a data model. What information are you going to store and how will you represent it?
2. Develop a collection of legal transactions on that model, such as inserts and updates.
3. Come up with a set of Web forms that let the user build up to one of those transactions.

STEP 1: THE DATA MODEL

You've decided to store e-mail address and real name. If you are a Defense Department-funded artificial intelligence researcher then you might spend a few years studying this "knowledge representation" problem. Otherwise, you'd probably budget two variable-length ASCII strings, one for the e-mail address and one for the name.

This is the step at which you decide whether or not you are going to allow two entries with the same e-mail address, whether you're going to assign some kind of guaranteed-unique key to each entry, and whether to also store the time and date of the entry. When I built a system like this for myself, I decided that there wasn't any point in having two entries with the same e-mail address. So the e-mail address could serve as the key. I also chose not to record the time and date of the entry, but partly because I knew that my database management software was keeping this information anyway.

STEP 2: LEGAL TRANSACTIONS

Users have to be able to add themselves to the list. So one legal transaction is the insertion of a name/e-mail pair into the database. Users should also be able to remove themselves. In the system I built, the e-mail address is the database key so the removal transaction is "delete the entry for joe@bigcompany.com." To simplify the user interface, I decided against having any update transactions. If a user changed his name or e-mail address, he could just remove the old entry and make a new one.

STEP 3: MAPPING TRANSACTIONS ONTO WEB FORMS

The only way that users can interact with your database is via the Web. So you have to come up with ways for them to formulate legal transactions using HTML forms. If the transaction is complicated and early choices change the possibilities for subsequent choices, then you may need a series of forms. In the case of this mailing list system, you probably can get away with two forms. The entry form has e-mail and name TEXT inputs. The removal form has only an e-mail TEXT input.

That's it. You've done the hard part.

THE EASY PART

You only have one thing left to do: Write a couple of programs that parse the HTML forms and turn them into actual database transactions.

Note that it is only during the easy part that you have to think about the particular technologies you are using on your server. The user has no way of knowing whether you are running the latest release of Oracle or whether all the form submissions actually turn into e-mail to someone who manually updates a regular file. The site will still work the same as far as the user is concerned.

In practice, you will probably be using some kind of relational database (see the next chapter). So your programs will be turning HTML form submissions into SQL and results from the database back into HTML. It is important to choose the best brand of database management system and the best Web connectivity tools for that system, but your site will not live or die by the choice. If you make the wrong choices, you will work harder at writing your programs and might have to buy a computer ten times larger than an efficiently constructed site would need, but whether a site is worth using or not depends mostly on the data model, transactions, and form design.

PROTOTYPING THE SITE, MY THEORY

You're building a database. You're modeling data from the real world. You're going to have to write computer programs in a formal language. You have to design a user interface for that computer program. If you have an MBA then your natural first step is . . . hire a graphic designer. After all, this computer stuff is confusing. Databases frighten you. What you really need is something that will look good at your next meeting. Graphic designers make pages that look good. You can always hire a programmer later to actually make the forms work.

The server logs of these MBAs would be a lot fatter if graphic design were the same thing as user interface design. You are building a program. The user interface happens to be Web pages. The links among the pages are part of the user interface. Whoever puts in those links has to understand whether the server can actually answer the query and, if so, how much crunching will be required.

Color Plates

Plate A: Here's me sitting in my apartment (described ad nauseum in http://money.rules-the.net/materialism/) with my dog Alex. This photo was taken by Rob Silvers to illustrate my one and only appearance as a dead trees media pundit in the Italian business weekly Il Mondo (see Chapter 15). Of course, the picture is completely fraudulent. I don't have a 10Base-T drop at my sofa so I never do any programming there. I never use my PowerBook 270c because the keyboard is too cramped.

Plate B: Parco dei Mostri, 1.5 hours north of Rome, described in the "Become Illiterate" section of Chapter 1.

Plate C: Another image from Parco dei Mostri. See http://webtravel.org/italy/ for 500 more of my photographs of this country.

Costa Rica

a Web Travel Review feature by Philip Greenspun.

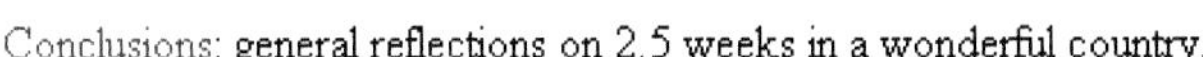

The Story

Map of Costa Rica: shows each region visited (80K)

- Miami: parrots, the wasteland, and President Nixon's vacation paradise.
- Central Valley: arrival in Costa Rica, touring the Central Valley, rafting the most scenic river in the world.
- Tortuguero: sloths and iguanas in the coastal Caribbean rainforest
- Corcovado: Scarlet Macaws convert me to the ecoreligion and we climb into the canopy for the first time.
- Monteverde Cloud Forest: Quakers, Ticos, clouds, and the most beautiful bird in the world.
- Arenal Volcano: we got within 2 km of one of the world's most active volcano and we still didn't see it.
- Hacienda Barú: an authentic Costa Rican ranch run by Colorado cattle ranchers turned rainforest preservationists.

Conclusions: general reflections on 2.5 weeks in a wonderful country.

Extras

Plate D: As I mentioned in Chapter 1, you need magnet content to attract readers and their comments. The magnet content for my Costa Rica site (http://webtravel.org/cr) is a 50-page personal story, 200 photos, and a long excerpt from a guidebook. Every .html file has a link to my comment server, but nobody would come to the site in the first place if I hadn't done a little work myself.

In ancient times (1993), we would have used a GIF like this, 14.7K, which takes 8-10 seconds to load on a 14.4 modem

Switching to JPEG format (LOW quality) reduces the file to 7K, 4 seconds to load.

Reducing to Black and White before JPEGing results in a 6.25K file, barely 10% smaller and faster to load than the 24-bit color JPEG. This is a consequence of the fact that there is much more information in the luminance of an image than in the chroma.

A B&W GIF is 19.2K in size, surprisingly larger than the color GIF.

Plate E: In Chapter 4 I promised to show you how image format affects file size. Here's a 130-pixel square image of South Beach (Miami). The original is a medium format Fuji Velvia transparency, which I snapped with my old Rollei 6008 camera system. The 6x6 cm original was scanned to Kodak Pro PhotoCD and thus the highest available resolution was 4,000 by 4,000. I converted these images with Adobe PhotoShop 3.0 on a Macintosh. Note that the JPEG is better quality and half the size of the GIF. Note further that a black-and-white JPEG is not significantly smaller than its color counterpart; a black-and-white GIF is actually much larger! [This plate is captured from an article that I wrote for *Web Tools Review*: http://webtools.com/wtr/img-format/]

A somewhat larger in-line GIF, rather porky at 47.8K (30 seconds at 14.4).

JPEGing at the LOW quality setting results in a 16.6K file, one third the size.

The B&W GIF is again huge, 68K.

JPEGing at the MED quality setting results in a 21.3K file, still less than half the size of the GIF.

A B&W LOW quality JPEG is 14.9K in size, again a savings of approximately 10% in size/time.

Plate F: The same rules apply to larger photographs. A 260-pixel square GIF occupies a minuscule portion of a modern 20-inch monitor, but it takes 30 seconds to download at 14.4 Kbits/second. Moving up to medium quality doesn't increase the image size too much and it does reduce the JPEG artifacts (note especially in the facade of the building). Still, none of the JPEGs have defects as gross as the upper-right hand portion of the sky in the color GIF.

TUDOR

Plate G: The original scan from the PhotoCD looks a lot better in print, doesn't it? Too bad the 20MB file doesn't download all that fast even with a T1. It is also too bad that I didn't quite catch the decisive moment (all of the motorcycle and the car in the frame at the same time). The Rollei is a nice camera, but you can't get a wide angle zoom lens for it and it doesn't handle as fast as a 35mm single-lens reflex. What do you want for $20,000?

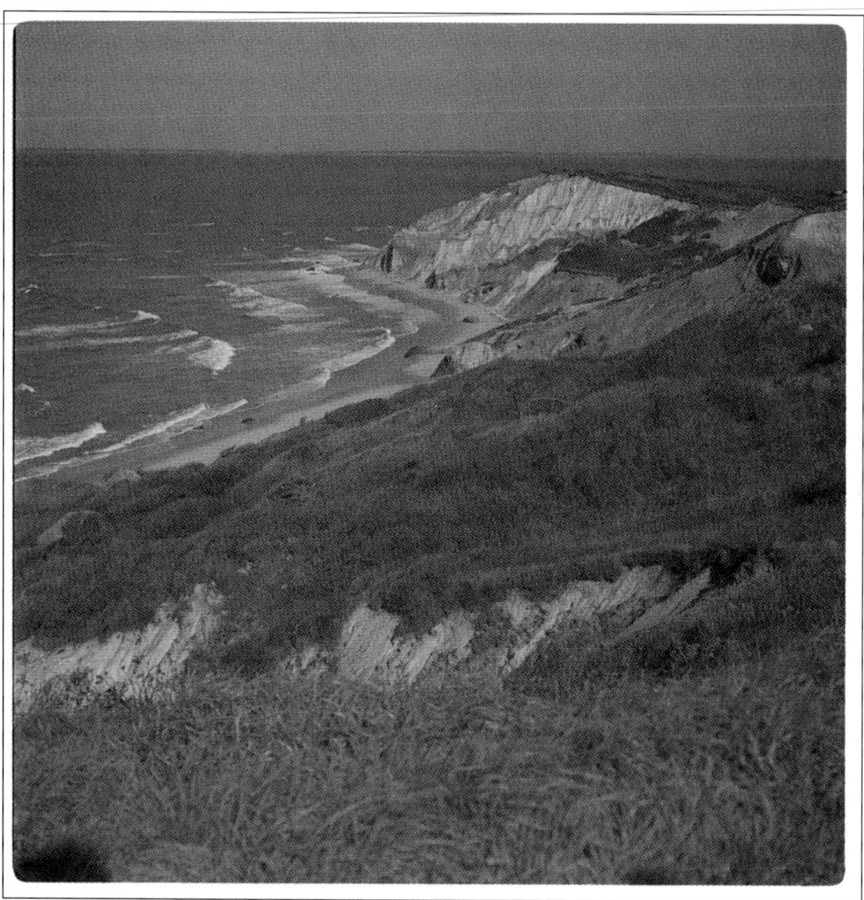

Plate H: Compare this image and the next one of Gay Head, Martha's Vineyard. This one is more or less straight off the PhotoCD. Note the warm purple sunset colors. What a dedicated photographer I must have been to stay out with a tripod until after sunset and then hike back to the car in the dark. Hold your acclaim, though, because this image was a snapshot taken at midday!

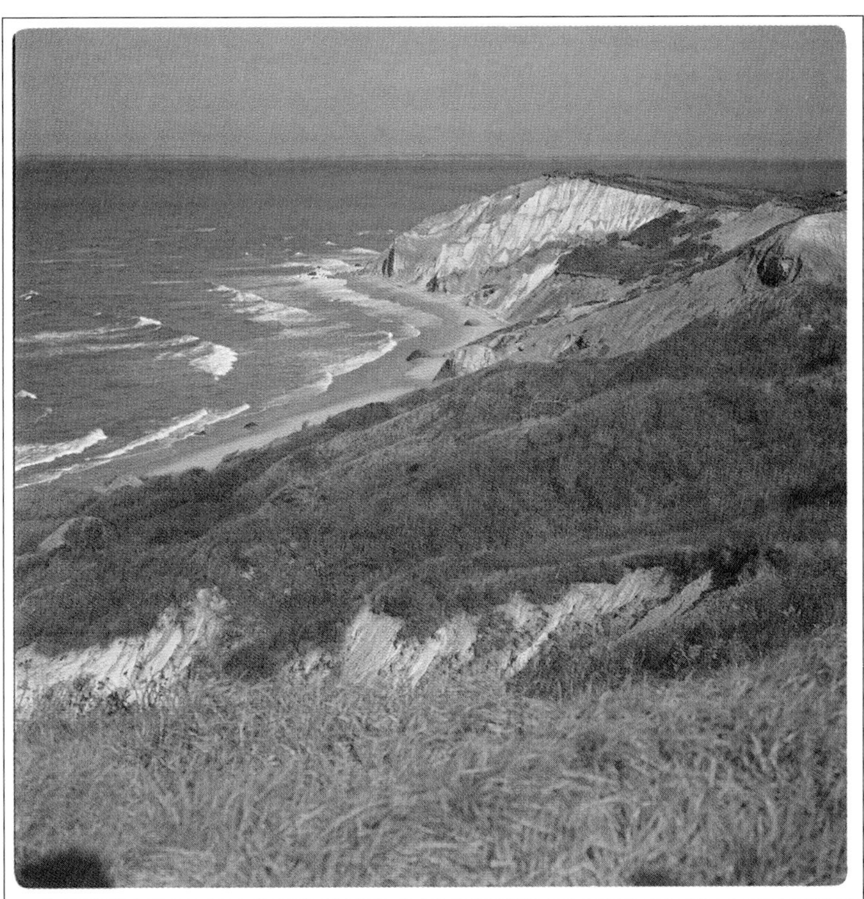

Plate I: Same photo, after an "Auto Levels" adjustment in Adobe PhotoShop. This is more or less how I remember the scene, and it is also how good quality prints from this negative appear. See my Web site: http://photo.net/philg/how-to-scan-photos.html.

Philip Greenspun's home page - Netscape
File Edit View Go Communicator Help
Back Forward Home Search Places Print Security Reload
Bookmarks: Location: http://www-swiss.ai.mit.edu/philg/index.html
What's New? What's Cool?
© 1995 philg@mit.edu
Philip Greenspun
I'm a graduate student at the AI Lab and Laboratory for Computer Science.
When I don't have any good ideas for research, I travel, write, or take pictures. I also teach probability and signal processing to EECS undergraduates and think about careers for engineers and computer scientists. I have my favorite links on the Web, of course.
In the good old days, I was interested in politics and litigation. One thing I'll never lose is my narcissism, which causes me to maintain a large album of pictures of myself, much to the horror of my friends.
What's New
My materialism and my narcissism (see the new Ask Philip site) have motivated me to write a real dead trees book on Web publishing.
I've added some images to my Achievement Gallery; my companion Alex says that he is shocked and horrified by this cheap attempt to use nude photography to build traffic.
If you think none of the above is interesting, you can search my entire Web server.
philg@mit.edu or phone/mail

Plate J: My home page, http://photo.net/philg/, essentially unchanged from three years ago. Note that the page is designed under the classical (1960s) model of hypertext: hypertext should read like regular prose. Thus the links are merely augmentations of words in sentences rather than list or menu items. Note that the phrase "click here" does not appear anywhere. The link to my local full-text search engine at the bottom of the page reflects a site-wide standard. I provide my phone numbers and maps to my home and office from the final "phone/mail" link. The inclusion of the phrase "cheap attempt to use nude photography to build traffic" is a joke. It accurately describes the new pictures in my Career Guide for Engineers and Scientists. However, it also is itself a cheap attempt to attract hits from people typing "nude photo" into Web-wide search engines.

My home page contains only one Netscape extension: the image on the left is marked up with "ALIGN=LEFT" so that text flows to the right of it. That makes my page inconvenient to view in ancient browsers but not unusable. The photo that preceded this one was of me lying naked with my old dog George (see "Using the Internet to Pick up Babes and/or Hunks" at http://webtools.com/wtr/getting-dates.html for how that worked out). I grabbed the top flower image with my old Rollei 6008 and Zeiss 120 macro lens. Francis Packer, an artist friend of mine from Hearst, had the idea of presenting it with a flipped copy turned digitally into a negative.

Light

a chapter in Making Photographs by Philip Greenspun

My personal definition of *photography* is "the recording of light rays." It is therefore difficult to take a decent picture if you have not chosen the lighting carefully.

Sunlight

"He spoke with the wisdom that can only come from experience, like a guy who went blind because he looked at a solar eclipse without one of those boxes with a pinhole in it and now goes around the country speaking at high schools about the dangers of looking at a solar eclipse without one of those boxes with a pinhole in it."
-- Joseph Romm

You can get plenty of light out of the sun, that's for sure. However, you might have to wait a bit if you want the light to have the *quality* that you need for your picture.

At high noon on a clear day, the sun is extremely strong. It generates a *hard light* with deep crisp shadows. It also is coming from directly overhead.

Portraits in Sunlight

The hardness of the light will generate dark shadows. The direction of the light will place those shadows in unattractive positions underneath the subject's eyes and nose. One solution is to move the subject into the shade where he will be lit by *skylight* rather than *sunlight*. Skylight comes from a large source and is therefore diffuse. Diffuse light does not cast strong shadows. Skylight is also rather blue and, if you are using color slide film, you might have to place a warming filter (e.g., 81D) over the lens to get natural skin tone.

If your goal is to record a subject in front of a sunlit object then you can't move him into the shade. There is too great a difference in illumination between shaded and sunlit objects. Photographic film and paper cannot handle the same range of contrast as your eyes. A picture that is correctly exposed for the sunlight object will render the

Landscape in Sunlight

It is difficult to see the shape of the landscape when the sun is directly overhead. Our eyes rely on shadows to recognize shapes. Nonetheless it is occasionally possible to get a good landscape photo at midday if the subject is reasonably compelling, especially if you are aiming at the kind of descriptive photos found in travel brochures.

Great Sand Dune National Monument, rather boring in the flat light of 11 am.

[BIG]

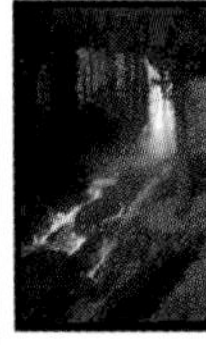

Vernal Falls, Yosemite National Park

Taken around 3 pm, the light in this image is pretty bad and casts harsh shadows. The cloudless and therefore uninteresting blue sky might make a Chamber of Commerce calendar but doesn't make art. Of course, the rainbow makes it all worthwhile and it might not have been there at sunset. Or the light might not have been falling on the waterfall.

Nikon 8008, 28mm AF lens, Fujichrome Velvia

Bachalpsee

Because of the saturated colors rendered by the then-new Fuji Velvia slide film, I'm not sorry that I had my Nikon out in the mid-afternoon in the Bernese Oberland (Switzerland).

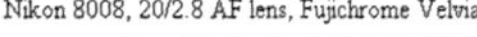

Nikon 8008, 20/2.8 AF lens, Fujichrome Velvia

Plate K: Sometimes it is nice to step back a bit from all of this database programming and collaborative service design and remember the simple pleasures of Web publishing: (1) it costs almost nothing; (2) you can say anything you want; (3) it is instant. I've got 4,000 pictures scanned and sitting on my Web server, mostly illustrating travel stories that I've written.

It was almost no extra effort to start a textbook for beginning photographers (http://photo.net/photo/tutorial). Each chapter just requires a few paragraphs of background text under each subhead and then a series of discussed examples pulled out of my other Web documents. I can link to a new chapter from my photo.net index page and get a few thousand readers in a matter of days. You don't get this economy of scale in print publishing. If you want to reuse a photo, you have to pay all of the 4-color printing costs again. You have to pay page designers again. You have to pay advertising and marketing costs again.

Plate L: You might think that this is the last plate because it shows the limitless horizons available on a new semantically tagged Web (Chapter 15). You might think that the rocks in the foreground are a metaphor for the dangers inherent in depending on Middleware/Junkware (Chapter 10). You might think that it is here because I give these pictures away to readers who donate money to Angell Memorial Animal Hospital (see http://webtravel.org/samantha/gift-shop.html), that it is part of my Final Plea to think of the Web as something other than a fast way to make a buck (Chapter 2). But you'd be wrong. It is here because I like it and because I'm bad at endings.

Here's my theory on how a database Web site gets developed:

1. Publisher/editor decides what service he or she wants to offer; for example, "automatic survey of camera reliability for readers of photo.net."
2. Programmer builds prototype with text-only user interface.
3. Publisher/editor critiques prototype.
4. Programmer refines user interface.
5. Graphic designer comes in to add graphics/layout, but without changing user interface.

Prototyping the Site, the Reality

I was asked to "make a classified ad system using a relational database that looks and works like this set of static HTML files we've put together." They had a category for each ad but decided that it "looked cleaner" to make full-text search the only option on the cover page. I tried to explain about the decades of information retrieval literature that demonstrated just how bad users were at formulating full-text queries. Full-text search was mainly useful when you weren't able to categorize. Since we had a big list of categories, why not make those primary and offer the full-text search as an alternative?

"We like the look."

Then I explained that full-text search was slow. The database could cough up all the ads in a category in about 1⁄20 of a second, but full-text search chewed up close to a full second of time on a $120,000 computer. And, by the way, we'd have to do the query twice: once to fill the space between <NOFRAMES> tags for the Netscape 1.1 crowd, and then again for the subwindows for users with frames-capable browsers. The same expensive query, twice!

"We like frames."

Do I Need a College Education to Understand Your System?

The next few chapters are going to get a little bit formal and technical. If you have been ingesting your daily quota of Web technology hype, then you know anyone can build a dynamic site without ever having to learn a programming language. Just fill out some forms, make a few strokes with your mouse, and presto: DB-backed Web site. The $50,000 may seem steep, but not when you compare it to the cost of a computer science education at Stanford.

If you can buy a $500 or $5,000 or $50,000 product, why bang your head against the wall trying to get through the next three chapters? Because there is no magic bullet. All the glossy brochures and PR budgets in the world can't disguise the fact that nobody has solved the automatic programming problem. There is no program that can take an English description of what you want done and turn that into software.

The fact that technology doesn't work is no bar to success in the marketplace, though, and tools that purport to automate programming have been selling well for decades. The worst of these tools simply don't work. You'd have been better off using EDSAC machine code. (The Electronic Delay Storage Automatic Computer was a vacuum-tube machine built in 1949, the first computer in which the program instructions were stored in memory along with the data.) The best of these tools are sort of like Lotus 1-2-3.

If your problem is very simple, it is much easier to code it up in a spreadsheet than it is to write a program from scratch. The spreadsheet generates the user interface. You just enter some rules for how cells relate to each other; the spreadsheet figures out in which order to perform the computations.

After a while, though, you become dissatisfied with your program. It looks and feels, well, like a spreadsheet. Rather than ask the user to just look at the row headings and type the data into the correct cells, you'd like a little series of interview dialog boxes. When the user gets through filling them all out, your little program will stuff the spreadsheet appropriately.

Only now do you find that the spreadsheet macro language will not let you do two or three of the things that you desperately need to do. Furthermore, documentation of what the language can and can't do is scant so you spend days looking for clever ways to accomplish your objective. Finally, you give up and start from scratch with a standard programming language.

WHY DON'T CUSTOMERS WISE UP?

After three decades of shelling out for magic programming bullets that fail, you'd think that corporate managers would wise up. Yet these products proliferate. Hope seems to spring eternal in the breasts of MBAs.

My personal theory requires a little bit of history. Grizzled old hackers tell of going into insurance companies in the 1960s. The typical computer cost at least $500,000 and held data of great value. When Cromwell & Jeeves Insurance needed custom software, they didn't say, "Maybe we can save a few centimes by hiring a team of guys in India." They hired the best programmers they could find from MIT and didn't balk at paying $10,000 for a week of hard work. Back in those days, $10,000 was enough to hire a manager for a whole year, a fact not lost on managers who found it increasingly irksome.

Managers control companies, and, hence, policies that irk managers tend to be curtailed. Nowadays, companies have large programming staffs earning, in real dollars, one-third of what good programmers earned in the 1960s. When even that seems excessive, work is contracted out to code factories in India. Balance has been restored. Managers are once again earning three to ten times what their technical staff earn. The only problem with this arrangement is that most of today's working programmers don't know how to program.

Companies turn over projects to their horde of cubicle-dwelling C-programming drones and then are surprised when, two years later, they find only a tangled useless mess of bugs and a bill for $3 million. This does not lead companies to reflect on the fact that all the smart people in their college class went to medical, law, or business school. Instead, they embark on a quest for tools that will make programming simpler. Consider the case of Judy CIO who is flying off to meet with the executives at Junkware Systems. Judy will book her airplane ticket using a reliable reservation system programmed by highly paid wizards in the 1960s. There is no middleware in an airline reservation system. There is no Microsoft software. There is no code written by C drones. Just one big IBM mainframe.

Judy changes planes in the new Denver airport. She could reflect on the fact that the airport opened a couple of years late because the horde of C programmers couldn't make the computerized baggage handling system work (it was eventually scrapped). She could reflect on the fact that the air traffic controllers up in the tower are still using software from the 1960s because the FAA can't get their new pile of C code to work—billions of dollars, 15 years, and acres of cubicles stuffed with $50,000-per-year programmers wasn't good for much besides a lot of memory allocation bugs. She could compare the high programmer salaries of the past and their still-working software to the low programmer salaries of the present and their comprehensive collection of bloated bug-ridden ready-any-year-now systems. However, these kinds of reflections aren't very productive for a forward-looking CIO. Judy uses her time at the airport to catch up on what passes for literature among MBAs: *The Road Ahead* and *Dollar Signs: An Astrological Guide to Personal Finance.*

Note: I'm not making up that last title. Here's the synopsis from the amazon.com site: "Financial astrology is used by many prominent investment houses to analyze and predict markets. Now, Yvonne Morabito, Penthouse's 'Cosmic Cashflow' columnist and a guest correspondent on financial astrology on CNBC, shows how anyone can use financial astrology to achieve greater success with this quick-reference guide." I don't myself believe in astrology. However, I think that's because I'm a Libra and Libras are always skeptical.

Judy CIO rushes from her last flight segment into the Junkware Systems demo room where their $100,000-per-year marketing staff will explain why the Junkware 2000 system, programmed by Junkware's cubicle drones, will enable her cubicle drones to write software ten times faster and more reliably. Judy rushes to take notes on this exciting product but becomes flustered when Windows 95 on her laptop crashes. Not to worry, Judy, the Macintosh OS running the Junkware Systems LCD projector also crashed . . .

IS THERE A BETTER WAY?

There *is* a better way: Learn to program (or hire someone who already knows how). The Junkware 2000 systems of the world might save you a few keystrokes here and there, but they don't attack the fundamental difficulty of correctly executing the three hard steps of designing a DB-backed Web site. Here they are again:

1. Develop a data model. What information are you going to store and how will you represent it?
2. Develop a collection of legal transactions on that model, such as inserts and updates.
3. Come up with a set of Web forms that let the user build up to one of those transactions.

Throughout these steps, the difficulty is never the putatively arcane syntax of SQL or HTML, both of which can be learned in a few days. The difficulty is thinking sufficiently formally about all the system requirements that you can boil them down to table and column definitions. The difficulty is in understanding the implications of adding and removing information from tables. The difficulty is in coming up with a user interface sufficiently perspicuous that a busy and unmotivated user won't get stuck halfway through a transaction. If you are capable of that kind of formal thinking, then you ought to be able to type

```
create table mailing_list (
        email           text,
        name            text
);
```

If you despair of understanding the profound mysteries of the preceding SQL statement, then Junkware 2000 is for you. Maybe it will interview you to learn that you want a two-column table, the first column of which should be called "email" and which will store a string, the second of which should be called "name" and also store a string. Then Junkware 2000 will crank out the above SQL code.

Fantastic!

But Junkware 2000 can't know that your organization will need to produce a Web page from this table sorted by last name. That means you really need to store first and last names in separate columns. Junkware 2000 can't know that your applications programs will fail if there are two entries with the same e-mail address. Somewhere during the data modeling process, you have to be thoughtful enough to tell SQL or Junkware 2000 to constrain the email column to be unique.

JUST SAY NO TO MIDDLEWARE

Any interesting Web/RDBMS problem can be solved using just the standard software shipped with the RDBMS. If you can't solve it with those tools, you can't solve it with any tool no matter how glitzy and turnkey. The critical element is not the tools, it is the programmer.

I wrote my first database-backed Web site in 1994 using Oraperl CGI scripts. Kevin Stock sat down for about two weeks and linked Perl 4 with the Oracle C libraries, adding about five new Perl functions in the process. He christened the new version "Oraperl" and distributed the source code for free.

In terms of maintainability, clarity of code, software development cycle, and overall Web server performance and reliability, Oraperl CGI scripts are better than any of the purpose-built Web/RDBMS tools that I have used, with the exception of AOLserver and Meta-HTML. Would I cry if I had to give up the brilliantly designed AOLserver and go back to Oraperl and NCSA HTTPD 1.3? Not really. Using AOLserver probably only cuts ten percent of the development time out of a big DB-heavy project. It gives me about a tenfold improvement in server throughput over a CGI-based approach (see Chapter 12), but it can't think and write software for me.

Would I cry if I had to use the latest and greatest hyped tools? Absolutely. Oraperl, AOLserver, and Meta-HTML let me change a script in Emacs and the new version is immediately live on the Web. The total solution of Netscape LiveWire would force me to recompile my application to test any change, slowing my development effort. If I were to shell out $70,000 for the complete Informix Universal Server and their award-winning Web Blade, I'd be using Netscape Navigator as a text editor for a programming language even more obscure and less powerful than Perl. My pages would deadlock with each other. I'd be thrust into a hell of system administration trying to figure out what was wrong.

A substantial portion of your investment in Web site programming can be wasted if you choose a middleware approach. Depending on SQL, C, Java, Lisp, Perl, or Tcl isn't dangerous. These languages have been around for years and exist in free and commercial versions for a wide variety of computer systems. But if your Web site is programmed in a *sui generis* language, let's call it "Middle Webbish," that can only be parsed by a commercial product that is only available for one kind of computer, you're in trouble. What if the company that sold you Middle Webbish is crushed by Microsoft? You don't have the source code for the Middle Webbish parser so you can't even hire a programmer to maintain your Web site. What if Middle Webbish fails to catch on and you're the only customer left? Your vendor isn't going to invest much in extending and porting Middle Webbish. Again, since you don't have the source code for the parser, you can't hire a programmer to extend and port Middle Webbish yourself.

Occasionally a product is sufficiently good and sufficiently stable and sufficiently likely to last that it is worth the dependency risk. But don't take that risk simply because you are afraid to think and program. Afraid or not, you will eventually have to think and program.

SUMMARY

This chapter was intended to inspire you to read the next three. Should I have failed to inspire a contempt for lucre in Chapter 2, it is worth reiterating that the most profitable sites on the Web are really databases. Furthermore, even if your own site loses money, once you've absorbed the lessons of the next three chapters you can pull in $1,250 per day as a Web/RDBMS programmer.

I hope that you'll steel yourself against the marketing assaults of junkware/middleware vendors by remembering that all the hard stuff is independent of specific technology and product choices. The next three chapters aren't all that technical. If you read them carefully, you won't turn into one of those people who are afraid to program and run into the arms of junkware peddlers.

If you already have an MBA and despair of learning how to do anything productive, then I hope that you've at least learned from this chapter that you should work with the programmer and user interface designer to build the site that fits your publishing model before bringing in a graphic designer to make it pretty. I hope I've also reminded you that we don't need the FBI to figure out why most modern software doesn't work.

If none of the above seems inspiring, I'll close with a quote from *The Magic Mountain*, possibly the most boring book ever written (writing a high-quality computer book like this naturally gives me license to criticize winners of the Nobel Prize for Literature). Thomas Mann clearly knew just how dull these

700 pages would seem to an audience spoiled by the 20th century because he wrote this in the foreword:

"We shall tell it at length, thoroughly, in detail—for when did a narrative seem too long or too short by reason of the actual time or space it took up? We do not fear being called meticulous, inclining as we do to the view that only the exhaustive can be truly interesting."

Relational Databases

What's Wrong with a File System (and Also What's Right)

Enter the Relational Database

How Does This RDBMS Thing Work?

SQL the Hard Way

Brave New World

Braver New World

Choosing an RDBMS Vendor

Paying an RDBMS Vendor

Performance

Don't Forget to Back Up

Reliability

Chapter 11

When you build an information system, of which a Web site is one example, you have to decide how much responsibility for data management your new custom software will take and how much you will leave to packaged software and the operating system. This chapter explains what kind of packaged data management software is available, covering files, flat file database management systems, relational database management systems (RDBMSs), object-relational database management systems, and object databases. Because RDBMS is the most popular technology, I cover it in the most depth and include a brief tutorial on SQL.

What's Wrong with a File System (and Also What's Right)

The file system that comes with your computer is a very primitive kind of database management system. Whether your computer came with the Unix file system, NTFS, or the Macintosh file system, the basic idea is the same. Data is kept in big, unstructured, named clumps. For example, suppose that you are storing a mailing list in a file system file. You could decide that no e-mail address or person's name can contain a newline character. Now you can store one entry per line. Then you could decide that no e-mail address or name may contain a vertical bar. That lets you separate e-mail address and name fields with the vertical bar character.

So far, everything is great. As long as you are careful to never try to store a newline or vertical bar, you can keep your data in this "flat file." Searching can be a slow and expensive, though. What if you want to see if philg@mit.edu is on the mailing list? Then you have to read through the entire file to check.

Let's say that you write a program to process "insert new person" requests. It works by appending a line to the flat file with the new information. Suppose, however, that several users are simultaneously using your Web site. Two of them ask to be added to the mailing list at exactly the same time. Depending on how you wrote your program, the particular kind of file system that you have, and luck, you could get any of the following behaviors:

1. Both inserts succeed.
2. One of the inserts is lost.
3. Information from the two inserts is mixed together so that both are corrupted.

In the last case, the programs you've written to use the data in the flat file may no longer work.

So what? Emacs may be ancient but it is still the best text editor in the world. You love using it so you might as well spend your weekends and evenings manually fixing up your flat-file databases with Emacs. Who needs concurrency control?

It all depends on what kind of stove you have.

Yes, that's right, your stove. Suppose that you buy a $268,500 condo in Harvard Square. You think to yourself, "Now my friends will be really impressed with me," and invite them over for brunch. Not because you like them, but just to make them envious of your large lifestyle. Imagine your horror when all they can say is, "What's this old range doing here? Don't you have a Viking stove?"

A *Viking stove?!?* They cost $5,000. The only way you are going to come up with this kind of cash is to join the growing ranks of online entrepreneurs. So you open an Internet bank. An experienced Perl script/flat-file wizard by now, you confidently build a system where all the checking account balances are stored in one file, checking.text, and all the savings balances are stored in another file, savings.text.

A few days later, an unlucky combination of events occurs. Joe User is transferring $10,000 from his savings to his checking account. Judy User is simultaneously depositing $5 into her savings account. One of your Perl scripts successfully writes the checking account flat file with Joe's new, $10,000 higher balance. It also writes the savings account file with Joe's new, $10,000 lower savings balance. However, the script that is processing Judy's deposit started at about the same time and began with the version of the savings file that had Joe's original balance. It eventually finishes and writes Judy's $5 higher balance but also overwrites Joe's new lower balance with the old high balance. Where does that leave you? $10,000 poorer, cooking on an old GE range, and wishing you had concurrency control.

After a few months of programming and reading operating systems theory books from the 1960s that deal with mutual exclusion, you've solved your concurrency problems. Congratulations. However, like any good Internet entrepreneur, you're running this business out of your house and you're getting a little sleepy. So you heat up some coffee in the microwave and simultaneously toast a bagel in the toaster oven. The circuit breaker trips. This is the time when you are going to regret having bought that set of Calphalon pots to go with your Viking stove rather than investing in an uninterruptible power supply for your server. You hear the sickening sound of disks spinning down. You scramble to get your server back up and don't really have time to look at the logs and notice that Joe User was back transferring $25,000 from savings to checking. What happened to Joe's transaction?

The good news for Joe is that your Perl script had just finished crediting his checking account with $25,000. The bad news for you is that it hadn't really gotten started on debiting his savings account. You're so busy preparing the public offering for your online business that you fail to notice the loss. But your underwriters eventually do and your plans to sell the bank to the public go down the toilet.

Where does that leave you? Cooking on an old GE range and wishing you'd left the implementation of transactions to professionals.

WHAT DO YOU NEED FOR TRANSACTION PROCESSING?

Data processing folks like to talk about the "ACID Test" when deciding whether or not a database management system is adequate for handling transactions. An adequate system has the following properties:

- *Atomicity*–Results of a transaction's execution are either all committed or all rolled back. All changes take effect, or none do. That means, for Joe User's money transfer, that both his savings and checking balances are adjusted or neither is.
- *Consistency*—The database is transformed from one valid state to another valid state. This defines a transaction as legal only if it obeys user-defined integrity constraints. Illegal transactions aren't allowed, and if an integrity constraint can't be satisfied then the transaction is rolled back. For example, suppose that you define a rule that, after a transfer of more than $10,000 out of the country, a row is added to an audit table so that you can prepare a legally required report for the IRS. Perhaps for performance reasons that audit table is stored on a separate disk from the rest

of the database. If the audit table's disk is offline and can't be written then the transaction is aborted.

- *Isolation*–The results of a transaction are invisible to other transactions until the transaction is complete. For example, if you are running an accounting report at the same time that Joe is transferring money, the accounting report program will either see the balances before Joe transferred the money or after, but never the intermediate state where checking has been credited but savings not yet debited.
- *Durability*–Once committed (completed), the results of a transaction are permanent and survive future system and media failures. If the airline reservation system computer gives you seat 22A and crashes a millisecond later, it won't have forgotten that you are sitting in 22A and also give it to someone else. Furthermore, if a programmer spills coffee into a disk drive, it will be possible to install a new disk and recover the transactions up to the coffee spill, showing that you had seat 22A.

That doesn't sound too tough to implement, does it? And, after all, one of the most refreshing things about the Web is how it encourages people without formal computer science backgrounds to program. So why not build your Internet bank on a transaction system implemented by an English major who has just discovered Perl?

Because you still need indexing.

FINDING YOUR DATA (AND FAST)

One facet of a database management system is processing inserts, updates, and deletes. This all has to do with putting information into the database. Sometimes it is also nice, though, to be able to get data out. And with popular sites getting 20 hits per second, it pays to be conscious of speed.

Flat files work OK if they are very small. A Perl script can read the whole file into memory in a split second and then look through it to pull out the information requested. But suppose that your online bank grows to have 250,000 accounts. A user types his account number into a Web page and asks for his most recent deposits. You've got a chronological financial transactions file with 25 million entries. Crunch, crunch, crunch. Your server laboriously works through all 25 million to find the ones with an account number that matches the user's. While it is crunching, 25 other users come to the Web site and ask for the same information about their accounts.

You have two choices: Buy an eight-headed DEC Alpha with 2GB of RAM, or build an index file. If you build an index file that maps account numbers to sequential transaction numbers, then your server won't have to search all 25 million records anymore. However, you have to modify all of your programs that insert, update, or delete from the database to also keep the index current.

This works great until two years later when a brand-new MBA arrives from Harvard. She asks your English major cum Perl hacker for a report of all customers who have more than $5,000 in checking, or live in Oklahoma and have withdrawn more than $100 from savings in the last 17 days. It turns out that you didn't anticipate this query so your indexing scheme doesn't speed things up. Your server has to grind through all the data over and over again.

ENTER THE RELATIONAL DATABASE

You are a Web publisher. On the cutting edge. You need the latest and greatest in computer technology. That's why you use, uh, Unix. Yeah. Anyway, even if your operating system harks back to the 1960s, you definitely can't live without the most modern database management system available. Maybe this guy E.F. Codd can help:

> "Future users of large data banks must be protected from having to know how the data is organized in the machine (the internal representation). . . . Activities of users at terminals and most application programs should remain unaffected when the internal representation of data is changed and even when some aspects of the external representation are changed. Changes in data representation will often be needed as a result of changes in query, update, and report traffic and natural growth in the types of stored information.
>
> "Existing noninferential, formatted data systems provide users with tree-structured files or slightly more general network models of the data. In Section 1, inadequacies of these models are discussed. A model based on *n*-ary relations, a normal form for database relations, and the concept of a universal data sublanguage are introduced. In Section 2, certain operations on relations (other than logical inference) are discussed and applied to the problems of redundancy and consistency in the user's model."

Sounds pretty spiffy, doesn't it? Just like what you need. That's the abstract to *A Relational Model of Data for Large Shared Data Banks*, a paper Codd wrote while working at IBM's San Jose research lab. It was published in the *Communications of the ACM* in June 1970.

Yes, that's right, 1970. What you need to do is move your Web site into the '70s with one of these newfangled relational database management systems. Actually, as Codd notes in his paper, most of the problems we've encountered so far in this chapter were solved in the 1960s by off-the-shelf mainframe software sold by IBM and the "seven dwarves" (as IBM's competitors were known). By the early 1960s, businesses had gotten tired of losing important transactions and manually uncorrupting databases. They began to think that their applications programmers shouldn't be implementing transactions and indexing on an ad hoc basis for each new project. Companies began to buy database management software from computer vendors like IBM. These products worked fairly well but resulted in brittle data models. If you got your data representation correct the first time and your business needs never changed then a 1967-style hierarchical database was great. Unfortunately, if you put a system in place and subsequently needed new indices or a new data format then you might have to rewrite all of your application programs.

From an application programmer's point of view, the biggest innovation in the relational database is that one uses a *declarative* query language: SQL (an acronym for Structured Query Language and pronounced "ess-cue-el" or "sequel"). Most computer languages are *procedural.* The programmer tells the computer what to do, step by step, specifying a procedure. In SQL, the programmer says, "I want data that meets the following criteria," and the RDBMS query planner figures out how to get it. There are two advantages to using a declarative language. The first is that the queries no longer depend on the data representation. The RDBMS is free to store the data however it wants. The second is increased software reliability. It is much harder to have a little bug in an SQL query than in a procedural program. Generally it either describes the data that you want and works all the time or it completely fails in an obvious way.

Another benefit of declarative languages is that less sophisticated users are able to write useful programs. For example, many computing tasks that required professional programmers in the 1960s can be accomplished by nontechnical people with spreadsheets. In a spreadsheet, you don't tell the computer how to work out the numbers or in what sequence. You just *declare* "This cell will be 1.5 times the value of that other cell over there."

RDBMSs can run very, very slowly. Depending on whether you are selling or buying computers, this may upset or delight you. Suppose that the system takes 30 seconds to return the data you asked for in your query. Does that mean you have a lot of data? That you need to add some indices? That the RDBMS query planner made some bad choices and needs some hints? Who knows? The RDBMS is an enormously complicated program that you didn't write and for which you don't have the source code. Each vendor has tracing and debugging tools that purport to help you, but the process is not simple. Good luck figuring out a different SQL incantation that will return the same set of data in less time. If you can't, call 1-800-DIGITAL and say, "I'd like an eight-processor DEC Alpha with 2GB of RAM." Alternatively, you could keep running the non-relational software you used in the 1960s, which is what the airlines do for their reservations systems.

How Does This RDBMS Thing Work?

Database researchers love to talk about relational algebra, n-tuples, normal form, and natural composition, while throwing around mathematical symbols. This patina of mathematical obscurity tends to distract your attention from their bad suits and boring personalities, but is of no value if you just want to use a relational database management system.

In fact, this is all you need to know to be a Caveman Database Programmer: A relational database is a big spreadsheet that several people can update simultaneously.

Each *table* in the database is one spreadsheet. You tell the RDBMS how many columns each row has. For example, in our mailing list database, the table would have two columns: "name" and "email." Each entry in the database consists of one row in this table. An RDBMS is more restrictive than a spreadsheet in that all the data in one column must be of the same type, such as integer, decimal, character string, or date. Another difference between a spreadsheet and an RDBMS is that the rows in an RDBMS are not ordered. You can have a column named "row_number" and ask the RDBMS to return the rows ordered according to the data in this column. But the row numbering is not implicit as it would be with Visicalc or its derivatives such as Lotus 1-2-3 and Excel. If there is a "row_number" column or some other unique identifier for rows in a table, then it is possible for a row in another table to refer to that row by including the value of the unique id.

Here's what some SQL looks like for the mailing list application:

```
create table mailing_list (
        email           text not null primary key,
        name            text
);
```

The table will be called "mailing_list" and will have two columns, both variable length character streams. We've added a couple of integrity constraints on the "email" column. The "not null" will prevent any program from inserting a row where "name" is specified but "email" is not. After all, the whole point of the system is to send people e-mail so it isn't much use to have a name with no e-mail address. The "primary key" tells the database that this column's value can be used to uniquely identify a row. That means that the system will reject an attempt to insert a row with the same e-mail address as an existing row. This sounds like a nice feature, but it can have some unexpected performance implications. For example, every time anyone tries to insert a row into this table, the RDBMS will have to look at all the other rows in the table to make sure that there isn't already one with the same e-mail address. For a really huge table, that could take minutes. If you had also asked the RDBMS to create an index for mailing_list on "email" then the check becomes almost instantaneous. However, the integrity constraint still slows you down because every update to the mailing_list table will also require an update to the index and there you'll be doing twice as many writes to the hard disk.

That is the joy and the agony of SQL. Inserting two innocuous looking words can cost you a factor of 1,000 in performance. Then inserting a sentence (to create the index) can bring you back so that it is only a factor of two or three.

Anyway, now that we've executed the Data Definition Language "create table" statement, we can move on to *Data Manipulation Language:* an INSERT.

```
insert into mailing_list (name, email)
values ('Philip Greenspun','philg@mit.edu');
```

Note that we specify into which columns we are inserting. That way if someone comes along later and does

```
alter table mailing_list add column phone_number text;
```

then our INSERT will still work. Note also that the string quoting character in SQL is a single quote. Hey, it was the '70s. If you visit the newsgroup comp.databases right now, I'll be that you can find someone asking, "How do I insert a string containing a single quote into an RDBMS?" Here's one I harvested from http://www.dejanews.com just a few minutes ago:

```
Subject:      HELP/BUG? Single Quotes in SQL
From:         "James Boswell" <j.boswell@ukonline.co.uk>
Date:         1997/02/11
Message-Id:   <01bc182d$98f21c50$8429bfc7@teme>
Newsgroups:   comp.lang.pascal.delphi.databases
[More Headers]

When submitting an SQL query through a Delphi TQuery component to an
Interbase database (using BDE), is there a problem with single quotes in parameters?
```

```
For example:
I want to put the following into a database field:

  John's record

And here's the code that I started with:

  strValue := 'John' + Chr(39) + 's record';
  with MyQueryObject do
  begin
       SQL.Clear;
       SQL.Add('INSERT INTO MYTABLE (MyStrFld) VALUES (' + strValue + ');
       Open;
  end;

The query looks like:

  INSERT INTO MYTABLE (MyStrFld) VALUES ('John's record');

which of course confuses the SQL interpreter.  So, normal programming
convention is to replace one quote character with two quote characters:

INSERT INTO MYTABLE (MyStrFld) VALUES ('John''s record');

But this puts two quotes into the database!!!

What is the convention in SQL, Interbase and BDE for allowing single quote
characters in paramters?

James Boswell
```

If you want to avoid humiliating yourself on Usenet, remember that doubling the single quote will let you insert one into the database . . .

```
insert into mailing_list (name, email)
values ('Michael O''Grady','ogrady@fastbuck.com');
```

So you've done DDL and DML statements. At last you are ready to experience the awesome power of the third type of SQL statement: a SELECT. Want your data back?

```
select * from mailing_list;
```

If you were to type this query into a standard shell-style RDBMS client program, like SQL*PLUS for Oracle or, in this case, MSQL for Illustra, here's what you'd get:

```
* select * from mailing_list;
-------------------------------------------
|email                |name                 |
-------------------------------------------
|philg@mit.edu        |Philip Greenspun     |
|ogrady@fastbuck.com  |Michael O'Grady      |
-------------------------------------------
2 rows selected
```

Now you realize that you want to also store phone numbers for these folks. Since this is the Internet, many of your users will have their pants hanging around their knees under the weight of their cell phones, beepers, and other personal communication accessories. So if you just added work_phone and home_phone columns, you wouldn't be able to accommodate the wealth of information users might want to give you.

The clean database-y way to do this is to define another table.

```
create table phone_numbers (
  email         text not null,
  number_type   text check (number_type in ('work','home','cell','beeper')),
  number        text
);
```

Note that in this table the email column is *not* a primary key. That's because we want to allow multiple rows with the same e-mail address. If you are hanging around with a database nerd friend, you can say that there is a *relationship* between the rows in the phone_numbers table and the mailing_list table. In fact, you can say that it is a *many-to-one relation* because many rows in the phone_numbers table may correspond to only one row in the mailing_list table. If you spend enough time thinking about and talking about your database in these terms, two things will happen:

1. You'll get an A in an RDBMS course at a mediocre state university.
2. You'll pick up readers of *Psychology Today* who think you are sensitive and caring because you are always talking about relationships.

Another item worth noting about our two-table data model is that we do not store the user's name in the phone_numbers table. That would be redundant with the mailing_list table and potentially self-redundant as well, as, for example, if "robert.loser@fastbuck.com" says he is "Robert Loser" when he types in his work phone and then "Rob Loser" when he puts in his beeper number, and "Bob Lsr" when he puts in his cell phone number while typing on his laptop's cramped keyboard. A database nerd would say that this data model is consequently in "Third Normal Form." Everything in each row in each table depends only on the primary key and nothing is dependent on only part of the key. The primary key for the phone_numbers table is the combination of email and number_type. If you had the user's name in this table, it would depend only on the email portion of the key.

Anyway, enough database nerdism. Let's populate the phone_numbers table:

```
insert into phone_numbers values ('ogrady@fastbuck.com','work','(800) 555-1212');
insert into phone_numbers values ('ogrady@fastbuck.com','home','(617) 495-6000');
insert into phone_numbers values ('philg@mit.edu','work','(617) 253-8574');
insert into phone_numbers values ('ogrady@fastbuck.com','beper','(617) 222-3456');
```

Note that we have used an evil SQL shortcut and not specified the columns into which we are inserting data. The system defaults to using all the columns in the order that they were defined. Except for prototyping and playing around, I don't recommend ever using this shortcut.

The first three INSERTs work fine, but what about the last one, where Mr. O'Grady misspelled "beeper?"

```
X23C00:integrity constraint violation:
  Constraint Name _CHECK_CONSTRAINT_ON_INSERT_TO_public_phone_numbers_
```

We asked Illustra at table definition time to check (number_type in ('work','home','cell','beeper')) and it did. The database cannot be left in an inconsistent state.

Let's say you want all of our data out. E-mail, full name, phone numbers. The most obvious query to try is a *join.*

```
select *
from mailing_list, phone_numbers;
--------------------------------------------------------------------------------
|email              |number_type|number        |email         |name            |
--------------------------------------------------------------------------------
|ogrady@fastbuck.com|work       |(800) 555-1212|philg@mit.edu|Philip Greenspun|
|ogrady@fastbuck.com|home       |(617) 495-6000|philg@mit.edu|Philip Greenspun|
|philg@mit.edu      |work       |(617) 253-8574|philg@mit.edu|Philip Greenspun|
|ogrady@fastbuck.com|work       |(800) 555-1212|ogrady@fastb*|Michael O'Grady |
|ogrady@fastbuck.com|home       |(617) 495-6000|ogrady@fastb*|Michael O'Grady |
|philg@mit.edu      |work       |(617) 253-8574|ogrady@fastb*|Michael O'Grady |
--------------------------------------------------------------------------------
6 rows selected
```

Yow! What happened? There are only two rows in the mailing_list table and three in the phone_numbers table. Yet here we have six rows back. This is how joins work. They give you the *Cartesian product* of the two tables. Each row of one table is paired with all the rows of the other table in turn. So if you join an *n*-row table with an *m*-row table, you get back a result with *n*m* rows. In real databases, *n* and *m* can be up in the millions so it is worth being a little more specific as to which rows you want:

```
select *
from mailing_list, phone_numbers
where mailing_list.email = phone_numbers.email;
---------------------------------------------------------------------
|email          |number_type|number         |email          |name           |
---------------------------------------------------------------------
|philg@mit.edu|work       |(617) 253-8574|philg@mit.edu|Philip Greenspun|
|ogrady@fastb*|work       |(800) 555-1212|ogrady@fastb*|Michael O'Grady |
|ogrady@fastb*|home       |(617) 495-6000|ogrady@fastb*|Michael O'Grady |
---------------------------------------------------------------------
3 rows selected
```

Probably more like what you had in mind. Refining your SQL statements in this manner can sometimes be more exciting. For example, let's say that you want to get rid of Philip Greenspun's phone numbers but aren't sure of the exact syntax.

```
delete from phone_numbers;
3 rows deleted
```

Oops. Yes, this does actually delete *all* the rows in the table. You probably wish you'd typed

```
delete from phone_numbers where email = 'philg@mit.edu';
```

but it is too late now. I guess there is one more SQL statement that is worth learning. Suppose that I move to Hollywood to realize my long-standing dream of becoming a major motion picture producer. Clearly a change of name is in order, though I'd be reluctant to give up the e-mail address I've had since 1976. Here's the SQL:

```
* update mailing_list set name = 'Phil-baby Greenspun' where email =
'philg@mit.edu';

one row updated
```

```
* select * from mailing_list;
-------------------------------------
|email              |name           |
-------------------------------------
|ogrady@fastbuck.com|Michael O'Grady|
|philg@mit.edu      |Phil-baby Gree*|
-------------------------------------
2 rows selected
```

As with DELETE, I don't recommend playing around with UPDATE statements unless you have a WHERE clause at the end.

SQL THE HARD WAY

So you've gotten your pathetic Web site up and running and are proud of yourself for your wimpy little SELECTs. You had planned to live on the advertising revenue from your site, but find that $1.37 a month doesn't go very far in Manhattan. So you say, "At least I've become a database wizard; I can work in the financial industry." The next day, you're interviewing for that $200,000-a-year database hacking job at CitiCorp. Everything is going smoothly until they ask you how you'd investigate a performance problem with a "self-join with subquery." Self-join? Subquery? Maybe you have a little more to learn about RDBMS. Here's an example drawn from my real-life suffering with Illustra.

My site would hand out a unique session key to every new user who arrived at the site. These keys were just an integer sequence. I realized that I could keep track of how many users came to the site by simply inserting an audit row every day showing the value of the session key generator. Here's the history table I created:

```
* create table history (
     sample_time     timestamp,     -- when did the cookie have the value
     sample_value    integer
);

* select * from history order by sample_time;
------------------------------------------
|sample_time               |sample_value |
------------------------------------------
|1996-02-15 19:02:08.000000|75000        |
|1996-02-16 19:02:08.000000|76000        |
|1996-02-17 19:02:08.000000|77000        |
|1996-02-18 19:02:08.347617|77276        |
------------------------------------------
```

I knew that I had the information I needed and waited a few days to write the trivial AOLserver Tcl script to barf out a report page. It turns out to be easy to extract the rows of a table in order, as in the last SELECT above. However, it is impossible for a row to refer to "the last row in this SELECT." I could have written a Tcl procedure to walk through the rows in order, just setting things up on the first pass through the loop and then doing the appropriate subtraction for subsequent rows. However, Tcl doesn't have primitives that understand SQL timestamps. If I'd been using Oracle, I could have written this in PL/SQL, a language with all the procedural expressiveness of Tcl plus all the datatypes and functions of SQL. But I was using Illustra so I had to resort to classical SQL techniques.

If the "history" table had *n* rows, I needed an interval table with *n*-1 rows. Each row would have the start time, end time, time interval, and cookie interval. Since I needed information from two different rows in the database, the most basic way to get it was with a join. Since there was only one table, though, this would have to be a self-join.

```
* select h1.sample_time, h2.sample_time
from history h1, history h2;
----------------------------------------------------
|sample_time               |sample_time              |
----------------------------------------------------
|1996-02-15 19:02:08.000000|1996-02-15 19:02:08.000000|
|1996-02-16 19:02:08.000000|1996-02-15 19:02:08.000000|
|1996-02-17 19:02:08.000000|1996-02-15 19:02:08.000000|
|1996-02-18 19:02:08.347617|1996-02-15 19:02:08.000000|
|1996-02-15 19:02:08.000000|1996-02-16 19:02:08.000000|
|1996-02-16 19:02:08.000000|1996-02-16 19:02:08.000000|
|1996-02-17 19:02:08.000000|1996-02-16 19:02:08.000000|
|1996-02-18 19:02:08.347617|1996-02-16 19:02:08.000000|
|1996-02-15 19:02:08.000000|1996-02-17 19:02:08.000000|
|1996-02-16 19:02:08.000000|1996-02-17 19:02:08.000000|
|1996-02-17 19:02:08.000000|1996-02-17 19:02:08.000000|
|1996-02-18 19:02:08.347617|1996-02-17 19:02:08.000000|
|1996-02-15 19:02:08.000000|1996-02-18 19:02:08.347617|
|1996-02-16 19:02:08.000000|1996-02-18 19:02:08.347617|
|1996-02-17 19:02:08.000000|1996-02-18 19:02:08.347617|
|1996-02-18 19:02:08.347617|1996-02-18 19:02:08.347617|
----------------------------------------------------
16 rows selected
```

A note about syntax is in order here. In an SQL FROM list, one can assign a correlation name to a table. In this case, I assign h1 and h2 to the two copies of history from which I am selecting. Then I can refer to h1.sample_time and get the sample_time column from the first copy of the history table.

The main problem with this query, though, has nothing to do with syntax. It is the fact that I have 13 rows too many. Instead of *n*-1 rows, I specified the Cartesian product and got *n***n* rows. I've successfully done a self-join and gotten all the pairings I need, but now I must specify which pairings are legal.

```
* select h1.sample_time as s1,
       h2.sample_time as s2
from history h1, history h2
where s2 > s1;
-------------------------------------------------------
|s1                         |s2                        |
-------------------------------------------------------
|1996-02-15 19:02:08.000000|1996-02-16 19:02:08.000000|
|1996-02-15 19:02:08.000000|1996-02-17 19:02:08.000000|
|1996-02-16 19:02:08.000000|1996-02-17 19:02:08.000000|
|1996-02-15 19:02:08.000000|1996-02-18 19:02:08.347617|
|1996-02-16 19:02:08.000000|1996-02-18 19:02:08.347617|
|1996-02-17 19:02:08.000000|1996-02-18 19:02:08.347617|
-------------------------------------------------------
6 rows selected
```

Note first that I've given correlation names to the columns as well. Not only is my report labeled with "s1" and "s2" but I also use these as shorthand in the WHERE clause, which states that we only want intervals where s2 is later than s1. That kills off ten of the rows from the Cartesian product but there are still three unwanted rows, such as the pairing of 1996-02-15 and 1996-02-18. I only want the pairing of 1996-02-15 and 1996-02-16. I can specify that with a different WHERE clause:

```
select h1.sample_time as s1,
       h2.sample_time as s2
from history h1, history h2
where s2 = (select min(h3.sample_time)
            from history h3
            where h3.sample_time > h1.sample_time)
order by s1;
-------------------------------------------------------
|s1                         |s2                        |
-------------------------------------------------------
|1996-02-15 19:02:08.000000|1996-02-16 19:02:08.000000|
|1996-02-16 19:02:08.000000|1996-02-17 19:02:08.000000|
|1996-02-17 19:02:08.000000|1996-02-18 19:02:08.347617|
-------------------------------------------------------
3 rows selected
```

At last, the self-join with subquery that the CitiCorp interviewer asked about. The self-join again is SELECTing "from history h1, history h2." The subquery is that we are now asking the database, for each of the 16 joined rows, to

```
select min(h3.sample_time)
from history h3
where h3.sample_time > h1.sample_time
```

This subquery will scan the history table yet again to find the oldest sample that is still newer than s1. In the case of an unindexed history table, this query should probably take an amount of time proportional to the number of rows in the table cubed (n^3). If we'd done this procedurally, it would have taken time proportional to n*log n (the limiting factor being the sort for the ORDER BY clause). There are a couple of lessons to be learned here:

1. Sometimes declarative languages can be difficult to use and vastly less efficient than procedural languages.
2. It is good to have a fast database server.

When I knew that I had the rows that I wanted, I added the trivial syntax to the SELECT list to subtract the times and cookie values.

```
select h1.sample_time as s1,
       h2.sample_time as s2,
       h2.sample_time - h1.sample_time as gap_time,
       h2.sample_value - h1.sample_value as gap_cookie
from history h1, history h2
where s2 = (select min(h3.sample_time)
            from history h3
            where h3.sample_time > h1.sample_time)
order by s1;
------------------------------------------------------------------------------
|s1                        |s2                        |gap_time  |gap_cookie|
------------------------------------------------------------------------------
|1996-02-15 19:02:08.000000|1996-02-16 19:02:08.000000|0-0       |1000      |
|1996-02-16 19:02:08.000000|1996-02-17 19:02:08.000000|0-0       |1000      |
|1996-02-17 19:02:08.000000|1996-02-18 19:02:08.347617|0-0       |276       |
------------------------------------------------------------------------------
3 rows selected
```

Illustra had decided that my time intervals were "0 years and 0 months" in length. Yes, thanks, that was just what I wanted to know. I spent a few hours trying various incantations and casts and spells but ultimately gave up. Nobody at Illustra support was ever able to make this query work either.

So before you apply for that $200,000-a-year database job, remember that

- Formulating SQL queries can be an art.
- You'll need time and experience to get good at thinking declaratively.
- RDBMSs do not always work as advertised.

Despite this last example, you probably won't have learned enough from this Caveman SQL Tutorial to pull down the big bucks. SQL is more than 20 years old and has been analyzed and explained for every possible kind of reader. I maintain a list of my current favorite SQL online tutorials and hard-copy books at http://webtools.com/wtr/bookshelf.html.

Brave New World

Training an African Grey parrot to function as an information systems manager can be very rewarding. The key sentence is "We're proactively leveraging our object-oriented client/server database to target customer service during reengineering." In the 1980s DB world, the applicable portion of this sentence was "client/server" (see next chapter). In the Brave New World of database management systems, the key phrase is "object-oriented."

Object systems contribute to software reliability and compactness by allowing programmers to factor their code into chunks that are used as widely as possible. For example, suppose that you are building a catalog Web site to sell magazines, videos, books, and CDs. It might be worth thinking about the data and functions that are common to all of these and encapsulating them in a "product" class. At the product level, you'd define characteristics such as product_id, short_name, and description. Then you'd define a "magazine" subclass that inherited all the behavior of "product" and added things like issues_per_year.

Programmers using modern computer languages like Smalltalk and Lisp have been doing this since the mid-1970s but the idea has only recently caught on in the RDMBS world. Here are some table definitions for the Illustra system (these would also work with the Informix Universal Server):

```
create table products of new type product_t
(
        product_id              integer not null primary key,
        short_name              text not null,
        description             text
);
```

Here's how we define new types and tables that inherit from products . . .

```
create table magazines of new type magazine_t (
        issues          integer not null,
        foreign_postage decimal(7,2),
        canadian_postage decimal(7,2)
)
under products;

create table videos of new type video_t (
        length_in_minutes       integer
)
under products;
```

Our data model is defined, so we can load some data.

```
* insert into magazines (product_id,short_name,description,issues)
values (Ø,'Dissentary','The result of merging Dissent and Commentary',12);
* insert into videos (product_id,short_name,description,length_in_minutes)
values (1,'Sense and Sensibility','Chicks dig it',11Ø);
* select * from products;
---------------------------------------------------
|product_id   |short_name           |description  |
---------------------------------------------------
|1            |Sense and Sensibility|Chicks dig it|
|Ø            |Dissentary           |The result o*|
---------------------------------------------------
```

Suppose that our pricing model is that magazines cost $1.50 an issue and videos cost $0.25 a minute. We want to hide these decisions from programs using the data.

```
create function find_price(product_t) returns numeric with (late)
as
return 5.5Ø;
```

So a generic product will cost $5.50.

```
create function find_price(magazine_t) returns numeric
as
return $1.issues * 1.5Ø;
create function find_price(video_t) returns numeric
as
return  $1.length_in_minutes * Ø.25;
```

The appropriate version of the function find_price will be invoked depending on the type of the row.

```
* select short_name, find_price(products) from products;
---------------------------------------
|short_name            |find_price     |
---------------------------------------
|Sense and Sensibility|          27.50|
|Dissentary           |          18.00|
---------------------------------------
```

This doesn't sound so impressive, but suppose you also wanted a function to prepare a special order code by concatenating product_id, price, and the first five characters of the title.

```
create function order_code(product_t) returns text
as
return $1.product_id::text ||
       '--' ||
       trim(leading from find_price($1)::text) ||
       '--' ||
       substring($1.short_name from 1 for 5);

* select order_code(products) from products;
-----------------
|order_code     |
-----------------
|1--27.50--Sense|
|0--18.00--Disse|
-----------------
```

This function, though trivial, is already plenty ugly. The fact that the find_price function dispatches according to the type of its argument allows a single order_code to be used for all products.

The Brave New World sounds great in DBMS vendor brochures, but the database folks have only recently gotten the object-oriented religion, and they never met Dave Moon. Who is Dave Moon? One of the world's best programmers, a pioneer in modern object systems, but alas not a patient man in his youth.

Moon was one of the chief architects of the MIT Lisp Machine, the world's easiest to program computer. It did things in 1978 that, if we are lucky, will be announced as innovations by Microsoft in the year 2005. A tiny company called Symbolics was spun out of MIT to commercialize the Lisp Machine and Moon was one of the founders. I was working there in 1984 when the company moved into a new building next to MIT. The facilities manager sent around some e-mail telling people not to tape posters to their office walls because we'd be moving to bigger quarters in a few years and didn't want the landlord to charge us for excessive wear. That night, the Foonly crashed. A Foonly was a clone of the PDP-10, a mainframe computer designed by Digital in the 1960s. MIT and Stanford people loved the PDP-10 but couldn't afford DEC's million-dollar price tags. So there were these guys in a basement in California smoking dope and wirewrapping clones that were one-third the speed and 1⁄20 the cost. Nobody ever figured out why they called the machines "Foonlies."

Moon was a superb hardware engineer and nobody doubted that he would get the Foonly up and running. Still, people were a bit surprised when a huge steel cylinder came crashing through the machine room wall. The cause of the crash had been one of those washing machine-sized Control Data T-300 disk packs. The cylindrical missile had been the spindle holding together the bad 12-inch platters. Moon had hurled it through the wall after determining its guilt in the crime of the Foonly crash. I went back to my office and taped up a poster.

This story illustrates that great programmers are not necessarily patient. One of the things that drove them crazy about the object systems of the 1970s (Smalltalk, Lisp Machine Flavors) was that if you changed a class definition, the existing instances of that class did not get modified. You'd have to restart your program, maybe even reboot your computer, if you changed your mind about how to represent something. You could lose 20 minutes or even more.

Thus the object systems of the 1980s, such as Common Lisp Object System, were designed to touch up running instances of classes if the class definition changed. At press-time, the only non-vaporware object-flavored relational database is Illustra 3.2. I built myself a beautiful table hierarchy more or less like what I've described above. Then six months later I needed to add a column to the products table. E.F. Codd understood back in 1970 that data models had to grow as business needs change. But the Illustra folks were so excited by their object extensions that they forgot. The system couldn't add a column to a table with dependent subclasses. What should I do, I asked the support folks? "Dump the data out of all of your tables, drop all of them, rebuild them with the added column, then load all of your data back into your tables." Uh thanks, I guess I could be back online by 1998 . . .

I had high hopes for the merged Informix/Illustra system. A year had passed since I'd pointed out that table inheritance was useless because of the brittleness of the resulting data models. So I figured surely they would have plugged this hole in the feature set. But it turned out that the new "solution to all of your problems" Informix Universal Server has the same limitation. I guess in the end it is much easier to hype 21st-century features than actually sit down and implement features from two decades back.

Braver New World

Oracle Release 8 is supposed to have some object extensions, but aside from "will be released sometime in 1997," the company isn't saying much about the product. In my experience, the Oracle system is very good about letting you change your data model, much better than Illustra. For example, you can change a column's type, add constraints, and drop a column. So here's hoping that they will deliver the benefits of table definition inheritance without locking users into their first-pass data models forever.

If you really want to be on the cutting edge, you can use a bona fide object database, like Object Design's ObjectStore (http://www.odi.com). These persistently store the sorts of object and pointer structures that you create in a Smalltalk, Common Lisp, C++, or Java program. Chasing pointers and certain kinds of transactions can be 10 to 100 times faster than in a relational database. If you believed everything in the object database vendors' literature, then you'd be surprised that Larry Ellison still has $100 bills to fling to peasants as he roars past in his Acura NSX. Oracle should have been crushed long ago under the weight of this superior technology, introduced with tremendous hype in the mid-1980s.

After ten years, the market for object database management systems is about $100 million a year, 1⁄50 the size of the relational database market. Larry Ellison isn't back to his old job teaching high school science because object databases bring back some of the bad features of 1960s pre-relational database management systems. The programmer has to know a lot about the details of data storage. If you know the identities of the objects you're interested in, then the query is fast and simple. But it turns out that most database users don't care about object *identities;* they care about object *attributes.* Relational databases tend to be faster and better at coughing up aggregations based on attributes. That said, I'm surprised that object databases aren't more popular. My personal theory is that the ascendance of C++ is responsible for the floundering of object databases. Anyone intelligent can quickly write a highly reliable program in Smalltalk or Common Lisp. But the world embraced C++, a language in which almost nobody has ever managed to write a reliable program. Corporations tend to be conservative about databases, among their most valuable assets. They never developed enough trustworthy C++ applications to make an object database worth buying and hence they continue to program in SQL.

Java to some extent restores programmers to where they were in 1978 with their Xerox Smalltalk environment or MIT Lisp Machine. Since Java seems to have enough money behind it to catch on and object databases are very naturally suited to backing up Java programs, I predict an increase in object database popularity.

If you want to sit down today and do something useful with an object database, probably the best thing to do is visit http://www.franz.com and download their Common Lisp system and Allegro Store, Franz Inc.'s bundled and Lisp-interfaced version of ObjectStore. Franz also has ODBC connectivity to any RDBMS and a Lisp Web server for which they will give you the source code. Now you have the world's most powerful computer language, a great programming environment, an object database tightly integrated with a safe language, access to RDBMS when you need it, and a Web server programmed and extendable in a safe language.

The price? Mostly free if you are running Linux.

What to do with it all? User tracking and personalization is where I'm going to start. This is a perfect example of when you care much more about an object's identity than you do about attributes. When a user #4758 visits your site, you need to quickly scoop up all the data about user #4758. Has this user seen /articles/new-page.html or not? Has this user seen /ads/screaming-banner.gif or not? With an RDBMS, you'd be sifting through 100MB tables to find all this stuff. Mind you, Informix is very good at sifting through 100MB tables, especially if they are properly indexed, but it will never be as good as an object database that doesn't have to sift through tables at all.

Anyway, I'm planning to do some interesting personalization, ad serving, and user tracking things with Franz and Allegro Store. Check http://webtools.com/wtr/ to see if I've made any progress. I should have source code to give away and probably a turnkey system.

Choosing an RDBMS Vendor

All the RDBMS vendors claim to understand exactly how a winning Web site should be built. You give them your money and they'll tell you what time it is on the Web. It all sounds really plausible until you look at the slow, content-free Web sites they've built for themselves. None of the Web crawlers were built by any of the database vendors, and, so far as I know, none of the Web crawlers even use any software made by the RDBMS vendors. As of 1997, six years after the Web was established, only Sybase (http://www.sybase.com) has figured out how to put their documentation on the Web.

What do you need out of an RDBMS? Although it isn't theoretically required that the SQL language come packaged with a relational database management system, it turns out that all commercial systems include SQL. SQL is more or less standard so that you can mechanically port 95 percent of your code from, say, Oracle to Informix to Sybase. I think that what really distinguishes a database for use behind a collaborative Web site is its ability to build a full-text index on the strings stored in the database. This is not part of standard SQL.

Suppose that a user says he wants to find out information on "dogs." If you had a bunch of strings in the database, you'd have to search them with a query like

```
select * from magazines where description like '%dogs%';
```

This requires the RDBMS to read every row in the table, which is slow. Also, this won't turn up magazines whose description includes the word *dog*. Finally, the modern text search engines are very smart about how words relate. So they might deliver a document that did *not* contain the word *dog* but did contain *Golden Retriever.* This makes services like classified ads, discussion forums, and so on, much more useful to users.

Unfortunately, as far as I know, the only relational database management systems that incorporate full-text search engines are Illustra/Informix with its PLS and Verity Blades and Oracle with its ConText option. My "text searching nerd" friends like to throw stones at Oracle/ConText for having bad linguistics but I'm not enough of an expert to level small criticisms at any product. I will say that Illustra/PLS is incredibly smart. I fed it 500 short classified ads for photography equipment then asked "What word is most related to *Nikon?*" The answer according to Illustra/PLS: *Nikkor* (Nikon's brand name for lenses).

It is moments like this that lead me to skip over the 211 other RDBMS vendors listed in Yahoo and only consider Informix and Oracle.

PAYING AN RDBMS VENDOR

This is the part that hurts. The basic pricing strategy of database management system vendors is to hang the user up by the heels, see how much money falls out, take it all and then ask for another $50,000 for "support." Ideally, they'd like to know how much your data is worth and how much profit you expect to make from making it available and then extract all of that profit from you. In this respect, they behave like the classic price-discriminating profit-maximizing monopoly from Microeconomics 101.

You can verify this by trying to get a price from an RDBMS vendor. Go ahead. You won't find prices on their Web sites. You have to talk to a salesperson who tries to figure out how much you're good for. Classically, they've priced these things per user. If you had a big company with 100 operators then you paid more than a small company with five operators. Oracle has 70 percent of the market and tends to be the leader in terms of setting prices. Suppose that you are Joe Smalltime with a Pentium box in your basement. You have a site with 17 hits a day. After a couple of hours with the Oracle Web site and 800 number, you will eventually be told that, since they can't tell how many users you have at any one time, you need an "unlimited users single processor license." That will be $64,000 please. Plus another $60,000 or so for ConText. However, if they see you walking away from the sale and getting into your beat-up Toyota and driving away, then they'll decide that $16,000 is better than nothing so they'll allow you informally to run with a minimum eight-user license. I've gone through this with a couple of friends of mine.

Microsoft is the only vendor that has the same price for everyone. You can go to their Web site and find a price for SQL Server: $1,400 for a five-user license. They explain clearly that if you are using it for the Internet, they want you to buy an Internet Connector for another $3,000 (prices on February 28, 1997). I'm not sure if this is the best deal in the world, but at least you can find the price in less than two days.

PERFORMANCE

According to their sales staff, Informix has "by far the fastest and most scalable core database engine in the world." This has an oddly familiar ring to it if you've just heard the Oracle guy note that "everyone agrees that the Oracle core code is the world's fastest and most scalable on multiprocessor machines." And if you go to the Sybase Web site, you'll see that their "Sybase System 11 has proved to be the leader in performance across a wide variety of hardware platforms." I suspect that somebody is not telling the truth.

Be assured that any RDBMS product will be plenty slow. I couldn't believe that my old Illustra system was capable of only about seven INSERTs per second into a three-column indexed table. This was on a 70-MIPS machine. Ten million instructions per INSERT! So I tried it with the latest and greatest Oracle 7.3 system. It could do 30 a second.

There are several ways to achieve very high performance. One is to buy a huge multiprocessor computer with enough RAM to hold your entire data model at once. Unfortunately, unless you decide to become a Microsoft SQL Server Achiever, your RDBMS vendor will give your bank account a reaming that it will not soon forget. The license fee will be four times as much for a four-CPU machine as for a one-CPU machine. When the basic fee is $60,000 to $100,000, multiplying by four can result in a truly staggering figure. Thus it might be best to try to get hold of the fastest possible single-CPU computer.

If you are processing a lot of transactions, all those CPUs bristling with RAM won't help you. Your bottleneck will be disk spindle contention. The solution to this is to chant "Oh what a friend I have in Seagate." Disks are slow.

Very slow. Literally almost one million times slower than the computer. Thus the computer spends a lot of time waiting for the disk(s). You can speed up SQL SELECTs simply by buying so much RAM that the entire database is in memory. However, the durability requirement in the ACID test for transactions means that some record of a transaction will have to be written to a medium that isn't erased in the event of a power failure. If a disk can only do 100 seeks per second and you only have one disk, your RDBMS is going to be hard-pressed to do more than about 100 UPDATEs a second.

The first thing you do is mirror all of your disks. If you don't have the entire database in RAM, this speeds up SELECTs because the disk controller can read from whichever disk is closer to the desired track. The opposite effect can be achieved if you use "RAID level 5" where data is striped across multiple disks. Then the RDBMS has to wait for four disks to seek before it can cough up a single row. So mirroring, or "RAID level 0," is what you want.

Once fully mirrored, you don't have to worry about media failure. If a disk dies, you just plug in a spare and experience zero off-the-Web time. However, you may still want snapshots of your database in case someone gets a little excited with a DELETE FROM statement. Or in case your facility is torched by a distraught user. Here's a technique that I learned from the Oracle studs at Boston Children's Hospital:

- Break the mirror.
- Back up from the disks that are offline as far as the database is concerned.
- Reestablish the mirror.

What if one of the online disks fails during backup? Are transactions lost? No. The redo log is on a separate disk from the rest of the database. This increases performance in day-to-day operation and ensures that it is possible to recover transactions that occur when the mirror is broken, albeit with some offline time. Children's Hospital has held on to their 60GB of data for quite a few years so I guess the procedure works.

The final decision that you must make is "How many disks?" The *Oracle DBA Handbook* (Loney; Oracle Press, 1994) recommends a 7x2 disk configuration as a minimum *compromise* for a machine doing nothing but database service. Their *solutions* start at 9x2 disks and go up to 22x2 (see Table 11.1). The idea is to keep files that might be written in parallel on separate disks so that one can do 2,200 seeks a second instead of 100.

Table 11.1: The *Oracle DBA Handbook*'s 17-Disk (Mirrored x2) Solution for Avoiding Spindle Contention

Disk	Contents
1	Oracle software
2	SYSTEM tablespace
3	RBS tablespace (rollback segment in case a transaction goes badly)
4	DATA tablespace
5	INDEXES tablespace (changing data requires changing indices; this allows those changes to proceed in parallel)
6	TEMP tablespace
7	TOOLS tablespace
8	Online Redo log 1, Control file 1 (these would be separated on a 22-disk machine)
9	Online Redo log 2, Control file 2
10	Online Redo log 3, Control file 3
11	Application software
12	RBS_2
13	DATA_2 (tables that tend to be grabbed in parallel with those in DATA)
14	INDEXES_2
15	TEMP_USER
16	Archived redo log destination disk
17	Export dump file destination disk

Even if you have lots of disks, you have to be very thoughtful about how you lay your data out across them. Oracle's installation procedure forces you to think about where your data files should go. On a computer with one disk, this is merely annoying and keeps you from doing development. But the flexibility is there because you know which of your data areas tend to be accessed simultaneously and the computer doesn't. So if you do have a proper database server with a rack of disk drives, an intelligent manual layout can result in a factor of five in increased performance.

Don't Forget to Back Up

Be afraid. Be very afraid. Standard Unix or Windows NT file system backups will not leave you with a consistent and therefore restorable database on tape.

Suppose that your RDBMS is storing your database in two separate Unix file system files, foo.db and bar.db. Each of these files is 200MB in size. You start your backup program running and it writes the file foo.db to tape. As the backup is proceeding, a transaction comes in that requires changes to foo.db and bar.db. The RDBMS makes those changes, but the ones to foo.db occur to a portion of the file that has already been written out to tape. Eventually the backup program gets around to writing bar.db to tape and it writes the new version with the change. Your system administrator arrives at 9 a.m. and sends the tapes via courier to an off-site storage facility.

At noon, an ugly mob of users assembles outside your office, angered by your introduction of frames and failure to include WIDTH and HEIGHT tags on IMGs. You send one of your graphic designers out to explain how "cool" it looked when run off a local disk in a demo to the vice president. The mob stones him to death and then burns your server farm to the ground. You manage to pry your way out of the rubble with one of those indestructible HP Unix box keyboards. You manage to get the HP disaster support people to let you use their machines for a while and confidently load your backup tape. To your horror, the RDBMS chokes up blood following the restore. It turned out that there were linked data structures in foo.db and bar.db. Half of the data structures (the ones from foo.db) are the old pre-transaction version and half are the new post-transaction version (the ones from bar.db). One transaction occurring during your backup has resulted in a complete loss of availability for all of your data. Maybe you think that isn't the world's most robust RDBMS design but there is nothing in the SQL standard or manufacturer's documentation that says Oracle, Sybase, or Informix can't work this way.

There are two ways to back up a relational database: offline and online. For an offline backup, you shut down the databases, thus preventing transactions from occurring. Most vendors would prefer that you use their utility to make a dump file of your offline database, but in practice it will suffice to just back up the Unix or NT file system files. Offline backup is typically used by insurance companies and other big database users who only need to do transactions eight hours a day. The Children's Hospital mirror-breaking example that I mentioned earlier in this chapter is another way of accomplishing the same thing.

Each RDBMS vendor has an advertised way of doing online backups. It can be as simple as "call this function and we'll grind away for a couple of hours building you a dump file that contains a consistent database but minus all the transactions that occurred after you called the function." That's what the Illustra 2.4 documentation said. But when I tested it by restoring from the dump file, a table that had been the subject of ten transactions during the dump came out broken. The dump file was not consistent. It took a year of wrangling with tech support, the testing of about ten "fixed binaries," and a new major release of the software (3.2) before the online backups would restore into legal databases.

The lessons here are several. First, whatever your backup procedure, make sure you test it with periodic restores. Second, remember that the backup and maintenance of an RDBMS is done by a full-time staffer at most companies, called the *DBA*, short for "database administrator." If the software worked as advertised, you could expect a few days of pain during the install and then periodic recurring pain to keep current with improved features. However, DBAs earn their moderately lavish salaries. No amount of marketing hype suffices to make a C program work as advertised. That goes for an RDBMS just as much as for a word processor. Coming to terms with bugs can be a full-time job at a large installation. Most often this means finding workarounds since vendors are notoriously sluggish with fixes. Another full-time job is hunting down users who are doing queries that are taking 1,000 times longer than necessary because they forgot to build indices or don't know SQL very well. Children's Hospital has three full-time DBAs and they work hard.

If all of this sounds rather tedious just to ensure that your data is still around tomorrow, then you might be cheered by the knowledge that Oracle DBAs are always in high demand and start at $60,000 to $80,000 a year. When the Web bubble bursts and your friends who are "HTML programmers" are singing in the subway, you'll be kicking back at some huge financial services firm.

RELIABILITY

If you've used the Web for any length of time, you might have noticed that database-backed Web sites are often unavailable. Furthermore, the least reliable sites are sometimes the biggest and most heavily funded corporate services with full-time staffs.

The first reason why well-funded sites die is that people tend to manage the risks they understand rather than the risks that are significant. Suppose that you start with a typical configuration: a low-end Unix workstation hooked up to a cheap Cisco router hooked up to a T1. Then you hire an MBA to form an "operations department." The MBA understands that the power could fail, that there might be an earthquake, or that the server's link to the Internet could be disrupted. So he spends $6,000 per month to rent a Unix box inside an earthquake-proof facility with conditioned power and redundant T1s. To properly do redundant network connectivity requires sophisticated routers arranged in an intelligent fashion. So the first consequence of this brilliant management decision is that latency is increased. Users are now hopping through a network of routers instead of just one Cisco. If your ISP has done everything correctly, the risk of outage due to a connectivity problem may be reduced.

Here's how Duffy Mazan (dmazan@elpress.com) was running things back in June 1995:

> "The key to our operation is redundancy at three levels. Our five T1s only run as far as a SONNET mux across the hall from our operations center and serve only to constrain our use of bandwidth to what we pay for. We can dial up or down with a day's notice. The actual connection to ANS is through two 100-Mbps fibers running out of opposite sides of the building.
>
> "Second, we run four Cisco routers connected to our Ethernet segments by two redundant Kalpana switches and redundant hubs. It is basically a star configuration that means we can lose any router or either switch with no impact on operations. And if we lose a hub, it only affects six machines.
>
> "Third, our connection to the ANS backbone is made on two different core node routers in two different cabinets.
>
> "Since we went to the fully redundant setup just after the first of the year we haven't had one second of down time. If we need to do maintenance, we can take a router or a network segment offline without affecting anything else. And when we do have problems, they are noncritical."

That's Duffy and Electric Press, though. Most ISPs are not this smart. They inadvertently arrange things so that in fact a whole pile of hardware has to be working for your site to be connected. Furthermore, this hardware is much more complicated and therefore much more likely to fail than the one-board Cisco and one-board Unix box that you used to have in-house. Remember that if you depend on components with a five percent per year chance of dying then your probability of running failure-free drops off quickly as you chain these components together. If you depend on five components, you'll have a 23 percent chance of failure. If you depend on ten components, you'll have a 40 percent chance. If you depend on 15 components, you'll have a 64 percent chance.

Suppose for the sake of argument that you've been lucky enough to hook up with Electric Press or a similar high-quality provider. You are bleeding some serious cash but can sleep knowing that your server is safe from earthquakes, power failure, and network outages.

Unfortunately, your operations manager managed the risks that he understood. Earthquakes, power failure, and network outages were never significant risks for your Web site. A T1 from a high-quality provider such as ANS might go for a year or two without any serious interruptions. I've never seen a dead low-end Cisco router. A single-board HP Unix workstation can run for five or ten years without any hardware failures. If set up properly, your workstation would automatically reboot and be serving pages after a power interruption (and in any case an uninterruptible power supply costs about $500).

Bugs in programs that you write are the most likely cause of failure for your DB-backed Web service. The second most likely cause of failure is a bug in the RDBMS or some other disruption of connectivity between your custom programs and the RDBMS. The third most likely cause is a system administration and/or operating system problem exposed by the continuous pounding that your service gives the computer and disk subsystem.

A typical ISP, even a $6,000-per-month ISP, cannot and will not do anything about bugs in your programs or database administration problems. Nor can even an experienced Unix system administrator do much about operating system problems without an intimate understanding of your service.

IF YOU HIRE AN ISP, BUY THE RIGHT SERVICE

If you shop your Web site out, make sure that you shop the whole thing out. Find an ISP who will undertake to keep a computer connected to the Internet, stably running an RDBMS, and stably running a Web server program connected to that RDBMS. This is going to be expensive. Being the database administrator for a heavily used RDBMS requires a lot of time and intimate knowledge of which tables are accessed and updated, and how often.

If you can't find an ISP who will take this level of responsibility for your machine, then just buy network connectivity and recognize that you will have to do everything else yourself. Don't fool yourself into thinking that the ISP's beeper number is good for anything other than kicking a dead router.

WHAT I DID FOR MYSELF

You might not find the details of this story relevant, but I will tell it to show the thought process that I went through in setting up a Web server in April 1997 (this was something like the 50th server that I'd set up).

Some friends of mine from MIT and I decided that we wanted to have our own Web/RDBMS server. We would use this machine to host a bunch of free public services, to develop and host a critical multi-hospital medical records site and also to develop and host sites for customers of our consulting company, ArsDigita (http://www.arsdigita.com). We decided to use SPARC/Solaris in order to have access to all of the latest software. We chose a Sun Ultra 2 with dual 167MHz UltraSPARC CPUs and 256MB of RAM. The most reliable disk subsystem would probably have been a single 9 or 27GB Seagate drive powered from the same power supply as the Ultra box. You might think that it would be more reliable to have two 9 or 27GB drives mirrored, but I think the added system administration complexity and potential for bugs from the mirroring software would result in more downtime than a disk that might fail once every five years.

We did not use a single 27GB drive inside the Ultra 2. For starters, a moby disk drive won't fit into an Ultra 2. The largest disk that will fit is an inch-high 3.5-inch drive (maximum of 4GB in April 1997). That wasn't enough space. More importantly, a single disk spindle was not going to provide adequately high performance for the RDBMSs we planned to run (Illustra, Informix Universal Server, and Oracle). We added the additional complexity and potential unreliability of a Sun external disk enclosure. This holds 12 thin disk drives, each up to 4GB in capacity. A computer that depends on 14 disk drives (two inside the Ultra; 12 in the SPARCstorage MultiPack) is a computer that doesn't work. So we installed Solstice Disk Suite to mirror the disk drives. We also reserved one physical disk as a "hot spare." Disk Suite will notice when one of the submirrors fails and instantly replace it with the hot spare. That means that we could lose any two disks and still have a fully functional machine.

Let me back up here and address the additional failure points that we introduced when we plugged in the external disk pack. The cable connecting the Ultra 2 to the external pack could fail. Fortunately, the cable connecting the DAT tape drive is identical so we always had a spare. The power supply inside the MultiPack was another source of failure. Third-party external disk enclosures generally have dual power supplies and a system will survive the loss of one. Sun does this too but only for their stratospherically priced SPARC Storage Array. Fortunately, the power supply in the MultiPack was user replaceable so we could just buy a spare and keep it next to the machine.

We plugged the whole thing into an uninterruptible power supply, thus protecting ourselves from power glitches but exposing ourselves to an additional point of failure if or when the UPS died. We dealt with this by parking the machine in a friend's T1-connected cluster. His office was only a few minutes' walk from our apartments and we had 24-hour access. We did not have to depend on beeping a harried ISP to unplug our machine from the dead UPS and plug it directly into the wall.

That brings up the question of network connectivity. We were not going to be serving prodigious quantities of images. We were going to be grinding through gigabytes of data but delivering only moderate-sized Web pages. So we wanted low latency, a network only a few milliseconds from the backbones, but didn't care too much about peak bandwidth. A T1 would be just fine. Nor did we worry too much about network redundancy. It would have been nice to be reachable from two backbones, for example, ANS and Sprint, but we were realistic about our programming and system administration skills. Our main source of downtime was going to be problems that we ourselves had caused. Our machine was directly connected to a simple router whose back-end was connected to a BBN Planet T1. The T1 in question was installed in May 1996 and has performed flawlessly ever since. Even if this particular T1 was up and running, that's of no help when the BBN Planet backbone itself was wedged, an event that happens with sufficient frequency for me to advise people to go with ANS instead. However, all of ArsDigita spends at least some time physically on the MIT campus. The MIT campus is wired to the Internet via BBN Planet. That meant that packets for running Emacs remotely did not have to go through New York or MAE East or any of the other traditionally congested spots for packet exchange among backbone providers.

Why did we decide to host other peoples' sites on our own machine? Mostly because it was so painful to use other peoples' computers. We were spending hours patching Solaris, installing needed tools, upgrading RDBMS software, and managing versions of our own function libraries. This was all wasted time that could have been better spent developing Web services. Furthermore, it would be much more reliable to run everything off a known-to-work installation. Our interests would be allied with our clients. If someone called us at 4 a.m. to say that their service was dead, we'd be delighted because that would mean that our public services were also dead. Finally, we did it for the money. It seemed stupid to let our customers pay $6,000 per month for hosting and not get what they really needed. We could take $5,000 per month, provide a much higher level of service by including the database administration, and it would cost us almost nothing because we had to do all the database administration for our own sites anyway.

How successful was this approach? Type http://www.arsdigita.com into your Web browser right now. If you don't get a response, then you'll know that we did something horribly wrong.

SUMMARY

Congratulations on wading through this chapter. I hope that you've found it worthwhile. Here is a recap of my main points:

- You and your programmers will make mistakes implementing transactions. You are better off focusing your energies on the application and leaving indexing, transactions, and concurrency to a database management system.
- The most practical database management software for Web sites is a relational database management system with a full-text indexer. Informix Universal Server and Oracle/ConText are the only two real contenders.
- If you can program a spreadsheet, you can program an RDBMS in SQL.
- RDBMSs are slow. Prepare to buy a big machine with a lot of disks.
- RDBMSs, though much more reliable than most user-written transaction processing code, are not nearly as reliable as a basic Unix system with a Web server pulling static files out of a file system. Prepare to hire a half- or full-time database administrator.

In the next chapter, we'll see how to best integrate an RDBMS with a Web server.

Interfacing a Relational Database to the Web

HOW DOES AN RDBMS TALK TO THE REST OF THE WORLD?

HOW TO MAKE REALLY FAST RDBMS-BACKED WEB SITES

CORBA: MIDDLEWARE MEETS VAPORWARE

SECURITY

WHAT DOES THIS STUFF LOOK LIKE?

SERVER-SIDE WEB/RDBMS PRODUCTS

BRING IN DA NOISE, BRING IN DA JUNK

Chapter

12

OK, you've got your RDBMS, 30 disk drives, and a computer connected to the Internet. It is time to start programming. Uh, but in what language? And what's the correct system architecture? And how do I get this Oracle thing to respond to an HTTP request? Maybe we'd better take a step back and look at the overall system before we plunge into detailed software design (Chapter 13).

How Does an RDBMS Talk to the Rest of the World?

Remember the African Grey parrot we trained in the last chapter? The one holding down a $250,000 information systems management position saying, "We're proactively leveraging our object-oriented client/server database to target customer service during reengineering?" The profound concept behind the "client/server" portion of this sentence is that the database *server* is a program that sits around waiting for another program, the database *client*, to request a connection. Once the connection is established, the client sends SQL queries to the server, which inspects the physical database and returns the matching data. These days, all connections are made via TCP sockets even if the two programs are running on the same computer (see Figures 12.1 and 12.2).

For a properly engineered RDBMS-backed Web site, the *RDBMS client* is the Web server program—AOLServer, for example (see Chapter 6 and/or http://www.aolserver.com/server). The user types something into a form on a

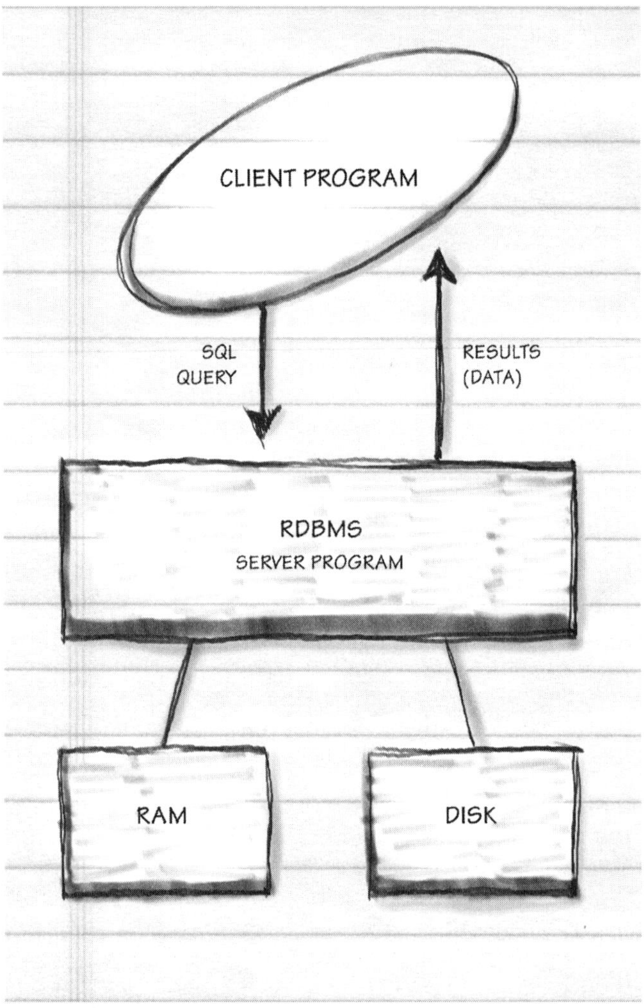

Figure 12.1: A basic relational database management system. The database client program sends SQL queries to the RDBMS server program. The RDBMS server program roots around among the data in its RAM cache and on the hard disk, then returns the requested data to the client program. The client and server programs are typically running on different physical computers and connecting over a network.

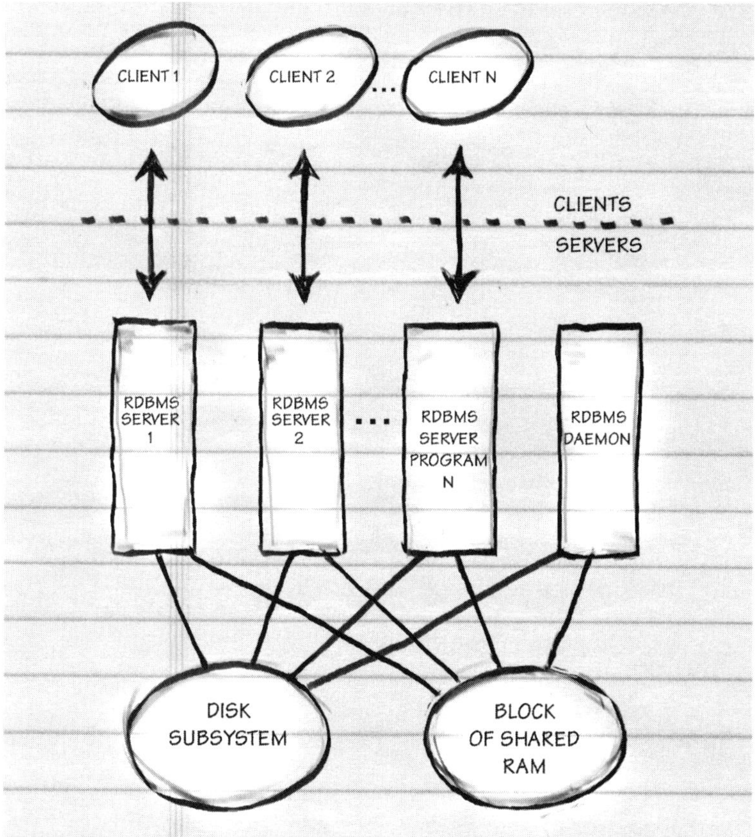

Figure 12.2: A classical RDBMS. The daemon program waits for requests from clients for connections. For each client, the daemon spawns a server program. All the servers and the daemon cache data from disk and communicate locking information via a large block of shared RAM (often as much as 256 MB). The raison d'être of an RDBMS is that *n* clients can simultaneously access and update the tables. Here we could have an AOLserver database pool taking up six of the client positions, a programmer using a shell-type tool such as SQL*Plus as another, an administrator using Microsoft Access as another, and a legacy CGI script as the final client. The client processes could be running on three or four separate physical computers. The database server processes would all be running on one physical computer (this is why Macintoshes and non-NT Windows machines are not used as database servers). Note that the trend is for database server programs to run as one process and use multiple kernel threads rather than operating system multitasking to service multiple clients. This is an implementation detail, however, and it doesn't affect the logical structure that you see in this figure.

Web client (such as Netscape Navigator) and that gets transmitted to the *Web server* which has an already-established connection to an *RDBMS server* (such as Oracle). The data then goes back from the RDBMS server to the RDBMS client, the Web server, which sends it back to the Web client (see Figure 12.3).

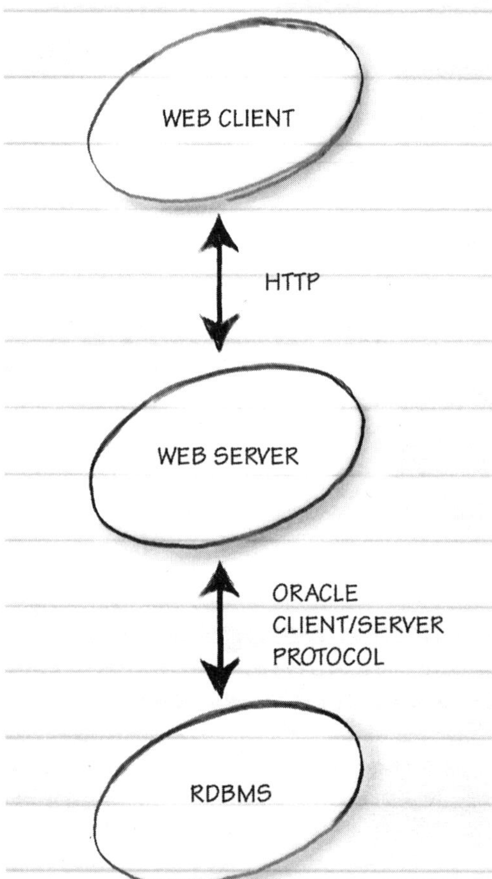

Figure 12.3: A high-performance RDBMS-backed Web site configuration. The Web server program itself is the database client. It opens a few connections to the database and keeps them open. When a Web page is requested from a Web client (such as Netscape Navigator), the Web server program (AOLserver, for example) finds a free database connection and gives it to a script that you've written. Your script can use that already-open connection to interact with the RDBMS.

Does that sound complicated and slow? Well, yes it is, but not as slow as the ancient method of building RDBMS-backed Web sites. In ancient times, people used CGI scripts. So the user would type "Submit" into his Web client (say, Netscape Navigator) causing the form to be transmitted to the Web server (NCSA 1.4, for example). The Web server would fork off a CGI script. The CGI script would then ask for a connection to the RDBMS, often resulting in the RDBMS forking off a server process to handle the new request for connection. The new RDBMS server process would ask for a username and password and authenticate the CGI script as a user. Only then would the CGI script start to transmit SQL and process results from the RDBMS server. A lot of sites were still running this way in 1997 but either they weren't popular or they felt unresponsive (see Figure 12.4).

How to Make Really Fast RDBMS-Backed Web Sites

The software architecture laid out in Figure 12.3 is the fastest currently popular Web site architecture. The Web server program maintains a pool of already-open connections to one or more RDBMS systems. You write scripts that run inside the Web server program's process instead of as CGI processes. For each URL requested, you save

- The cost of starting up a process ("forking" on a Unix system) for the CGI script.
- The cost of starting up a new Web server process. (Note: Oracle 7 and imitators pre-fork server processes; Oracle on NT and Informix on any operating system need only start a new thread which is much faster.)
- The cost of establishing the connection to the database, including a TCP session and authentication (databases have their own accounts and passwords).
- The cost of tearing all of this down when it is time to return data to the user.

As of April 1997, there were a handful of server vendors who'd realized this and produced more or less buggy implementations of the "hand out open RDBMS connections" code. See the server-side products section later in this chapter for specific product recommendations.

If you are building a richly interactive site and want the ultimate in user responsiveness, then Java is the way to go. You can write a Java applet that, after

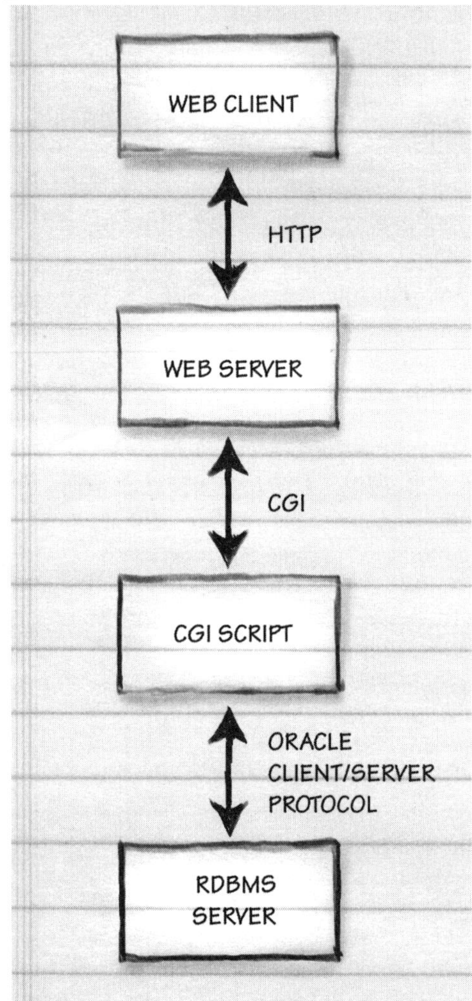

Figure 12.4: An old-style RDBMS-backed Web site. The Web client makes a request of the Web server. The Web server forks a CGI script to handle the request. The first thing the CGI program must do is open a connection to the relational database server. Modern computers are very fast, but think about how long it takes to start up a word processing program versus making a change to a document that is already open. Even with an enormous server computer, this kind of architecture results in a site that feels unresponsive to users. That said, the average Perl/CGI site is a lot faster and more reliable than the average site built with a special Web/RDBMS integration tool (see Chapter 10 and the later portions of this chapter for more derision of middleware/junkware).

a painful and slow initial download, starts running inside the user's Web client. The applet can make its own TCP connection back to the RDBMS, thus completely bypassing the Web server program. The problems with this approach include security, licensing, performance, and compatibility.

The client/server RDBMS abstraction barrier means that if you're going to allow a Java applet that you distribute to connect directly to your RDBMS, then in effect you're going to permit any program on any computer anywhere in the world to connect to your RDBMS. To deal with the security risk that this presents, you have to create a PUBLIC database user with a restricted set of privileges. Database privileges are specifiable on a set of actions, tables, and columns. It is not possible to restrict users to particular rows. So in a classified ad system, if the PUBLIC user has enough privileges to delete one row, then a malicious person could easily delete all the rows in the ads table.

The magnitude of the licensing problem raised by having Java applets connect directly to your RDBMS depends on the contract you have with your database management system vendor and the vendor's approach to holding you to that contract. Had you stuck with a classical DB-backed Web site architecture, the Web server might have counted as one user even if multiple people were connecting to the Web site simultaneously. Certainly, it would have *looked* like one user to fancy license manager programs even if there was legal fine print telling you have to pay for the multiplexing. Once you "upgrade to Java," each Java applet connecting to your RDBMS will definitely be seen by the license manager program as a distinct user. So you might have to pay tens of thousands of dollars extra even though your users aren't really getting anything very different.

A standard RDBMS will fork a server process for each connected database client. Thus if you have 400 people playing a game where each user interacts with a Java applet connected to Oracle, your server will need enough RAM to support 400 Oracle server processes. It might be more efficient in terms of RAM and CPU to program the Java applets to talk to AOLserver Tcl scripts via HTTP and let AOLServer multiplex the database resource among its threads.

The last problem with a Java applet/RDBMS system is the most obvious: Users without Java-compatible browsers won't be able to use the system. Users with Java-compatible browsers behind corporate firewall proxies that block Java applet requests will not be able to use the system. Users with Java-compatible browsers who successfully obtain your applet may find their machine (Macintosh, Windows 95) or browser process (Windows NT, Unix) crashing.

CORBA: MiddleWare Meets VaporWare

A variant of the Java-connects-directly-to-the-RDBMS architecture is Java applets running an Object Request Broker (ORB) talking to a Common Object Request Broker Architecture (CORBA) server via Internet Inter-ORB Protocol (IIOP). The user downloads a Java applet. The Java applet starts up an ORB. The ORB makes an IIOP request to get to your server machine's CORBA server program. The CORBA server requests an object from the server machine's ORB. The object, presumably some little program that you've written, is started up by the ORB and makes a connection to your RDBMS and then starts streaming the data back to the client.

CORBA is the future. CORBA is backed by Netscape, Oracle, Sun, Hewlett-Packard, IBM, and 700 other companies (except Microsoft, of course; Windows is the only standard that anyone needs, isn't it?). CORBA is so great, its proponents proudly proclaim it to be . . . "middleware":

> "The [ORB] is the middleware that establishes the client-server relationships between objects. Using an ORB, a client can transparently invoke a method on a server object, which can be on the same machine or across a network. The ORB intercepts the call and is responsible for finding an object that can implement the request, pass it the parameters, invoke its method, and return the results. The client does not have to be aware of where the object is located, its programming language, its operating system, or any other system aspects that are not part of an object's interface. In so doing, the ORB provides interoperability between applications on different machines in heterogeneous distributed environments and seamlessly interconnects multiple object systems."
>
> —from http://www.omg.org/

The basic idea of CORBA is that every time you write a computer program you also write a description of the computer program's inputs and outputs. Modern business managers don't like to buy computer programs anymore so we'll call the computer program an "object." Technology managers don't like powerful computer languages such as Common Lisp so we'll write the description in a new language: Interface Definition Language (IDL).

Suppose that you've written an object (computer program) called "find_cheapest_flight_to_paris" and declared that it can take methods such as "quote_fare" with arguments of city name, department, and date and "book_ticket" with the same arguments plus credit card number and passenger name.

Now a random computer program (object) out there in Cyberspace can go hunting via ORBs for an object named "find_cheapest_flight_to_paris". The foreign object will discover the program that you've written and then ask for the legal methods and arguments and start using your program to find the cheapest flights to Paris.

The second big CORBA idea is that one can wrap services such as transaction management around arbitrary computer programs. As long as you've implemented all of your programs to the CORBA standard, you can just ask the Object Transaction Service (OTS) to make sure that a bunch of methods executed on a bunch of objects all happen or that none happen. You won't have to do everything inside the RDBMS anymore just because you want to take advantage of its transaction system.

COMPLEXITY (OR "IT PROBABLY WON'T WORK")

Given the quality of the C code inside the Unix and Windows NT operating systems and the quality of the C code inside RDBMS products, it is sometimes a source of amazement to me that there is even a single working RDBMS-backed Web site on the Internet. What if these sites also had to depend on two ORBs being up and running? Netscape hasn't yet figured out how to make a browser that can run a simple Java animation without crashing, but we're supposed to trust the complicated Java ORB that they are putting into their latest browsers?

Actually I'm being extremely unfair. I've never heard, for example, of a bug in a CORBA Concurrency Control Service, used to manage locks. Perhaps, though, that is because seven years after the CORBA standard was first proposed, nobody has implemented a Concurrency Control Service. CORBA circa 1997 is a lot like an Arizona housing development circa 1950. The architect's model looks great. The model home is comfortable. You'll have water and sewage hookups real soon now.

WHAT IF IT DID WORK?

Assume for the sake of argument that all the CORBA middleware actually worked. Would it usher in a new dawn of reliable, high-performance software systems? Yes, I guess so, as long as your idea of a new dawn dates back to the late 1970s.

Before the Great Microsoft Technology Winter, there were plenty of systems that functioned more or less like CORBA. Xerox Palo Alto Research Center produced SmallTalk and the InterLISP machines. MIT produced the Lisp Machine. All of these operating systems/development environments supported powerful objects. The objects could discover each other. The objects could ask each other what kinds of methods they provided. Did that mean that my objects could invoke methods on your objects without human intervention?

No. Let's go back to our find_cheapest_flight_to_paris example. Suppose the foreign object is looking for "find_cheap_flight_to_paris". It won't find your perfectly matching object because of the slight difference in naming. Or suppose the foreign object is looking for "find_cheapest_flight" and expects to provide the destination city in an argument to a method. Again, your object can't be used.

That was 1978, though. Isn't CORBA an advancement over Lisp and SmallTalk? Sure. CORBA solves the trivial problem of objects calling each other over computer networks rather than from within the same computer. But CORBA ignores the serious problem of semantic mismatches. My object doesn't get any help from CORBA in explaining to other objects that it knows something about airplane flights to Paris.

This is my personal theory for why CORBA has had so little practical impact during its seven-year life.

AREN'T OBJECTS THE WAY TO GO?

Maybe CORBA is nothing special, but wouldn't it be better to implement a Web service as a bunch of encapsulated objects with advertised methods and arguments? After all, object-oriented programming is a useful tool for building big systems.

The simple answer is that a Web service is already an encapsulated object with advertised methods and arguments. The methods are the legal URLs, "insert-msg.tcl" or "add-user.tcl", for example. The arguments to these methods are the form variables in the pages that precede these URLs.

A more balanced answer is a Web service is already an encapsulated object but that its methods and arguments are not very well advertised. We don't have a protocol whereby my server can ask your server, "Please send me a list of all your legal URLs and their arguments." Hence, CORBA may one day genuinely facilitate server-to-server communication. For the average site, though, it isn't clear whether the additional programming effort over slapping something together in AOLserver Tcl or Oraperl is worth it. You might decide to completely redesign your Web service before CORBA becomes a reality.

In concluding this CORBA for Cavemen discussion, it is worth noting that the issues of securing your RDBMS are the same whether you are using a classical HTTP-only Web service architecture or CORBA.

Security

I hope that we have spent most of our time in this book thinking about how to design Web services that will be popular and valued by users. I hope that I've also conveyed some valuable lessons about achieving high performance and reliability. However, a responsive, reliable, and popular Web server that is spitting out data inserted by your enemies isn't anything to e-mail home about. So it is worth thinking about security occasionally. I haven't written anything substantial about securing a standard Windows NT or Unix server. I'm not an expert in this field, but there are plenty of good books on the subject, and ultimately it isn't possible to achieve perfect security so you'd better have a good set of backup tapes. However, running any kind of RDBMS raises a bunch of new security issues that I *have* spent some time thinking about so let's look at how Harry Hacker can get into your database.

Before Harry can have a data modeling language (INSERT, UPDATE, DELETE) party with your data, he has to do two things: (1) successfully connect to the IP address and port where the RDMBS is listening, and (2) once connected, present a username and password pair recognized by the RDBMS.

If you are remarkably incompetent, you would be running the RDBMS on the same machine as your Web server, both binding to the same IP address. You wouldn't bother changing the default port numbers on which your RDBMS listens. You would have well-known usernames (for example, "oracle" for Oracle or "miadmin" for Illustra) with no passwords and/or well-known passwords.

To achieve Step 1, connecting to the RDBMS, Harry need only use the same IP address as your Web site and the default port number as published in the documentation for the RDBMS that you are using. To achieve Step 2, Harry need only try a well-known username/password pair.

Is anyone out there on the Internet really this incompetent? Sure! I have done at least one consulting job for a company whose Web server had been set up and left like this for months. The ISP was extremely experienced with both the Web server program and the RDBMS being used. The ISP was charging my client thousands of dollars per month. Was this reasonably popular site assaulted by the legions of crackers one reads about in the dead trees media? No. Nobody touched their data. The lesson: Don't spend your whole life worrying about security.

However, you'll probably sleep better if you spend at least a little time foiling Harry Hacker. The easiest place to start is with the username/password pairs. Obviously you want to set these to something hard to guess. Unfortunately, these aren't super secure because they often must be stored as clear text in CGI scripts or cron jobs that connect to the database. Then anyone who gets a Unix username/password pair can read the CGI scripts and collect the database password. On a site where the Web server itself is the database client, the Web server configuration files will usually contain the database password in clear text. This is only one file so it is easy to give it meager permissions but anyone who can become root on your Unix box can certainly read it.

A worthwhile parallel approach is to try to prevent Harry from connecting to the RDBMS at all. You could just configure your RDBMS to listen on different ports from the default. Harry can't get in anymore by just trying port 7599 because he saw the little "backed by Sybase" on your home page and knows that Sybase will probably be listening there. Harry will have to sweep up and down the port numbers until your server responds. Maybe he'll get bored and try someone else's site.

A much more powerful approach is moving the database server behind a firewall. This is mostly necessary because RDBMSs have such lame security notions. For example, it should be possible to tell the RDBMS, "Only accept requests for TCP connections from the following IP addresses . . ." Every Web server program since 1992 has been capable of this. However, I'm not aware of any RDBMS vendor who has figured this out. They talk the Internet talk, but they walk the *intranet* walk.

Because Oracle, Informix, and Sybase forgot to add a few lines of code to their product, you'll be adding $10,000 to your budget and buying a firewall computer. This machine sits between the Internet and the database server. Assuming your Web server is outside the firewall, you program the firewall to "not let anyone make a TCP connection to port 7599 on the database server except 18.23.0.16 [your Web server]." This works great until someone compromises your Web server. Now they are root on the computer that the firewall has been programmed to let connect to the database server. So they can connect to the database.

Oops.

So you move your Web server inside the firewall, too (see Figure 12.5). Then you program the firewall to allow *nobody* to connect to the database server for any reason. The only kind of TCP connection that will be allowed will be to port 80 on the Web server (that's the default port for HTTP). Now you're *reasonably* secure.

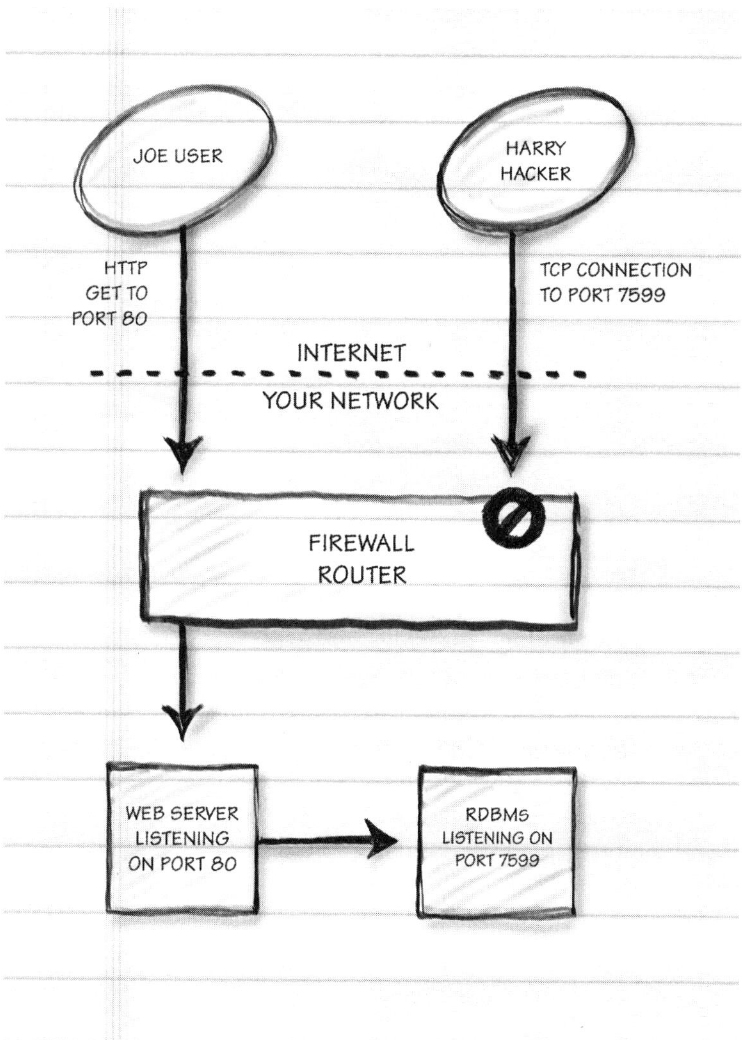

Figure 12.5: You don't want Harry Hacker connecting directly to your RDBMS. The vendors of relational databases don't allow you to restrict access based on IP address. So you need a firewall router (usually a standard Unix box running software; see the Trusted Information Systems site http://www.tis.com for explanations, free source code for a firewall toolkit, and packaged firewall products). The router selectively forwards packets from the Internet. You can instruct your firewall to reject everything except requests for connections to port 80 of a specific IP address where your Web server is listening. Then Harry Hacker's request for a connection to the port where your RDBMS is listening will be blocked.

WHAT DOES THIS STUFF LOOK LIKE?

Here's a typical AOLserver Tcl API DB-backed page. Tcl is a safe language and an incorrect Tcl program will not crash AOLserver or result in a denial of service to other users. This program reads through a table of e-mail addresses and names and prints each one as a list item in an unnumbered list. If this is placed in a file named "view.tcl" in the Greedy Corporation's Web server root directory then it may be referenced at http://www.greedy.com/view.tcl.

```
# send basic text/html headers back to the client
# Note that the AOLserver has already bound the Tcl
# local variable CONN to the connection for the
# user who requested this page.
    ns_write $conn "HTTP/1.0 200 OK
MIME-Version: 1.0
Content-Type: text/html

"

# write the top of the page
# note that we just put static HTML in a Tcl string and then
# call the AOLserver API function ns_write
ns_write $conn "<title>Entire Mailing List</title>
<h2>Entire Mailing List</h2>
<hr>
<ul>
"

# get an open database from the AOLserver
# and set the ID of that connection to the local variable DB
set db [ns_db gethandle]

# open a database cursor bound to the local variable SELECTION
# we want to read all the columns (*) from the mailing_list table
set selection [ns_db select $db "select * from mailing_list
order by upper(email)"]

# loop through the cursor, calling ns_db getrow to bind
# the Tcl local variable SELECTION to a set of values for
# each row; it will return 0 when there are no more rows
# in the cursor
while { [ns_db getrow $db $selection] } {

    # pull email and name out of SELECTION
    set email [ns_set get $selection email]
    set name [ns_set get $selection name]
```

```
    ns_write $conn "<li><a href=\"mailto:$email\">$email</a> ($name)"

}

ns_write $conn "</ul>

<hr>
<address><a href=\"mailto:philg@mit.edu\">philg@mit.edu</a></address>
"
```

Not exactly rocket science, was it? Still, there are some fine points here. One is that the program returns headers and the top portion of the page before asking AOLserver for a database connection or asking the database to do anything. This kind of construction ensures that users aren't staring at a blank Netscape window. A second fine point is that we wrap the e-mail address in a MAILTO tag. Maybe nobody will ever actually want to send e-mail from here, but at least nobody will say, "What a bunch of losers who don't know how to use MAILTO tags." Third, a microfine point is that there is an advertised author for this page. I've put my e-mail address at the bottom so if it isn't working, the user can tell me. Finally, even if there were a Tcl compiler, it wouldn't be able to check the correctness of this program. Tcl doesn't know anything about the database so it doesn't know if the mailing_list table exists or what the names of the columns are. So you won't find typos until you test the page or a user follows a branch you didn't test (ouch!). The plus side of this is that a Tcl program is free to construct SQL queries on the fly. Because Tcl makes no attempt to test program correctness before execution, you can easily write a Tcl program that, for example, takes a table_name argument from a user and then puts it into a query.

Let's try something similar in Oracle WebServer 2.0. We're going to use PL/SQL, Oracle's vaguely ADA-inspired procedural language that runs inside the server process. It is a safe language and an incorrect PL/SQL program will usually not compile. If an incorrect program gets past the compiler, it will not run wild and crash Oracle unless there is a bug in the Oracle implementation of PL/SQL (and I've tripped over a couple). This PL/SQL program is from a bulletin board system. It takes a message ID argument, fetches the corresponding message from a database table, and writes the content out in an HTML page. Note that in Oracle WebServer 2.0 there is a one-to-one mapping between PL/SQL function names and URLs. This one will be referenced via a truly ugly URL of the following form

```
http://www.greedy.com/public/owa/bbd_fetch_msg
```

Nobody ever said Oracle was pretty . . .

```
-- this is a definition that we feed directly to the database
-- in an SQL*PLUS session.  So the procedure definition is itself
-- an extended SQL statement.  The first line says I'm a Web page
-- that takes one argument, V_MSG_ID, which is a variable length
-- character string
create or replace procedure bbd_fetch_msg ( v_msg_id IN varchar2 )
AS
  -- here we must declare all the local variables
  -- the first declaration reaches into the database and
  -- makes the local variable bboard_record have
  -- the same type as a row from the bboard table
  bboard_record bboard%ROWTYPE;
  days_since_posted integer;
  age_string varchar2(100);
BEGIN
  -- we grab all the information we're going to need
  select * into bboard_record from bboard where msg_id = v_msg_id;
  -- we call the Oracle function "sysdate" just as we could
  -- in a regular SQL statement
  days_since_posted := sysdate - bboard_record.posting_time;
  -- here's something that you can't have in a declarative
  -- language like SQL...  an IF statement
  IF days_since_posted = 0 THEN
    age_string := 'today';
  ELSIF days_since_posted = 1 THEN
    age_string := 'yesterday';
  ELSE
    age_string := days_since_posted || ' days ago';
  END IF;
  -- this is the business end of the procedure.  We
  -- call the Oracle WebServer 2.0 API procedure htp.print
  -- note that the argument is a big long string produced
  -- by concatenating (using the "||" operator) static
  -- strings and then information from bboard_record
  htp.print('<html>
<head>
<title>' || bboard_record.one_line || '</title>
</head>
<body bgcolor=#ffffff text=#000000>

<h3>' || bboard_record.one_line || '</h3>

from ' || bboard_record.name || '
(<a href="mailto:' || bboard_record.email || '">'
 || bboard_record.email || '</a>)
```

```
<hr>

' || bboard_record.message || '

<hr>

(posted '|| age_string || ')

</body>
</html>');

END bbd_fetch_msg;
```

The first thing to note in this program is that we choose "v_msg_id" instead of the obvious "msg_id" as the procedure argument. If we'd used msg_id, then our database query would have been

```
select * into bboard_record from bboard where msg_id = msg_id;
```

which is pretty similar to

```
select * from bboard where msg_id = msg_id;
```

Does that look a little strange? It should. The WHERE clause is inoperative here because it is tautological. *Every* row in the table will have msg_id = msg_id so all the rows will be returned. This problem didn't arise in our AOLserver Tcl program because the Tcl was being read by the Tcl interpreter compiled into the AOLserver and the SQL was being interpreted by the RDBMS back-end. With a PL/SQL program, the whole thing is executing in the RDBMS.

Another thing to note is that it would be tough to rewrite this procedure to deal with a multiplicity of database tables. Suppose you decide to have a separate table for each discussion group. So you have photo_35mm_bboard and photo_medium_format_bboard tables. Then you'll just add a v_table_name argument to the procedure. But what about these local variable declarations?

```
bboard_record bboard%ROWTYPE;
```

This says, "Set up the local variable bboard_record so that it can hold a row from the bboard table." No problem. You just replace the static bboard with the new argument

```
bboard_record v_table_name%ROWTYPE;
```

and voilá . . . you get a compiler error: "v_table_name could not be found in the database." All of the declarations have to be computable at compile time.

The spirit of PL/SQL is that you give the compiler enough information at procedure definition time that you won't have any errors at run-time.

You're not in Kansas anymore and you're not Web scripting, either. This is programming. You're declaring variables. You're using a compiler that will be all over you like a cheap suit if you type a variable name wrong. Any formally trained computer scientist should be in heaven. Well, yes and no. Strongly typed languages like ADA and Pascal result in more reliable code. This is great if you are building a complicated program like a fighter jet target-tracking system. But when you're writing a Web page that more or less stands by itself, being forced to dot all the i's and cross all the t's can be an annoying hindrance. After all, since almost all the variables are going to be strings and you're just gluing them together, what's the point of declaring types?

I don't think it is worth getting religious over which is the better approach. For one thing, as discussed in Chapter 10, "When Is a Site Really a Database?," this is the easy part of building a relational database-backed Web site. You've developed your data model, defined your transactions, and designed your user interface. You're engaged in an almost mechanical translation process. For another, if you were running AOLserver with Oracle as the back-end database, you could have the best of both worlds by writing simple Tcl procedures that called PL/SQL functions. We would touch up the definition bbd_fetch_msg so that it was designed as a PL/SQL *function*, which can return a value, rather than a procedure, which is called for effect. Then instead of htp.print we'd simply RETURN the string. We could interface it to the Web with a five-line AOLserver Tcl function:

```
# grab the input and set it to Tcl local variable MSG_ID
set_form_variables

# get an open database connection from AOLserver
set db [ns_db gethandle]

# grab one row from the database.  Note that we're using the
# Oracle dummy table DUAL because we're only interested in the
# function value and not in any information from actual tables.
set selection [ns_db 1row $db "select bbd_fetch_msg($msg_id) as moby_string from
dual"]

# Since we told the ns_db API call that we only expected
# one row back, it put the row directly into the SELECTION
# variable and we don't have to call ns_db getrow
set moby_string [ns_set get selection moby_string]
```

```
# we call the AOLserver API call ns_return to
# say "status code 200; MIME type is text/html"
# and then send out the page
ns_return $conn 200 text/html $moby_string
```

As I write this, the America Online folks who bought NaviSoft are still waiting to see if this Oracle fad catches on. Thus, they've not written an Oracle driver for AOLserver. So this combination of AOLserver Tcl API and PL/SQL would only work on a Windows NT box where the ODBC standard (see below) lets AOLserver and Oracle talk to each other. Still, you could use the same approach any time you have a database server with a good procedural language (rumor has it that Oracle 8 will let you run Java inside the server in addition to PL/SQL) and a Web server with the basic ability to serve the result of an SQL query as the entire page.

Server-side Web/RDBMS Products

I don't think I made enough enemies in Chapter 10 by saying that commercial Web/RDBMS integration products in general are inferior to thrown-together public-domain hacks. So now I'll review some specific products.

ORACLE WEBSERVER 2.0

Oracle has a rich history of claiming that they understand the Web better than any other company. They took one look at HTML and Netscape Navigator and said, "This stuff is no good for database applications; we'll build our own standard and our own Oracle PowerBrowser." As a sop to people who clung pathetically to the idea that HTML was going to catch on, Oracle distributed a "Web toolkit" of public-domain server-side software, including Kevin Stock's Oraperl (see Chapter 10). Kevin hadn't touched the code since the old Oracle 6 days so my friend Eric was really excited to download the toolkit from the Oracle site and start using it with Oracle 7, the then-current release of the RDBMS server.

Eric couldn't get Oraperl to work with Oracle 7 so he called Oracle support.

"We don't support the Web toolkit. It is just a free add-on."

Had they paid Kevin Stock or anyone else to spend a few days making Oraperl work with the latest version of Oracle?

"No. We just collected the stuff in the toolkit from other Web sites and make it available for download in one file."

I suppose that part of the reason Oracle didn't want to buy a few days of Kevin's time is that they were shortly to come out with their own Web server: Oracle WebServer. Their PR staff worked tirelessly to convince customers to switch from all these unsupported public-domain packages and enjoy the total quality solution of Oracle software engineering and Oracle support from RDBMS to Web server to Web browser. However, the word on the street about WebServer 1.0 was so bad that I didn't bother to try it. Neither apparently was Oracle Corporation itself too eager to try WebServer 1.0:

```
philg-sub-47> telnet www.oracle.com 80
Trying...
Connected to www-2.us.oracle.com.
Escape character is '^]'.
HEAD / HTTP/1.0

HTTP/1.0 200 Document follows
Date: Wed, 06 Mar 1996 22:37:51 GMT
Server: NCSA/1.5
Content-type: text/html
```

Note: This is the standard way to find out what Web server a site is running. You telnet from a shell to the hostname, in this case www.oracle.com, port 80. Then you type in a request line like "GET / HTTP/1.0<return><return>". The "Server:" header in this response tells us that Oracle was using the NCSA 1.5 server as of March 6, 1996 (more than six months after introducing a competitive product). NCSA 1.5 was distributed with source code, and hence I'm kind of surprised that Oracle didn't at least remove the line of C code that writes this embarrassing header.

By the time some friends of mine were sitting down to rebuild http://www.comdex.com (to handle online registration for the big COMDEX trade show), Oracle was touting WebServer 2.0: "Even more perfect than WebServer 1.0." We decided to give it a try.

Installation and configuration took days and would not have been a success without assistance from some of my friends on the Oracle WebServer development team. Once installed, WebServer 2.0 demands a relatively painful development cycle. Each dynamic Web page is a single PL/SQL procedure. You edit the foobar.sql file in Emacs then have to cut and paste the definition into an SQL*Plus session to define the procedure foobar in the database. Then and only then does the dynamic Web page become accessible at http://www.greedy.com/public/owa/foobar. If you are accustomed to AOLserver Tcl or Perl/CGI then you often find yourself fixing a PL/SQL bug in Emacs and then wondering why the online page is still broken. You usually only waste a minute or two before realizing that you need to feed Oracle the new procedure definitions.

Once we got used to the software development cycle, things proceeded moderately smoothly until we hit two interlocking WebServer 2.0 shortcomings: lack of flexibility and lack of support. Lack of flexibility meant that there was only one way to issue an HTTP 302 redirect. Lack of support meant that when we discovered a server-crashing bug in this one facility, it wasn't until six months later that Oracle got around to releasing a new version of the server that wouldn't crash trying to issue a redirect.

Lack of flexibility also made it impossible to deal with problems like the inadvertent hiding from search engines that I discussed in Chapter 5. With AOLserver, I can register an arbitrary URL or families of URLs to a Tcl procedure. That's not possible in Oracle WebServer and you never know when you might need it (in addition to Chapter 5, see the discussion of my Loquacious comment server in Chapter 14).

Oracle's design philosophy for the API is questionable. For example, a PL/SQL procedure that sits behind an HTML form is supposed to have one argument for each INPUT name. Check box values come through as an array. However, they didn't think carefully about what happens if a user doesn't check any of the boxes. We expected that the PL/SQL would be set to NULL and that we could test for this in our procedure. Instead, the PL/SQL procedure aborts with an error because it doesn't get enough arguments. Our software never even had a chance to consider the user-entered data. We discovered this about 2 a.m. one night and worked around it by putting

```
<INPUT TYPE=HIDDEN NAME=FOOBAR VALUE=ORACLESUCKS>
```

whenever there were check box inputs named "FOOBAR" in one of our forms. This struck us as repulsive so we asked Oracle what the correct way to do this was. After a few weeks, we got our answer: Put in a hidden variable with the same name as the check boxes and a value of "NOBOXCHECKED". They didn't even acknowledge that this was a less than elegant implementation.

Even where the API is elegant, it is not complete. You cannot do the things that you need to do, such as send e-mail or grab a Web page from another site. Where the API is complete, it is not robust. I wrote out a couple of set-cookie headers with the API and then forgot to call the "close header" function. I should have ended up with one broken page and/or an error message. Instead, I got a crashed server and denial of service to all users.

For all of Oracle's talk about how great an RDBMS is, WebServer 2.0 doesn't make too much use of one. It writes its access and error logs into the file system, not into the database (Microsoft Internet Information Server lets you choose which you prefer). HTTP authentication usernames and passwords are not stored in database tables that you can extend, query from your Web site scripts, or join with other tables. Rather, these username/password pairs and group memberships are stored in custom-formatted Unix files that you can't touch or query (AOLserver also uses a Unix file but at least they give you API hooks to add users, check passwords, and so on).

We were never happy with the performance we got from Oracle WebServer 2.0/Oracle7.3. Even in development on an idle workstation, our site was much less responsive than production AOLserver/Illustra-backed sites on an overloaded Unix box with a load average of 3. Oracle is a faster RDBMS than Illustra, hence we laid the blame at WebServer 2.0's door. In fact, I think that my old CGI-based sites running Oraperl scripts and Oracle 6 on a discarded antediluvian SPARC were significantly faster.

Can I say anything good about WebServer 2.0? Yes. If a PL/SQL procedure is accepted without errors by the Oracle compiler, almost always the Web page will run without errors. It is easier to have confidence in the correctness of a collection of PL/SQL programs than it is to have confidence in a collection of purely interpreted Tcl scripts. With the Tcl script, the interpreter won't even look at the half of a conditional that isn't relevant. A glaring syntax error can go unnoticed for months unless you are very rigorous about testing.

The bottom line? Oracle WebServer is a reasonably good product, but I wouldn't use it again. Larry Ellison spends a lot of time taunting Bill Gates and Microsoft for their ignorance of all things Internet. I could take these taunts more seriously if it weren't possible to download about 50 files from www.microsoft.com (IIS-backed) in the time that it takes to grab the first page from www.oracle.com (Oracle WebServer 2.1-backed as of March 1997).

INFORMIX WEB DATABLADE

My general rule, "Don't depend on any Web software from a company that hasn't figured out how to put its documentation online," saved me from personally losing with the Web DataBlade, an idea that Informix acquired when it bought Illustra in early 1996. My first in-depth exposure to the Web Blade came when I was asked to analyze the utter failure of a DB-backed Web site built by expensive New York consultants. Let's call it http://www.deadlocked.com.

The Web Blade is yet another server-side extension to HTML. If you read Chapter 9 then you know that I think semantically augmented HTML is the future of server-side programming. However, the Web Blade isn't exactly what I had in mind. Rather than a full-featured programming language with HTML syntax a la Meta-HTML (http://www.mhtml.com), Informix delivers an ad hoc design that lets you embed SQL queries in HTML. You store these templates in a database table. In response to user queries, the WebDaemon will pull the relevant piece of extended HTML out of the database, parse it, do the SQL queries specified by your HTML, and then return standard HTML to the requesting client.

The first part of the Web Blade that you'll see as a developer is the "application builder." This lets you edit your Web Blade templates via HTML forms. The template itself occupies a TEXTAREA in your Netscape Navigator.

If you spent the last 20 years learning Emacs then you'll find that Netscape Navigator is a very poor substitute as a text editor. The Netscape Find command does not even search through text in a TEXTAREA. So if you want to search for a part of a complicated page, you have to do it with your eyes only.

The one good thing that I can say about the application builder is that it is easy to throw away. If you just extract your templates into static Unix files, then you end up with a development cycle similar to that of Oracle WebServer. You edit your templates in Emacs, being careful to escape all the single quotes because eventually you'll have to put the entire template into an SQL INSERT or UPDATE. When you are satisfied with your page, you feed it to Illustra in an MSQL session as an INSERT or UPDATE to the webPages table. Then you go to your Web browser and reload the page to see how it works. Not as convenient as AOLserver Tcl or CGI, but not unusable and you can still use all of your familiar Unix software development utilities.

Assuming you are able to make peace with the Web Blade's development cycle, you are still stuck with its baroque syntax. Here's an example of grabbing the e-mail address and subject line for a particular message from a database table of bboard messages:

```
<?MISQL SQL = "SELECT email, subject FROM bboard where msg_id = 37;">
$2 (from $1)
<?/MISQL>
```

The business end of this code is the "$2 (from $1)". This is horrible data abstraction. It might not look that bad now, but what if you had a complicated query and then produced 30 lines of HTML? Do you really want to see $13 on line 28 and try to figure out which column it is? In Oraperl, AOLserver Tcl, or PL/SQL for Oracle WebServer 2.0, you'd instead be able to say "$subject (from $email)".

Conditionals and control structure are even worse. The heart and soul of this thing is declarative but a lot of times you need to do procedural stuff. Feast your eyes on this:

```
cond=$(OR,$(NXST,$email),$(NXST,$name),$(NXST,$subject))
```

I never expected to be nostalgic for Tcl or Perl . . .

You'd think that the whole point of a tool like the Web DataBlade would be that you could say, "Make sure this input is an integer not null and, if not, give the user a nice error message." But you can't. You have to put in all these gnarly conditionals yourself and write your own error messages. It isn't any worse than using raw Perl but the authors of Perl never made any claim that theirs was a Web/DB integration tool.

Another thing you'd expect from a Web/RDBMS tool is good database integration. As documented above, Oracle WebServer has its share of shortcomings, but at least the form variables come to you the programmer as PL/SQL variables. They can contain any ASCII, and you can insert them without further worry. Oracle understands RDBMS. Perl and Tcl don't, so you have to manually double the apostrophes (the SQL quoting character) before attempting a string insert, that is, you have to change 'don't' to 'don''t'. For AOLserver, I wrote a magic little Tcl function that lets me say "$Qqsubject" when I want the double-quoted version of the "subject" form variable. The Web DataBlade isn't as powerful a language as Tcl and it doesn't understand RDBMS like PL/SQL, so you have to do this:

```
<?mivar delimit="'" replace="''" name=subject>$subject<?/mivar>
```

for every variable that you insert into the database. Ugh!

Note: You can define a function call to do this a little more cleanly but it would still be much more painful than my Tcl hack and neither solution is as good as Oracle's.

Having noted the glacial performance of other Web Blade-backed sites (including http://www.informix.com), I was prepared for my client's site to be sluggish. Informix claims that the software will work plugged into the Netscape Enterprise Server's API. However, customers report that their systems become unstable when they try this configuration. Some of the product folks at Informix swore that the Web Blade is reliable when used with NSAPI but I noticed that they are using it in CGI-mode themselves:

```
http://www.informix.com/infmx-cgi/Webdriver?MIval=products_and_technology
```

(I cut and pasted this URL on March 9, 1997; they were running the Enterprise 2.01 server at the time).

The overhead of CGI should only have degraded responsiveness by a factor of ten. However, http://www.deadlocked.com was at least a factor of 100 slower than expected. In fact, it was only able to serve one user at a time.

Every Page a Transaction I discovered that Informix designed each Web Blade page to execute as a single SQL transaction. So if you SELECT FROM a table at the top of the page and then try to UPDATE or INSERT into the same table lower down, you will deadlock. That's because the SELECT grabs a read lock on the table. Another copy of the same page can be running simultaneously. It also grabs a read lock on the same table. Then the UPDATE or INSERT tries to get the write lock, which only one RDBMS connection can have at once. It waits for all read locks to be freed up. The simultaneously running copy, holding one of those read locks, is also waiting for the write lock. So two copies of the same page will wait for each other forever (or until the deadlock timer kills them both).

This isn't a problem in Oraperl or AOLserver Tcl. You probably don't need the whole page to run as a transaction and if you don't do anything special then the SELECT up top and the UPDATE down below are separate. They aren't part of the same transaction block and hence will get serialized just fine with the SELECTs and UPDATEs from simultaneously running pages. That was the whole point of using an RDBMS!

Web Blade Workaround 1: EXEC Perl The expensive New York Web site developers apparently didn't like the Web Blade's limited procedural language facilities. So when they wanted to check an input against a regular expression, they just EXECed a Perl script. Yes, that means that the Unix box has to fork right in the middle of a database transaction. Worse yet, they often forked off a Perl script that then needed to look up some information in the database. They could have installed the Informix/Illustra equivalent of Oraperl and read from the database directly. Instead they had the Perl script fork MSQL, the Illustra shell-level tool. The Perl script would fork MSQL, collect the human-readable output, REGEXP like crazy to pull the data out into Perl variables, and then perhaps fork MSQL a few more times!

All of this while holding down table locks in the middle of a transaction.

Web Blade Workaround 2: Convert to AOLserver I installed AOLserver and wrote a Tcl script to pull the Web Blade templates out of the RDBMS and stick them into ordinary Unix files. Now they were accessible to grep, Perl, and Emacs. I then wrote a Perl script to batch convert these files into pidgin AOLserver Tcl API URLs. I could have done this in my original AOLserver Tcl script but it turns out that Perl is a much better tool for the job than Tcl. Why? Perl offers the option of non-greedy REGEXP matching. This means that you can easily match "from <FOO> to the first </FOO>". If you use {<FOO>(.*)</FOO>} as a Tcl REGEXP pattern then the "(.*)" matches the entire file between the very first "<FOO>" to the very last "</FOO>". You get the same bad behavior in Perl unless you remember to use the magic "*?" operator: <FOO>(.*?)</FOO>.

Tip: If you aren't afraid of your friends' scorn, pick up a copy of Mastering Regular Expressions (Friedl; O'Reilly, 1997). I wouldn't call it great literature, but it covers Tcl, GNU Emacs, Python, and (mostly) Perl. It is a lot better than the man pages and the books on the individual languages.

I was then able to touch up the Perl output in Emacs at the rate of about 20 DB-backed URLs a day. End result? The site was about ten times more responsive at times of light load and was no longer plagued with deadlocks. The site went from being able to perform no more than one query at a time to being able to easily handle ten or more queries per second.

Note: If you have a suffering Web Blade site and would like a copy of my Tcl and Perl scripts to assist in a conversion to AOLserver, just send me some e-mail.

Web Blade Workaround 3: Convert to Meta-HTML Since the Web Blade is just an extended HTML, probably the cleanest way to port a Web Blade site to something reasonable would be to sit down for a few days with Meta-HTML (http://www.mhtml.com) and write a bunch of Meta-HTML tag definitions to correspond to the Informix tags. I didn't do this because I'm much more experienced with AOLserver and it was therefore a more conservative path to getting www.deadlocked.com back up and running.

Web Blade Bottom Line The Web Blade is the worst-conceived, worst-performing piece of Web/RDBMS integration software that I have used. I would much rather go back to 1994, Oraperl, and Oracle 6 than use this product, which has serious deficiencies in

- Expressivity of language
- Development cycle
- Ease of debugging
- Reliability and performance

Informix Universal Server promises to be a very nice RDBMS, but just say no to this way of connecting your Web site to it.

NETSCAPE LIVEWIRE

I covered LiveWire fairly thoroughly in Chapter 6. All of the deficiencies I noted there apply here. I should add that my repeated attempts to get LiveWire to connect to Oracle ended in failure. I had to have all kinds of Oracle software installed on both the client and server computers. It had to be exactly the right version. I eventually ran out of Oracle CD-ROMs and patience.

Since I couldn't get LiveWire to work, it seems only fair to give a real user the last word:

```
Date: Fri, 28 Feb 1997 20:29:13 -0500
From: Dave Mitchell <davem@magnet.com>
Organization: Magnet Interactive Communications

I just finished (I hope) a largish commerce project in livewire
(solaris/informix) and it was HELL! Livewire blows goats! I'm still
spending every day fixing yesterday's little bugs and todays big bugs
and creating tomorrows little bugs that expose yesterdays bigger bugs!

. . .

In any case, the problems we had were with bizarre variable
scoping problems (remove var statement to fix problem... sometimes),
such as building an array of objects, only to find that when you're
done, you've got an array of .... something. Strange things also happen
              if you redeclare a variable that already exists - such as "var" in a
loop. Usually it just crashes when it gets there, but sometimes it
just works and things appear to be fine, but the values don't get
updated properly?

I only wish I could provide test code to demonstrate the problems -
but I can't!! Every test function I ever wrote works fine.

Or how about this one - how can I find out what kind of object I
have? how about what methods I can call on it? If you try to call
a method on an object it doesn't have the app just crashes!
```

META-HTML

As I noted in Chapter 9, I think the future of server-side programming is semantically enhanced HTML and the best current example is Meta-HTML (http://www.mhtml.com). The PowerStrip version of Meta-HTML is compiled with the OpenLink ODBC libraries for transparent access to just about any RDBMS. Many of my friends from MIT have built high-traffic database-backed sites with Meta-HTML so I'm pretty sure that it works. Meta-HTML also has a lot of high-level Web programming features like session variables.

However, I haven't done too much myself with it because I've got so much experience and source code for AOLserver that it is more efficient for me to continue using the tools that I know.

WEBOBJECTS, MICROSOFT IIS, AND OTHERS

A lot of big rich companies use WebObjects (http://www.next.com) for their dynamic sites. Most of the WebObjects-backed site I've come across have been unacceptably slow. WebObjects definitely provides for RDBMS connectivity, although when you add the sluggishness of the average RDBMS to the apparent sluggishness of WebObjects, it is tough to imagine the final result being good for much besides corporate vanity.

The most common method of building an RDBMS-backed page with Internet Information Server (http://www.microsoft.com/iis) is through *Active Server Pages.* You are talking to one of these any time you see a URL that ends in .asp. ASPs work with just about any scripting language or standard programming language and let you define and maintain session variables. There is specific support for JavaScript, Visual Basic, and connections through to ODBC databases. ASPs run inside the Web server process and hence avoid the forking overhead of CGI. NT Server 4.0 does at least one very clever thing, which is to notice when an ASP page has changed in the file system and arrange with the running IIS to deliver the new version. The development cycle problems I noted with LiveWire have not been lost on Microsoft:

> "How does Active Server Pages compare to Netscape LiveWire?
>
> "Netscape LiveWire requires the use of JavaScript, while Active Server Pages supports the use of virtually any scripting language, with native support for VBScript and Jscript. Active Server Pages supports components written in any language while LiveWire supports only Java components.
>
> "LiveWire applications must be manually compiled after each change, and then the application stopped and restarted. Active Server Pages recognizes when an ASP file changes, and automatically recompiles the application at the next request."
>
> —from http://www.microsoft.com/iis/

I don't have enough experience with Windows NT to evaluate IIS and this whole way of doing server-side programming. Generally every Microsoft product I've ever used has sounded much better on paper than it has worked in practice. However, I suppose that if you've already sold your soul to Microsoft then IIS + ASP + Visual Basic probably isn't a bad way to go.

I haven't kept up with all the Web "technology" being pushed by various vendors and every document of this nature is necessarily out of date. So don't be surprised if the latest tantalizingly hyped product isn't mentioned above. Try to keep in mind the caveats I laid down in Chapter 10. No junkware/middleware/Webware product can do your thinking for you. Once you've done the thinking, it isn't too hard to do the programming with standard and simple tools. Also try to keep in mind the caveats I laid down in Chapter 6 against commercial products for which source code is not distributed. You do not want to put yourself at a vendor's mercy, especially a vendor who has never built a high-volume Web site for itself.

AOLSERVER

I saved my personal choice for last. I use AOLserver, which has been tested in thousands of production sites since May 1995. I have personally used AOLserver for about a dozen heavily used RDBMS-backed sites (together they are responding to about 100 requests a second as I'm writing this sentence). AOLserver provides the following mechanisms for generating dynamic pages:

- CGI, which is mostly good for using packaged software and/or supporting legacy apps
- "*.tcl" Tcl procedures that are sourced by the server each time a URL is requested
- Tcl procedures that you can register to arbitrary URLs, and which are loaded at server startup and after explicitly reinitializing Tcl
- Java byte code that is interpreted in the server process (not until the 2.2 version, slated for June 1997)
- C functions loaded into the server at start-up time

All but the first mechanism (CGI) provide access to the AOLserver's continuously connected pools of connections to relational databases and thus provide users with the fastest possible Web service.

Choosing among the latter four is relatively easy. The C API is out because you run the risk that an error in your little program will crash the entire AOLserver. Tcl and Java are slower than compiled C, but these inefficiencies are irrelevant for most RDBMS-backed Web applications. Delays in processing by the RDBMS and delays in transmitting data over the Internet will swamp any delays caused by interpreters. I don't use the Java API because it hasn't been written yet! That leaves two varieties of Tcl. The language and the API are exactly the same but the software development cycle is different. I use the "sourced at start-up" Tcl for applications like my comment server where I want DB-backed URLs such as /com/philg/foobar.html ("philg" and "foobar.html" are actually arguments to a procedure). I use the "*.tcl" variety for most applications because a change to a file is reflected the next time a URL such as /bboard/fetch-msg.tcl is loaded.

The first shortcoming of AOLserver is that it doesn't provide a lot of help for things like session variables. Meta-HTML, LiveWire, and a lot of middleware/junkware systems are more programmer-friendly if you want to do things like build up shopping carts. This isn't a serious shortcoming for me because I want to keep all of my software system's persistent information in the relational database anyway. At most, I need to be able to set and read magic cookies containing keys to relational database tables. This can be accomplished with fewer than ten lines of Tcl code.

The second shortcoming of AOLserver is that it is mostly being developed for internal AOL consumption. That means they aren't planning to develop any new versions for Windows NT. They aren't going to renew their contract with Informix that lets them distribute a free RDBMS from their Web site (people who went to http://www.aolserver.com/ before May 1997 were able to grab a full copy of Illustra 3.2).

They are publicly committed to continuing distribution of Unix releases (at least SGI Irix, HP/UX, Digital Unix, Sun Solaris, and Linux) and the program sits behind heavily accessed AOL sites, but they are no longer making a serious effort to compete in the general-purpose server market and aren't giving away the source code so that anyone else can take up the torch.

Despite these shortcomings, as of April 1997, I think AOLserver is the best overall development environment.

Note: I maintain an entire server with example applications in AOLserver Tcl, complete with source code at http://demo.webho.com. If you want to try out any of the examples in this book, you will want to at least download my utilities.tcl file from there.

CHOOSING

Picking the best choice from the above-mentioned products isn't easy. Whatever your choice, be sure that it will probably be wrong a year from now. There will be a superior product on the market. However superior this new product is, be sure that it will probably be a mistake to switch. Once you build up a library of software and expertise in Tool X, you're better off ignoring Tools Y and Z for a year or so. You know all of the bugs and pitfalls of Tool X. All you know about Tool Y and Z is how great the hype sounds. Being out of date is unfashionable, but so is having a down Web server, which is what most of the leading edgers will have.

Table 12.1 provides a summary comparison of the technologies mentioned above. "Software Development" looks at the lifecycle of writing dynamic Web pages. The best tools for loosely specified constantly changing programs like Web sites require you only to edit a file. The worst tools require you to edit a file, recompile an application, and restart the Web server program. "Safety" considers how likely your programming error is to trash Web services for everyone else. A high-quality API for experienced programmers is one that is very flexible with lots of powerful building blocks. A good programmer can always make an impressive application if it is possible to write bytes directly to the connection, send e-mail out of the server, grab a Web page from another site, and define new functions and data structures. Good programmers can build their own infrastructure quickly. Novice programmers need a different kind of API, though. For them it is best if the API advertises mechanisms for session variables, for example. That way they don't have to learn about the magic cookie protocol and other ways to figure out if a series of requests have been made by the same user.

Bring in Da Noise, Bring in Da Junk

Now that everything is connected, maybe you don't want to talk to your RDBMS through your Web server. You may want to use standard spreadsheet-like tools. There may even be a place for, dare I admit it, junkware/middleware. First a little context.

An RDBMS-backed Web site is updated by thousands of users "out there" and a handful of people "back here." The users "out there" participate in a small number of structured transactions, for each of which it is practical to write a series of Web forms. The people "back here" have less predictable requirements. They might need to fix a typo in a magazine title stored in the database, for example, or delete a bunch of half-completed records because your forms-processing code wasn't as good about checking for errors as it should have been.

Every RDBMS-backed Web site should have a set of admin pages. These provide convenient access to the webmasters when they want to do things like purge stale threads from discussion groups. But unless you are clairvoyant and

Table 12.1: Comparison of Technologies for Building RDBMS-Backed Web Sites

Product	Software Development	Safety	Performance
Oraperl CGI	Rapid	High	Medium
AOLserver Tcl	Rapid	High	High
AOLserver Java	Slow (must compile)	High	High
AOLserver C	Glacial	Low	High
Oracle Web Server 2.x	Medium	High	Medium
Informix Web DataBlade	Medium	Low (crashes)	Low (deadlocks and CGI overhead)
Netscape LiveWire	Slow	Medium (crashes)	Medium-high (inefficient use of RDBMS connections)
Meta-HTML	Rapid	High	Medium
IIS + ASP	Depends on language used	Depends on language used	High

API Quality (for experienced programmers)	API Quality (for novices)	Price	Bottom Line
Low (no simple hooks)	Low (no infrastructure)	Free	Low-risk, portable, but you can do better
High (email, geturl, passwordcheck)	Medium (no session variables)	Free	Low-risk, blazing speed, but better for good programmers
High	Medium	Free	Not available until June 1997
High	Medium	Free	Server API programming in C is to be shunned
Low (no flexibility)	Medium (no session variables)	$2,500	Painful installation, administration; bad support
Low (weak procedural capabilities)	Low (no session vars; no automatic double-quoting or defaulting)	Part of $15,000–$70,000 server package	Just plain bad
Medium (no email, geturl)	High (session variables)	$300-$1,500	A half-baked solution
Medium	High (session variables)	$2,500	The technology to watch
Low	Low	Free with NT Server	Inelegant but seems fundamentally sound; only for very experienced NT programmers

can anticipate webmaster needs two years from now or you want to spend the rest of your life writing admin pages that only a couple of coworkers will see, it is probably worth coming up with a way for webmasters to maintain the data in the RDBMS without your help.

CANNED WEB SERVER ADMIN PAGES

Some RDBMS/Web tools provide fairly general access to the database right from a Web browser. Both Oracle WebServer 2.0 and AOLServer, for example, provide some clunky tools that let the webmaster browse and edit tables. These won't work, though, if you need to do JOINs to see your data, as you will if your data model holds user e-mail addresses and user phone numbers in separate tables. Also, if you would like the webmasters to do things in structured ways, involving updates to several tables, then these kinds of standardized tools won't work.

SPREADSHEET-LIKE ACCESS

Fortunately, the RDBMS predates the Web. There is a whole class of programs that will make the data in the database look like a spreadsheet. This really isn't all that difficult because, as discussed in the previous chapter, a relational database really is just a collection of spreadsheet tables. This is the kind of program that can make it very convenient to make small, unanticipated changes. Microsoft Excel and Microsoft Access can both be used to view and update RDBMS data in a spreadsheet-like manner.

FORMS BUILDERS

If you need more structure and user interface, then you might want to consider the junkware/middleware tools discussed in Chapter 10. There are literally thousands of these tools for Macintosh and Windows machines that purport to save you from the twin horrors of typing SQL and programming user interface code in C. With middleware/junkware, it is easy to build forms by example and wire them to RDBMS tables. These forms are then intended to be used by, say, telephone sales operators typing at Windows boxes. If you're going to go to the trouble of installing a Web server and Web browsers on all the user machines, you'd probably just want to make HTML forms and server-side scripts to process them. Some of the people who sell these "easy forms for SQL" programs have realized this as well and provide an option to "save as a bunch of HTML and Web scripts." The plus side of these forms packages is that they often make it easy to add a lot of input validation. The down side of forms packages is that the look and user interface might be rather clunky and standardized. You probably won't win any awards if you generate your public pages this way.

CONNECTING

Both spreadsheet-like database editors and the applications generated by "easy forms" systems connect directly to the RDBMS from a PC or a Macintosh. This probably means that you'll need additional user licenses for your RDBMS, one for each programmer or Web content maintainer. In the bad old days, if you were using a forms building package supplied by, say, Oracle then the applications generated would get compiled with the Oracle C library and would connect directly to Oracle. These applications wouldn't work with any other brand of database management system. If you'd bought any third-party software packages, they'd also talk directly to Oracle using Oracle protocols. Suppose you installed a huge data entry system, then decided that you'd like the same operators to be able to work with another division's relational database. You typed the foreign division's server's IP address and port numbers into your configuration files and tried to connect. Oops. It seems that the other division had chosen Sybase. It would have cost you hundreds of thousands of dollars to port your forms specifications over to some product that would generate applications compiled with the Sybase C library.

From your perspective, Oracle and Sybase are interchangeable. Clients put SQL in; clients get data out. Why should you have to care about differences in their C libraries? Well, Microsoft had the same thought about five years ago and came up with an *abstraction barrier* between application code and databases called ODBC. Well-defined abstraction barriers have been the most powerful means of controlling software complexity ever since the 1950s. An abstraction barrier isolates different levels and portions of a software system. In a programming language like Lisp, you don't have to know how lists are represented. The language itself presents an abstraction barrier of public functions for creating lists and then extracting their elements. The details are hidden and the language implementors are therefore free to change the implementation in future releases because there is no way for you to depend on the details. Very badly engineered products, like DOS or Windows, have poorly defined abstraction barriers. That means that almost every useful application program written for DOS or Windows will depend intimately on the details of those operating systems. It means more work for Microsoft programmers because they can't clean up the guts of the system, but paradoxically a monopoly software supplier can make more money if their products are badly engineered in this way. If every program a user has bought requires specific internal structures in your operating system, there isn't too much danger that the user will be able to switch operating systems.

Relational databases per se were engineered by IBM with a wonderful abstraction barrier: Structured Query Language (SQL). The whole raison d'être of SQL is that application programs shouldn't have to be aware of how the database management system is laying out records. In some ways, IBM did a great job. Just ask Oracle. They were able to take away most of the market from IBM. Even when Oracle was tiny, their customers knew that they could safely invest in developing SQL applications. After all, if Oracle tanked or the product didn't work, they could just switch over to an RDBMS from IBM.

Unfortunately, IBM didn't quite finish the job. They didn't say whether or not the database had to have a client/server architecture and run across a network. They didn't say exactly what sequence of bytes would constitute a request for a new connection. They didn't say how the bytes of the SQL should be shipped across or the data shipped backed. They didn't say how a client would note that it only expected to receive one row back or how a client would say, "I don't want to read any more rows from that last SELECT." So the various vendors developed their own ways of doing these things and wrote libraries of functions that applications programmers could call when they wanted their COBOL, Fortran, or C program to access the database.

ODBC

It fell to Microsoft to lay down a standard abstraction barrier in January 1993: Open Database Connectivity (ODBC). Then companies like Intersolv (http://www.intersolv.com) released ODBC drivers. These are programs that run on the same computer as the would-be database client, usually a PC. When the telephone operator's forms application wants to get some data, it doesn't connect directly to Oracle. Instead, it calls the ODBC driver which makes the Oracle connection. In theory, switching over to Sybase is as easy as installing the ODBC driver for Sybase. Client programs have two options for issuing SQL through ODBC. If the client program uses "ODBC SQL" then ODBC will abstract away the minor but annoying differences in SQL syntax that have crept into various products. If the client program wants to use a special feature of a particular RDBMS like Oracle ConText, then it can ask ODBC to pass the SQL directly to the database management system. Finally, ODBC supposedly allows access even to primitive flat-file databases like FoxPro and dBASE.

You'd expect programs like Microsoft Access to be able to talk via ODBC to various and sundry databases. However, this flexibility has become so important that even vendors like Oracle and Informix have started to incorporate

ODBC interfaces in their fancy client programs. Thus you can use an Oracle-brand client program to connect to an Informix or Sybase RDBMS server.

The point here is not that you need to rush out to set up all the database client development tools that they use at Citibank. Just keep in mind that your Web server doesn't have to be your only RDBMS client.

Summary

- It takes a long time to fork a CGI process and watch it connect to an RDBMS server; fast Web sites are built with already-connected database clients.
- Running a relational database is a security risk; you may not want to allow anyone on the Internet to connect directly as a client to your RDBMS server.
- Writing the HTML/SQL bridge code in Tcl or PL/SQL is straightforward.
- Most Web/RDBMS software does not perform as advertised and will shackle you to an incompetent and uncaring vendor; just say no to middleware (becoming my personal "Delenda est Carthago").

In the next chapter, we'll look at the design decisions that went into a few sites.

Case Studies

Case 1: The Mailing List

Case 2: The Mailing List

Case 3: The Birthday Reminder System

Case 4: The Bulletin Board

Case 5: The Bulletin Board (Again)

Case 6: The Bulletin Board (Full-text Indexed)

Case 7: Classified Ads

Chapter 13

This chapter contains seven case studies, each with some actual source code. I present user interface, interaction design, and data modeling ideas that should be useful to you in many contexts. This chapter is not a step-by-step guide. If it were, it would be 800 pages long, absurdly boring, and extremely tool-specific. My classified ad system case (number 7) has some source code that works with the Illustra RDBMS and the AOLserver. But any of the ideas can be used with an object database and a Franz Common Lisp-based server. Most of the ideas are useful for building systems that don't have anything to do with classified ads.

Because I'm afraid that your eyes will glaze over and you'll skip this, I'll try to give you a hint of what is in store:

- Case 1 is straightforward and dull. It is intended to help you understand how AOLserver Tcl works with a simple mailing list registration application. Feel free to skip it if you already get it.
- Case 2 shows how to generalize this application so that many static Web services can share a single RDBMS-backed service. It is a powerful idea that I have used at least a dozen times.
- Case 3, the birthday reminder system, introduces the idea that less can be more. It does less than a calendar management program but is easier to use. Case 3 also demonstrates how to build a back-end to loop through a database table and send e-mail when necessary. In doing so, it addresses in a practical way an important question about concurrency and RDBMSs.

- Case 4, the bulletin board system, hammers home the less-is-more theme, showing how a less powerful Q&A forum can be much more useful to readers than fully threaded discussions.
- Case 5, the bulletin board system extended with user-requested features, pulls together a lot of threads from previous cases: generalizing a service with distributed maintenance; using e-mail to pull a community together around a Web site; sending e-mail alerts by a nightly sweeping function.
- Case 6 gets nuts-and-bolty with the full-text search capabilities of a modern RDBMS.
- Case 7 uses classified ads to show how most Web sites overdo their data modeling and search form. It also demonstrates the construction of an auction system and talks about which transactions are legal given referential integrity constraints.

I hope that you're inspired. If you don't have the patience to read the source code then please at least skim the text underneath each new case headline.

CASE 1: THE MAILING LIST

We went through this in the first chapter on RDBMS-backed sites, but now we'll do it over again with actual code. Remember that you want a mailing list system for your site. Users can add and remove themselves, supplying e-mail addresses and real names. You want to be the only one who can view the list and the only one who can send mail to the list.

STEP 1: THE DATA MODEL

```
create table mailing_list (
        email           text not null primary key,
        name            text
);
```

STEP 2: LEGAL TRANSACTIONS

Here are examples of the two types of transactions:

```
insert into mailing_list (email,name)
values ('philg@mit.edu','Philip Greenspun');

delete from mailing_list where email = 'philg@mit.edu';
```

STEP 3: MAPPING TRANSACTIONS ONTO WEB FORMS

A form (see Figure 13.1) to add someone to the list . . .

```
<html>
<head>
<title>Add yourself to the mailing list</title>
</head>
<body bgcolor=#ffffff text=#000000>

<h2>Add yourself to the mailing list</h2>

<form method=post action=add.tcl>
<table>
<tr><td>Name<td><input name=name type=text size=35>
<tr><td>email<td><input name=email type=text size=35>

</table>
<p>
<input type=submit value="Add Me">
</form>

</body>
</html>
```

Figure 13.1: Add Me form rendered by Netscape Navigator

. . . and a form (Figure 13.2) so that someone can delete himself from the list . . .

```
<html>
<head>
<title>Remove yourself from the mailing list</title>
</head>
<body bgcolor=#ffffff text=#000000>

<h2>Remove yourself from the mailing list</h2>
```

```
<form method=post action=remove.tcl>
<table>
<tr><td>email<td><input name=email type=text size=35>

</table>
<p>
<input type=submit value="Remove Me">
</form>

</body>
</html>
```

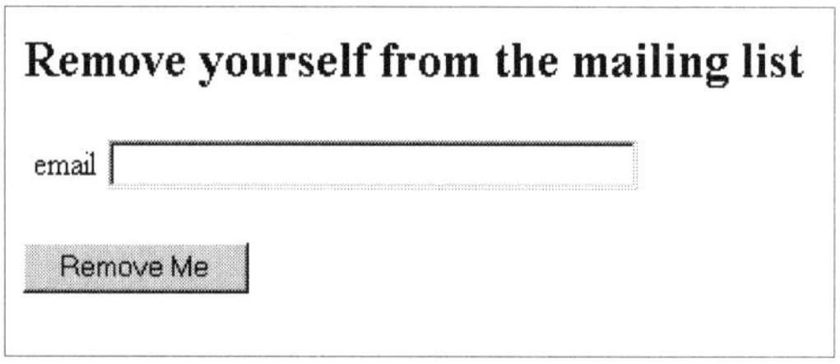

Figure 13.2: Delete Me form rendered by Netscape Navigator

STEP 4: WRITING CODE TO PROCESS THE FORMS

This is supposed to be the easy part and it really is. However, looking at someone else's source code is always confusing. Don't infer from your confusion that these are complex programs. The only real art to them is how they handle errors and ill-formed input.

Here is a AOLserver Tcl script to process the "add me" form. The script will do the following:

1. Check for user input errors in Tcl before sending anything to the database so that more attractive error messages can be returned.
2. Formulate an SQL INSERT.
3. Send the INSERT to the database.
4. Report success or failure to the user.

Here's the full program:

```
# call philg's magic functions to set local variables
# to what the user typed into the form
set_form_variables
set_form_variables_string_trim_DoubleAposQQ
```

```
# name, email, QQname, QQemail are now set
# get an open database connection from the AOLserver
set db [ns_db gethandle]

# Check for errors in user input before doing anything else

# we use the Tcl REGEXP command to see if the email variable
# has the following form:  1 or more ASCII characters (.+) followed
# by the "at sign" (@) then 1 or more ASCII characters (.+)
# followed by at least one period (\.) then 1 or more ASCII characters (.+)
if { ![regexp {.+@.+\..+} $email] } {
    # the REGEXP didn't match
    ns_return $conn 200 text/html "<html>
<head><title>Problem Adding $email</title></head>
<body bgcolor=#ffffff text=#000000>

<h2>Problem Adding $email</h2>

Your email address doesn't look right to us.  We need your full
Internet address, something like one of the following:

<code>
<ul>
<li>Joe.Smith@att.com
<li>student73@cs.stateu.edu
<li>francois@unique.fr
</ul>
</code>
<hr>
<address>webmaster@greedy.com</address>
</body>
</html>
"
    # RETURN terminates the AOLserver source.tcl command
    # so none of the code below this point will be executed
    # if the email address had an incorrect form
    return
}

# if we got here, that means the email address was OK
if { $name == "" } {
    # the variable NAME was an empty string
    ns_return $conn 200 text/html "<html>
<head><title>Problem Adding $email</title></head>
<body bgcolor=#ffffff text=#000000>

<h2>Problem Adding $email</h2>
```

```
You didn't give us your name.  Please back up using your
browser and make a more complete entry.
</body>
</html>
"
    # this terminates the AOLserver source.tcl command
    return
}

# Error checking complete; ready to do real work

# construct the SQL query using the versions of the form
# variables where apostrophes have already been doubled
# so that names like "O'Grady" don't cause SQL errors
set insert_sql "insert into mailing_list (email, name)
                values ('$QQemail','$QQname')"

# we execute the insert inside the Tcl function CATCH
# if the database raises an SQL error, the AOLserver API
# call ns_db dml will raise a Tcl error that would result
# in a "Server Error" page being returned to the user.  We
# don't want that, so we catch the error ourselves and return
# a more specific message
if [catch { ns_db dml $db $insert_sql } errmsg] {
        # the insert went wrong; the error description
        # will be in the Tcl variable ERRMSG
        ns_return $conn 200 text/html "<html>
<head><title>Problem Adding $email</title></head>
<body bgcolor=#ffffff text=#000000>

<h2>Problem adding $email</h2>

<hr>

The database didn't accept your insert, most likely because your email
address is already on the mailing list.

<p>

Here was the message:
<pre>

$errmsg

</pre>
```

```
<hr>

<address>webmaster@greedy.com</address>
</body>
</html>
"

} else {
   # the insert went fine; no error was raised
   ns_return $conn 200 text/html "<html><head><title>$email Added</title>
</head>
<body bgcolor=#ffffff text=#000000>

<h2>$email Added</h2>

<hr>

You have been added to the <a href=/index.html>www.greedy.com</a>
mailing list.

<hr>

<address>webmaster@greedy.com</address>
</body>
</html>
"
```

The AOLserver Tcl script to process the "delete me" form is much simpler.

```
set_form_variables
set_form_variables_string_trim_DoubleAposQQ

# now email and QQemail are set as local variables

# ask for a database connection
set db [ns_db gethandle]

# note that the dual calls to the SQL UPPER function
# ensure that the removal will be case insensitive
set delete_sql "delete from mailing_list
                where upper(email) = upper('$QQemail')"

# execute the delete statement in the database
ns_db dml $db $delete_sql

# call the special AOLserver API call ns_ill resultrows
# to find out how many rows were affected by the delete
```

```
if { [ns_ill resultrows $db] == 0 } {
    # 0 rows were affected
    ns_return $conn 200 text/html "<html>
<head><title>Problem Deleting $email</title></head>
<body>

<h2>Problem deleting $email</h2>

<hr>
We could not find <code>\"$email\"</code> on the mailing list (and our search is
<em>not</em> case-sensitive).

<hr>

<address>webmaster@greedy.com</address>
</html>
</body>
"

} else {
  # the delete affected at least one row so removal must
  # have been successful
  ns_return $conn 200 text/html "<html><head><title>$email Removed</title>
</head>
<body bgcolor=#ffffff text=#000000>

<h2>$email Removed</h2>

<hr>

You have been removed from the <a href=/index.html>www.greedy.com</a>
mailing list.

<hr>

<address>webmaster@greedy.com</address>
</body>
</html>
"

}
```

Case 2: The Mailing List

"Mailing list?" This sounds vaguely like Case 1. It is. Vaguely. It turns out that you need mailing lists for four other services that you offer. Also, ten of your friends want to run mailing lists for their sites. You'd be happy to give them your code, but you know that they aren't willing to endure the pain of maintaining a relational database management system just for this one feature. They are grateful, but "oh, while you're at it, would you mind allowing us to also store snail mail information?"

Could you make the code generic? You just need an extra table to store information about each of your and your friends' services.

```
create table spam_domains (
        domain          text not null primary key,
        backlink        text,    -- a URL pointing back to the  page
        backlink_title  text,    -- what to say for the link back
        blather         text,    -- arbitrary HTML text
        challenge       text default 'Your mother''s maiden name',
        response        text,
        maintainer_name         text,
        maintainer_email        text,
        notify_of_additions_p   boolean default 't',
        list_type       text     -- 'basic', 'snail_too', 'snail_plus_demographics'
);
```

Each domain is identified with a string, such as "photonet" for the magazine *photo.net*. Then you store the URL, http://photo.net/photo/, in the backlink column and the title, *photo.net*, in backlink_title. You provide a space for some descriptive HTML for the top of the "add me" form, something like, "You will get mail once every month describing new articles in *photo.net*."

Rather than a password, which your friends might forget and then bug you to manually retrieve from the database, you store a challenge question of their choice, such as "mother's maiden name," and their response.

You keep track, per domain, of the name and e-mail address of the list maintainer. If the notify_of_additions_p column is set to true, then your "add me" script will send e-mail to the maintainer when someone new adds himself to the list. Finally, you keep track of how much data is stored in the list_type column. A "basic" list is only name and e-mail. A "snail_too" list also asks for and stores a physical mail address. A "snail_plus_demographics" list also asks for age and sex.

Once that new table is defined, you need to beef up the mailing list table as well. It would be possible to build this system so that it defined a separate table for each new domain, but I think it is cleaner to add a domain column to the mailing list table as long as we're adding all the extra columns for physical mail and demographics:

```
create table spam_list (
  domain          text not null references spam_domains, -- which list is this
entry for
  email           text not null,
  name            text,
  -- info for 'snail_too'
  line1           text,
  line2           text,
  city            text,
  state           text,
  postal_code     text, -- ZIP+4 better, but five digits ok. Canada, too!
  country         char(2),        -- ISO country code
  -- info for snail_plus_demographics
  birthday        date,
  sex             text check(sex in ('M','F')),
  primary key( domain, email )
);
```

Note that you have to remove the primary key constraint on the e-mail column. There is no reason why philg@mit.edu can't be in the mailing list table ten times, each time for a different domain. However, you don't want philg@mit.edu on the photo.net list ten times. Thus the "primary key(domain, email)" constraint at the end of the table definition.

How does this all work? If you visit you can see the whole system in action. Here's an example of how the add-me.html form has been replaced by a Tcl procedure:

```
set_form_variables_string_trim_DoubleAposQQ

# "domain" was the one form argument so QQdomain is set

set db [ns_db gethandle]

# ask for all the columns in the domains table for this domain
set selection [ns_db 1row $db "select unique * from spam_domains
                               where domain='$QQdomain'"]

# call philg's magic function to set local variables for all columns
set_variables_after_query

# these are the basic fields, "name" and "email", that every mailing
# list will have.  If this domain requires more, they will be appended
set form_fields "<tr><td>Name<td><input name=name type=text size=35>
<tr><td>email<td><input name=email type=text size=35>"
```

```
if { $list_type == "snail_too" || $list_type == "snail_plus_demographics" } {
    # this domain wants a more complicated list; add Snail Mail fields
    append form_fields "<tr><td>Address Line 1<td><input name=line1 type=text
size=35>
<tr><td>Address Line 2<td><input name=line2 type=text size=35>
<tr><td>City, State, Postal Code<td><input name=city type=text size=12>
<input name=state type=text size=6>
<input name=postal_code type=text size=8>
<tr><td>Country<td><input name=country type=text size=3 limit=2> (ISO Code, e.g.,
\"us\", \"fr\", \"ca\", \"au\", etc.)"
}

if { $list_type == "snail_plus_demographics" } {
    append form_fields "<tr><td>Birthday<td><input name=birthday type=text
size=12> (YYYY-MM-DD format must be exact)
<tr><td>Sex<td><input name=sex type=radio value=M CHECKED> Male
<input name=sex type=radio value=F> Female
"
}

# finally return the page to the user
ns_return $conn 200 text/html "<html><head><title>Add Yourself to the Mailing
list</title></head>
<body bgcolor=#ffffff text=#000000>
<h2>Add Yourself</h2>

to <a href=\"home.tcl?domain=[ns_urlencode $domain]\">the mailing list</a>
for <a href=\"$backlink\">$backlink_title</a>

<hr>

<form method=post action=add-2.tcl>
<input type=hidden name=domain value=\"$domain\">
<table>
$form_fields
</table>
<input type=submit value=Submit>
</form>

<hr>
<address>
<a href=\"mailto:$maintainer_email\">
$maintainer_name ($maintainer_email)
</a>
</address>
</body>
</html>
"
```

Note how the final HTML page is strewn with values from the database, such as $maintainer_email, $backlink, and $backlink_title. Now it looks to all intents and purposes like it is part of your friend's service and you won't be getting e-mail from the confused. See Figure 13.3 for an example.

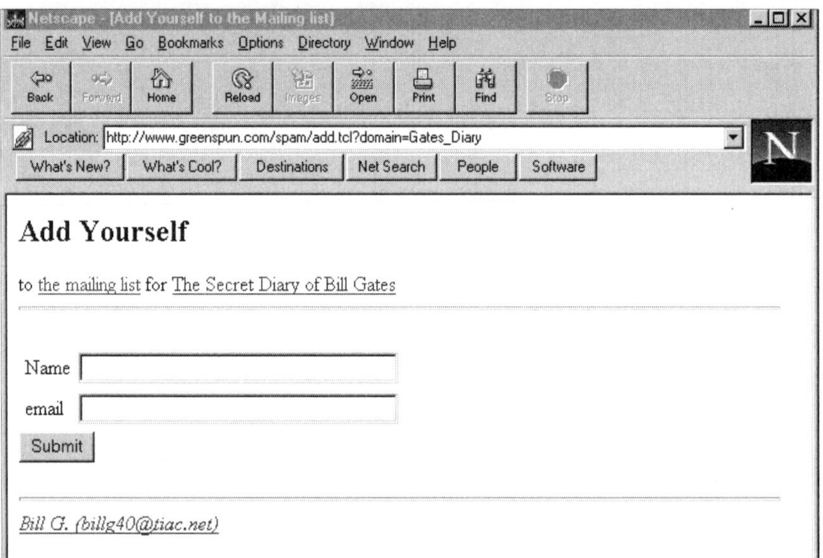

Figure 13.3: My mailing list system being used by another Web publisher (billg40@tiac.net). If users were to look carefully at the location box, they might notice that they were being bounced from www.tiac.net to www.greenspun.com after clicking the "join mailing list" link. Billg40 can keep his Secret Diary of Bill Gates at Tiac, where they don't run an RDBMS, and yet look just like a high-tech Web publisher with a staff of programmers and a database administrator.

CASE 3: THE BIRTHDAY REMINDER SYSTEM

Olin refused to give Alex (http://photo.net/photo/alex.html) a sample off his plate at brunch. "You're just a dog, Alex," Olin said. We pressed Olin as to his reason for feeling superior to Alex. Olin thought for a few minutes and all he could come up with was "I have a Ph.D. and he doesn't."

Olin demonstrated the practical value of his Carnegie-Mellon computer science degree by turning down Jim Clark's 1994 offer to become Employee #3 at a little start-up called Mosaic Communications (grab http://www.netscape.com

if you want to see how Jim and Co. are doing now). Consequently, his resort to credentialism set off howls of laughter throughout the room.

"Let's see what value society places on your Ph.D., Dr. Shivers," I said. "We'll take both you and Alex to Harvard Square and hang signs around your necks. Alex's sign will read 'Needs home.' Your sign can read 'Needs home. Has Ph.D.' Which one of you do you think would have to sit out there longer?"

"Nooooo contest," opined Olin's girlfriend.

Anyway, Olin clung to his belief that his Ph.D. was worth something despite the fact that the marketplace was crushing him under a burden of poverty to correspond to his burden of ignorance of how to build an RDBMS-backed Web service.

I kept offering to show Olin but he was too busy writing papers for academic journals that even he didn't bother reading. We began to joke that Olin was "afraid to be rich." Then one night Olin came over to my house and said, "Let's jack into this World Wide Cybernet thing."

We sat down to build a toy AOLserver/Illustra-backed birthday reminder system. Sure there are plenty of fancy calendar management systems that incorporate one-time events, recurring events, and reminders. But most of these calendar management programs require you to maintain them on a Macintosh or Windows machine. If you switch from computer to computer, they don't do you much good. We all read our e-mail no matter where we are, so why not build a system that feeds reminders into our e-mailbox? Again, it turns out that there are Web-based calendar management systems that will do just that. But these programs are very complicated. I don't have a job. I don't make appointments. I don't plan in advance. I don't want to invest in learning and using a calendar management program. I just want an e-mail message a week before my friend's birthday so that I can send him a card.

Olin and I sat down at 9 p.m. to build RemindMe. We were finished by midnight. Then we showed the text-only system to Ulla Zang (http://www.ullazang.com) and asked her to do a spiffy graphic design. Now we have a nice public service to offer.

STEP 1: THE DATA MODEL

Note: The syntax is for the Illustra 3.2 RDBMS.

```
--
-- this table has one row for each person using the system
-- the PRIMARY KEY constraint says that there can't be two
-- rows with the same value in the EMAIL column
--
```

```
create table bday_users (
       email          text not null primary key,
       password       text not null
);

--
-- we index bday_users because of the integrity constraint
-- on bday_reminders (so that an insert to bday_reminders
-- doesn't have to do a sequential scan of bday_users)
--

create index bday_users_by_email on bday_users using btree ( email );

create table bday_reminders (
       email                 text references bday_users,
       event_description     text,
       event_date            date,
       remind_week_before_p boolean default 'f',
       remind_day_before_p  boolean default 'f',
       remind_day_of_p      boolean default 'f',
       last_reminded        date
);
```

The first item of interest in this data model is the integrity constraint that values in the email column of bday_reminders must correspond to values in the email column of bday_users. That's what "references bday_users" tells the database. After a row in bday_reminders is inserted or updated, the RDBMS will check to make sure that this integrity constraint is true. If not, the transaction will be aborted. Also, nobody will be able to delete a row from bday_users if there are still rows in bday_reminders that contain the same e-mail address.

Integrity constraints are critical if you have users typing data into a shell database tool. But here users will only be able to access the RDBMS through our Web pages. Why can't we just write our forms-processing software so that it never allows bad data into the database? Well, we can and we will. But unless you are the rare programmer who always writes perfect code, it is nice to have the RDBMS's integrity constraint system as a last line of defense.

Thomas Jefferson did not say, "Eternal vigilance is the price of liberty." That's because he wasn't John Philpot Curran (Irish statesman who never set foot in the United States). Nor did Jefferson say, "Eternal sluggishness is the price of integrity." That's because he wasn't an RDBMS programmer.

Let's focus a bit on "values in the email column of bday_reminders must correspond to values in the email column of bday_users." It is not magic fairies who maintain integrity but rather plodding, stupid computer programs.

During every attempt to insert a row into bday_reminders, the plodding, stupid relational database management system will grind through every row in bday_users to see if the proposed value for the EMAIL column matches one of those rows. This is an "order *n*" operation, requiring time proportional to the number of rows in the bday_users table. If, however, we create an index on the bday_users table thusly

```
create index bday_users_by_email on bday_users using btree ( email );
```

then the plodding, stupid RDBMS can check the index instead of the full table. For the binary tree index we just created, this takes "order log *n*" time. If you have 64,000 rows, *n* is 64,000 and log *n* is about 16.

STEP 2: LEGAL TRANSACTIONS

You'd think that the most obvious legal transaction would be "add user to bday_users table." However, I decided to not make that one of the legal transactions. I don't want a table full of e-mail addresses for people who aren't really using the system. Thus it is only legal to add a user atomically with at least one reminder:

```
begin transaction;
insert into bday_users
(email, password)
values
('philip@greenspun.com','hairysamoyed');
insert into bday_reminders
(email, event_description,
event_date,remind_week_before_p,remind_day_before_p,remind_day_of_p)
values
('philip@greenspun.com','remember to finish PhD',
'1997-09-01','t','t','t');
end transaction;
```

This transaction inserts the user "philip@greenspun.com" with password "hairysamoyed" and a reminder to finish his Ph.D. by September 1, 1997. Reminders will be sent a week before, a day before, and the day of.

Suppose the user doesn't want to be reminded the day of? That's another legal transaction:

```
update bday_reminders
set remind_day_of_p = 'f'
where oid = '2056.2017'
```

OID? That's a non-standard Illustra hidden column, the "object identifier." It uniquely identifies a row. Pages leading up to this transaction can get all the columns of bday_reminders plus the oid by querying "select oid,* from bday_reminders." Mind you, if I were a good database programmer, bday_reminders would have a unique key. Either that or I would demand that the triple of EMAIL, EVENT_DESCRIPTION, and EVENT_DATE be unique and then use those as the key. Or I would add a REMINDER_ID column to the table and then assign unique values to this column from a sequence generator.

It is possible to index the table by EMAIL, EVENT_DESCRIPTION, and EVENT_DATE, then use a triple as a key. However, it makes for rather unwieldy looking update statements. Had I been using Oracle, I would have used a REMINDER_ID column and then inserted "reminder_id_sequence .NextVal" for the value. This takes advantage of a built-in Oracle sequence generation facility. Illustra doesn't have anything like this so I'd have to define a separate sequence generator table and complicate my transactions.

Where do I draw the line at vendor-specific kludges like this? On the client/server boundary. If other tables needed to refer to rows in bday_reminders, I'd create a REMINDER_ID column. I would never use an OID as a pointer from one database row to another because then my data model wouldn't be portable to Oracle or Sybase. However, in this case I'm just going to use the OID temporarily in my client Tcl program. If I move the system to another RDBMS, I'll add a key column to the data model and rewrite the two Tcl pages in question.

A reminder system with only one reminder isn't anything to write home about. We ought to be able to add new events:

```
insert into bday_reminders
(email, event_description,
event_date, remind_week_before_p, remind_day_before_p, remind_day_of_p)
values
('philip@greenspun.com','Wash dog whether he needs it or not',
'1997-12-01','t','f','t')
```

A week before December 1, I'll be reminded to buy shampoo for my Samoyed (he usually requires an entire bottle). I disabled the day-before reminder so that's "f," but I'll be reminded on December 1 itself.

One last legal transaction: deleting a reminder. Suppose that I finish my Ph.D. thesis (to which supposition my friends invariably respond, "Suppose the sun falls out of the sky"):

```
delete from bday_reminders where oid = '2056.2017'
```

Again, we're using the OID but just for the user interface.

STEP 3: MAPPING TRANSACTIONS ONTO WEB FORMS

My general philosophy is to have as few pages as possible. This keeps the user interface simple. Figure 13.4 shows the interaction flow for the RemindMe system. Oftentimes, the system uses redirects to pages that reflect current status rather than separate confirmation pages. For example, after a user disables a week-before alert, there is no confirmation page. Instead, after doing the database update, the Tcl script issues a 302 redirect back to the reminder summary page where the alert is shown to be disabled. Come add yourself as a RemindMe user (the system will be linked from http://webtools.com/wtr/ and http://arsdigita.com/) and then let me know if you think the interaction design is a success.

Figures 13.5 and 13.6 illustrate the evolution of our user interface.

STEP 4: WRITING CODE TO PROCESS THE FORMS

Here is the .tcl page that summarizes a user's reminders (see Figures 13.7 and 13.8):

```
set_form_variables
set_form_variables_string_trim_DoubleAposQQ

# email, password

set db [ns_db gethandle]
if { [database_to_tcl_string $db "select unique upper(password)
from bday_users
where upper(email) = upper('$QQemail')"] != \
     [string toupper $password] } {
    ns_returnredirect $conn \
                      "bad-password.tcl?email=[ns_urlencode $email]"
    # we've returned a 302 redirect to the user, now exit this thread
    return
}

# if we got here it means that the password checked out OK

# we're going to use this a bunch of times so let's save some work

set emailpassword \
    "email=[ns_urlencode $email]&password=[ns_urlencode $password]"

# we return the headers and top of the page before doing a query
# into the BDAY_REMINDERS table; that way the user isn't staring at
# a blank screen

# note: ReturnHeaders is one of my magic functions from utilities.tcl,
# available from http://demo.webho.com
```

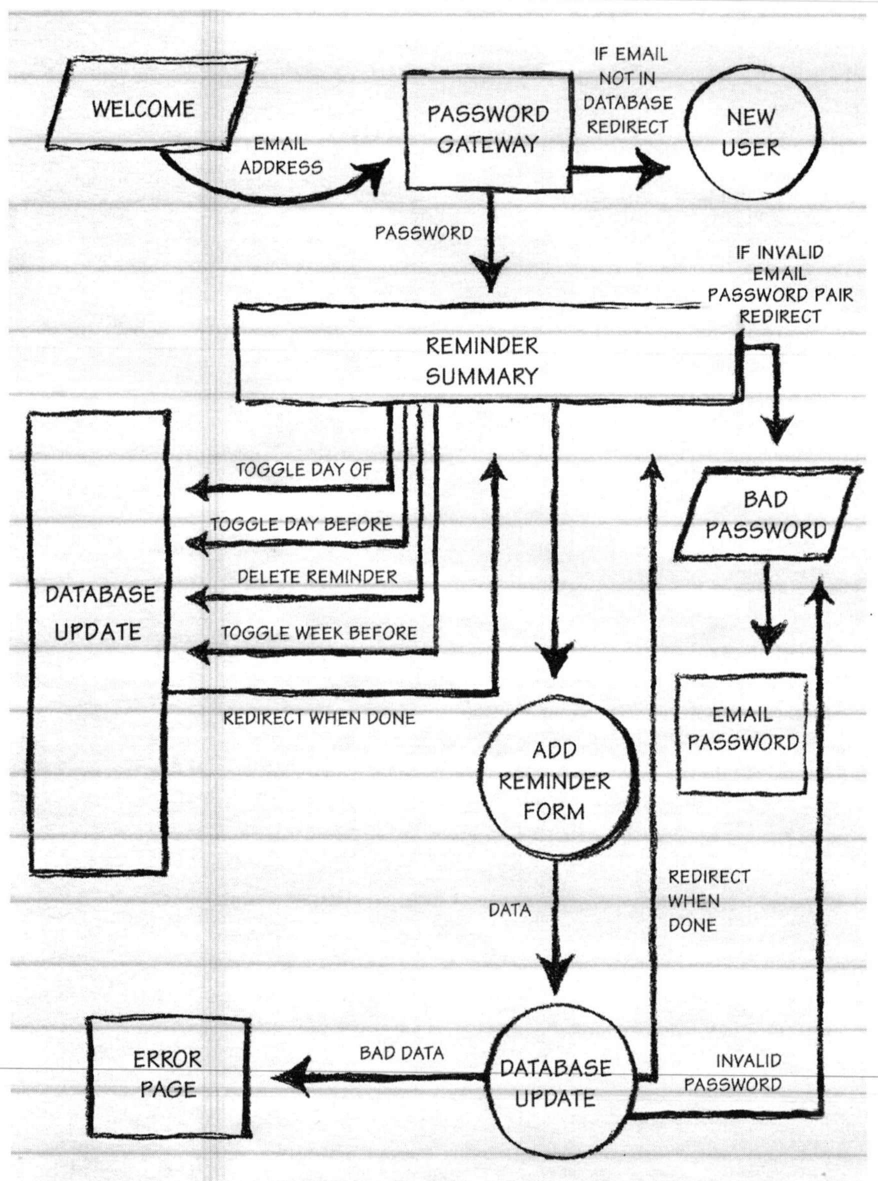

Figure 13.4: Interaction for the RemindMe system. Note the extensive use of redirects when bad input is received and/or after a simple update.

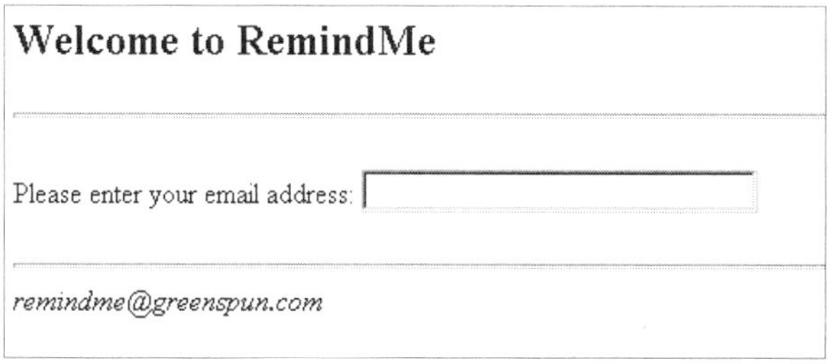

Welcome to RemindMe

Please enter your email address:

remindme@greenspun.com

Figure 13.5: The text-only welcome page, built by me and Olin

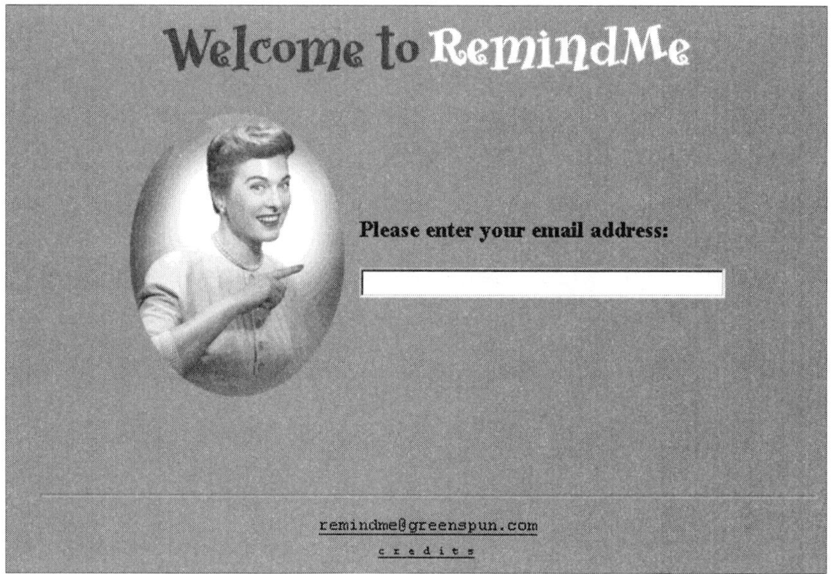

Figure 13.6: The welcome page, design by Ulla Zang; we saved a lot of time and heartache by completing our interaction design with a text-only site before consulting a graphic designer. Ulla turns out to be one of the few graphic designers I've worked with who is also an excellent interaction designer. Nonetheless, by having finished the programming beforehand, we were able to use Ulla's time to maximum advantage.

Reminders

for philg@mit.edu, held by RemindMe

- Mom's Birthday : May 20, 1934 [Week Before: On][Day Before: Off][Day Of: On][DELETE]
- Most Glorious Day Ever : September 28, 1963 [Week Before: On][Day Before: On][Day Of: On][DELETE]

- Add new reminder

remindme@greenspun.com

Figure 13.7: The reminders summary page, core of the user interface. Olin and I weren't satisfied with this design but decided to dump the user interface issue onto Ulla.

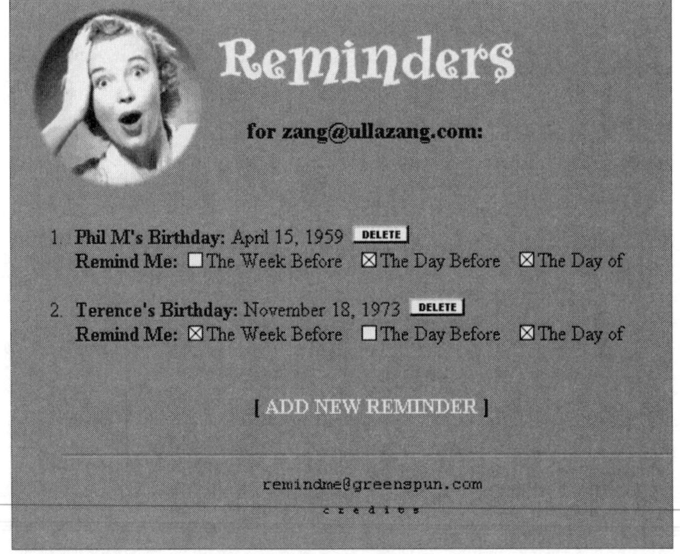

Figure 13.8: Ulla's reminders summary page. Much bigger than our text-only version, but also much cleaner. We'll be able to take her simplifications and translate them back into the text-only site as well. (That's another advantage of doing a full text-only site first; you always have something to satisfy the 28.8 modem crowd even if your graphic designer goes wild with huge images.)

```
ReturnHeaders $conn

ns_write $conn "<html>
<head>
<title>Reminders for $email</title>
</head>

<body bgcolor=#ffffff text=#000000>
<h2>Reminders</h2>

for $email

<hr>

<ul>
"

set selection [ns_db select $db \
"select *,
        oid,
        extract(month from event_date) as event_month,
        extract(day from event_date) as event_day
from bday_reminders
where upper(email) = upper('$QQemail')
order by event_month, event_day"]

while {[ns_db getrow $db $selection]} {
    set_variables_after_query
    ns_write $conn "<li>$event_description : [util_IllustraDatetoPrettyDate
$event_date] "
    # it would have been cleaner to think more and come up with
    # a general-purpose action.tcl function, but I think it is
    # also OK to do what we've done, use a separate .tcl page for
    # each kind of action

# for each reminder, we test to see if it is already set,
    # then present an appropriate current status hyperlinked to
    # a URL that will toggle the state of that reminder
    # note that we're using the Illustra OID as a key
    if { $remind_week_before_p == "t" } {
       ns_write $conn "\[Week Before: <a href=\"week-before-
off.tcl?oid=[ns_urlencode $oid]&$emailpassword\">On</a>\]" } else {
       ns_write $conn "\[Week Before: <a href=\"week-before-
on.tcl?oid=[ns_urlencode $oid]&$emailpassword\">Off</a>\]" }
    if { $remind_day_before_p == "t" } {
       ns_write $conn "\[Day Before: <a href=\"day-before-
off.tcl?oid=[ns_urlencode $oid]&$emailpassword\">On</a>\]" } else {
```

```
        ns_write $conn "\[Day Before: <a href=\"day-before-
on.tcl?oid=[ns_urlencode $oid]&$emailpassword\">Off</a>\]" }
    if { $remind_day_of_p == "t" } {
        ns_write $conn "\[Day Of: <a href=\"day-of-off.tcl?oid=[ns_urlencode
$oid]&$emailpassword\">On</a>\]" } else {
        ns_write $conn "\[Day Of: <a href=\"day-of-on.tcl?oid=[ns_urlencode
$oid]&$emailpassword\">Off</a>\]" }

    ns_write $conn "\[<a href=\"delete.tcl?oid=[ns_urlencode
$oid]&$emailpassword\">DELETE</a>\]"

}

ns_write $conn "

<P>

<li>

<a href=\"add-reminder.tcl?$emailpassword\">Add new reminder</a>

</ul>

<hr>
<a href=\"mailto:[bday_system_owner]\">
<address>[bday_system_owner]</address>
</a>
</body>
</html>"
```

Most of the interesting points about this procedure are documented in the comments above. The only thing worth stressing is that this is the meat of the user interface. The links from this page mostly just update the RDBMS and then redirect back to this page. For example, here's week-before-off.tcl:

```
set_form_variables

# email, password, oid

set db [ns_db gethandle]

# do a password check here as in the above procedure (code omitted)

ns_db dml $db "update bday_reminders
set remind_week_before_p = 'f'
where oid = '$oid'"
```

```
ns_returnredirect $conn "domain-top.tcl?email=[ns_urlencode
$email]&password=[ns_urlencode $password]"
```

This procedure just checks the password, updates the bday_reminders row, then redirects back to the reminder summary page.

STEP 5: STEP 5?

Yes, there is a Step 5 for this system: Making it work. If you are an Internet entrepreneur who has just raised $40 million for your WebJunkware System 2001 then Step 5 is optional. You only need a front-end good enough to show to venture capitalists and a screen capture program so that you can insert some screen shots into the initial public offering prospectus. If, however, you are a cringing little engineer whose ego is pathetically dependent upon producing a useful service, you need to write a back-end to send out reminders.

Almost all back-ends require that a function run every day at a set hour. I like to write my back-end code using the same tools as the rest of the system. In the old days, I would write the nightly sweeper or whatever as a dynamic Web page. Then I'd use the Unix cron facility to run a shell script every night (the Windows NT equivalent is the At command). The shell script would call htget (a Perl script) to grab this dynamic Web page.

AOLserver, however, has a built-in cron-like function. I prefer to use it rather than an operating system facility because it means less system administration when moving a service from one physical computer to another. Also, my code is portable across operating systems, and I won't need to install Perl scripts like htget.

It should be easy:

```
ns_schedule_daily 5 0 bday_sweep_all
```

This tells the AOLserver to run the function bday_sweep_all at 5:00 a.m. every day.

The first and most obvious problem with this statement is that the server might be down at 5 a.m. If we are careful to define bday_sweep_all so that it won't send out duplicates, we can just schedule it for a bunch of times during the day:

```
ns_schedule_daily 5 0 bday_sweep_all
ns_schedule_daily 9 0 bday_sweep_all
ns_schedule_daily 13 0 bday_sweep_all
```

The second problem is an AOLserver bug (my opinion) or feature (Doug McKee's opinion; he's one of the server's authors): If these statements are executed multiple times, the function will be multiply scheduled. For example, if you put these schedule requests in the Tcl directory that gets sourced on server startup and then reinitialize Tcl five times (to test changes in other code), you will find that bday_sweep_all is called six times at 5 a.m.

Here's my workaround:

```
global bday_scheduled_p

if { ![info exists bday_scheduled_p] } {
    ns_schedule_daily 5 0 bday_sweep_all
    ns_schedule_daily 9 0 bday_sweep_all
    ns_schedule_daily 13 0 bday_sweep_all
    set bday_scheduled_p 1
}
```

I tell the Tcl interpreter that the variable bday_scheduled_p is to be global among all the AOLserver threads. If it has not been set yet ("![info exists"), I schedule the sweep at 5 a.m., 9 a.m., and 1 p.m. Then I set the flag to 1 so that subsequent loads of this Tcl file won't result in redundant scheduling.

All we have to do now is write the bday_sweep_all procedure. We can expect the algorithm to be more or less for all three reminder types, so we posit a basic bday_sweep procedure that takes the reminder type as an argument:

```
proc bday_sweep_all {} {
    bday_sweep "day_of"
    bday_sweep "day_before"
    bday_sweep "week_before"
}
```

Now we just have to write the sweeper per se:

```
proc bday_sweep {message_type} {
    # message_type can be "week_before", "day_before", "day_of"

    switch $message_type {
       week_before { set sql_clause "remind_week_before_p
and event_month=extract(month from (current_date + interval '7' day))
and event_day=extract(day from (current_date + interval '7' day))"
                  set subject_fragment "NEXT WEEK"
                  set body_fragment "next week"
              }
       day_before { set sql_clause "remind_day_before_p
and event_month=extract(month from (current_date + interval '1' day))
and event_day=extract(day from (current_date + interval '1' day))"
                  set subject_fragment "TOMORROW"
                  set body_fragment "tomorrow"
              }
       day_of { set sql_clause "remind_day_of_p
```

```
and event_month=extract(month from current_date)
and event_day=extract(day from current_date)"
                set subject_fragment "TODAY"
                set body_fragment "today"
               }

    }

    # grab two database connections, one to look for reminders,
    # and one for updates to mark reminders as having been done
    set db_connections [ns_db gethandle [philg_server_default_pool] 2]
    set db [lindex $db_connections 0]
    set db_sub [lindex $db_connections 1]

    # we're going to keep track of how many reminders we sent and when
    set email_count 0
    set start_stamp [database_to_tcl_string $db "return current_timestamp(0)"]

    # we use our first database connection to look for relevant reminders
    # note that $SQL_CLAUSE is set in the SWITCH statement above
    # note also the final clause that prevents us from sending two
    # reminders on the same day for the same event
    set selection [ns_db select $db "select oid,*,extract(month from event_date)
as event_month, extract(day from event_date) as event_day
from bday_reminders
using (isolation level read uncommitted)
where $sql_clause
and (last_reminded <> current_date or last_reminded is null)"]

    while {[ns_db getrow $db $selection]} {
       set_variables_after_query
       # now all the columns from the DB are accessible as Tcl vars

       # we wrap a Tcl CATCH around the call to sendmail; we don't
       # want one error (e.g., a really badly formed email address
       # stopping the entire sweep)
       if [catch { ns_sendmail $email [bday_system_owner] "$event_description is
$subject_fragment" "Reminder:

$event_description ($event_date)

is $body_fragment.

This message brought to you by [bday_system_name].

If you don't want to receive these reminders in the future,
just visit [bday_system_url].
```

```
"
    } errmsg] {
       # failed to send email
       # this AOLserver API call writes an entry into the error log
       ns_log Error "[bday_system_name] failed sending to $email: $errmsg"
    } else {
       # succeeded sending email, mark the row as reminded
       # note that we are using the $DB_SUB database connection
       # so as not to disturb our sweep through the reminders
       ns_db dml $db_sub "update bday_reminders
set last_reminded = current_date
where oid = '$oid'"
        incr email_count
    }
  }

  # we're all done, let's log the work
  ns_db dml $db "insert into bday_log (message_type, message_count, start_stamp,
end_stamp)
values
('$message_type',$email_count,'$start_stamp',current_timestamp(0))"
  # we call these directly because bday_sweep_all calls this fcn
  # three times in succession and otherwise AOLserver won't allow
  # the ns_db gethandle to go through
  ns_db releasehandle $db
  ns_db releasehandle $db_sub

}
```

An interesting highlight of this sweeping function is that we add "using (isolation level read uncommitted)" to the first SELECT. Illustra uses a page locking system rather than the row level locking selectable (per table) in heavier duty RDBMSs such as Informix and Oracle. We want to make sure that we don't deadlock ourselves by trying to read from the table and update it simultaneously. The "read uncommitted" tells Illustra not to grab any locks on the table when doing the SELECT.

Oh yes, in case you were wondering, we do have to define the bday_log table:

```
create table bday_log (
       message_type    text,
       message_count   integer,
       start_stamp     timestamp(0),
       end_stamp       timestamp(0)
);
```

CASE 4: THE BULLETIN BOARD

In 1982, I tried Usenet news for the first time. I'd just graduated from MIT and took up my cubicle at HP Labs in Palo Alto. Though I had access to good operating systems (TOPS-20 and the Lisp Machine), for some reason I decided to ask for an account on the VAX, which was running Unix. I think it was my friend Luigi who signed me up to net.jokes. After two days, I counted one funny joke, five not funny jokes, 20 people complaining that Joke X was inappropriate for the list because it was racist/sexist/not funny/whatever, and 80 people complaining that the complainers should not have complained.

My Concurrency Question

Suppose I have two database connections open.

- Connection 1 does a SELECT * FROM BIG_TABLE; and then is slowly sweeping through it. The value of the FOOBAR column is 56 for all rows.
- Just as Connection 1 is reaching the 1,000th row, Connection 2 does an UPDATE BIG_TABLE SET FOOBAR = 15 WHERE ROW_ID = 2000.

Connection 1 eventually reaches the 2,000th row, maybe one minute later. Does Connection 1 find that the FOOBAR column has the old value of 56 or the updated value of 15? And is this behavior required by the SQL standard?

Answer from My Friend Who Works at Oracle

"OK: When you execute a query, the first thing the kernel does is take note of the time you started the query. As the query progresses through the table, it will look at the SCN ('system change number') of each row, which indicates when it has last been updated. If it finds that the row was updated after the query began, the kernel goes to the rollback buffer to fetch the last value the row held *before* the query began. So in your example, Connection 1 will not see the update made by Connection 2 if the update is done after the query begins.

"In fact, even after the query finishes and you start another, it *still* won't see the change . . . not until you explicitly commit the update. (I shouldn't say 'explicitly' since closing the connection cleanly will also perform a commit.) But even if you commit while the query is running, it still won't get the new value. However, the next time you query, it will catch the change.

(Continued)

I was so impressed with Unix and Usenet that I went to talk to the sysadmin, a paunchy black-T-shirted guy who sat in his cube all day reading science fiction novels. He'd been saying for years that he would upgrade the DEC-20's operating system to Digital's latest release, but instead the stack of novels just grew larger. Even top managers didn't dare challenge his terrifying power. He knew PDP-10 assembler and they didn't. It took all of my courage to even approach the man, but I decided that conquering my terror would be worth it. "Would you please delete my Unix account?" I asked.

About a decade later, my 18th year on the Internet, my officemate at MIT showed me the alt.sex hierarchy. I had no idea . . .

(Continued from previous page)

"But wait, there's more. Let's say you don't do a 'commit' in Connection 2, but you enter the same query as before, this time in Connection 2. While that's running, you also run the query in Connection 1. The results will differ. Why? Because the query running in Connection 2 *knows* you've made an update, and sees those SCNs rather than the ones stored in the permanent table structure. (Technically, before a commit, the results of a write operation are stored in the ITL, or Interested Transaction Layer. A session has access to the portion of those results performed in that session *only;* these operations are 'presumably committed' for the purposes of whatever you do in that session. It cannot, however, see anything in other sessions, which is why Connection 1 has no clue what you've done until you truly commit it.) This illustrates one of the challenges of concurrent programming with databases. Lesson 1: Always commit your changes as soon as you know they're permanent. (Corollary: Always have frequent backups for those plentiful occasions when they weren't and aren't reversible.)

"Regarding locks (a subject which I know for a fact varies among database vendors), Connection 1 will not lock the table, unless the person executing the query has explicitly done so beforehand by doing 'select * from table_name for update'. If so, it would be released after an explicit commit is typed, and Connection 2 would wait and/or time out while the lock is held.

"Most likely, you would not want to lock an entire table for a query. The only reasons I can dream of doing this are if

- You need to run a very long query (many hours).

(Continued)

With this deep affinity for and experience with bboard systems, then, who could have predicted that one day I would write my own?

CAN 30 MILLION USENET USERS REALLY BE WRONG?

Given the high average quality of information on Usenet, the obvious intelligence of the people posting, the high performance and reliability of news servers, and the quality user interface of such programs as rn (the incredibly primitive original Unix news reader), it is tough to believe that anyone would dare try improving on Usenet. Nonetheless, there are a few areas in which a database-backed bboard can be an improvement over Usenet:

- Have an optional "mail me when a response is posted" field.

(Continued from previous page)

- There are tons of transactions going on simultaneously.
- Those transactions are less important than the query results.
- You have a *very* small amount of rollback space.

"Remember that point where it finds a newer SCN and fetches the old value from the rollback? If the rollback doesn't go back far enough, the query errors out with an 'ORA-1555 : snapshot too old' error. So as long as the entire table isn't locked, and no other connections are locking the rows you need to update, Connection 2 will do its update right away.

"When Connection 2 does update, it will either lock the entire table or just the row it is trying to update, depending on the database's system and session parameters, such as whether something like 'ROW_LOCKING=ALWAYS' is in your oracle.ini file. I think the default is to lock the table, but don't quote me on that (it would be silly if we did, since row locking is a big thing for Oracle).

"The question of yours regarding the SQL standard: That I don't know. I've never read the ANSI standards for SQL or SQL92, but I do not believe there are any rules regarding the behavior of concurrent sessions. If there are, though, I'm fairly confident we're doing what it says. (If we weren't, we'd be fixing it, and I've heard of no intentions to do so.)"

My Conclusion

Thank God I don't have to write my own RDBMS.

- Provide full-text indexing (assuming your RDBMS supports it).
- Control access via all the usual HTTP mechanisms,
- Do secure transmission of data to and from the bboard via SSL.
- Use the admin pages to delete stale/ugly/whatever messages.

If you have enough money to buy and maintain an RDBMS, it is a fairly safe bet that you have enough money to buy Netscape News and Collabra Servers. These are reasonably full-featured products. However, they don't come with source code or much customization ability. If you want to learn how to design and build a collaboration environment that suits your users, keep reading . . .

STEP 1: THE DATA MODEL

```
create table bboard (

        msg_id          char(6) not null primary key,
        refers_to       char(6),
        email           text,
        name            text,
        one_line        text,
        message         text,
        notify          boolean default 'f',
```

Where's the Beef?

The only thing hard about building a threaded bboard system is sorting into threads. If all you have is a binary "response to" relation (that is, that Message N is a response to Message J), then you need to calculate the transitive closure of this relation to find the thread. I like using the phrase "transitive closure" because it makes me feel that computer science graduate school *really was* the best ten years of my life. Anyway, the transitive closure of a relation X is just the set of things that are related under relation X.

So what?

Well, transitive closure in the worst case (where all the messages are one thread) provably requires computing resources that grow as the cube of the number of messages ("order *n*-cubed" or $O[n^3]$). That's bad. It could be very expensive for the server and slow for the user if one had to calculate the threads every time the bboard was surfed.

My program cheats by calculating a sort key every time a message is added to the bboard. Then the thread sort is done with a simple SQL "order by" clause. This kind of sorting is "$O[n \log n]$" or maybe 100 times faster for a moderate-sized bboard.

```
        posting_time    timestamp(0),
        sort_key        text

);

create index bboard_index on bboard using btree ( msg_id );

create table msg_id_generator (

        last_msg_id     char(6)

);

insert into msg_id_generator values ('000000');
```

If you are using Oracle or Sybase, you'll need to use VARCHAR(2000) instead of TEXT for some fields and will have to decide if you want your message column to be LONG or VARCHAR (limited to 2,000 bytes in Oracle).

STEP 2: LEGAL TRANSACTIONS

There is only one legal user transaction:

```
begin transaction;
select unique last_msg_id from msg_id_generator
using ( lock = table, exclusive);
update msg_id_generator set last_msg_id = '00001n';
insert into bboard
(msg_id,refers_to,email,
name,one_line,
message,
notify,sort_key,posting_time)
values
('00001n',NULL::char(6),'philg@mit.edu',
'Philip Greenspun','generating some queries for my book',
'I''m posting this so that I can look in the server.log
and harvest the queries for my book...',
't','00001n',current_timestamp(0));
end transaction;
```

The first portion of the transaction is a bit odd. For message IDs, I'm using six-character strings. This bboard has been in use for awhile so the latest message had an ID of 00001m. The next ID after that is 00001n, which is what our new message will bear. Each character cycles through the integers, then the capital letters, then the lowercase letters. So after 00001z the next message is 000020, nine messages later, 000029, then 00002A, and 00002Z will be followed by 00002a.

This kind of sequence is rather tough to generate in standard SQL so I do it all in Tcl. However, that means that I have to read from the msg_id_generator table, do some computation, then write to the msg_id_generator table. That's the classic recipe for deadlock. We have to tell the database to lock the msg_id_generator table immediately and not start any other transactions using this table. That's why I added the "using (lock = table, exclusive)" clause to the first SELECT. (Note: in Oracle, we'd just use "SELECT .. FOR UPDATE" to accomplish the same goal.)

Sort keys deserve some discussion. The sort key for a top-level message like this is just the message ID, 00001n. For messages that respond to the top level, the sort keys are 00001n.00, 00001n.01, . . . , 00001n.09, 00001n.0A, . . . , 00001n.0Z, 00001n.0a, . . . , 00001n.0z, 00001n.10, . . . There are 62 possibilities for each character and two characters per thread level. So any one message can have 3,844 immediate responses. A response to a response will have a sort key with two extra characters, for example, 00001n.0900 would be the first response to the ninth response to top-level message 00001n.

This sort key enables me to get the messages out in thread-sorted order with

```
select msg_id, one_line, sort_key from bboard order by sort_key
```

and the level of a message can be calculated simply as a function of the length of the sort key.

The administrator is able to delete messages subject to the constraint that threads or subthreads must be removed together. In other words, it is not possible to remove a message if it has dependent messages. The user interface offers an option "Remove this message and its four dependents?" That way we make sure that no message ever has a REFER_TO column pointing to a nonexistent message.

Here's the kind of deletion that works:

```
delete from bboard b1
where msg_id in
 (select b2.msg_id from bboard b2 where b2.sort_key like '0000e6.%');
```

Just to be on the safe side, we've used correlation names for the two different uses of the table bboard. Because of the way the sort keys are constructed, this query will remove the message with ID 0000e6 and the entire thread that it supports.

STEP 3: MAPPING TRANSACTIONS ONTO WEB FORMS

I initially conceived my bboard system as a kind of runt Usenet. I went to a lot of trouble to make fully threaded discussions work and was going to deliver all of that power to users. So I dragged out the big Web user interface iron: frames. I'd use the top frame to show subject lines and the bottom frame to show the full message, just like all the Usenet clients (including the one built into Netscape Navigator itself). See Figures 13.9 and 13.10 for examples of Usenet and my bboard software.

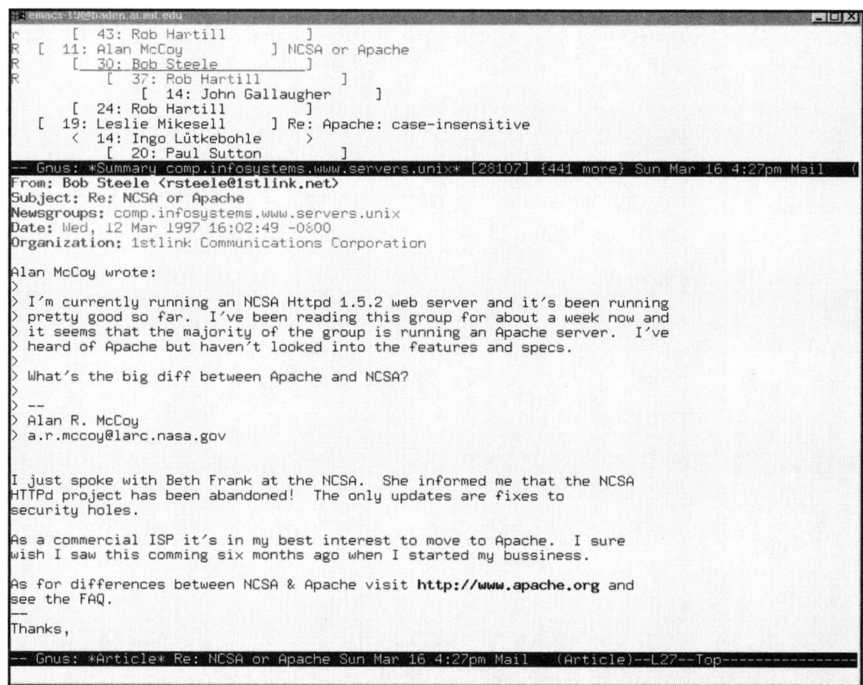

Figure 13.9: A view of the Usenet group comp.infosystems.www.servers.unix, presented by GNUS, the news reader built into GNU Emacs (a good programmer never leaves Emacs for any reason!). Subject lines for about 450 messages are available in the top window, the full text of one posting in the bottom window. Here Alan McCoy of NASA's Langley Research Center has asked about the difference between NCSA 1.5 and Apache. Bob Steele, who apparently runs a commercial ISP, tells him that NCSA has shut down their HTTP server project and points McCoy to the FAQ at www.apache.org. Despite what you might hear from politicians, this kind of exchange constitutes the overwhelming majority of Network News Transfer Protocol (NNTP) traffic.

After observing the forums in operation for a while, I realized that actually threads were annoying and overly complicated. A bboard anchored to some Web content was best presented as a question and answer forum. The questions would mostly be directed at the author but other readers might wish to answer as well. It would be a real user-interface convenience to be able to see the question and all the answers on one page. See Figure 13.11 for an example.

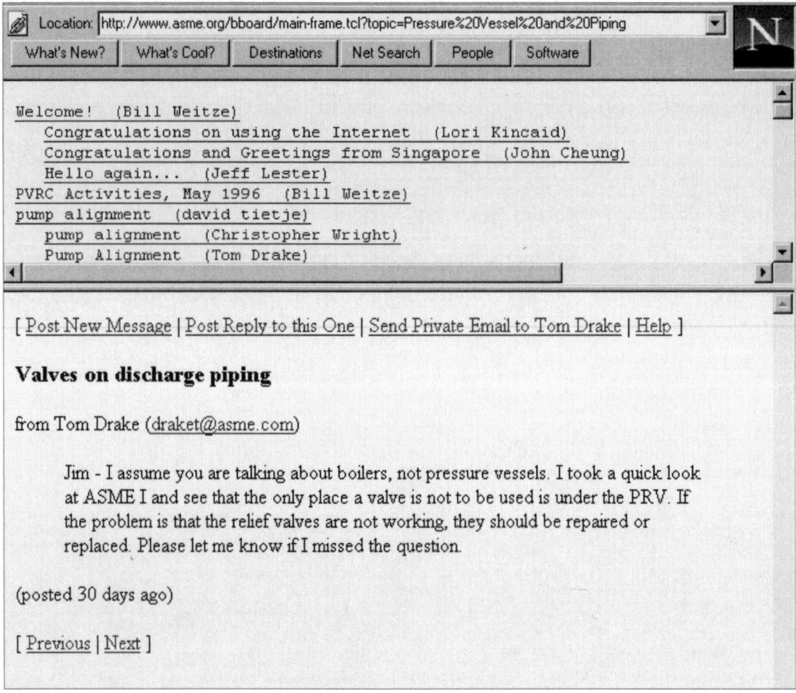

Figure 13.10: My bboard software in use at The American Society of Mechanical Engineers (http://www.asme.org/). ASME runs more than 40 public and private forums, mostly using the full threads interface. Casual inspection of the topics, though, reveals that most discussions have only two levels (question, answer, answer, answer, question, answer, answer, answer, . . .).

For a few minutes, I thought about starting from scratch to write a Q&A forum. Then I realized that I could drive the same data model from both threaded and Q&A user interfaces. Furthermore, I could make them interoperate. A posting from the threaded interface would be visible in the Q&A interface and vice versa!

How did I do it? An answer added from the Q&A interface has a subject line of "Response to $original_question_subject_line" automatically inserted. This is never displayed to users of the Q&A interface but threads users will see it in the subject frame. An answer added from the threads interface will have a custom subject line. This is displayed in boldface between answers in the Q&A interface.

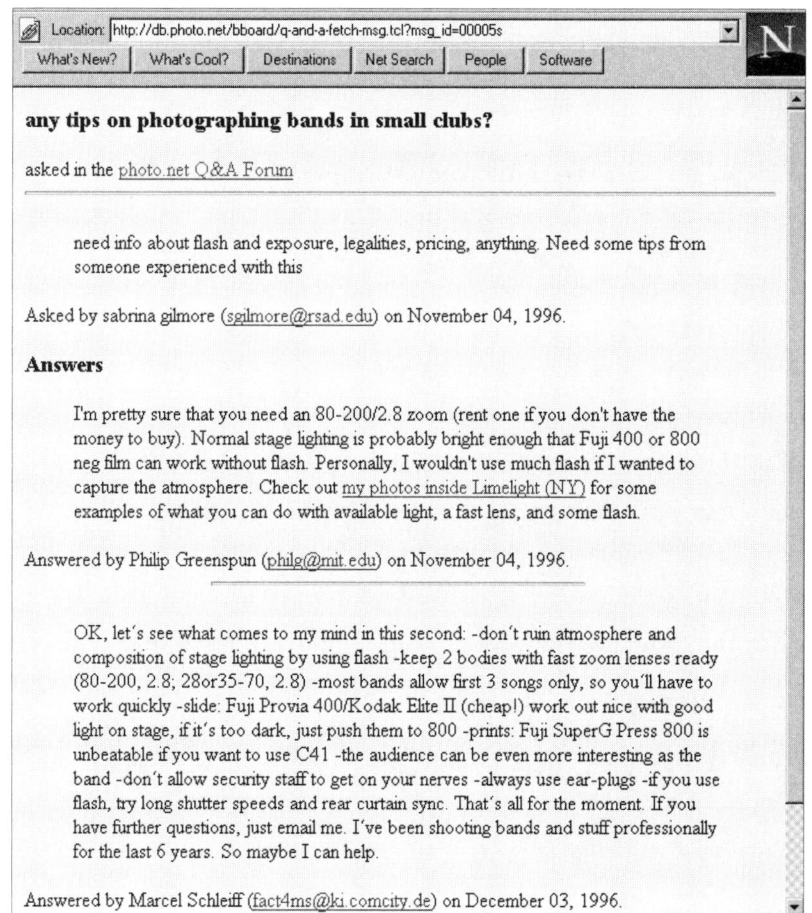

Location: http://db.photo.net/bboard/q-and-a-fetch-msg.tcl?msg_id=00005s
What's New? | What's Cool? | Destinations | Net Search | People | Software
any tips on photographing bands in small clubs?
asked in the photo.net Q&A Forum
need info about flash and exposure, legalities, pricing, anything. Need some tips from someone experienced with this
Asked by sabrina gilmore (sgilmore@rsad.edu) on November 04, 1996.
Answers
I'm pretty sure that you need an 80-200/2.8 zoom (rent one if you don't have the money to buy). Normal stage lighting is probably bright enough that Fuji 400 or 800 neg film can work without flash. Personally, I wouldn't use much flash if I wanted to capture the atmosphere. Check out my photos inside Limelight (NY) for some examples of what you can do with available light, a fast lens, and some flash.
Answered by Philip Greenspun (philg@mit.edu) on November 04, 1996.
OK, let's see what comes to my mind in this second: -don't ruin atmosphere and composition of stage lighting by using flash -keep 2 bodies with fast zoom lenses ready (80-200, 2.8; 28or35-70, 2.8) -most bands allow first 3 songs only, so you'll have to work quickly -slide: Fuji Provia 400/Kodak Elite II (cheap!) work out nice with good light on stage, if it's too dark, just push them to 800 -prints: Fuji SuperG Press 800 is unbeatable if you want to use C41 -the audience can be even more interesting as the band -don't allow security staff to get on your nerves -always use ear-plugs -if you use flash, try long shutter speeds and rear curtain sync. That's all for the moment. If you have further questions, just email me. I've been shooting bands and stuff professionally for the last 6 years. So maybe I can help.
Answered by Marcel Schleiff (fact4ms@ki.comcity.de) on December 03, 1996.

Figure 13.11: A typical question and answer in the http://photo.net/photo/ Q&A forum. You can see the question and all the responses on the same page. Note that I personally answered the question on November 4, 1996. One month later, a much more experienced photographer from Germany contributed a much better answer. Both answers were sent by e-mail to the woman who asked the question. This interoperates with the threaded discussion user interface against the same data model. That is, a posting in the threaded interface is visible in the Q&A interface and vice versa.

STEP 4: WRITING CODE TO PROCESS THE FORMS

I'm reluctant to give you a tour of this software because it is available for download from http://demo.webho.com.

CASE 5: THE BULLETIN BOARD (AGAIN)

The bboard project taught me something profound: When you build something in three days, you tend to leave out some important features. I released the bboard software to what I thought would be an adoring public. Instead they came back with

- Why can't I run multiple forums?
- Why can't I password-protect a forum?
- Can you send me e-mail every time there is a new message?
- Now that you've added password protection, why can't I use the Web server's user/password database for authentication?
- Why can't older postings in the Q&A forum be sorted by category?
- Why can't you show the poster's name or e-mail address in the subject line?

STEP 1: THE DATA MODEL

In order to support multiple forums, I need to store some information about each forum. No longer can I assume that the person who installed the software is the moderator. I need to support distributed moderation. So we at least need to store a maintainer_name, maintainer_e-mail, and admin_password for each group. Also, each forum needs to have a name and some links back to the static content with which it is associated. Finally there are some columns associated with Q&A presentation. Here's a new table in which information about bboard_forums is represented:

```
create table bboard_topics (
  topic          text not null primary key,
  backlink       text, -- a URL pointing back to the relevant page
  backlink_title text,  -- what to say for the link back
  blather        text, -- arbitrary HTML text for top of page
  admin_password    text,
  user_password     text,  -- for restricted bboards
  ns_perm_group     text,  -- for using AOLserver's permissions system
  -- non-null if we added a custom group when creating this topic
  ns_perm_group_added_for_this_forumtext,
  maintainer_name             text,
```

```
  maintainer_email      text,
  subject_line_suffix  text,  -- e.g., 'name'
  -- send email to the maintainer when a message is added?
  notify_of_new_postings_p    boolean default 't',
-- HTML encouraging user to search elsewhere before posting
  pre_post_caveat              text,
  -- present the Q&A or threads from the top level list?
  q_and_a_primary_p    boolean default 'f'
  -- stuff just for Q&A use
  -- note that the sort_order has an integrity constraint that
  -- prevents it from containing values other than 'asc' and 'desc'
  q_and_a_sort_order   text default 'asc' not null
         check (q_and_a_sort_order in ('asc','desc')),
  q_and_a_categorized_p boolean default 'f',
  -- defines what is considered "new" and therefore displayed above
  -- that older, categorized, questions
  q_and_a_new_days     integer default 7,
  -- at posting time, do we ask the user to suggest a category?
  q_and_a_solicit_category_from_userboolean default 't',
  -- do we allow users to type in new categories?
  q_and_a_categorization_user_extensible_pboolean default 'f'
);
```

Now that bboard messages can be categorized, we need to keep track of what the legal categories are:

```
create table bboard_q_and_a_categories (
   topic          text not null references bboard_topics,
   category       text not null,
   primary key (topic, category)
);
```

Note the integrity constraint that rows here must have a TOPIC column value that is present in bboard_topics. Also note the primary key constraint that prevents two rows from having the same TOPIC and CATEGORY.

We'll have to add two columns, TOPIC and CATEGORY, to the BBOARD table:

```
create table bboard (
  msg_id         char(6) not null primary key,
  refers_to      char(6),
  topic          text not null references bboard_topics,
  category       text,  -- only used for categorized Q&A forums
  email          text,
  name           text,
  one_line       text,
  message        text,
```

```
  notify         boolean default 'f',
  posting_time   timestamp(0),
  sort_key       text
);
```

Note that the CATEGORY column is only relevant for top-level posts in Q&A forums.

It was always my intent that the bboard system support casual collaboration by sending posters e-mail copies of responses to their messages. Also, the forum maintainer can opt to receive immediate e-mail notification of new postings. However, a lot of users asked for periodic summaries of postings. Here's the table that registers their interest:

```
create table bboard_email_alerts (
       email  text not null,
       topic  text not null references bboard_topics,
       -- we set this to 'f' if we get bounces
valid_p  boolean default 't',
       frequency text,
       keywords  text
);
```

Fundamentally this registers EMAIL's interest in TOPIC. Frequency is one of instant, daily, Monday/Thursday, or weekly. If I sign up for a weekly alert for the photo.net topic then I'll get a summary prepared early Monday morning. If I add a string to the KEYWORDS column, I'll get only those new messages that also match in the full-text index (see below). For example, I can restrict any frequency alert to only return messages related to "nikon." Instant alerts are e-mailed individually as new messages are posted.

We need a housekeeping table to implement the alerts. This contains the last time that alerts were mailed, used when querying for new messages, plus a count of all the messages that have been sent.

```
create table bboard_email_alerts_last_updates (
       weekly timestamp(0),
       weekly_total integer,
       daily timestamp(0),
       daily_total integer,
       monthu timestamp(0),
       monthu_total integer
);
```

STEP 2: LEGAL TRANSACTIONS

Not much has changed. If the user provides a category when posting a new question from the Q&A interface, we insert that into the bboard table. There are a bunch of new admin functions to manage categorization. There are a bunch of obvious transactions on the alerts table when users add and disable alerts.

STEP 3: MAPPING TRANSACTIONS ONTO WEB FORMS

Nothing too surprising here. I'll let the figures (13.12, 13.13, and 13.14) do the talking.

Administration for "photo.net"

a discussion group in LUSENET

[user page (threads) | user page (Q&A)]

Information about this BBoard

Backlink	http://photo.net/photo/ (a URL; whichever page this discussion group will be associated with)
Backlink Title	photo.net (the title of the above URL)
Maintainer Name	Philip Greenspun (the full name of the bboard administrator/moderator/owner, presumably this will be you)
Maintainer Email Address	philg@mit.edu (email address of the above person)
Admin Password	aardvark (administration password)
User Password	(user password; if you leave this blank, the bboard will be public; if you set it to something then only users who know the password will be able to use the system)
Subject Line Suffix	(legal values are blank, "name", "email")
Notify Maintainer of New Postings?	Yes No (the administrator will get email each time a post is made)
Default to Q&A format?	Yes No (any forum can be presented to users either as Q&A or as threads)

Update this Information in the Database

Figure 13.12: Top of the main administration page for the photo.net forum. Note that the administration can choose whether or not the Q&A interface is primary. There is a separate administration section for items that are only relevant to the Q&A code (see Figure 13.13).

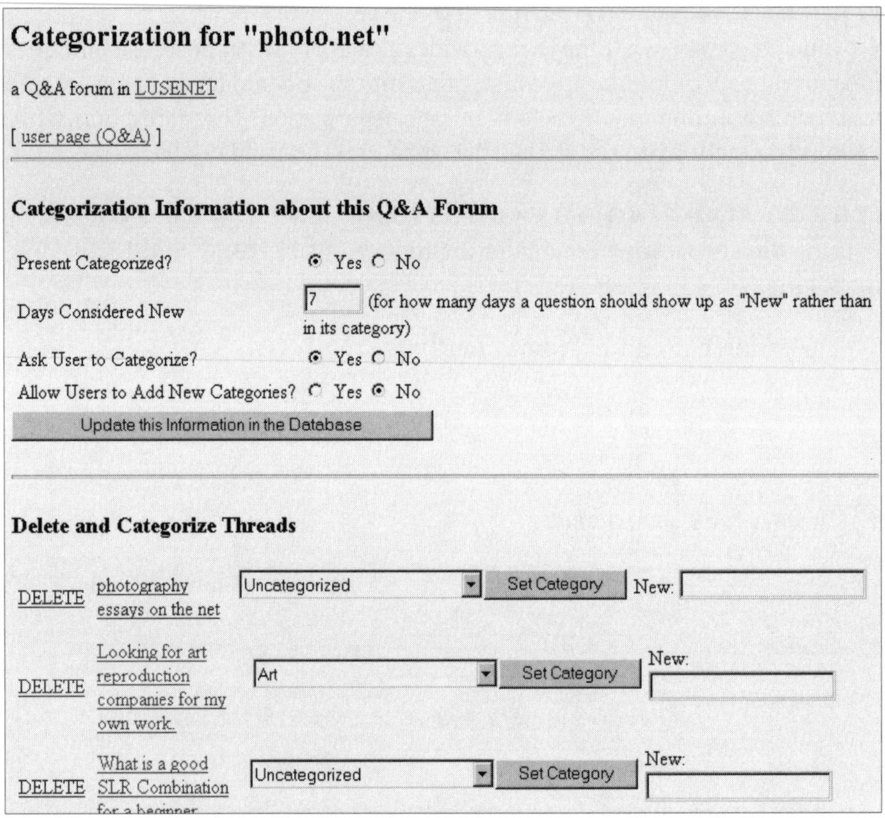

Categorization for "photo.net"

a Q&A forum in LUSENET

[user page (Q&A)]

Categorization Information about this Q&A Forum

Present Categorized? Yes No

Days Considered New 7 (for how many days a question should show up as "New" rather than in its category)

Ask User to Categorize? Yes No

Allow Users to Add New Categories? Yes No

Update this Information in the Database

Delete and Categorize Threads

DELETE photography essays on the net Uncategorized Set Category New:

DELETE Looking for art reproduction companies for my own work. Art Set Category New:

DELETE What is a good SLR Combination for a beginner Uncategorized Set Category New:

Figure 13.13: Q&A forum administration for photo.net. The top-level threads are listed below the "forum personality" slots from the bboard_topics table. Each thread can be deleted or categorized by the administrator.

STEP 4: WRITING CODE TO PROCESS THE FORMS

I noticed that a lot of naïve users were posting the same message two or even three times. Hence I added a check to insert-msg.tcl to see if there was already a row with the same TOPIC, ONE_LINE, and MESSAGE:

```
if [catch { set n_previous \
               [database_to_tcl_string $db \
                                "select count(*) from bboard
where topic = '$QQtopic'
and one_line = '$QQone_line'
and message = '[bboard_convert_plaintext_to_html $QQmessage]'"]} \
    errmsg] {
    ns_log Notice "failed trying to look up prev posting: $errmsg"
```

Add an Alert

for the photo.net Q&A Forum

If you'd like to keep up with this forum but don't want to check the Web page all the time, then this forum will come to you! By filling out this form, you can ask for email notification of new postings that fit your interests.

Step 1: decide how often you'd like to have your mailbox spammed by this server:

○ Instant (as soon as a posting is made)
or...
○ Daily ◉ Monday and Thursday ○ Weekly

Step 2: decide if you want to limit results by keyword

Keywords: [ ] (separate by spaces)

[Note: if you type anything here, you will *only* get notified when a posting matches *at least one* of the keywords. Keywords are matched against the subject line, message body, author name, and author email address.]

Final Step: Tell us your Email Address: [ ]

[Add My Alert]

Edit Previous Alerts

Not interested in this subject anymore? Going on vacation? You can put your alerts on hold.

Start by entering your email address: [ ]

Figure 13.14: Forms to let users specify new e-mail alerts and disable old ones. Instant notification is done by a thread that stays alive following each new posting to the forum. Daily, weekly, and Monday/Thursday notifications are done by a procedure scheduled inside the AOLserver.

```
    } else {
    # lookup succeeded
    if { $n_previous > 0 } {
       incr exception_count
       append exception_text "<li>There are already $n_previous
messages in the database with the same subject line and body.
Perhaps you already posted this?  Here are the messages:
<ul>
"
        set selection [ns_db select $db \
                          "select name, email, posting_time
```

```
from bboard
where topic = '$QQtopic'
and one_line = '$QQone_line'
and message = '[bboard_convert_plaintext_to_html $QQmessage]'"]
        while {[ns_db getrow $db $selection]} {
           set_variables_after_query
           append exception_text "<li>$posting_time by $name ($email)\n"
        }
        append exception_text "</ul>
If you are sure that you also want to post this message, then back up
and change at least one character in the subject or message area,
then resubmit."

    }
}
```

Note that this check doesn't have too much confidence in itself. It offers the user a list of the previous messages and ultimately relies on human intelligence. Input validation is nice but there is always a risk that it will outsmart itself and squash legitimate postings.

CASE 6: THE BULLETIN BOARD (FULL-TEXT INDEXED)

When the LUSENET software is installed at a site with the Illustra PLS Blade for full-text indexing, I take advantage of it by adding a PLS index on the bboard table:

```
create index bboard_pls_index on bboard using pls
( one_line, message, email, name );
```

This means that all the words in all four of the named columns will be indexed. How do you query using the index? Here's an example:

```
select msg_id, one_line
from PlsQueryOrdered('bboard_pls_index',
                    'Canon macro lenses')::setof("Table bboard")
where topic='photo.net';
```

This user is looking for a discussion of "Canon macro lenses" in the http://photo.net/photo/ bboard (see Figure 13.15). The function PlsQueryOrdered returns a set of rows from the bboard_pls_index that match this query, ordered by relevance. For obscure reasons known only to Illustra, these must be explicitly type-cast to "set of rows from the bboard table" with

```
setof("Table bboard")
```

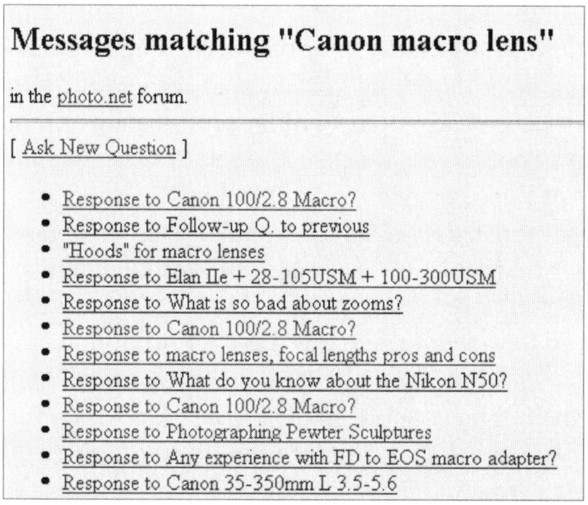

Messages matching "Canon macro lens"

in the photo.net forum.

[Ask New Question]

- Response to Canon 100/2.8 Macro?
- Response to Follow-up Q. to previous
- "Hoods" for macro lenses
- Response to Elan IIe + 28-105USM + 100-300USM
- Response to What is so bad about zooms?
- Response to Canon 100/2.8 Macro?
- Response to macro lenses, focal lengths pros and cons
- Response to What do you know about the Nikon N50?
- Response to Canon 100/2.8 Macro?
- Response to Photographing Pewter Sculptures
- Response to Any experience with FD to EOS macro adapter?
- Response to Canon 35-350mm L 3.5-5.6

Figure 13.15: The brilliant Illustra/PLS Blade finds all the messages relevant to the query string "Canon macro lens." My software makes each search hit a link to the full question and answer page so that users see answers in context. The subject line "Response to Canon 100/2.8 Macro?" appears several times because several of the six responses to this message are relevant to the query string. I could reformulate the query to eliminate duplicates but in some ways the repetition is good because it encourages the user to look at that thread.

After the cast, we can do anything we want with these rows. We can restrict the SELECT with WHERE clauses, in this case to messages from the photo.net topic. We can restrict the columns retrieved with the FROM list. We can JOIN with another table.

Although in general Illustra/PLS is clever enough that I don't have to even try to be clever, I did do one intelligent thing in my implementation of full-text search for my bboard system. In the Q&A interface, when the user's query matches a response to a message, clicking on the search hit takes the user to the standard page with the full question plus all the responses. In the threads interface, the user gets the option of seeing the full thread or just the message in question.

Case 7: Classified Ads

Once you have an RDBMS that can index the strings, it would be a crime if you didn't build a good classified ad system. I've built about five classified systems and think I've learned one or two useful things.

First is a publishing philosophy point. People who come from the dead-trees world always want to charge money for online classifieds. Their dead-trees publication makes a huge profit selling classifieds to readers and they think that they can cup their palms then lap up similar profits online. In meetings with such folks, I'd point out the existence of Usenet. Anyone who is online has access to hundreds of free classified services, including Usenet newsgroups. Why should they pay to be listed in a Web classifieds system that surely gets less traffic than ba.market.vehicles (1,000 messages a month; *ba* stands for "Bay Area"—San Francisco, that is) or rec.photo.marketplace (5,000 messages a month)?

It then occurred to me that there was a deeper point to be made. Given that Web publishers pay nothing for paper and printing, someone placing a classified ad is doing the publisher a big favor. The ad placer is contributing content. The publisher can use that content to build traffic, sell ads, and lure readers into other services. If anything, the publisher should be paying advertisers to post classifieds.

That's Useful Thing 1: Don't think about charging money unless you have some kind of monopoly.

My second epiphany is that full-text search engines work well enough that you don't need much structure in your data model. Typical RDBMS-backed Web sites appear to have been developed by 15-year-olds who unpacked their Oracle boxes and said, "Cool, I can have lots of different columns and then limit my searches based on values in those columns." The casual user of such a site is very quickly confronted with a 15-input search form. Fifteen inputs to fill out? All the user wanted to do was browse around and see what was in the system. After making those fifteen choices, the complicated query is submitted to a relational database management system that works heroically to produce…zero matches.

This design might have been great if there were 275,000 ads in the database, but not if there are only 300. For some kinds of classifieds systems, personals, for example, part of the fun is browsing ads that aren't 100-percent relevant.

Oracle ConText Instead

With Oracle ConText, the syntax is a bit hairier for creating the index:

```
execute ctx_ddl.create_policy('BBOARD_POLICY', BBOARD.MESSAGE);
execute ctx_ddl.create_index('BBOARD_POLICY');
```

but then somewhat simpler for queries:

```
select * from BBOARD where contains(MESSAGE, 'Canon macro lenses')>0;
```

Forms that encourage overconstrained searches rob users of their fun. Furthermore, the heavy structure of the data model imposes a burden on users when they are entering ads.

Useful Thing 2: Don't add columns to your data model if you won't be allowing users to constrain searches based on those values.

At this point, you're probably nodding your head and wondering how someone who belabors the obvious to the extent that I do can get published on real dead trees. Yet in February 1997 I was asked by a publisher, call them Naif News, to evaluate a bunch of commercial classified ad systems. Naif News publishes more than 100 small newspapers so they were being wooed heavily. Millions of dollars were about to change hands. The vendors had already sold systems to dozens of newspapers and were online with graphics-heavy user interfaces.

What did I find? All of these vendors had fallen into the "15-year-old with Oracle" trap. It was very difficult to construct a query that would return any ads at all, even when they had thousands of ads in their database. Furthermore, their structured systems weren't able to use the structure to do simple things such as return Chevrolet and Chevy ads to someone querying for "Chevy" in the manufacturer column (any full-text search engine would have figured out for itself that Chevy and Chevrolet are related words after seeing a few hundred ads).

Enough about how stupid everyone else is . . . let's talk about how stupid I am.

CLASSIFIEDS IDEA: CATEGORIZE

My generic classified ads system depends first upon categorization of ads. User interface research back in the 1960s concluded that humans are very bad at formulating boolean queries, for example "Nikon AND NOT microscope AND NOT 'integrated circuit mask stepper'". The Holy Grail of information retrieval was supposed to be the full-text search engine that is so common today. Just type in a string that reflects your curiosity, look at some results, then refine by picking a good result and asking for "more like this."

Why then categorize? Why bother to make users of my http://photo.net/photo/ classifieds say whether they are placing an ad for Underwater Equipment or Darkroom? Why can't the search engine direct people to appropriate ads?

It turns out that users have trouble coming up with that initial query string. It is a lot easier to browse than to think. It is also a lot more efficient for the RDBMS to grab all ads in the Underwater category rather than send PLS off looking for "flash for my Nikonos V." There are only about ten ads in the Underwater section most of the time so why not let the user see all of them?

How to come up with the right set of categories? I made "user_extensible_categorization" a settable option. If set, users of the classified service in question can type in arbitrary new categories that then become available as menu options for everyone else.

CLASSIFIEDS IDEA: AUTOMATIC MANAGEMENT

I don't want to spend the rest of my life managing my classified ad system. Users post ads using forms. Users edit and delete their obsolete ads by typing in a password. If the password isn't the same as what they typed when they posted the ad, my software offers to e-mail it to them.

How well does this work? My system has handled about 4,100 ads so far. I've gotten about ten e-mail messages asking me to edit ads. In all but one or two cases, the user was able to edit his own ad after I pointed him to the forms.

CLASSIFIEDS IDEA: E-MAIL ALERTS

With only a few hundred current ads in my database, I have to do something to distinguish myself from rec.photo.marketplace with its 1,000 current ads at any time. Starting a couple of years ago, I offered to mail out e-mail alerts to people who were interested in seeing all the ads, just ads in a particular category, or just ads that match a query string (according to PLS). There are 205 people currently requesting alerts (options are daily, Monday/Thursday, and weekly as with the RemindMe system).

CLASSIFIEDS IDEA: SHOW OFF NEW ADS

One-line summaries of the newest ads should be displayed on the very first page of the system. Users shouldn't have to click to see ads.

CLASSIFIEDS IDEA: AUCTION

One thing that Web classifieds can do that newspaper classifieds can't is turn into an auction. Users of my system can choose at posting time whether or not they'd like Philip's Classifieds to record bids. A bid is instantly e-mailed to the seller and is also displayed underneath the ad for subsequent displays (see Figure 13.16).

STEPS 1–4

My classified system is a bit too complicated to describe in a book. However, I think it is worth showing off a few points, starting with the cover page (see Figures 13.17 and 13.18).

Cannon EOS 300 2.8L Pristine Cond.$3800 B/O

advertised 12 days ago in the photo.net Classifieds by EricZ@EZarakov.XO.Com (Eric Zarakov)

Barely used EOS 300 2.8L lens. This is literally a flawless lens that I bought new and used just a few times. Rather than sit in my closet, it belongs in the hands of someone who has a need for it, wants a new lens and is looking for a bargin.

Place a bid | Reply privately to EricZ@EZarakov.XO.Com

Note: if you place a bid using the whizzy auction software, email will be sent immediately to EricZ@EZarakov.XO.Com notifying him/her of the new bid.

Bids

- 2750.00 US dollars bid by Majik1187@aol.com (Mathew Joseph) at 1997-03-11 23:37:10 in Yonkers,NY
- 2600.00 US dollars bid by homefs@cei.net (Lee Moore) at 1997-03-11 22:48:01 in Fort Smith
- 2500.00 US dollars bid by billyy@worldnet.att.net (Bill McCloe) at 1997-03-10 10:40:16 in New York
- 2400.00 US dollars bid by mer@mail.odyssey.net (John Merriman) at 1997-03-08 23:19:51 in New York
- 2300.00 US dollars bid by billyy@worldnet.att.net (Bill McCloe) at 1997-03-07 15:47:50 in NY City
- 2000.00 US dollars bid by lscottmann@aol.com (L. Scott Mann) at 1997-03-03 20:56:16 in Texas
- 10.00 US dollars bid by EricZ@EZarakov.XO.Com (TestBid for Eric) at 1997-03-03 19:33:03 in San Francisco

Figure 13.16: My generic classified ad system can be configured to run auctions for advertised items. Eric Zarakov is auctioning a delicious Canon EOS 300/2.8L lens. They cost about $4,600 new. Mr. Zarakov is asking $3,800 or best offer. Over eight days, he has received six bids (the highest so far is $2,750). (Note: this is not the most expensive item sold in the http://photo.net/photo classifieds; that distinction belongs to a $20,000 Zeiss 300mm lens. The seller was so grateful that he wanted to send me some money. I told him that the classifieds were a free service. He insisted. I asked him to write a check for whatever amount he deemed appropriate to Angell Memorial Animal Hospital. I didn't hear from him for a few weeks. Eventually I and Angell got the check. It turned out that the seller had a millionaire relative who'd died and left all of her money to an animal charity, rather disappointing the family. My request was a painful reminder!)

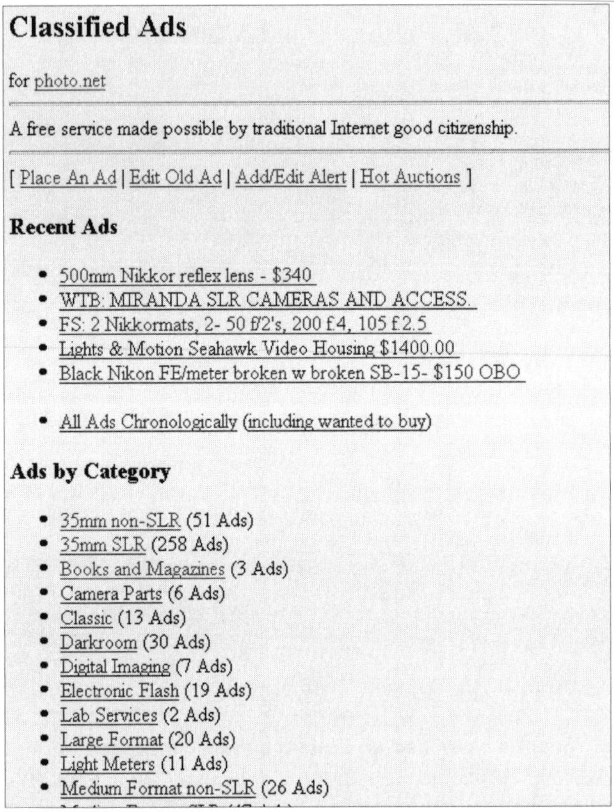

Classified Ads

for photo.net

A free service made possible by traditional Internet good citizenship.

[Place An Ad | Edit Old Ad | Add/Edit Alert | Hot Auctions]

Recent Ads

- 500mm Nikkor reflex lens - $340
- WTB: MIRANDA SLR CAMERAS AND ACCESS.
- FS: 2 Nikkormats, 2- 50 f/2's, 200 f.4, 105 f.2.5
- Lights & Motion Seahawk Video Housing $1400.00
- Black Nikon FE/meter broken w broken SB-15- $150 OBO

- All Ads Chronologically (including wanted to buy)

Ads by Category

- 35mm non-SLR (51 Ads)
- 35mm SLR (258 Ads)
- Books and Magazines (3 Ads)
- Camera Parts (6 Ads)
- Classic (13 Ads)
- Darkroom (30 Ads)
- Digital Imaging (7 Ads)
- Electronic Flash (19 Ads)
- Lab Services (2 Ads)
- Large Format (20 Ads)
- Light Meters (11 Ads)
- Medium Format non-SLR (26 Ads)

Figure 13.17: Top-level page for a domain in my generic classifieds system. Note that the user gets a tremendous amount of information right on the first page: one-line summaries of recent ads, a listing of the available categories, a count of the number of ads in each category. See Figure 13.18 for the bottom of the page.

The Cover Page First, here's a table that defines an ad *domain*. I run classifieds for photo.net, Web Tools Review, and Web Travel Review all from the same server (http://classifieds.photo.net/gc/) and from the same tables. Each of these publications is a domain as far as my generic classified system is concerned. Here's what I represent for each domain:

```
create table ad_domains (
  domain               text not null primary key,
  maintainer_name      text,
  maintainer_email     text,
  maintainer_telephone text,
```

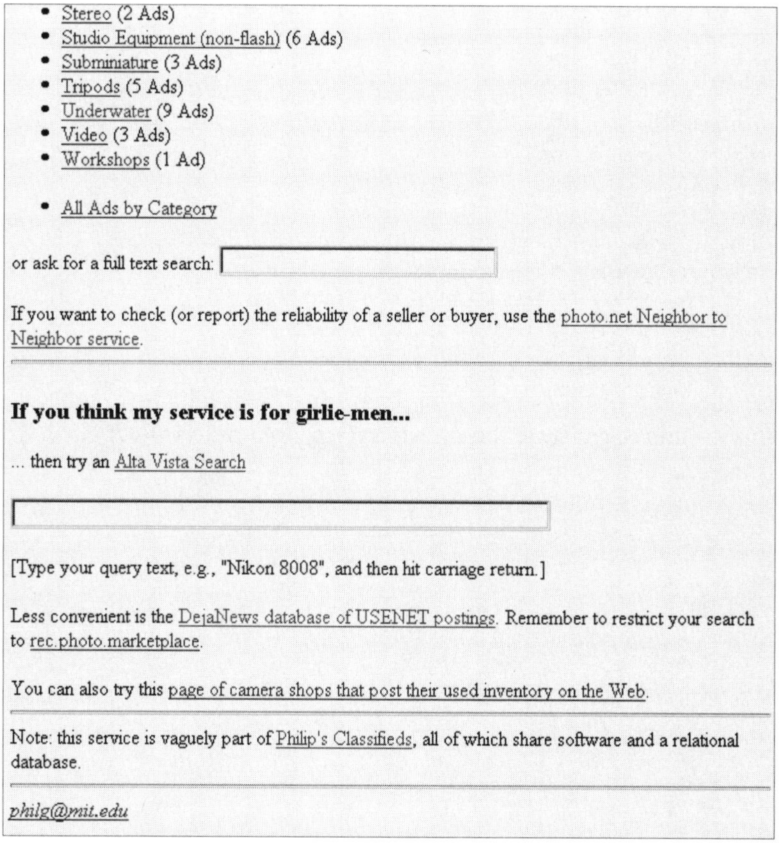

- Stereo (2 Ads)
- Studio Equipment (non-flash) (6 Ads)
- Subminiature (3 Ads)
- Tripods (5 Ads)
- Underwater (9 Ads)
- Video (3 Ads)
- Workshops (1 Ad)

- All Ads by Category

or ask for a full text search:

If you want to check (or report) the reliability of a seller or buyer, use the photo.net Neighbor to Neighbor service.

If you think my service is for girlie-men...

... then try an Alta Vista Search

[Type your query text, e.g., "Nikon 8008", and then hit carriage return.]

Less convenient is the DejaNews database of USENET postings. Remember to restrict your search to rec.photo.marketplace.

You can also try this page of camera shops that post their used inventory on the Web.

Note: this service is vaguely part of Philip's Classifieds, all of which share software and a relational database.

philg@mit.edu

Figure 13.18: The bottom portion of the first page for a domain in my generic classified system (see Figure 13.17 for the top). Note that only here is the full-text search engine made available. Users can browse just by clicking the mouse on the links above. Note also that I provide a link to the AltaVista search engine. My form targets a little script of mine that tacks on additional syntax to restrict AltaVista's search to the rec.photo.marketplace newsgroup. So a user typing "Canon macro lens" on my page results in a 302 redirect to http://www.altavista.digital.com/cgi-bin/query?pg=aq&what=news&fmt=.&q=newsgroups:rec.photo.marketplace+AND+Canon+macro+lens

```
  display_telephone    text,  -- maybe a customer service 800 number
  backlink_url         text,  -- if this is part of a bigger service
  backlink_title       text,
  blurb                text,  -- top of the front page
  blurb_bottom         text,  -- top of the front page
  insert_form_fragments text,  -- HTML form INPUTs
  ad_deletion_blurb    text,  -- printed out after an ad is deleted
  default_expiration_days       integer default 100,
  -- how many levels of categorization (if they just
  -- use primary_category then it is 1)
  levels_of_categorization integer default 1,
  user_extensible_categorization_p  boolean default 'f'
);
```

Here's the Tcl script for the top-level page that pulls data from the ad_domain table to generate the user interface, then pulls information from the ads table.

```
#
# parameters

# this probably should be a column in the ad_domains table but it
# isn't; so a change in the .tcl file will affect all the domains

set how_many_recent_ads_to_display 5

set_form_variables
set_form_variables_string_trim_DoubleAposQQ

# domain

set db [ns_db gethandle]
set selection [ns_db 1row $db "select * from ad_domains where domain =
'$QQdomain'"]
set_variables_after_query

# now all the properties of the domain are available as Tcl local vars

# we're doing some expensive database queries; we don't want users
# staring at a blank window, so return headers and some text

ReturnHeaders $conn


ns_write $conn "<html>
<head>
<title>$backlink_title Classified Ads</title>
```

```
</head>
<body bgcolor=#ffffff text=#000000>
<h2>Classified Ads</h2>

for <a href=\"$backlink_url\">$backlink_title</a>

<hr>

$blurb

<hr>

\[ <a href=\"place-ad.tcl?domain=$domain\">Place An Ad</a> |

<a href=\"edit-ad.tcl?domain=$domain\">Edit Old Ad</a> |

<a href=\"add-alert.tcl?domain=$domain\">Add/Edit Alert</a>

\]


<h3>Recent Ads</h3>

<ul>

"

# we only want the first 5 ads, but there is no clean way to specify
# that in SQL. So we just ask for all the unexpired ads in this domain
# ordered by descending classified_ad_id

set selection [ns_db select $db "select classified_ad_id,one_line
from classified_ads
where domain = '$QQdomain'
and (current_date <= expires or expires is null)
order by classified_ad_id desc"]

set ad_counter 0
while {[ns_db getrow $db $selection]} {
    incr ad_counter
    if { $ad_counter > $how_many_recent_ads_to_display } {
       # we've already displayed enough recent ads, so we shouldn't
       # read anymore rows from the preceding SELECT.  However, we
       # can't just walk away from an "open cursor". That can leave
       # all kinds of garbage around in the RDBMS client and server.
       # We call the AOLserver function "ns_db flush" which will in
       # turn inform the RDBMS server that no more rows are wanted.
```

```
        ns_db flush $db

        # call a Tcl function to break out of the while loop
        break
    }
    # we still have some recent ads to display
    set_variables_after_query
    ns_write $conn "
<li><a href=\"view-one.tcl?classified_ad_id=$classified_ad_id\">
$one_line
</a>
"

}

# we're done displaying the recent ads

ns_write $conn "<p>
<li><a href=\"domain-all.tcl?domain=$domain&by_category_p=f&wtb_p=f\">
All Ads Chronologically</a>
(<a href=\"domain-all.tcl?domain=$domain&by_category_p=f&wtb_p=t\">
including wanted to buy</a>)

</ul>

<h3>Ads by Category</h3>

<ul>"

# this is a very expensive database query using the GROUP BY feature
# of SQL.  We are asking the RDBMS to gather up the ads, group them
# by PRIMARY_CATEGORY, count the ads in each category, then return
# the count and the category name, ordering the returned rows by
# UPPER( PRIMARY_CATEGORY ) so that capitalization doesn't affect
# sorting. This query necessarily involves the RDBMS scanning the
# entire table.  It can still be very fast if you have a smart RDBMS
# on a computer with a lot of RAM. It is even tolerably fast with
# Illustra (a very stupid RDBMS when it comes to caching) because my
# table is pretty small and my RDBMS server box has 4 CPUs

# SQL nerd note 1: if you don't have OR EXPIRES IS NULL then you won't
# get any rows where EXPIRES is NULL.  A profound concept, to be sure,
# but one that escaped me at first.

# SQL nerd note 2: if you don't have a good name for something in the
# FROM list, you can just refer to it by position.  Here ORDER BY 3
# says "order by the 3rd thing in the FROM list" which is to say
```

```
# ORDER BY UPPER(PRIMARY_CATEGORY)

set selection [ns_db select $db "select count(*) as count,
primary_category as category,
upper(primary_category)
from classified_ads
where domain = '$QQdomain'
and (current_date <= expires or expires is null)
group by primary_category
order by 3"]

while {[ns_db getrow $db $selection]} {
    set_variables_after_query
    if { $count == 1 } {
       set pretty_count "1 Ad"
    } else {
       set pretty_count "$count Ads"
    }
    ns_write $conn "<li>
<a href=\"view-category.tcl?domain=[ns_urlencode
$domain]&primary_category=[ns_urlencode $category]\">
$category
</a>
($pretty_count)
"
}

ns_write $conn "<p>
<li>
<a href=\"domain-all.tcl?domain=$domain&by_category_p=t&wtb_p=t\">
All Ads by Category
</a>

</ul>

<form method=post action=search.tcl>
<input type=hidden name=domain value=\"$domain\">
or ask for a full text search:
<input type=text size=30 name=query_string>
</form>

$blurb_bottom

<hr>
```

```
Note: this service is vaguely part of
<a href=index.tcl>Philip's Classifieds</a>,
all of which share software and a relational database.

<hr>

<a href=\"mailto:$maintainer_email\">
<address>$maintainer_email</address>
</a>
</body>
</html>"
```

Note how the returned document will adopt the personality of the ad domain. The signature at the bottom is $maintainer_email (from the database). The links up at the top are to $backlink_url (from the database). There are blurbs at the top and bottom that come straight from the RDBMS. Go over to http://photo.net/photo/ right now and see how responsive the pages are. It is surprisingly fast to pull the ad_domain row out of the RDBMS. I've not yet been tempted to do any clever caching in Tcl global variables.

The Auction System Recording bids is straightforward:

```
create table classified_auction_bids (
  classified_ad_id      integer not null references classified_ads,
  bid                   numeric(9,2),
  currency              text default 'US dollars',
  bid_time              timestamp(0),
  location              text, -- e.g., 'New York City'
  email                 text,
  name                  text
);
```

Note the integrity constraint that this table can't contain bids for ads that don't exist in the classified_ads table. Assuming the RDBMS is behaving itself, we won't be able to delete an ad without first deleting bids for that ad. Here is a legal transaction in the augmented data model:

```
begin transaction;
delete from classified_auction_bids where classified_ad_id = 17;
delete from classified_ads where classified_ad_id = 17;
end transaction;
```

Summary

From reading any of these cases, I hope you've come away thinking that interaction design is the heart and soul of good service. I also hope that the straightforward nature of the Tcl code in all of these examples convinces you that it is indeed tough to hang yourself with the software if you start out with a decent data model. Finally, I hope that the RemindMe system example has convinced you of the virtues of the management philosophy laid out in Chapter 10: Programmers do a text-only site; the graphic designer comes in after it is working and makes it pretty.

If you didn't like staring at my software, you'll be pleased to learn that the next two chapters take us back to the tone and level of the beginning of the book.

Sites That Don't Work (And How to Fix Them)

User Feedback

Related Links

General Lessons

Chapter 14

This chapter looks at the evolution of the systems that I've used for three years to manage user feedback and related links. It demonstrates that solutions appropriate to a new site with 10,000 hits per day are time-consuming failures when applied to a mature site with 500,000 hits per day. I'm going to share with you a bunch of site and software design ideas that eventually failed, study why they failed, and then share my ultimate solution.

User Feedback

I peppered my first Web projects with user feedback forms: "Click here to tell me how you liked *Travels with Samantha*." From this, I learned two things:

- Ten percent of Internet users do not know their own e-mail address; ergo, your carefully crafted reply will bounce.
- The 1,000th response is less thrilling than the first; the 10,000th makes you question the wisdom of having solicited comments in the first place.

I reduced the severity of the first problem by changing to a "mailto" tag instead of a form. After I made the change, I would only get bounces when replying to users who haven't correctly filled out their browser's options dialog box. I reduced the severity of the second problem (sheer volume) by discreetly burying my e-mail address at the bottom of pages and refraining from explicitly requesting feedback. Users with a really heartfelt response to something would generally take the initiative and send me long thoughtful messages. Users who'd formerly just sent a line or two didn't bother. Every now and then I'd mine the most thoughtful comments from my e-mail archives and add them to http://webtravel.org/samantha/other-voices/.

So much for comments. That still left me with 10 or 20 questions every day. These fell into the following categories:

1. I scanned some pictures for my Web site and they look terrible. Yours look much better and they are one-third the size. How did you do it?
2. I was thinking about buying Camera X for purpose Y and want to know if you think this is a good idea.
3. My routine job is numbing my brain. I want to have a fabulous varied life full of travel and new experiences like yours. How do I do it?

Note: Throughout this chapter I'm going to refer to my personal site (http://photo.net/philg). I thought it would be helpful background to present five graphical snapshots of the site taken at various times from 1994 through 1997 (Figures 14.1 to 14.5).

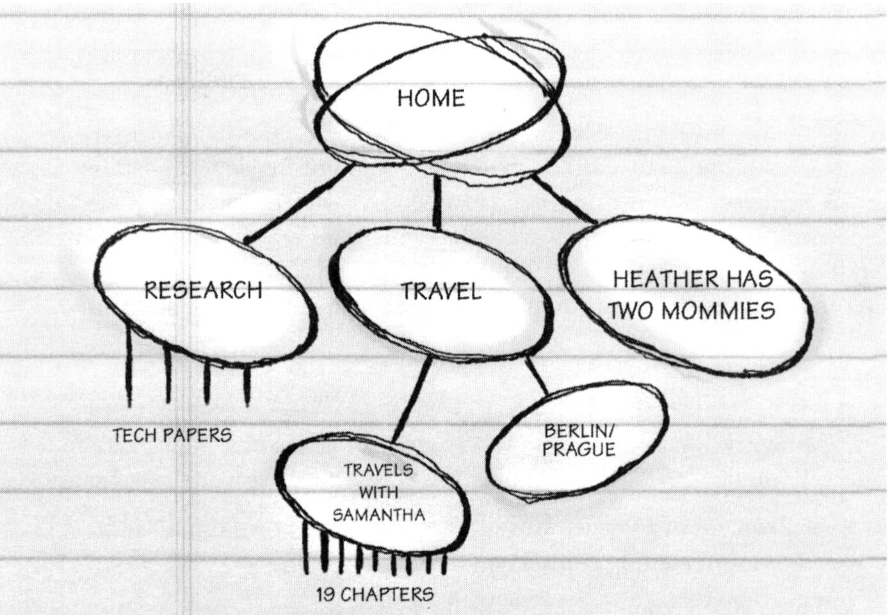

Figure 14.1: My pathetically wimpy Web site in early 1994. I offered a bunch of research papers that I'd written as big PostScript files. Most of the traffic was for two travelogues with photos and an exhibit of zoo photos, Heather Has Two Mommies. The latter was my attempt to write a charming children's book. After about one hour, though, I discovered that I was missing something fundamental: talent. So I changed the title to the funniest children's book title I could find and turned it into an uninspired parody of political correctness. It all happened between midnight and 6 a.m. on one strange night. To this day I get e-mail from folks saying "I listen to Rush Limbaugh every day and I'm so happy to have found a kindred soul on the Internet." I'm half-tempted to delete it but it gets at least 5,000 hits a day.

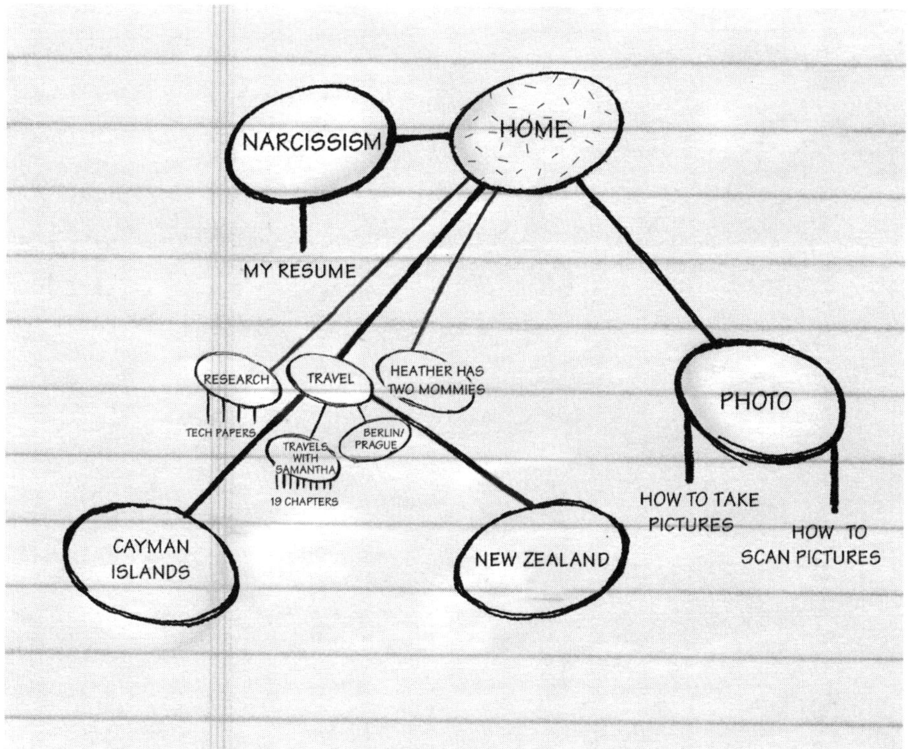

Figure 14.2: After *Travels with Samantha* won Best of the Web '94, I decided to respond to Internet demand for more travelogues with an extensive New Zealand story and a short piece on the Cayman Islands. Meanwhile, I added a photography section in hopes of more efficiently dealing with e-mailed questions (see text). I also started a narcissism section containing my resume and other personal information to answer another category of e-mailed questions.

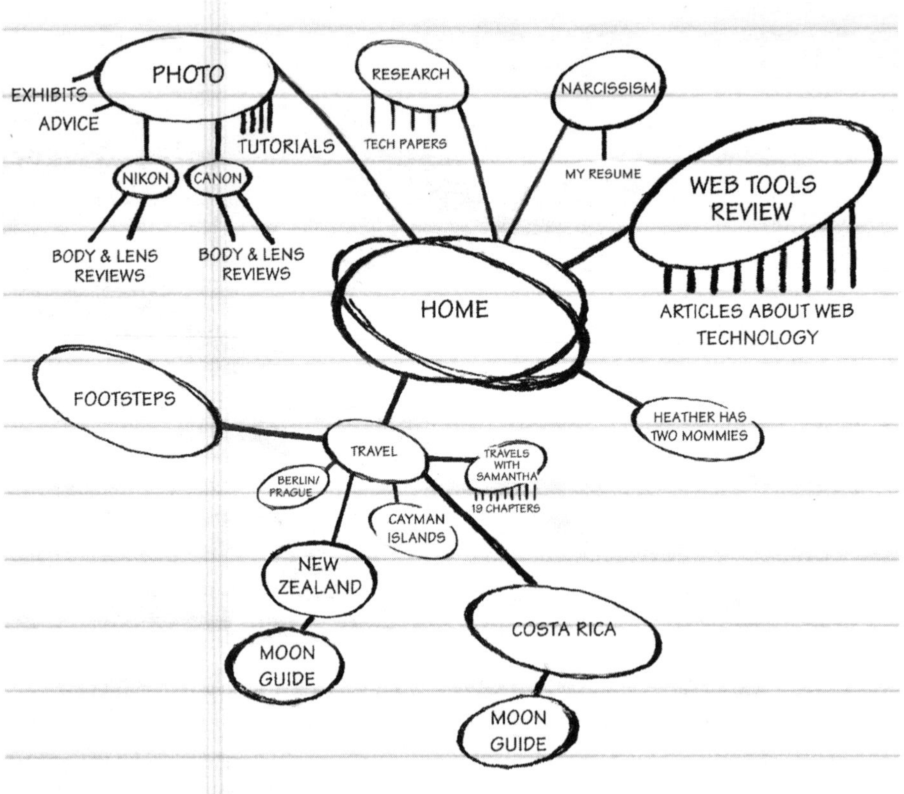

Figure 14.3: By mid-1995, I had decided to experiment a bit with my travelogues, making them more useful as travel planning tools. I struck a deal with Moon Publications to reprint portions of their guidebooks to Costa Rica and New Zealand. I arranged with some experts on the ground in Costa Rica to answer questions. I also got serious about offering Web publishing advice and started the *Web Tools Review* page that grew into this book.

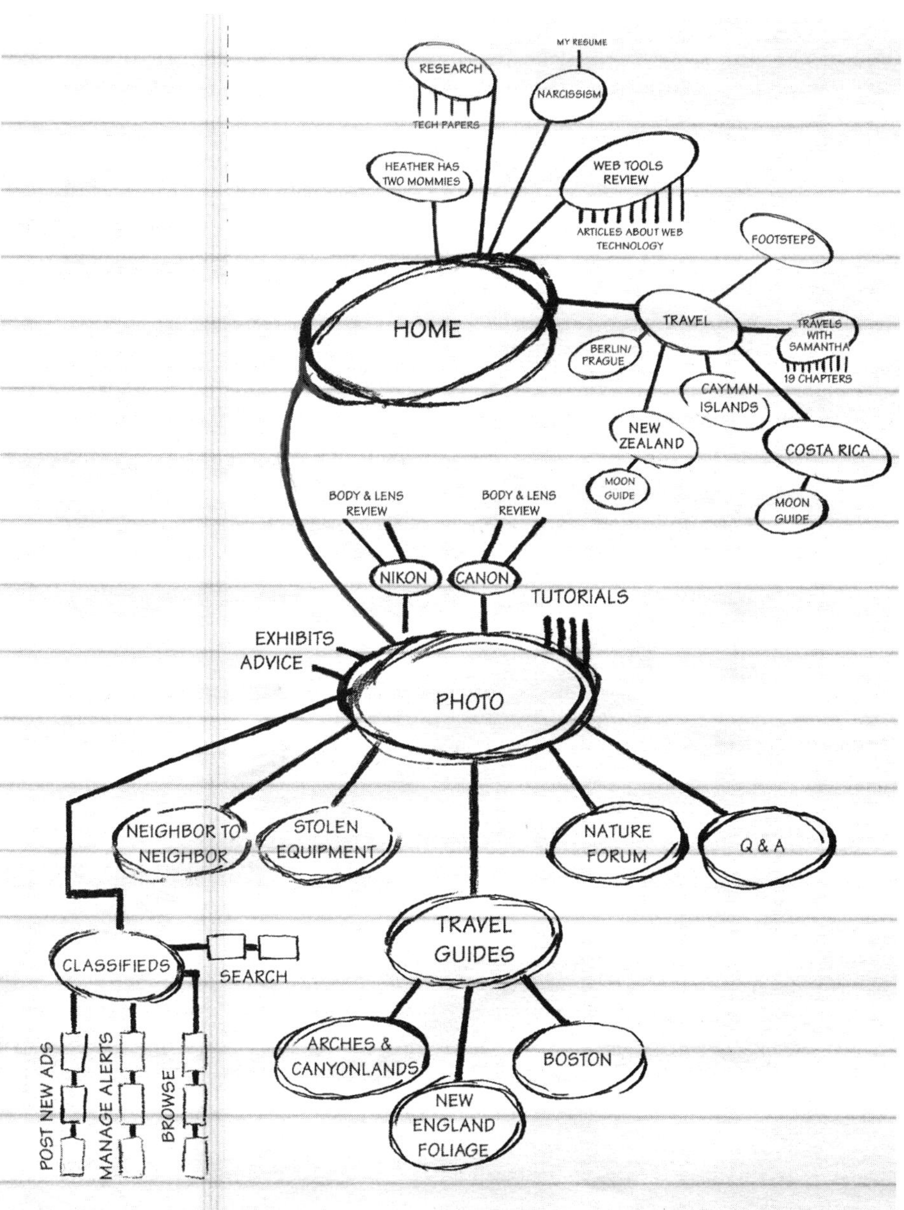

Figure 14.4: Toward the end of 1995, I got bored with adding more static pages. I started to use my personal site as a proving ground for Web collaboration ideas. I added a classified ad system, threaded discussion/Q&A forums, a registry for stolen cameras, and a neighbor-to-neighbor service for people to record their experiences with camera retailers, wedding photographers, individuals selling equipment on the Internet, and so forth.

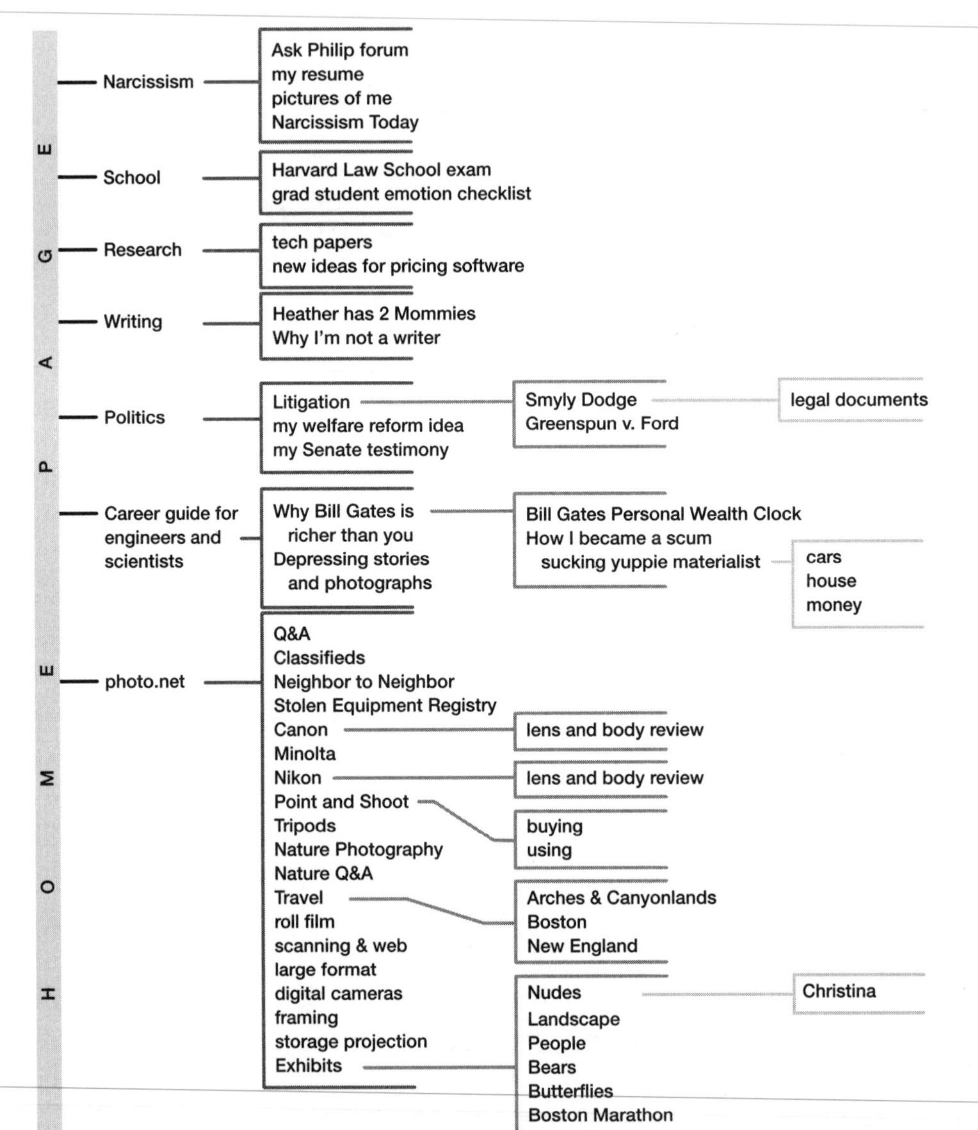

Figure 14.5: My personal site as of March 1997. The interesting trends to note are that I've added collaboration to virtually every page on my server. Users can add comments and/or related links to my pages. I'm running the classified ad software for Help Wanted web developer ads in *Web Tools Review,* for travel services in *Web Travel Review,* and for cameras in photo.net. I've added an Ask Philip Q&A forum under Narcissism. I'm offering all of these collaboration tools free to other Web publishers as services running from my server at Primehost. I'm publishing more content from other

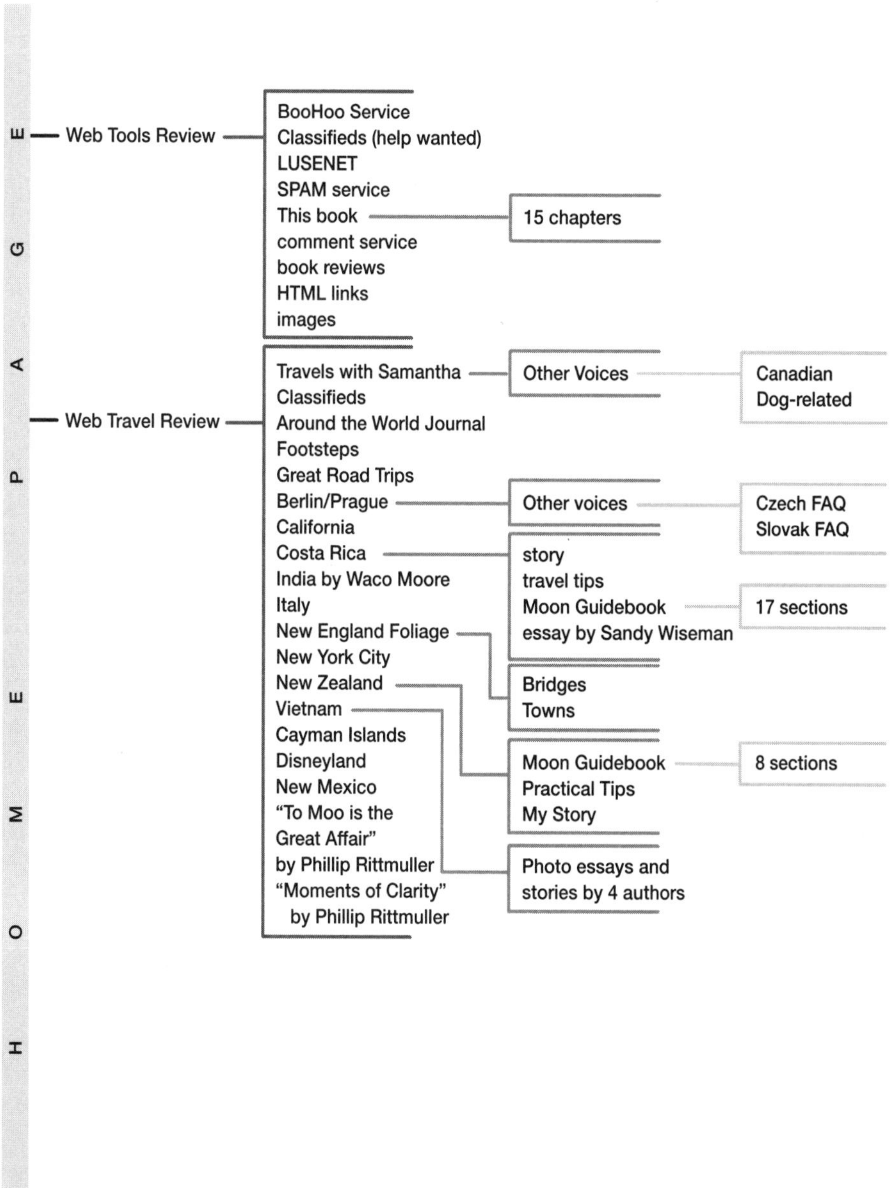

authors, ranging from travelogues to camera reviews. I've also rediscovered the joy of writing static pages and have added new travel sites of my own (Italy and California) plus an entire materialism section reflecting my experience as a consumer.

CATEGORY 1: HOW TO SCAN?

I disposed of Category 1 questions and a few other very specific ones by writing a FAQ for *Samantha* and linking from there to an explanation of my process for batch-converting images from Kodak PhotoCD (http://photo.net/philg/how-to-scan-photos.html; sort of like Chapter 4 of this book). That cut down the number of people asking by a factor of seven or eight. The remaining "how to scan" questions that did come through were easier to answer after I augmented my Emacs a little bit so that a few keystrokes adds the appropriate URL to an e-mail reply.

CATEGORY 2: GENERAL PHOTOGRAPHY QUESTIONS

So satisfied was I with this situation that I attempted to deal with the Category 2 questions in the same manner. I built a photography page (http://photo.net/photo/) and added material to it every time someone asked a question. Eventually, I figured, people would answer their own questions by browsing my page and the photo question stream would trickle out. Instead what happened is that my content spurred more questions. If I said that I liked my Yashica T4 point-and-shoot camera, that spurred literally hundreds of people to ask, "How does it compare to the Pentax/Olympus/Minolta YadaYada-15X point-and-shoot camera?" If I said that you needed a large aperture lens to do portraiture, that spurred a moderate number of questions about what I meant by "aperture." Here's one that came in a few days ago:

> "I recently inherited a Ciro-flex 120 box camera (model F). It says made in Deleware, OH, it has a Wollensak lens, 83mm f 3.2. I have taken a few rolls of Kodak color prints which seem to be OK, but I am not experienced enough with 120 film to know what I am doing at this point. Do you know anything about this camera? Is it good quality that I can use for outdoor photography or should I keep my 35mm point-and-shoot?"

The interesting thing about this question is that the guy asking it is probably the only person on the Internet, perhaps the only person in the world, capable of answering it. He has an apparently functioning example of an obscure camera that hasn't been manufactured for at least 50 years. He has taken "a few" rolls of pictures with the camera. He presumably has compared these pictures to those from his modern 35mm camera. I'm never going to get another question like this and, even if I did get a regular stream of questions about "Ciro-flex" cameras, I lack the experience to answer them myself.

My next attempt to deal with this flood was my Q&A forum software. I would use this to dispense photo advice too fragmented to put into .html files in photo.net. As with an .html file, though, I'd only have to answer each question once. Users on the point of asking a question would instead find the answer already posted in the forum. Furthermore, I'd capture wisdom and experience from other readers (maybe even some who'd used a Ciro-flex camera!).

At first, the forum was a tremendous success. I was surprised at the depth of knowledge of many of my readers and their eagerness to help novices. I no longer had to explain what an aperture was. Remember that my forum software directly e-mails responses to the original poster. It uses the ns_sendmail AOLserver API call and fakes headers so that if the novice replies with a follow-up, it goes to the responding reader. They can have a lengthy e-mail exchange without my even seeing it.

Should one of my eager answerers say something that is inaccurate, I can just add my own answer. An answer from philg@mit.edu sorts right at the top (since I'm the forum maintainer). So I can leave a partly correct answer below if it has any pedagogical value. Alternatively, I can just delete erroneous answers from the admin interface.

Everyone was winning. I was answering more distinct questions. My sophisticated readers were directly answering my naive readers. A lot of folks were checking the archives before posting duplicate questions.

After collecting about 2,000 postings (both questions and answers), the Q&A forum seemed to be failing. A lot of users were covering the same ground with "What kind of camera should I buy" questions? At first, I dealt with this by adding a generic "Please search this bboard before asking a question" form. This helped a bit, but in the end I added a column to the bboard_topics table with a customizable "pre_post_caveat." See Figure 14.6 for what the "Post New" form looks like now.

Am I done? I don't think so. There are 478 top-level postings in the forum. Even with the categorization, that's becoming far too many for users to browse. Furthermore, I haven't been savage enough in my editorial judgment. There are a lot of threads that might be worth keeping around for the full-text search but that aren't worth presenting at top level. For example, one reader asks whether a Tamron 90/2.8 macro lens is any good. Another reader responds that he likes his older Tamron 90/2.5 lens, which is a different optical design. That's the whole thread. I'd hate for someone to stumble into it because it doesn't really teach anything. On the other hand, I don't want to delete it because it might be useful to someone in the market for a used Tamron 90/2.5 lens.

I think it is time to add a column to my bboard table. It will be called interesting_p and will be "t" if the thread is interesting, "f" if not. Then I can reprogram my top-level page to only show the interesting threads. The full-

Post a New Message

into the photo.net forum

Note: before you post a new question, you might want to make sure that it hasn't already been asked and answered...

Full Text Search:

The form above will let you search through this forum. You might also want to browse the articles in photo.net and/or do a full-text search through the photo.net articles.

The most commonly asked questions are answered in the following photo.net articles:

- What Camera Should I Buy?
- Point & Shoot Cameras, buying and using
- Canon versus Nikon
- Where Should I Buy This Camera?
- Recommended Film
- Recommended Photo Labs

Anyway, this isn't meant to discourage you from asking an interesting question. There are hundreds of good photographers who'd love to see a question about the best way to capture a scene. But nobody wants to have to tell you that cheap lenses are not as good as expensive lenses, that it is not smart to choose a camera system based on which body happens to be cheaper right now, or that none of us have used the latest point & shoot wonder zoom, model XYZ-145x.

Your Email Address

Your Full Name

Subject Line (summary of question)

Category Don't Know (this helps build the FAQ archives)

Figure 14.6: After collecting about 2,000 postings, my http://photo.net/photo/ Q&A forum began to fall apart. Users were posting new questions that had already been asked and answered. At first, I added the generic "search this forum first" note. Later, I decided that I needed the ability have a custom pre_post_caveat for each bboard topic. This figure shows the user interface in place as of March 1997.

text search service will still consider all the postings in the table. So the average reader won't be distracted by this posting whereas the searcher for "Tamron macro" will find it instantly.

Who is going to decide whether a thread is interesting? I could do it, but I'm already spending 30 minutes a week maintaining the forum (mostly deleting uninteresting postings and categorizing miscategorized threads). I think I will build in a facility to allow the group to collaboratively decide that a posting is uninteresting and/or allow a group of experts selected by the maintainer to decide.

Note: In addition to starting photo.net to handle the photography questions, I started Web Tools Review (http://webtools.com/wtr/) to handle the Web publishing questions. It worked pretty well for a while but then the information started to get out of date and the page became an embarrassment. Then Simon Hayes at Ziff-Davis Press approached me with the idea of revamping the material and turning it into a book. You're reading it now. So what started out as a way to save time answering reader e-mail turned into the job of writing 450 manuscript pages of text plus figures and screen shots. How much fun is that? Winston Churchill had something to say on this subject: "Writing a book is an adventure. To begin with, it is a toy and an amusement; then it becomes a mistress, and then it becomes a master, and then a tyrant. The last phase is that just as you are about to be reconciled to your servitude, you kill the monster, and fling him out to the public." Anyway, I guess I have to say that the idea of building Web Tools Review as a timesaver has failed miserably.

CATEGORY 3: HOW TO MAKE MY LIFE AS COOL AS YOURS?

These are the questions that break my heart. Some poor guy trapped at a desk job 40 hours a week. He has read all 19 chapters of *Travels with Samantha* and my 60-page New Zealand story and my 50-page Costa Rica story. Now he wants to bust out and be a footloose free spirit like me.

I really ought to program my Emacs to autorespond with "All you have to do to be a free spirit like me is develop 50 RDBMS-backed Web sites. Then you can be woken up in the morning by a former customer whose full-time programmer has quit and left them with a bug; they want you to telnet into their Unix box and poke around and fix it. Then you can spend 120 hours a week at your desk maintaining various Web servers. Then you can go away for the weekend and find 250 e-mail messages from your readers in your inbox."

BUT WHAT ABOUT COMMENTS? (LOQUACIOUS, VERSION 1.0)

My big objective through all of the preceding endeavors was ducking e-mail. This would have been fine if I still had an interesting life to write about. Then I could have enhanced my site periodically with new stories. Unfortunately, as I noted above, I'd taken to spending entire weeks at home in front of my terminal. I'd become so boring that I started to quote Andrei Gromyko. (When he was Soviet ambassador to the U.S. and a reporter asked him a question about his family, he'd say, "My personal life doesn't interest me.")

I decided to turn to my readers. They would invigorate my site by adding interesting comments to each of my pages. I could use a relational database to collect and organize these comments, then some simple programs to present them. But my personal server was on an old HP-UX machine at the MIT Laboratory for Computer Science. This computer was already struggling to handle my static pages. It certainly couldn't handle running an RDBMS that got queried on every page load. A script-and-RDBMS-backed site is never as reliable as a static site. I didn't want to reduce the reliability of my large body of static material in order to serve a small body of dynamic material. I didn't want to spend the rest of my life doing system and database administration either.

I ended up building a comment server on a separate computer, a multiprocessor SPARCserver 1000 already running Illustra and AOLserver to reliably deliver a million RDBMS-backed hits per day. Conveniently, this box had an on-call system/database administrator paid for by the commercial Web publisher who owned it. What would have been a lifetime project if done at MIT could now be accomplished with a few days of programming.

How does my Loquacious system end up working? Suppose I have a static page such as http://photo.net/photo/point-and-shoot.html. I simply add a reference to the comments page at http://db.photo.net/com/philg/photo/point-and-shoot.html.

The "/com" tells the AOLserver listening on db.photo.net that the user is requesting the Loquacious comment service (as opposed to the other services delivered by this host). The "/philg" tells the Loquacious software that the referencing page is part of the "philg" realm (previously defined and stored in a comment_realms table). The last portion of the comment reference, "/photo/point-and-shoot.html," is a URL stub that, if glued to the realm base, will form the complete URL of the referencing page. For example, in the case of the "philg" realm, the URL base ("server_prefix") in the comment_realms table is "http://photo.net/". The first time a comment page is referenced, the Loquacious system attempts to grab the static file and REGEXP out the title. That way it can provide a backlink that says "Comments on Point & Shoot Cameras" rather than "Comments on http://photo.net/photo/point-and-shoot.html" (see Figure 14.7).

As soon as I'd finished building the AOLserver Tcl/SQL scripts that implement the Loquacious system, I wrote a Perl script to grind over my 1,000 or so static .html files at MIT. The Perl script inserted a legal comment server reference to the bottom of each page. Now virtually all of my pages could accept comments.

Where did this flurry of programming get me? Right back to where I was in 1994. A torrent of comments flooded in, mostly one or two sentences of the "I love this page" ilk. These cluttered up my inbox just as in 1994 because my software e-mails the realm maintainer every time there is a new posting. But

Comments

on Point & Shoot Cameras (made possible by Loquacious)

I agree strongly with the T-4 assessment. I carry one in my briefcase, my wife carries one in her purse and each of my children have one for their bookbags or backpacks. Great little camera, with a definite cult following. Cheap too.

Contributed by Kimball Corson (kandj@goodnet.com) on December 15, 1996.

I've got a Pentax IQzoom 38-90 WR, which has been on the market about 4 years now. I've never been particularly happy with its autofocus, and the poor parallax compensation on Macro mode; its always cutting off tops and bottoms. Pictures are acceptably sharp. Last but not least, The rubber shutter release cover fell off, rendering the Water resi- stance feature useless. Repair cost US110.00, because of the way it's designed the whole front case needs replacement.

My Dad's got a Ricoh P&S, fits in his pocket and takes great pictures. Check it out.

Contributed by Isaac L. Kaplan (ilkaplan@pacbell.net) on December 27, 1996.

Figure 14.7: http://db.photo.net/com/philg/photo/point-and-shoot.html, the database-generated dynamic comment page for the static page http://photo.net/photo/point-and-shoot.html. Note that the backlink to "Point & Shoot Cameras" was automatically generated by the comment server. The first time a user requested the comment page from Loquacious, it fetched the static page from my static server and REGEXPed out the title. That's why you don't see "comments on http://photo.net/photo/point-and-shoot.html".

now I had to also go to the back-end admin pages and delete these observations from my database.

In an attempt to stop the ratings, I put in cautionary language saying, "This is not meant to collect ratings but only alternative perspectives that might be of interest to other readers." The flood continued unabated.

LOQUACIOUS, VERSION 2.0

My next step was to add a second submit button, offering users the option of sending private e-mail to the realm maintainer (see Figure 14.8). This cut down on the amount of crud dumped into the RDBMS but increased my junk e-mail load. A lot of users (at least 30 percent) would submit a public comment, look at the confirmation page that said, "Thanks and, by the way, I've just sent e-mail to philg@mit.edu," then back up and resubmit the same comment as "private e-mail to philg@mit.edu" (Figures 14.9 and 14.10). My defense against garbage in the database remained a couple of very fast back-end administration pages (Figures 14.11 and 14.12).

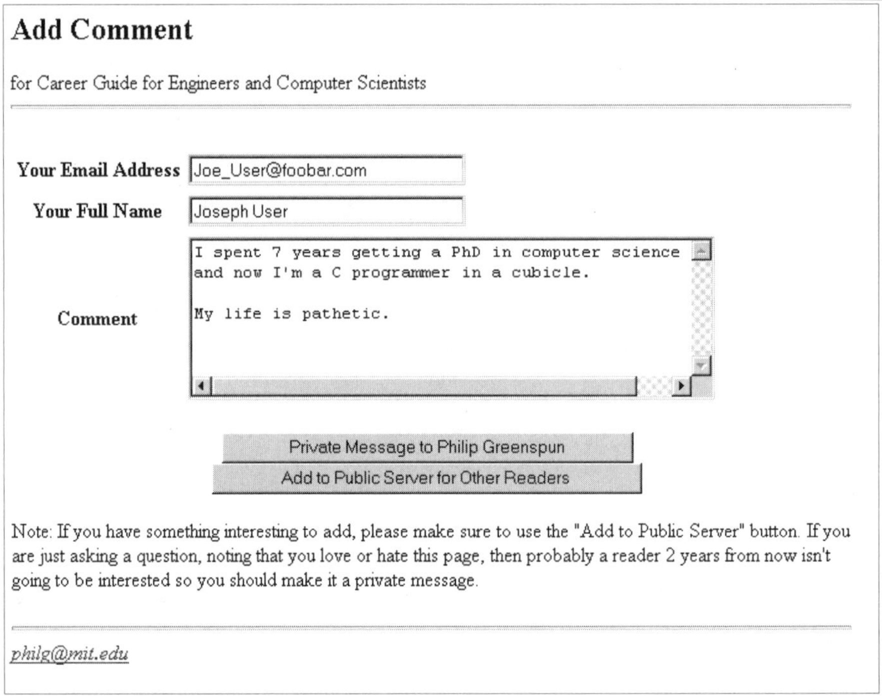

Add Comment

for Career Guide for Engineers and Computer Scientists

Your Email Address Joe_User@foobar.com

Your Full Name Joseph User

Comment

```
I spent 7 years getting a PhD in computer science
and now I'm a C programmer in a cubicle.

My life is pathetic.
```

Private Message to Philip Greenspun

Add to Public Server for Other Readers

Note: If you have something interesting to add, please make sure to use the "Add to Public Server" button. If you are just asking a question, noting that you love or hate this page, then probably a reader 2 years from now isn't going to be interested so you should make it a private message.

philg@mit.edu

Figure 14.8: My second attempt at an "add my comment" form; I've added the option of sending private e-mail to the comment realm maintainer (in this case "philg@mit.edu") instead of adding something to the persistent database.

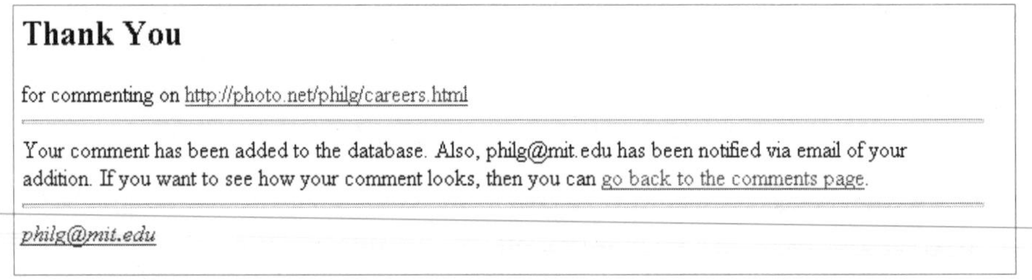

Thank You

for commenting on http://photo.net/philg/careers.html

Your comment has been added to the database. Also, philg@mit.edu has been notified via email of your addition. If you want to see how your comment looks, then you can go back to the comments page.

philg@mit.edu

Figure 14.9: Confirmation page from Loquacious following addition of a public comment. Note that the user is explicitly informed that the comment realm maintainer (in this case "philg@mit.edu") has been notified via e-mail. Nonetheless, at least 30 percent of commenters backed up and resubmitted the same comment as a private e-mail message!

Subject: Comment on http://photo.net/photo/point-and-shoot.html
Resent-Date: 25 Mar 1997 10:24:18 -0500
Resent-From: philg@martigny.ai.mit.edu
Resent-To: philg-pop@martigny.ai.mit.edu
Date: Tue, 25 Mar 1997 07:40:24 -0500
From: tzeho@pacific.net.sg
To: philg@MIT.EDU

```
A comment on

http://photo.net/photo/point-and-shoot.html

was added to the philg comment realm:

What about the Minolta TC-1? I love its small size, but I've not heard anyth

from tzeho@pacific.net.sg (Tze Ho Tan)

---------------------

If you want to delete it, go to the admin page:

http://db.photo.net/com/admin/philg/photo/point-and-shoot.html
```

Figure 14.10: A typical e-mail notification of a new comment received. Note that this was a public comment, rather than a private message, and it is a question rather than the informed alternative perspective that I seek. When reading this message in Netscape Navigator, I am just one click away from the administration page (see Figure 14.11).

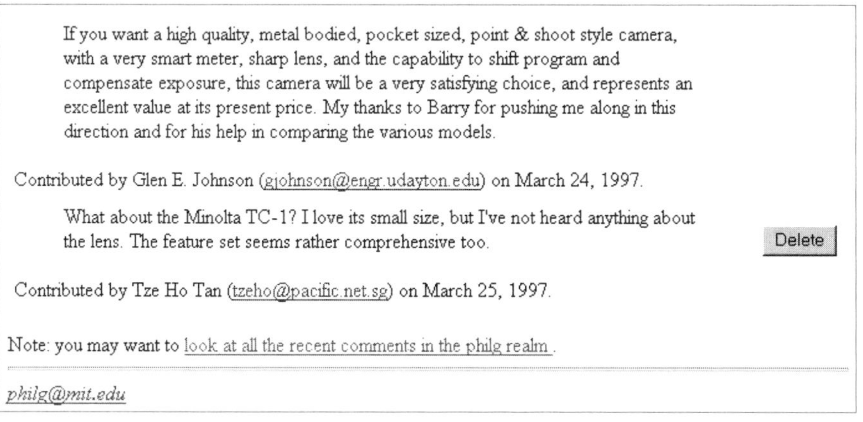

If you want a high quality, metal bodied, pocket sized, point & shoot style camera, with a very smart meter, sharp lens, and the capability to shift program and compensate exposure, this camera will be a very satisfying choice, and represents an excellent value at its present price. My thanks to Barry for pushing me along in this direction and for his help in comparing the various models.

Contributed by Glen E. Johnson (gjohnson@engr.udayton.edu) on March 24, 1997.

What about the Minolta TC-1? I love its small size, but I've not heard anything about the lens. The feature set seems rather comprehensive too.

Delete

Contributed by Tze Ho Tan (tzeho@pacific.net.sg) on March 25, 1997.

Note: you may want to look at all the recent comments in the philg realm .

philg@mit.edu

Figure 14.11: The administration back-end for comments on just one page. This is not a very convenient way to edit five recently received and bogus comments, though, which is why I built the quicker interface in Figure 14.12.

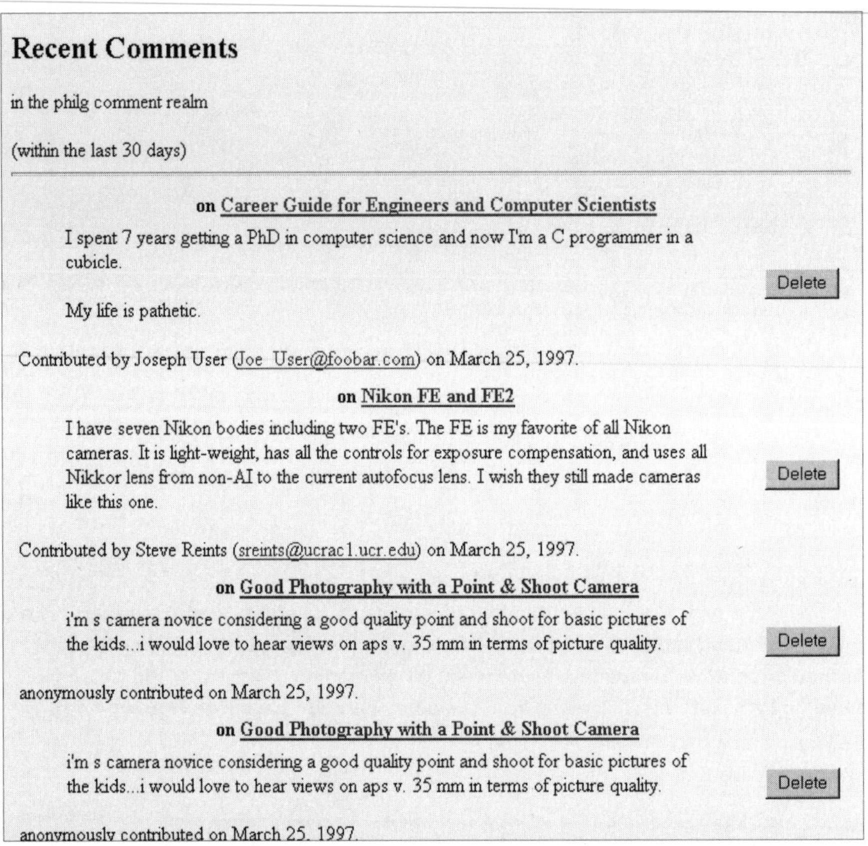

Recent Comments
in the philg comment realm
(within the last 30 days)
on Career Guide for Engineers and Computer Scientists
I spent 7 years getting a PhD in computer science and now I'm a C programmer in a cubicle.
My life is pathetic.
Delete
Contributed by Joseph User (Joe_User@foobar.com) on March 25, 1997.
on Nikon FE and FE2
I have seven Nikon bodies including two FE's. The FE is my favorite of all Nikon cameras. It is light-weight, has all the controls for exposure compensation, and uses all Nikkor lens from non-AI to the current autofocus lens. I wish they still made cameras like this one.
Delete
Contributed by Steve Reints (sreints@ucrac1.ucr.edu) on March 25, 1997.
on Good Photography with a Point & Shoot Camera
i'm s camera novice considering a good quality point and shoot for basic pictures of the kids...i would love to hear views on aps v. 35 mm in terms of picture quality.
Delete
anonymously contributed on March 25, 1997.
on Good Photography with a Point & Shoot Camera
i'm s camera novice considering a good quality point and shoot for basic pictures of the kids...i would love to hear views on aps v. 35 mm in terms of picture quality.
Delete
anonymously contributed on March 25, 1997.

Figure 14.12: With this super administration page, I can go through a whole month's worth of comments, deleting duplicates, questions, and otherwise uninteresting material.

At this point, I stepped back from the system and let it sit for a few months. I had accumulated several hundred interesting comments and therefore could not account Loquacious a failure. On the other hand, I was spending up to 30 minutes each week deleting redundant e-mail and cleaning the database. People wanted to rate my content even though I told them that I wasn't interested in positive comments. Oftentimes, people would say, "This page is great. I want to encourage you to keep it available." I think the average person's experience of the Web is that links go dead within a few months. They presumably assume that the reason for the short-livedness of links is that authors aren't getting enough encouragement and therefore fold up their server tents and go home.

LOQUACIOUS, VERSION 3.0

My friend Neil suggested that "Hey, if people are determined to rate your content, why don't you add a system whereby they can rate your content?" So I added a table to my RDBMS and wrote a couple of new Tcl procedures and you can see the result in Figures 14.13 and 14.14. I don't have enough experience with the new system to say whether my feedback problems are finally solved, but I'm optimistic.

> **Note:** If you want to run a Loquacious comment realm for your own static site, you can just add a realm to my database server. Just visit http://webtools.com/wtr/ and fill out a form. It will cost you nothing. I maintain the comment server and RDBMS.

RELATED LINKS

When the Web was young, publishers linked to everyone they could find. You linked to people whose content complemented yours. You linked words in your documents to foreign servers with deeper explanations. You built favorite links pages to highlight work that you admired. You did all of this in an attempt to create a richer hypertext environment for your readers.

That worked pretty well when 95 percent of the publishers were students and researchers and there wasn't a get-rich-quick-with-banner-ads stampede.

Nowadays, if you operate a popular Web site, you'll get at least 20 messages per day requesting a link exchange. This is kind of a strange concept if you are operating under the original Web model. You've linked to publishers whose content complements your own and will therefore help your readers. Should you pull those links if the linked-to publishers don't like your site? Suppose I publish a page about Minolta cameras (http://photo.net/photo/minolta/index.html) in which I link to http://www.minoltausa.com/. My page notes that I think almost everyone would be better off buying a Canon or Nikon 35mm single-lens reflex system rather than a Minolta Maxxum. Should I expect Minolta to link back to me? Should I pull my link to them if they won't?

Unable to look at all of the URLs offered, I programmed Emacs to autorespond something to the effect of "I don't try to maintain a comprehensive list of links to the rest of the Internet, even in one subject area. Even if I did, what would be the utility of this to my readers? They have Yahoo. They have AltaVista. Why do they need my half-heartedly maintained list?"

Then one day I had a brilliant insight: The people who started Yahoo are a lot richer than I am. Given that it would take me about one hour to program a

What Kind of Comment?

for How to be a Web Whore Just Like Me

I just want to say whether I liked this page or not: Add a rating.

I just want to send some email to the page author: Send email to philg@mit.edu (note: Philip Greenspun is the maintainer of this comment realm; he or she might not be the author of "How to be a Web Whore Just Like Me")

I have an alternative perspective to contribute, something that will be of interest to other readers of this page two or three years from now: Add a persistent comment.

I have a question: probably you are best off asking the page author directly with an email message.

philg@mit.edu

Figure 14.13: I replaced the "Add Comment" form with a gateway page, encouraging users to think for a moment about what they want to express. Note that the very first option is simply to add an integer rating, something that won't result in my getting an e-mail message.

Rate

How to be a Web Whore Just Like Me on a scale from 0 (bad) to 10 (good).

Your Rating [ ] (integer from 0 to 10)

Your Email Address [ ]

Your Full Name [ ]

Submit Query

philg@mit.edu

Figure 14.14: Here's the new "Add Rating" form. Note that I collect user e-mail addresses and full names. These are optional fields but might be useful if I change the commented-on page and want to spam everyone who has ever rated it. For example, "You rated foobar.html a 9 on March 26, 1997. I've made a bunch of changes and you'll probably want to come back and re-rate it as a 2."

self-maintaining Yahoo-style links directory and that there were apparently thousands of people willing to go to the effort of adding entries, I built the BooHoo system.

Here were my design objectives:

- No dead links (which have made Yahoo itself almost useless over the years)
- Instant updates
- Resistance to spamming
- Extendable to distributed management (like Loquacious)

NO DEAD LINKS

The BooHoo system works its way through the links every night or two. If a link is unreachable, its status goes from "live" to "coma." If it had already been marked "coma" by a previous sweep, it is marked "dead" and an e-mail notification is sent to the person who posted it. Dead links are no longer displayed to users. When the sweep gets to a link that is already marked "dead," it is either restored to "live" status (if the server has come back) or removed from the database (actually there is an administrative command to "really remove" the dead links and/or restore them all to "live" status; this ensures that all of your links are not lost if my server or the entire Internet has a few "bad hair days").

INSTANT UPDATES

I get instant updates for free since BooHoo is fully RDBMS-backed. After a user finishes working through the "Add URL" forms, the data gets stuffed into a database table. The next time a reader requests the related links for that particular page, the new row is pulled from the database.

Why doesn't Yahoo work this way? Probably partly because of history. Yahoo was started by a couple of Stanford graduate students in electrical engineering. Universities are generally a couple of decades behind the times when it comes to database management technology.

Even if Yahoo were engineered with the latest and greatest RDBMS software, it would require a tremendously huge server farm to handle the hundreds of queries per second that an "Internet anchor" service gets. It is vastly cheaper in terms of hardware requirements to periodically grind the data out of the database into static .html files, which is what Yahoo in fact does.

SPAM RESISTANCE

Suppose that Joe Artiste adds a link from photo.net to his site. Unfortunately Joe is hosting on a slow server, has neglected to add WIDTH and HEIGHT tags to his IMGs (see Chapter 4), has chosen a truly offensive background GIF, and offers only the shallowest content. BooHoo instantly notifies me (the owner of the photo.net page) by e-mail when a related link is added. The e-mail notification includes an instant link to the administration page where the link to Joe Artiste may be removed with a mouse click.

More interestingly, suppose that Bill Gates is very enthusiastic about launching Windows 98. He thinks everyone should know about it and therefore believes that his page announcing Windows 98 is related to just about all of my pages. So he has some of his serfs make http://www.microsoft.com/win98/, a related link to all of my pages. BooHoo's blacklisting capability saves me from having to read a flurry of e-mail and then make a flurry of removal mouse clicks. As the administrator of a BooHoo realm, I can say "reject any link that matches the pattern *microsoft.com*". I can specify this pattern for just one page or for all pages known to a BooHoo installation. My software will grind over the database and delete all the links that contain "microsoft.com". Furthermore, any fresh attempts to insert related URLs containing "microsoft.com" will be rejected with an error message to the user.

DISTRIBUTED MANAGEMENT

Like everything else I've written for my personal site, I want BooHoo to be usable by other Web publishers. Consequently, I have a BooHoo system that is designed to run on one server (see http://webtools.com/wtr/) and treat each page as a separately managed item. This means that some nice features, for example, "blacklist microsoft.com site-wide", aren't available. On the other hand, it saves publishers from the pain of having to install and maintain an RDBMS.

HOW DOES IT WORK?

In terms of cutting down on my e-mail, BooHoo has worked fantastically well. I don't get as many requests for reciprocal links. When I do, I can just autorespond with a description of the BooHoo system. The system has collected hundreds of links. Figure 14.15 shows some of the links users have added to my top-level photo.net page. Figure 14.16 shows the form they use to add a link.

Why don't I consider BooHoo a success? Mostly because I have been too lazy to add Related Links buttons to my static pages. Every time I want to add a new page to BooHoo, I have to fill out a Web form. I am too lazy to do this for the hundreds of static pages on my site that deserve related links buttons. I really ought to rewrite BooHoo to function more like Loquacious so that I need only write one Perl script to add Related Links buttons to all of my static pages in one fell swoop. But I've been too lazy to do that . . .

Related Links

to photo.net

Catch-all for photography-related links. A good place for other magazines, photographers, manufacturers, museums, etc.

- Nikkor Club Deutschland - Sites of the NCD
- M&M Photo Source Home Page - Comprehensive reference and commercial page for all photographers
- Photo-Tech Camera Service Inc. (Canadian) - Western Canada's friendly full line camera service center. Factory authorized warranty service for Canon, Minolta, Ricoh, Olympus, Sekonic, Tamron and others. Factory trained technicians for Nikon and Pentax. If we can't service it, we'll do our best to find someone who can!
- AP-TS, Inc. Photography Links Page! - Links to the Photographic Industry including: Camera & Photo Equipment, Film & Batteries, Video, Digital Imaging, Newsgroups, Online Magazines and
- Desktop Images at pcpix.com - A new photograph (in four different resolutions) and tileable background is posted every day. An Photo Gallery - Personal photo gallery of Krzysztof Marcinkiewicz photographer from Poland
- Wee Keng Hor's Photo Page - Tips for buying photography equipment in Singapore. Guide for joining photography clubs in Singapore. It also features some photographs taken by the web author.
- Gilles LUCATO's photo page - In **french**, **advices** for newcomers in Photography, '*what to buy*', '*how to do*' made simple by examples: '*depth of field*', '*overexposure*', '*open flash*'.
- Eliadis Archaeological Photography - The art in the Archaeological Photography. Sculptures, Coins, Icons, Nature, UV Photography,Articles and Links.
- York Photo - York provides mail order photo processing products and services. Their site also has games, customer photo submissions, photography tips and much more!
- Toomas Tamm's photo page -
  - How to recognize (and prevent) molds and dust mites from inhabiting your lens.
  - Canon EOS Feature list.
  - Electronic Flash FAQ - the basics and beyond.
- Jim and Janet's Planet - Photo gallery from various locations in the Mid Atlantic region of the United States.

Figure 14.15: The BooHoo system displays related links to http://photo.net/photo/.

GENERAL LESSONS

Nobody is smart enough to predict all of the implications of a software design decision. The first joy of developing Web software is that you find out immediately when you've made a mistake. The second joy is that you never distribute a CD-ROM to thousands of people. Thus you only have to fix your code on the server and all of your users will benefit instantly.

If God had meant you to get it right the first time, He would not have put "alter table" into SQL. If fixing bugs and adding features to online systems handling 20 hits a second were easy, you would not be getting paid $1,250 a day.

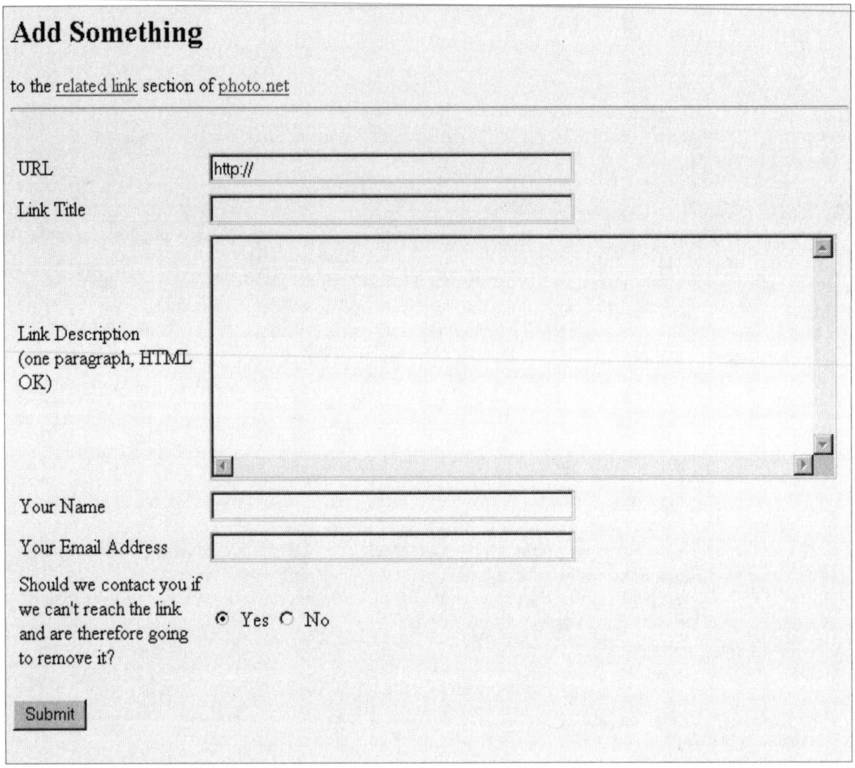

Add Something

to the related link section of photo.net

URL http://

Link Title

Link Description (one paragraph, HTML OK)

Your Name

Your Email Address

Should we contact you if we can't reach the link and are therefore going to remove it? Yes No

Submit

Figure 14.16: Anyone can add a link from photo.net to their own site simply by filling out this form.

A Future So Bright You'll Need to Wear Sunglasses

Should Software Really Be Sold Like Tables and Chairs?

Your User's Browser: a GE Range

Personalization

Collaboratively Exchanged Data Models

Collaboratively Evolved Data Models

Grand Conclusion

Chapter 15

Eric Rabkin, Professor of English at University of Michigan, surveyed science fiction and found only one case in which a science fiction writer had accurately predicted an invention: Arthur C. Clarke's 1945 proposal for geostationary communication satellites, the first of which was launched in 1965. All the other writers credited with scientific invention were merely extrapolating implications of technologies that had already been invented.

The most successful Internet punditry is a lot like Rabkin's survey of science fiction. University labs got corporate money in the 1980s to invent virtual reality. Magazines and newspapers got advertising dollars in the 1990s to tell the public about the amazing new development of virtual reality. All of this was greatly facilitated by Ivan Sutherland and Bob Sproull. They placed an array of sensors in a ceiling to track the user's head postion and attitude. With a head-mounted display and real-time information about the user's position, Sutherland and Sproull were able to place synthetic chairs in the room (Sutherland joked that the ultimate computer display would let the user sit down in the chair). They built a completely functioning virtual reality system, using government research funds, and published the results to the world with papers, photographs, and movie demonstrations. The year? 1966.

Note: You can read more about Ivan Sutherland at http://www.eu.sun.com/960710/feature3/.

I've made a careful study of book and magazine Internet punditry. I've graphed the author's wealth and fame versus the novelty of the ideas presented. Based on this research, here are my predictions for the future:

- Have you ever picked up a small plastic device and heard a voice from the other side of the planet? You will. (Alexander Graham Bell, 1876)

- Have you ever had a friend in the office next door type a message and watched an image of the typed letters form seconds later on a cathode-ray tube in front of your eyes? You will. (Various e-mail systems of the 1960s)
- Have you ever cooperated with a friend in another city, each of you typing on a computer keyboard, drawing with a mouse, talking to each other, and looking at a little inset video picture of your collaborator on the screen? You will. (Douglas Engelbart at the December 1968 Fall Joint Computer Conference in San Francisco; demonstrated to a room of 2,000)
- Have you ever clicked a mouse on a hypertext document or graphic? You will. (Engelbart, same 1968 demo)
- Have you ever imagined that the mouse click could grab a file from halfway across the Internet? You will. (Engelbart, same 1968 demo)

Can we learn anything general from my results? Absolutely. Armies of hardware engineers will work anonymously in cubicles like slaves for 30 years so that the powerful computers used by pioneers in the 1960s will be affordable to everyone. Then in the 1990s rich people and companies will use their PR staffs to take credit for the innovations of the pioneers in the 1960s, without even having the grace to thank the hardware geeks who made it possible for them to steal credit in the first place. Finally, the media will elect a few official pundits who are (a) familiar enough with the 1960s innovations to predict next year's Cyberlandscape for the AOL crowd, but (b) not *so* familiar with the history of these innovations that they sound unconvincing when crediting them to the rich people and companies of the 1990s.

Where does that leave me? I'm not one of the pioneers of the 1960s—I was born in 1963. I'm not a rich person of the 1990s—I forgot to get rich during the Great Internet Boom. I'm not an official pundit, except once for an Italian newsweekly (see http://photo.net/philg/narcissism/narcissism.html for the full story)—I guess I must have done a bad job for those Italians.

I may be a failure, but they can't take away my aspirations. There isn't much point in aspiring to be a pioneer of the 1960s. The '60s are over, even if some folks in my hometown (the People's Republic of Cambridge, Massachusetts) haven't admitted it. There isn't much point in my aspiring to be an official real dead-trees media pundit. My friends would only laugh at me if I started writing for *Wired* magazine. However, being a rich person of the 1990s has a certain indefinable appeal for me. Perhaps it is this comment I made on one of my Web pages: "Not being a materialist in the U.S. is kind of like not appreciating opera if you live in Milan or art if you live in Paris. We support materialism better than any other culture. Because retailing and distribution are so efficient here, stuff is cheaper than anywhere else in the world. And then we have huge houses in which to archive our stuff."

Materialism is definitely more fun when one is rich. How to get there, though. Conventional wisdom in Italy has it that "There are three ways to make money. You can inherit it. You can marry it. You can steal it." Based on my survey of the computer industry, the third strategy seems to be the most successful. With that in mind, here are some ideas that I've stolen from smarter people.

Should Software Really Be Sold Like Tables and Chairs?

Steve Ward is probably the only MIT computer science professor that any undergraduate would ever want to be like. If you walk into the average MIT CS lecture, you'll see what looks like a troll in used clothing mumbling out equations to a sea of somnambulant nerds. Ward, on the other hand, stands over six feet tall, is crisply dressed, and speaks coherently. He looks like he would know what wines to order with a seven-course French dinner.

Talking to Ward about computer science reminds me of what it must have been like to be an Irish monk when the Roman Empire was disintegrating and Europe descended into barbarism. It doesn't matter what your idea is. Steve has a more elegant one, and he had it in the 1980s. Here's one thing I've learned from Professor Ward.

The Nub

We software developers live in a pre-industrial age. We don't build on each other's work, we reinvent the wheel over and over again—and the bumps in the wheel. Ultimately, it is the user who gets the stuffing beaten out of him.

It is the way that software is sold that keeps software development mired in the 1950s. Software is put into packages and sold like tables or chairs. That's great because we have a highly efficient distribution and retail system for tables and chairs and because we've been buying things like tables and chairs for centuries. It would all work out beautifully for everyone if only tables and chairs needed periodic upgrades, if tables and chairs required documentation and support, if tables and chairs could be downloaded over networks, if users developed significant investments in the interfaces of tables and chairs, and if it cost $30 million to develop a slightly better table or chair from scratch.

Look at the choices that current software pricing forces people to make.

Johnny the User Johnny the user is a university student. He wants to use Adobe PhotoShop for a class project and has a Macintosh on the Internet in his dorm room. He can buy PhotoShop for $500, he can steal it from a friend, or he can drive to Kinko's to rent a Macintosh for a few hours.

Suppose that Johnny buys PhotoShop. Adobe gets $500 and is happy. Johnny gets manuals and support and he's working efficiently. Johnny doesn't have to drive anywhere so society doesn't suffer from increased pollution and traffic congestion. Unfortunately, probably not too many students are happy about paying $500 for software that they're only going to use for a day or two. Also, when Johnny next wants to use the software, he'll probably find that the version he has no longer runs with Apple's new operating system, or that Apple has gone belly-up and his version doesn't run on his new Windows NT machine, or that the instructor wants him to use a program feature that is only in the latest version of PhotoShop.

Let's be realistic. Johnny probably isn't going to buy PhotoShop. He's going to steal it from Adobe by borrowing the CD-ROM from his friend's friend. He'll spend his $500 on a spring break trip to Florida. Unfortunately for Johnny, PhotoShop is almost impossible to use without the manuals. Johnny drives to the bookstore and spends $30 on an "I stole the program and now I need a book on how to use it" book. Johnny wastes some time; Adobe gets no money; society has to breathe Johnny's exhaust fumes and wait behind his jalopy at intersections.

If Johnny is remarkably honest, he may go to Kinko's and rent a Macintosh running PhotoShop. This is great except that the network was supposed to free users from having to physically move themselves around. Johnny is inconvenienced and society is inconvenienced by the externalities of his driving.

Amanda the User Interface Programmer Amanda is writing some user interface code for an innovative new spreadsheet program. She wants it to appeal to the users of Microsoft Excel and Lotus 1-2-3 but knows that they have spent years learning the user interface quirks of those programs. Amanda has to choose between copying the user interface and spending ten years in federal court or making her new program work in a gratuitously different manner (in which case each user has to spend several days relearning commands that they already knew in their old programs).

Joey the Image Editor Programmer Joey wants to make a nice program for quickly converting all the images on a PhotoCD. Adobe PhotoShop does 99 percent of what his program needs to do. Unfortunately, lacking that last one percent, PhotoShop is useless for the task at hand. Adobe had no incentive to make the pieces of PhotoShop callable by other programs, so Joey has to start from scratch or abandon his project. Should Joey succeed, his program will contain duplicates of code in PhotoShop. Joey's software, though, will have bugs that Adobe stamped out in 1991. It will ultimately be the user who is pushing the Macintosh restart button and losing work.

Adobe the Software Publisher Adobe wants to maximize its revenue under the "tables and chairs" software vending model. It will do this by keeping manuals and documentation out of the hands of users who don't pay, by not putting full documentation up on the Web, for example. Adobe will withhold support from users who stole the binary. Adobe will sue companies who copy the PhotoShop user interface. Adobe will not share its internal program design with anyone.

CHOICES SUMMARY

Selling software like tables and chairs forces users to make a buy/steal choice with a threshold of $500. It forces thousands of confusing new user interfaces into the marketplace every year. It forces programmers to start from scratch if they are to market anything at all.

A BETTER WAY

Suppose that Jane's Software Consortium (JaneSoft) negotiated deals with a bunch of software authors. Users would pay a fixed $x per year to JaneSoft for the right to use any software that they wished. Each user's computer would keep track of which company's programs were actually executed and file a report once a month with JaneSoft. Based on those usage reports, JaneSoft would apportion its revenues to software publishers and authors.

Let's revisit the same people under the new model . . .

Johnny the User Johnny can decide whether to (a) pay his $x a year and get everything, or (b) buy a few important packages under the tables-and-chairs model and steal/rent everything else. Assuming he pays the $x a year, Johnny may legally run any software that he finds useful. It gets delivered via the Internet to his machine along with any documentation and support that he may need.

Amanda the User Interface Programmer Amanda still wants her users to be able to employ the familiar Lotus user interface. It is now in Lotus's interest to tell other programmers how to call their user interface code. Because licensing consortium revenues are apportioned according to usage, every time a Lotus menu is displayed or command is run, Lotus is going to get some extra money from the consortium. Amanda's company will get paid when her new spreadsheet core program is executing. Lotus and Amanda's company are sharing revenue and it is in both of their interests to make the user productive.

Joey the Image Editor Programmer Adobe now has an incentive to document the internal workings of PhotoShop. Joey can tap into these and add his one percent. Because PhotoShop is an old and well-debugged program, the user gets a much more reliable product. Joey only gets 1 percent of the revenue derived from any user's session with "his" software, but he only did one percent of the work so he can move on to other projects. Furthermore, because he doesn't have to come up with an attractive physical package, his cost of entering the software market is considerably reduced.

Adobe the Software Publisher Adobe's main goal now is to get as many people as possible to run PhotoShop and for as long as possible. Remember that a user won't pay extra to run PhotoShop more frequently, but if a user spends a greater percentage of his time in PhotoShop then Adobe will get a greater percentage of the licensing consortium's revenues. Adobe's first likely action would be to put the PhotoShop manuals on the Web, possibly open only to people who are licensing consortium subscribers. Making telephone and e-mail support fast and effective becomes a priority because Adobe doesn't want any user to give up on PhotoShop and run Doom instead. Hardcopy manuals are mailed out free or at nominal cost.

Adobe sponsors conferences to help other software developers call PhotoShop's internals. Adobe will not file any look-and-feel lawsuits because they're getting paid every time someone uses their user interface code.

NEW WORLD ORDER

Five years after software licensing consortia are in place, the world looks very different. Fewer programs are written from the ground up, fewer users stab away cluelessly at stolen programs for which they lack documentation, fewer look-and-feel lawsuits are filed, fewer bugs are created. Roughly the same amount of money is flowing to the software publishing industry, but the industry has better information about who its customers are and how useful they find their products.

My personal prediction is that two kinds of consortia would emerge. One kind would cater to business. Users would pay $x per year and get the old familiar software. Consortia catering to home users, however, would offer a $0 per year deal: You can use any software you want, but we're going to replace those startup screens and hourglasses with ads for McDonald's and Coke. Ask for a spell check in your word processor? While it is loading, an ad for Rolaids will ask you how you spell relief. Ask PhotoShop to sharpen a big PhotoCD scan? That thermometer progress bar will be buried underneath an ad reminding you how sharp you'd feel if you were dressed from head to toe in L.L. Bean clothing.

A LESS RADICAL APPROACH

Renting *software* rather than the physical machines on which it is installed would achieve some of the same goals as blanket licensing and metering. Certainly a casual user would prefer to spend $1 an hour trying out PhotoShop than $500 for "the package" and then $100 a year for updates. Adobe would then have many of the same incentives to make documentation and support readily available.

However, renting software would not solve the deeper problem created by software developers standing on each other's toes rather than each other's shoulders.

PRIVACY

I probably wouldn't want my employer to know that I spent 95 percent of my time running Netscape and Doom when I was supposed to be using Word and Excel. So I want to make sure that a public-key encryption system can be designed so that nobody can figure out which programs were run on my machine. Anonymity is good, but it opens the door to fraud by software publishers. Suppose that I write a text editing program. It isn't nearly as good as Emacs, so nobody uses it. But if I can figure out a way to file false usage reports that fool the consortia into thinking that 100,000 people ran my text editor for 2,000 hours each, I'll get a much larger than deserved share of license revenue. Again, public-key encryption and digital signatures can be used to fraud-proof the system.

WE HAVE A NETWORK; WE CAN DO BETTER

Selling software like tables and chairs is a fairly new idea. In the mainframe decades, customers rented software so that they could be sure of getting support and updates. The idea of selling software like tables and chairs was an innovation that came with the personal computer and it worked pretty well for a while. However, it doesn't make sense in a networked world.

Note: If you want to see how absurd the current system has gotten, visit the IBM Patent Server (http://patent.womplex.ibm.com/) and look at the patents assigned to your favorite software vendor.

YOUR USER'S BROWSER: A GE RANGE

Your reader's house will be a Class C subnet. Every device in the typical American home will have an IP address. The washing machine, the microwave oven, the VCR, the stove, the clock radio, the thermostat. Any device with an IP address is a potential Web client. As a Web publisher, you have to think about how your content can be used by browsers that aren't keyboard, mouse, and monitor.

Do I believe in this explosion of Internetworking because I'm a technology optimist? Have I decided to write for *Wired* magazine after all? No. I believe this because I've become a technology pessimist.

PRODUCT ENGINEERING: THEORY VERSUS REALITY

When I graduated from MIT in 1982, I was a technology optimist. I was a genius doing brilliant engineering. My work would go out the door into the arms of an adoring public whose lives would be enriched by my creations. Experience taught me that I had at least the first part of this right: New products indeed go out the doors of companies. As to the rest, well, sometimes those products work. Sometimes the documentation is adequate. Sometimes the consumer can figure out how to make it work. But mostly every time consumers buy a new gizmo they are in for a few days of misery and waiting in tech support phone queues. Our society can engineer lots of things that it can't support.

An engineer's age is thus determinative of his or her attitude toward home networking. Young engineers think that we'll have home appliance networking because it will make life easier for consumers. Gerry Sussman, my old advisor at MIT, is getting a little bit grizzled and probably wouldn't argue with my characterization of him as an old engineer. Gerry loves to pull a huge N ("Navy") RF connector out of his desk drawer to show students how it can be mated with the small BNC ("Bayonet Navy Connector") for expediency. "These were both designed during World War II," Gerry will say. "You don't get strain relief but it makes a perfectly good contact in an emergency. The guys who designed these connectors were brilliant. On the other hand, there has been a commission meeting in Europe for 15 years trying to come up with a common power-plug standard."

The problems of home appliance networking are human and business problems, not technical problems. There is no reason why a Sony CD player shouldn't have been able to communicate intelligently with a Pioneer receiver ten years ago. Both machines contain computers. How come when you hit "Play" on the CD player, the receiver doesn't turn itself on and switch its input to CD?

Why can't a Nikon camera talk to Minolta's wireless flash system? Or, for that matter, why can't this year's Nikon camera talk intelligently to last year's Nikon flash?

Computer engineers are confused into thinking that companies care about interoperability. In fact, the inherently monopolistic computer industry was dragged kicking and screaming toward interoperability by the United States federal government, the one buyer large enough to insist on it. Many of the standards in the computer industry are due to federal funding or conditions in government purchasing contracts. Buyers of home appliances are too disorganized to insist on standards. General Electric's appliance division, the market leader in the U.S., isn't even a sponsor of the Consumer Electronics Bus consortium. IBM is. AT&T Bell Labs is. Hewlett-Packard is.

Does this mean you have to figure out how to fry an egg on your PC or telephone before you'll have a really smart house? No. As I hinted up top, I think that companies such as GE will start to put Internet interfaces into their appliances as soon as about 20 percent of American households are wired for full-time Internet, for example, with cable modems (see Chapter 6). But they won't do it because they think it is cool for your GE fridge to talk to your Whirlpool dishwasher. They'll do it because it will cut the cost of tech support for them. Instead of paying someone to wait on the 800 line while you poke around with your head underneath the fridge looking for the serial number, they'll want to ping your fridge across the Internet and find out the model, its current temperature, and whether there are any compressor failures.

WHAT KINDS OF THINGS CAN HAPPEN IN A NETWORKED HOUSE?

My GE Profile range (see http://money.rules-the.net/philg/materialism/kitchen.html) already has a tall backsplash with an LED display. If GE had put a 10base-T outlet on the back to provide technical support then the next logical step would be to replace the LED display with a color LCD screen. Then I would be able to browse recipe Web sites from my stove top. Once I'd found the desired recipe, I would press "start cooking." A dialog box would appear: "JavaScript Alert: Preheat oven to 375?" After I'd confirmed that, the recipe steps would unfold before me on the LCD.

WHAT DOES THIS MEAN TO ME AS A WEB PUBLISHER?

Ubiquitous Internet and therefore ubiquitous Web browsers imply that publishers will have to adhere to Tim Berners-Lee's original vision of the Web: The browser renders the content appropriately for the display. This idea seemed laughable when the "weirdo displays" were VT100 terminals in the hands of physics post-docs. Who cares about those pathetic losers? They don't have enough money to buy any of the stuff we advertise on our site anyway.

So I watched as the sites I'd built for big publishers got tarted up with imagemaps and tables and frames and flashing GIFs and applets. If it looks OK in Netscape Navigator on a Mac or a PC, then ship it. Don't even worry whether it is legal HTML or not. Then one day WebTV came out. Suddenly there was a flurry of e-mail on the group mailing lists. How to redesign their sites to be compatible with WebTV? I had to fight the urge to reply, "I looked at my personal site on a WebTV the other day; it looked fine."

WebTV was a big shock to a lot of publishers. Yet WebTV is much more computer-like than any of the other household appliances that consumers will be connecting to the Web. Be ready: Focus on content. Standard HTML plus semantic tags can make your content useful to household devices with very primitive user interface capabilities.

PERSONALIZATION

Though I love to diss the bloated MIT administration and the hubris of computer science academics, I can say sincerely that one of the greatest privileges life can offer is teaching a section of MIT undergraduates.

My favorite course to TA is 6.041. Yes, all the courses at MIT are just numbers (the "6" refers to the Department of Electrical Engineering and Computer Science so it really isn't that much more dehumanizing than the "EECS 041" that you might find at another university). One of the reasons that I love 6.041 is the professor, Al Drake. He is one of the fully-human human beings that never seem to get past tenure committees these days. He's been teaching 6.041 for decades and he wrote the text: *Fundamentals of Applied Probability Theory.*

Note: Despite the name, Drake's book (McGraw-Hill, 1967) is the world's clearest statistics text. I tried to learn statistics about four times and gave up. Statistics books and courses cater to two audiences: People who are presumed unable to think and/or learn probability theory, and people who are mathematics graduate students. Drake only devotes one chapter to statistics but a few hours spent with it is much more illuminating than any of the MIT stats courses.

Each week in 6.041, I would meet with students in small groups. I'd make them go up to the blackboard and work through problems that they hadn't seen before. Partly the idea was to see how they were thinking and offer corrections.

Partly the idea was to prepare them to give engineering presentations and communicate their ideas. The student at the board wasn't really supposed to solve the problem, just coordinate hints from other students at the conference table.

One day I gave a problem to a quiet Midwestern girl named Anne. She studied it for a moment, walked over to the board, and gave a five minute presentation on how to solve it, mentioning all of the interesting pedagogical points of the problem, writing down every step of the solution in neat handwriting. Her impromptu talk was better prepared than any lecture I'd ever given in the class.

Anne and I were chatting one day before class.

"What did you do on Sunday?" she asked.

"Oh, I don't know. Ate. Brushed the dog. Watched *The Simpsons.* And you?" I replied.

"Me and my housemates decided to have a hacking party. We do this every month or so. Since we have a network of PCs running Unix at home, it is easy to get lots of people programming together. We couldn't decide what to build so I said 'Well, we all like science fiction novels. So let's build a system where we type in the names of the books that we like and a rating. Then the system can grind over the database and figure out what books to suggest.'" She said.

And?

"It took us the whole afternoon, but we got it to the point where it would notice that I liked Books A, B, and C but hadn't read Book D which other people who liked A, B, and C had liked. So that was suggested for me. We also got it to notice if you and I had opposite tastes and suppress your recommendations."

This was back in 1994. Anne and her friends had, in one afternoon, completed virtually the entire annual research agenda of at least two professors whom I knew at MIT (neither in my department, I'm relieved to note).

The first lesson to be drawn from this example is that Anne is a genius. The second is that an afternoon hack, even by a genius, isn't enough to solve the personalization problem. Yet if you cut through the crust of hype that surrounds any of the expensive Web server personalization software "solutions" available in 1997, all that you find underneath is Anne's afternoon hack. Nor am I aware of any publisher who has done better with software developed in-house (though I know Pathfinder is trying).

What's wrong with Anne's system? First, it imposes a heavy burden of logging in and rating on users. Given that we're going to lose our privacy and have an unfeeling computer system know everything about our innermost thoughts and tastes, can't it at least be a painless process?

Suppose we did get everyone in the world to subscribe to Anne's system and tirelessly rate every Usenet posting, every Web site, every musical composition, every movie, every book. Does this help me make the choices that matter? If

I've typed in that I like the *Waldstein* sonata, probably Anne's software can tell me that I wouldn't like the Pat Boone cover of AC/DC's *It's a Long Way to the Top (If You Wanna Rock and Roll)*. But will it help me pick among Beethoven's other 31 piano sonatas? Is it meaningful to rate Beethoven's sonatas on a linear scale: *Pastoral* good, *Appassionata* great, *Moonlight*, somewhere in between?

Suppose my tastes change over time? Consider that old French saying that "If you're not a liberal when you're young, then you have no heart; if you're not a conservative when you're old, then you have no mind." Perhaps I liked Guy de Maupassant and Dickens when I was foolish and young but now that I'm old, I've come to see the supreme truth of Ayn Rand. I don't want Anne's system recommending a bunch of sissy books about people helping each other when I could be reading about a perfect society where rich people rent rather than loan their cars to friends.

That's no big deal. We'll just expire the ratings after ten years. But what if my tastes change over the course of a few days? Last week I was content to sit through four hours of *Hamlet*. This week the InterNIC, with that mix of greed and incompetence peculiar to unregulated monopolies, ripped my (fully paid up) domain WEBTRAVEL.ORG out of their database. I need a comedy.

READER RATINGS: A BIG MISTAKE?

Why do we ask readers to explicitly rate content? Each American is being watched by so many computers so much of the time that if we have to ask a person what he or she likes, then that only reveals the weakness of our imagination and technology.

Ken Phillips, a professor at New York University, has been thinking about these issues since the late 1970s when he set up a massive computer network for Citibank. He asked me what I thought was AT&T's most valuable asset. I tried to estimate the cost of undersea cables versus the fiber links the crisscross the continent. Ken laughed.

"AT&T gives you long distance service so they know which companies you call and how long you spend on the phone with each one. AT&T gives you a credit card so they know what you buy. AT&T owns Cellular One so, if you have a cell phone, they know where you drive and where you walk. By combining these data, AT&T can go to a travel agency and say 'For $100 each, we can give you the names of people who drive by your office every day, who've called airline 800 numbers more than three times in the last month, who have not called any other travel agencies, and who have spent more than $10,000 on travel in the last year.'"

Ken is a lot smarter than I am.

As discussed in Chapter 7, Web publishers and marketers are trying to do some of this with persistent magic cookies issued by central ad delivery/tracking services. However, these systems are extremely crude compared to traditional direct marketing databases. Judging from last week's harvest of junk snail mail, I'd say that the world's IBM mainframes know that I recently bought a condo, that I won't go to a store to buy anything, that I will buy stuff from a catalog, and that I shave with a blade. Judging from last week's harvest of junk e-mail, I'd say that the world's Unix and NT servers have decided that I'm a regular reader of Web sites that in fact I haven't visited for two years, that I enter contests (I don't), that I buy junkware/middleware and Web authoring software (I don't), and that I'm in the market for a Russian or Ukranian bride (one out of four isn't bad, I guess).

My behavior on the Web is much more consistently logged than my behavior in real life. Why then is my Web profile so much less accurate? Partly because Web data is fragmented. Information about which files I've downloaded is scattered among many different sites' server logs. But mostly because people don't know what to do with their data. Server-side junkware and Web site marketers are invariably expert at telling a story about all the wonderful data that they can collect. Occasionally they actually do collect and store this data. However, once the data goes into the big Oracle table, it seldom comes back out.

Why not? Partly because of technology. Web sites are generally implemented in a stateless fashion, as per the spirit of the original protocols. Each request from a user is handled in isolation. Producing an up-to-date profile on User X requires sifting through all the available data for User X. A typical implementation would use a bunch of RDBMS tables to store this data. These will grow to hundreds of megabytes in size. Sifting through these tables and JOINing them with each other is not going to be quick no matter how smart your RDBMS software. Certainly it is not something that you can afford to do on every page request.

Switching to an object database for storing user profiles is potentially beneficial. I talk about this a bit in Chapter 11 and in fact am planning some experiments myself in this area, using Franz Common Lisp to drive ObjectStore. Certainly Lisp is a huge improvement in software development technology over the mishmash of Tcl, Perl, Java, and C that sit behind the average Web site. And certainly an object database could be orders of magnitude faster for certain kinds of queries. But the main barriers to working personalization are inadequate data models, inadequate user models, inadequate thinking about obtaining data from off-the-Web sources, and inadequate characterization of Web site content. The last barrier on the list ought to be easy to surmount. If my Web pages are in the Unix file system, nothing stops me from creating a database table with one row per Web page. The row would contain the Unix file name and some kind of description of its content. It sounds easy but if you think about it a bit, it is tough to imagine how to do a better job than just dumping all the words into a full-text indexer such as Excite for Web Servers. Anyway, even if we solve the content characterization problem, that still leaves all the hard user and data modeling problems.

What are the biggest, most sophisticated Web publishers doing right now to address these problems? Most of them are still trying to figure out how to add WIDTH and HEIGHT tags to their IMGs. Does the incompetence of publishers mean that hope is lost for personalization? Absolutely not. In fact, the best place for most "quiet personalization research" is at the client end.

CLIENT-SIDE PERSONALIZATION

My desktop machine knows that it is running Windows NT. If publishers added semantic tags to their sites (see Chapter 3), my Web browser could warn me that the software whose blurbs I was investigating wasn't available for NT. My desktop machine knows not only which Web pages I've downloaded, but also how long I've spent viewing each one. It knows which Web pages I've saved to my local disk. My desktop machine knows that I've sent a bunch of e-mail today to friends telling them how the InterNIC took my money and then shut down my domain. It can listen to my phone line and figure out that my autodialer has called the InterNIC 50 times and gotten a busy signal. It has watched me program one of my AOLservers to send InterNIC e-mail every 15 minutes. You'd think that my desktop machine could put all this together to say, "Philip, you should probably check out http://www.internicsucks.com. It also looks like you're going a little non-linear on this InterNIC thing. You ought to relax tonight. I notice from your calendar program that you don't have any appointments. I notice from your Quicken database that you don't have any money so you probably shouldn't be going to the theater. I notice that *Naked Gun* is on cable tonight. I don't see any payments in your Quicken database to a cable TV vendor so I assume you aren't a Cable Achiever. I remember seeing some e-mail from your friend David two months ago containing the words "invite" and "cable TV" so I assume that David has cable. I see from watching your phone line's incoming caller line ID that he has called you twice in the last week from his home phone so I assume he is in town. Call him up and invite yourself over."

I trust my desktop computer with my e-mail. I trust it with my credit card numbers. I trust it to monitor my phone calls. I trust it with my financial and tax data. I can program it to release or withhold this information. I don't have to rely on publishers' privacy notices. If publishers would stop trying to be clever behind my back, I would be happy to give them personal information of my choosing. Publishers could spend a few weeks sitting down to come up with a standard for the exchange of personalization information. Netscape would add a Profile Upload feature to Navigator 6.0. Then a magazine wouldn't have to go out and join an ad banner network to find out what I like; they could just provide a button on their site and I'd push it to upload my profile. This would be useful for more mundane transactions as well. For example, instead of each publisher spending $150,000 developing a shopping basket system and order form, they could just put an "upload purchase authorization and shipping address" button on their site. I'd type my credit card and mailing address just once into the browser's Options menu rather than 1,000 times into various publishers' forms.

Note: If I didn't tend to always use the same browser/computer to surf and/or was heavily dependent on mobile computing, I would probably want to designate a single hard-wired computer as my personalization proxy, more or less like the Internet Fish that Brian LaMacchia built back in 1995 (see http://www-swiss.ai.mit.edu/~bal). These are "semi-autonomous, persistent information brokers; users deploy individual IFish to gather and refine information related to a particular topic. An IFish will initiate research, continue to discover new sources of information, and keep tabs on new developments in that topic. As part of the information-gathering process the user interacts with his IFish to find out what it has learned, answer questions it has posed, and make suggestions for guidance." As far as a Web publisher is concerned, a proxy such as an Internet Fish looks exactly the same as a client.

WHAT DOES THIS MEAN TO ME AS A WEB PUBLISHER?

Take two tacks. First, count on the client-side (and proxy) personalization systems getting smart and pervasive. This is where the most useful systems are going to be built. You can help client-side systems by adding semantic tags to your content. As discussed in Chapter 3 and in http://photo.net/philg/research/shame-and-war-revisited.html, computers can't understand natural language and aren't likely to learn how any time soon. Thus you need to express, in a formal language, "This is a list of features for a commercial computer program; this program is only available for Intel processors running Windows 95; this program costs $95."

Sadly, even if you wanted to do the right thing as a publisher, it isn't possible today. There is no agreed-upon language for tagging the semantics of Web documents. People who set the Web standards have instead invested the past five years in devising ways to support more garish advertising. You can publish colored text. You can publish blinking text. You can publish blinking pictures. You can publish blinking pictures that make noise. You can publish moving blinking pictures that make noise. You just can't publish anything that is meaningful to another computer and that therefore might save a human being some time.

One day users will get tired of this. You can be ready for that day by keeping your content in a more structured, more semantically meaningful form than HTML.

In the meantime, you can take the second tack: banking on server-side personalization being done better and on a larger scale. Record user click streams. Record user click-throughs (see Chapter 7). Then sell the information! Remember the example of AT&T. Even if they made no money delivering cellular phone service, long distance service, and credit card transactions, they could still get quite fat by selling information about their users. With a sufficiently evil and refined system pervading the Internet, you might be able to make a living from a popular site without ever putting in a single banner ad. Just tell Honda that users A, B, and C downloaded several large JPEGs of the Acura NSX from http://money.rules-the.net/philg/cars/nsx.html, Canon that users D and E were studying the Nikon F4 review in http://photo.net/photo/, and American Airlines that users F, G, and H were reading the full story on Costa Rica in http://webtravel.org/cr/.

Collaboratively Exchanged Data Models

As discussed briefly in Chapter 2, corporations have been squandering money on computers for years and don't have too much to show for their investment. Suppose that Spacely Sprockets wants to buy widgets from Acme Widgets. Spacely Sprockets has an advanced computerized purchasing system. An employee in purchasing works through some online forms to specify that Spacely needs 2,500 widgets, Spacely part number W147, Acme model number A491, to be delivered on June 1. The order is stored in a relational database.

Acme is also a modern company. They have an integrated order entry, inventory, and billing system backed by an RDBMS. As soon as the order goes into the system, it sets into motion a synchronized chain of events in the factory.

How does the data for the 2,500-widget order get from Spacely to Acme? Each decade had its defining technology:

- In the 1970s, a Spacely employee printed out the order from the advanced Spacely system, stuck it into an envelope and mailed it to Acme.

An Acme employee opened the envelope and keyed the order into the Acme system, typing "25,000" instead of "2,500."

- In the 1980s, a Spacely employee printed out the order from the advanced Spacely system and faxed it to Acme. An Acme employee grabbed the order from the fax machine output bin and keyed the order into the Acme system, typing "25,000" instead of "2,500."
- In the 1990s, a Spacely employee pulls the order out of the advanced Spacely system and e-mails it to Acme. An Acme employee grabs the order from his or her inbox and rekeys the order into the Acme system, typing "25,000" instead of "2,500."

If this all sounds a little more efficient than the business world with which you're familiar, keep in mind that the whole process is repeated in the opposite direction when Acme wants to invoice Spacely for the 25,000 widgets.

What stops Spacely's computer from talking directly to Acme's? Pre-Internet, one would give up when faced with the difficulty of getting bits back and forth. Post-Internet, one *could* give up when faced with the difficulties of security. Can we be sure that Spacely's computer won't attempt any naughty transactions on Acme's computer? For example, if Spacely had full access to Acme's RDBMS, it could mark lots of invoices as having been paid. The issue of security is an anthill, however, compared to the craggy mountain of data model incompatibility.

Column names may be different. Acme's programmers choose "part_number" and Spacely's use "partnum." To us they look the same, but to the computer they might as well be completely different. Worse yet are differences in the meaning of what is in that column. Acme has a different part number for the same widget than does Spacely. Nor need there be a one-to-one mapping between columns. Suppose Spacely's data model uses a single text field for shipping address and Acme's breaks up the address into line_1, line_2, city, state, postal_code, and country_code columns? Nor finally need there be a one-to-one mapping between tables. Spacely could spread an order across multiple tables. An order wouldn't contain an address at all, just a factory ID. You'd have to JOIN with the factories table if you wanted to print out one order with a meaningful shipping address. Acme might just have one wide table with some duplication of data. Multiple orders to the same factory would just contain duplicate copies of the factory address.

We could fix this problem the way GM did. Go over to Germany and buy some data models from SAP (http://www.sap.com/). Then make every division of the company use these data models and the same part numbers for the same screws. Total cost? About one billion dollars. A smart investment? How can you doubt GM? This is the company that spent $5 billion on robots at a time when they could have purchased all of Toyota for about the same sum. Anyway, the bureaucrats at MIT were so fattened by undergrads paying $23,000 a year and so impressed by GM's smart move that they bought SAP data models, too. My advisor was skeptical that data models designed for a factory would work at a university. "Sure they will," I said, "You just have to think of each major as an assembly line. You're probably being modeled as a painting robot."

Was my faith in SAP shaken when, two calendar years and 40 person-years into the installation process, MIT still wasn't really up and running? Absolutely not. SAP is the best thing that ever happened to computer people. It appeals to businesses that are too stupid to understand and model their own processes but too rich to simply continue relying on secretaries and file cabinets. So they want to buy SAP or a set of data models from one of SAP's competitors. But since they can't understand their business processes well enough to model them themselves, they aren't able to figure out which product is the best match for those processes. So they hire consultants to tell them which product to buy. A friend of mine is one of these consultants. If I score a $1,250 a day Web consulting gig, I don't bother to gloat in front of David. His time is worth $6,500 a day. And he doesn't even know SQL! He doesn't have to do any programming. He doesn't have to do any database administration. He doesn't have to do any systems administration. David just has to fly first class around the world and sit at conference tables with big executives and opine that perhaps Oracle Financials would be better for their company than SAP.

There are plenty of rich stupid companies on the Web. Is it therefore true that the same "convert everyone to one data model" approach will achieve our objective of streamlined intercompany communication? No. There is no central authority that can force everyone to spend big bucks converting to a common data model. Companies probably won't spend much voluntarily either. Company X might have no objection to wasting billions internally but management is usually reluctant to spend money in ways that might benefit Company Y.

What does that leave us with? n companies on the Web technically able to share data but having n separate data models. Each time two companies want to share data, their programmers have to cooperate on a conversion system. Before everyone can talk to anyone, we'll have to build $n*(n-1)$ unidirectional converters (for each of n companies we need a link to n-1 other companies, thus the $n*(n-1)$). With just 200 companies, this turns out to be 39,800 converters.

If we could get those 200 companies to agree on a canonical format for data exchange then we'd only need to build 400 unidirectional converters. That is a much more manageable number than 39,800, particularly when it is obvious that each company should bear the burden of writing two converters (one into and one out of its proprietary format).

The fly in the ointment here is that developing canonical data models can be extremely difficult. For something like hotel room booking, it can probably be achieved by a committee of volunteer programmers. For manufacturing, it apparently is tough enough that a company like SAP can charge tens of millions of dollars for one copy of its system (and even then they haven't really solved the problem because they and the customers heavily customize their systems). For medical records, it is a research problem (see http://www.emrs.org/).

That's why the next section is so interesting.

Collaboratively Evolved Data Models

When I was 14 years old, I was the smartest person in the world. I therefore did not need assistance or suggestions from other people. Now that I've reached the age of 33, my mind has deteriorated to the point that I welcome ideas from other minds with different perspectives and experience.

Suppose I wanted to build a database for indexing photographs. When I was 14, I would have sat down and created a table with precisely the correct number of columns and then used it forever. Today, though, I would build a Web front-end to my database and let other photographers use my software. I'd give them the capability of extending the data model just for their images. After a few months, I'd look at the extensions that they'd found necessary and use those to try to figure out new features that ought to be common in the next release of the software.

Note: If this example sounds insufficiently contrived, it is because it is one of my actual back burner projects; check http://photo.net/photo to see if I've actually done it.

Ditto for my SPAM mailing list manager system (http://www.greenspun.com/spam/), described *ad nauseum* in Chapter 13. The interesting thing to do with it would be to let each publisher add extra columns to his or her private data model and then see what people really wanted to do with the system.

A much more challenging problem is building a computer system that can find commonality among the extensions that users have made to a data model and automatically spit out a new release of the canonical data model that subsumes 85 percent of the custom modifications (you want as much capability in the canonical data model as possible because off-the-shelf software will only be convenient when working with the standard portions of the model).

Why this obsession with data modeling? Computers can't do much to help us if we can't boil our problems down to formal models. The more things that we can formally model, the more that computers can help us. The Web is the most powerful tool that we've ever had for developing models. We don't need focus groups. We don't need marketing staff reading auguries. We don't need seven versions of a product before we get it right. We have a system that lets users tell us directly and in a formal language exactly what they need our data model to do.

GRAND CONCLUSION

The Internet is going to be big. You heard it here first.

Did you expect something more profound? Perhaps we should listen to an MIT professor who was asked the following:

Q: "Do you see the new technologies, by helping to increase the flow of information, to be a force toward decentralization of power or toward more democracy?"

A: "Certainly not in the rich countries. . . . It's not a big secret that the economy is moving very fast, in fact, from what used to be mainly national economies to an increasingly internationalized economy. So take the United States: Thirty years ago the question of international trade was not a big issue because the national economy was so huge in comparison with trade that it didn't matter all that much. You didn't have big debates about trade policy. Now that's changed. The international economy is enormous. In fact, it's not really trade, so about 40 percent of U.S. trade, as it's called, is actually internal to big transnational corporations. It means like one branch of the Ford Motor Company moving things to another branch which happens to be across a border. Forty is not a small amount and it's the same worldwide. But, in any event, the economy's becoming much more internationalized. It's much easier to move capital abroad. The effect of that is that production can be shifted much more easily to low-wage/high-repression areas elsewhere. And the effect of that is to bring the third-world model home to the United States and other rich countries. It means that these countries themselves are drifting toward a kind of a third-world model in which there is a sector of great wealth and privilege and a growing mass of people who are basically superfluous. They're not necessary for a profit either as producers or consumers. You can produce more cheaply elsewhere and the market can easily become the international wealthy sectors. You end up with south-central Los Angeles . . ."

I do apologize for that potentially unsettling bit. It seems that all the official Internet pundits who happen to be MIT professors were giving interviews to reporters from dead-trees magazines. So I turned to MIT's most cited professor: Noam Chomsky. The quote above comes from a 1993 interview printed in *Chomsky for Beginners* (David Cogswell, 1996; Writers and Readers; see http://www.worldmedia.com/archive/ for an extensive on-line collection of Chomsky's ideas).

I talked to Chomsky a bit about the above quote and it turns out that it doesn't really represent his thinking today on the subject of Internet:

"The answers depend on whose hands will be at the controls. Advanced technology, more integrated world economy (NB: relative to GNP, it's not so different now than early in this century), Internet/Web, etc., are in themselves neutral with regard to the rich/poor. They can liberate or oppress, like—say—a hammer. In the hands of a carpenter, it can help build a house for someone. In the hands of a torturer, it can bash in the person's skull. These are questions for action, not speculation, which is idle."

I had an MIT kid over to my house a few weeks ago. He said that he'd been working as a consultant to Netscape writing software to stream video. It turned out that Netscape was itself doing a consulting project for Hustler Magazine and that the ultimate application was streaming pornography.

"How do you feel about that morally?" asked one of my sincere liberally educated neighbors.

"Well, they paid me a lot of money," was Stuart's reply.

This gets us back to Noam Chomsky's answer in *Secrets, Lies and Democracy* (David Barsamian 1994; Odonian) to "What do you think about the Internet?"

> "I think that there are good things about it, but there are also aspects of it that concern and worry me. This is an intuitive response—I can't prove it—but my feeling is that, since people aren't Martians or robots, direct face-to-face contact is an extremely important part of human life. It helps develop self-understanding and the growth of a healthy personality.
>
> "You just have a different relationship to somebody when you're looking at them than you do when you're punching away at a keyboard and some symbols come back. I suspect that extending that form of abstract and remote relationship, instead of direct, personal contact, is going to have unpleasant effects on what people are like. It will diminish their humanity, I think."

INDEX

A

abstraction barriers, 249–250
active server pages (ASPs), 242
Adams, Ansel, 46
Adobe PhotoShop. *See* PhotoShop
ADSL (Asymmetrical Digital Subscriber Line), 107–108
advertising. *See* marketing and advertising
Allegro Store, 202
AltaVista, 41, 68
  graphic design, lack of recognition of, 141
  images, lack of recognition of, 141
  Java applets, lack of recognition of, 141
Amazon.com, 24–27
An Essay Concerning Human Understanding (Locke), 135
animation, 141–142
AOLserver, 97–99, 243–244
  API for, flexibility of, 154
  CGI scripts on, 98
  database-backed web sites created with, 177
  HTML (Hypertext Markup Language), programming in, 162–163
  Informix Web DataBlade, AOLserver conversion as workaround to, 239–240
  Netscape Enterprise/FastTrack compared, 100, 102
  RDBMS connectivity, 98
  redirect capability of, 154
  source code availability for, 98
  speed of, 99
  support for, 98
  Tcl software for, 97–98
  virtual servers, 99
Apache, 99
API (Application Programming Interface), 93–95
  calls, sample, 97–98
  different APIs on each server program, problems due to, 152
  flexibility of, 154
  Netscape Enterprise/FastTrack, 99–100
  Oracle WebServer 2.0, 235
  RDBMS integration products, API as factor in choice of, 245
  Tcl scripts. *See* Tcl scripts
  Web sites' creativity due to, 161
A Relational Model of Data for Large Shared Data Banks (Codd), 185–186
ArsDigita, 210, 212
ASP (active server pages), 242
Asymmetrical Digital Subscriber Line (ADSL), 107–108
automatic programming, 174

B

banner ads, 71, 73
Berners-Lee, Tim, 155, 341
birthday reminder system, creation of, 264–278
BooHoo system, 327–328
  dead links, 327
  e-mail notification of links with, 328
  instant updates, 327
  management distribution with, 328
  spam resistance, 327–328
browsers. *See* Web browsers
bulletin board systems
  e-mail notification, 288–294
  multiple forum support, 288–294
  user-requested features, implementation of, 288–294

C

C, 94–95
  APIs created with, 152
  Java compared, 139
  unreliability of, 136
cable modems, 107
calendar management systems, 264–278
cameras, digital, 50
Career Guide for Engineers and Scientists (Greenspun), 156
Cartesian product, 192, 195

case studies
birthday reminder system, creation of, 264–278
classified ad system, creation of, 295–306
full-text indexed bulletin boards, 294–295
categorization of classified ads, 297–298
CD-ROMs
Flashpix-format scans, 52
Kodak PhotoCD, 47–48
user interface, 39–40
CGI (Common-Gateway Interface) scripting, 93, 150–151
AOLserver, on, 98
Kodak PhotoCD, 49
new process started for each CGI script, 151–152
Perl CGI script, sample of, 151
RDBMS connections, 152
Tcl scripts. *See* Tcl scripts
CGI Programming on the World Wide Web (Gundavaram), 150
Chomsky for Beginners (Cogswell), 353
Chomsky, Noam, 353
Clark, Jim, 33
click-through servers, 117
client-side personalization, 346–347
Codd, E. F., 185–186, 200
Common Lisp Object System, 200
Common Object Request Broker Architecture. *See* CORBA (Common Object Request Broker Architecture)
compilers, 133, *134*, 135
computer languages (generally), 133–136
concurrency control, 182–183
connectivity, 104. *See also* RDBMS connectivity
ADSL (Asymmetrical Digital Subscriber Line), 107–108
cable modems, 107
flat-file databases, ODBC (Open Database Connectivity) access to, 250
ISDN (Integrated Services Digital Network), 104–106
ISP (Internet service provider) connectivity problems, risk of, 209–210
ODBC (Open Database Connectivity), 250–251
T1 lines, 106, 210
Consumer Electronics Bus consortium, 341
content of site, samples of, 1–4
cookies
marketing and advertising, as information source for, 121–125, 345
Microsoft Internet Explorer cookie files, 125
Netscape Navigator cookie files, 121, 125
personalization, as information source for, 345
server logs issuing, 115–116, 121–125
copyright infringement, 64–65
CORBA (Common Object Request Broker Architecture), 222–223, 224
Concurrency Control Service, 223
semantic mismatches, 224

D

database administrator (DBA), 208
database-backed Web sites, 170
AOLserver used to create, 177
data models, 171
designing, 171–173, 176–177
failure in, causes of, 210
form design, 171–172
full-text searches on, 173
Meta-HTML used to create, 177. *See* Meta-HTML
middleware, use of, 177–178
Oraperl used to create, 177
prototype for, creation of, 172–173
relational database management system backed Web sites. *See* RDBMS-backed Web sites
SQL statements for, 176
Tcl program for, sample, 228–229
transactions, 171
database management systems, 181–183
atomicity property of, 183
consistency of, 183–184
data retrieval from, 184–185
durability of, 184
illegal transactions, handling of, 183–184
index files, 184–185
isolation property of, 184
object-oriented database management systems. *See* object-oriented database management systems
relational database management systems. *See* RDBMS (relational database management systems)
servers, 215
transaction processing, requirements for, 183–184
database table, backend loop through, 275–278
data models
collaboratively evolved, 351–352
customizing, 351–352
incompatibility between, 349–351
information exchanged between, 349–351
object database management systems, adding data models to, 200
DBA (database administrator), 208
dbANYWHERE, 140
Debabelizer, 55–56
declarative languages, 186
Dertouzos, Michael, 33–34
development environments, 140
digital cameras, 50
digital image library, 47
Kodak PhotoCD, 47–48
uploading, 49–50
digital signatures, 339
Dollar Signs: An Astrological Guide to Personal Finance (Morabito), 175
Double Click, 125
Drake, Al, 342
drum scanners, 50

E

EDSAC (Electronic Delay Storage Automatic Computer), 174
Electric Press, 209
Electronic Document Interchange (EDI), 14
Ellison, Larry, 201, 236
Emacs, 85
e-mail
alerts, 298
birthday reminder system, 264–278

BooHoo system, notification of links to, 328
bulletin board systems, e-mail notification of new postings to, 288–294
classified ads, alerts for, 298
list, Tcl program to create, 228–229
MAILTO tags, 229
spam resistance, 327–328
Engelbart, Douglas, 334
examples. *See* case studies
Exploring Java (Niemeyer and Peck), 141

F

file systems, 181–183
Filo, David, 78
Flashpix, 51–52
flat-file databases, 181–183
data retrieval from, 184
ODBC (Open Database Connectivity) access to, 250
Fox, Brian, 165
Franz Inc., 202
full-text indexing
bulletin board systems, 294–295
Oracle ConText, 296
relational database management systems (RDBMS), 202–203
search engines, 70
Fundamentals of Applied Probability Theory (Drake), 342

G

Gates, Bill, 6, 33, 82, 90, 122, 155–157, 236
GIF files, 51, 53
GNNserver. *See* AOLserver
graphic design
AltaVista, lack of recognition by, 141
user interface design compared, 172
graphics, search engines not reading, 71–72

H

hardware, 89, 93
Hayes, Simon, 319
Hewlett-Packard, 50, 88, 90
hierarchical databases, 186
home appliance networking, 340–341
home pages. *See* Web sites
HTML (Hypertext Markup Language), 34
AOLserver programming in, 162–163
basic HTML document, sample of, 36
document structure, 35–39
extended version of, programming in, 162
formatting, 38–39
HEIGHT attribute for images, 62
image attributes, 62–63
Informix Web DataBlade as server-side extension to. *See* Informix Web DataBlade
Meta-HTML. *See* Meta-HTML
NetCloak's use of, 165–166
programming language, as, 163–166
semantic tags, 38, 347–348
server-parsed HTML, 162–163
SQL queries embedded in, 236–237
Web Tools Review, 34–35
WIDTH attribute for images, 62
HTTP (Hypertext Transfer Protocol), 145
Hypertext Markup Language. *See* HTML (Hypertext Markup Language)

I

IBM, 155, 250
IIOP (Internet Inter-ORB Protocol), 222
IIS (Internet Information Server), 242
Illustra
online backups with, 207–208
SQL techniques, use of, 194
Illustra/Informix, 200, 203
ImageMagick, 56–60
images/photographs
AltaVista's lack of recognition of, 141
attention of readers, as means of attracting, 45–46
copyright information, adding, 60
digital cameras, 50
digital image library. *See* digital image library
drum scanners, 50
Flashpix, 51–52
GIF files, 51, 53
HEIGHT attribute for, 62
ImageMagick, 56–60
JPEG files, 51
Kodak PhotoCD. *See* Kodak PhotoCD
library, digital image. *See* digital image library
Live Picture, 50–51
loading, 53, 62
Meta-HTML used to code, 164
monitors, contrast range of, 46–47
NIFRGB, 51
PhotoCD. *See* Kodak PhotoCD
PhotoShop. *See* PhotoShop
Photo YCC, 51
Picture Imaging Workstations (PIWs), 48
prints, contrast range of, 46
scanners, 47
single color compression, 51
slides, contrast range of, 46
Travels with Samantha, 46, 61, 68
WIDTH attribute for, 62
WWWis program, 62
index files, 184–185
indexing, full-text. *See* full-text indexing
Informix/Illustra, 200, 203
Informix Universal Server, 200
Informix Web DataBlade, 236–238
AOLserver conversion as workaround to, 239–240
deficiencies in, list of, 240
EXEC Perl as workaround to, 239
Meta-HTML conversion as workaround to, 240
quotes in, 238
syntax, 237
transaction, each page executing as single, 239
Integrated Services Digital Network (ISDN), 104–106
interlaced GIFs, 53
Internet Fish, 347
Internet Information Server (IIS), 242
Internet interfaces on appliances, 341–342
Internet Inter-ORB Protocol (IIOP), 222
Internet service provider (ISP). *See* (ISP) Internet Service Provider
interpreted languages, *134,* 135
intranets, 144–145
IP addresses
home devices having, 340
server logs, 115, 126
ISDN (Integrated Services Digital Network), 104–106
ISP (Internet Service Provider)

connectivity problems, risk of, 209–210
Electric Press, 209
requirements for, 210

J

Java, 133–135, 133–136. *See also* Java applets
animation, limitations on usefulness of, 141
browser crashing due to, 139
Class Loader as security component for, 138
C programs compared, 139
custom user interface with, 143, 146
documentation for, 140–141
example of use of, 144–146
interpreter, as, 136
longterm importance of, 141
multithreading feature of, 139
object database management systems, Java as programming language for, 201
ORB (Object Request Broker), 223
RDBMS-backed Web sites, compatibility of Java connections, 221
real-time responses as factor in using, 143
real-time updates as factor in using, 143–144
Security Manager as security component for, 138
security system, 138–139
type inference, 138
Unix ability to withstand crashes due to, 140
unreliability of, 139
user interface as factor in using, 143, 146
uses of, 142
Verifier as security component for, 138
widespread installation of, 136
Windows NT ability to withstand crashes due to, 140
Java applets
AltaVista's lack of recognition of, 141
Kodak PhotoCD, Java applets used to reference, 49
RDBMS-backed Web sites connections, 219, 221
unreliability of, 139
Java Language Reference (Grand), 141
The Java Language Specification (Gosling, Joy, and Steele), 141
Java Network Programming (Harold), 141
Java Threads (Oaks and Wong), 141
The Java Tutorial (Campione and Walrath), 141
JPEG files, 51
ImageMagick used to create, 59–60
photographs, use of JPEG files for, 53
PhotoShop conversion of PhotoCD Image Pacs to, 53–55
progressive JPEGs, 53
Web servers, organization on, 61–62
junkware, 177–178, 248–249

K

Kodak PhotoCD, 47–48
CGI scripts used to reference, 49
Java applets used to reference, 49
JPEG files, PhotoShop conversion of PhotoCD Image Pacs to, 53–55
uploading images from, 49–50
vendors, 48
Web support for, 49–50
WWWis run on, 62

L

LaMacchia, Brian, 347
line art, use of GIF files for, 53
links, 325, 327
BooHoo system, 327–328
Netscape links to your Web site, 161
redirects, linking to, 153–155
Yahoo, 325, 327
Linux operating system, 88
Lisp, 135, 139
abstraction barrier, as, 249
Common Lisp Object System, 200
object database management systems, Lisp Web servers for, 202
programming with, ease of, 199
Live Picture, 50–51
LiveWire, 100–102, 241
Locke, John, 135
log analyzer programs, 126–127
net.Analysis, 129
relational database-backed tools, 128–130
source code, availability of, 127
stand-alone log analyzers, 127
substrate-based log analyzers, 127
WebReporter, 128
wwwstat, 127–128
Loquacious system, 319–325

M

Macintosh
Knoll Gamma Corrector, 53–54
NeXT operating system, 84
Photoshop requirements, 53
Web servers, as, 84
mailing list system, creation of, 254–260, 261–264
marketing and advertising, 15, 73
banner ads, 71, 73
cookies as information source for, 121–125, 345
server log as information source for, 116–121
Web servers, personalization of, 343–344
Mastering Regular Expressions (Friedl), 240
Mazan, Duffy, 209
memory leaks, 86–87
Meta-HTML, 163–166, 241–242
images, coding, 164
Informix Web DataBlade, Meta-HTML conversion as workaround to, 240
RDBMS integration products, as, 241–242
search engines, META elements added to increase hits with, 74–75
Microsoft, 50, 242–243, 249–250
Microsoft Internet Explorer, cookie files of, 125
middleware, 177–178, 248–249
Minsky, Henry, 165
mirrored disks, 89, 93, 205
Moon, Dave, 199–200
multithreading, 139

N

NaviServer. *See* AOLserver
net.Analysis, 129
NetCloak, 165–166
net.Genesis, 129
Netscape Enterprise/FastTrack
AOLserver compared, 100, 102
APIs for, 99–100
client objects, 101–102
database connectivity, 102
development cycle for, 100
LiveWire, 100–102, 241
objects, use of, 101
project objects, 101
redirect capability of, 153–154
request objects, 101
server objects, 101
shrink-wrapped software for, 103
source code availability of, 103
speed of, 103
support for, 103
Windows NT, process run on, 102
Netscape LiveWire, 100–102, 241
Netscape Navigator, 52
cookies files, 121, 125
links to your Web site from, 161
text editor, as, 237
NeXT operating system, 84

O

object-oriented database management systems, 197–200
attributes of object, 201
C++ applications for, 201
class definitions, changing, 200
Common Lisp Object System, 200
data models, adding, 200
data storage, 200
functions, examples of, 198–199
identities of object, 201
INSERT statements, 198
Java as programming language for, 201
Lisp Web servers for, 202
personalization with, 202
RDBMS connectivity, 202
relational database management system compared, 201
SELECT statements, 198–199
table definitions, examples of, 197–198
user profiles stored on, 345
user tracking, 202
ODBC (Open Database Connectivity), 250–251
OpenMarket, 129
Oracle, 201
connectivity, 249–250
ConText option, 203, 296
PL/SQL, use of, 194
pricing methods of, 203–204
Oracle DBA Handbook (Loney), 205–206
Oracle WebServer 2.0, 103–104, 233–236
API design, 235
PL/SQL program, sample, 229–231
URLs, inability to register, 235
ORB (Object Request Broker), 222

P

Perl, 150
CGI script, sample of, 151
Informix Web DataBlade, EXEC Perl as workaround to, 239
Oraperl used to create database-backed Web sites, 177
personalization, 343–344, 348
client-side personalization, 346–347
cookies as information source for, 345
reader ratings, need for, 344
user profiles, 345–346
Web site content, characterization of, 345–346
Phillips, Ken, 344
PhotoCD. *See* Kodak PhotoCd
photographs. *See* images/photographs
PhotoShop, 50–51, 146, 336–337
Action Lists, 55
GIF files, conversion of PhotoCD Image Pacs to, 53–55
JPEG files, conversion of PhotoCD Image Pacs to, 53–55
PhotoCD Image Pacs, conversion of, 53–55, 59–61
requirements for, 53
Picture Imaging Workstations (PIWs), 48
Pinkerton, Brian, 68, 76
procedural programs, 186
product engineering, 340–341
profit-generating Web sites
categories of, 15–21
medical example, 23–24
real estate example, 23
travel example, 22–23
programming history, 174–175
proxy servers, 114–115
public key encryption, 339
publishing models
collaborative information sites, 15–16, *18*, 20, 169
medical example, 24
multiple database query sites, 17, 20, *21*, 170
real estate example, 23
server-side program sites, 17, *19*, 20, 169–170
traditional information sites, 15, *16*, 20, 169, 170
travel example, 22, 23

Q

query processor, 71

R

Rabkin, Eric, 333
RDBMS-backed Web sites, 215–219
abstraction barriers, 249–250
administration of, tools for. *See* RDBMS/Web tools
architecture for fast, *218*, 219
birthday reminder system, creation of, 264–278
BooHoo system. *See* BooHoo system
building, comparison chart of technologies for, *246–247*
bulletin board systems, creation of. *See* bulletin board systems
classified ad system, creation of, 295–306
compatibility of Java connections, 221
connectivity, 249–250
CORBA servers. *See* CORBA (Common Object Request Broker Architecture)
diagram of, 218
IIOP (Internet Inter-ORB Protocol), 222
Java applet connections, 219, 221

licensing issues with use of Java applet connections, 221
mailing list system, creation of, 254–260, 261–264
ODBC (Open Database Connectivity), 250–251
ORB (Object Request Broker), 222
performance drain with Java applet connections, 221
PUBLIC database on, 221
RDBMS client, 215–219
RDBMS server, 215–219
security risk of Java applet connections, 221
static Web services sharing single, 261–264
tools for. *See* RDBMS/Web tools
Web client, 215–219
Web server, 215–219

RDBMS client, 215–219

RDBMS connectivity, 95
AOLserver, 98
CGI (common-gateway interface) script, 152
object database management systems, 202
Web server programs, as factor in choice of, 95

RDBMS integration products
AOLserver. *See* AOLserver
API as factor in choice of, 245
choosing, factors in, 244–245
Informix Web DataBlade. *See* Informix Web DataBlade
Internet Information Server (IIS), 242
Meta-HTML, 241–242
Netscape LiveWire, 100–102, 241
Oracle WebServer 2.0. *See* Oracle WebServer 2.0
WebObjects, 242

RDBMS (relational database management system). *See* relational database management system (RDBMS)

RDBMS server, 215–219

RDBMS vendors
choice of, 202–203
full-text search engines as factor in choice of, 202–203
license fees, 204
Microsoft, pricing methods of, 204
online backups, methods of, 207–208
Oracle, pricing methods of, 203–204
pricing methods of, 203–204
SQL, inclusion of, 202–203

RDBMS/Web tools, 245–246
canned web server admin pages, 248
junkware, 177–178, 248–249
middleware, 177–178
spreadsheet-like database editors, 248

redirects, 113, 153–155

referer URL, 72–73

registration to access sites, 77

relational database management system (RDBMS), 185–193
backups for, 206–208
bugs in RDBMS as cause of failure in database-backed Web sites, 210
Cartesian product as result of query in, 192, 195
click-through server connections, 117–121
client programs, 215–219
concurrency control, 182–183, 279–281
creation of, 187–193
database administrators, 208
database-backed bulletin board systems, 281–288
diagrams of, *216–217*
disk configurations to increase performance of, 205–206
disk mirroring to increase performance of, 205
firewalls as security management for, 226–227
full-text indexing on, 202–203
Informix Web DataBlade. *See* Informix Web DataBlade
integration products for. *See* RDBMS integration products
license fees for, 204
log analyzer programs as, 128–130
maintenance, tools for. *See* RDBMS/Web tools
Netscape LiveWire. *See* Netscape LiveWire
object database management systems compared, 201
offline backups, 207
online backups, 207–208
operating system problems as cause of failure in database-backed Web sites, 210
Oracle WebServer 2.0. *See* Oracle WebServer 2.0
passwords as security management for, 225–226
performance of, methods of increasing, 204–206
redundant network connectivity, 208–209
reliability of, 208–210
security issues, 225–226
server programs, 215–219
speed of, methods of increasing, 204–206
spreadsheets compared, 187
SQL, use of. *See* SQL (Structured Query Language)
system administration problems as cause of failure in database-backed Web sites, 210
tables in, 187
tools for maintenance. *See* RDBMS/Web tools
usernames as security management for, 225–226

remote servers, 81

The Road Ahead (Gates), 175

S

SAP, 349–350

scanners, 47
drum scanners, 50
Kodak PhotoCD, 47–48

SCSI controllers, 89

search engines, 67–68
advertising by buying words on, 73
AltaVista, 41, 68, 141
banner ads, 71, 73
components of, 68–71
crawlers, 68
exposure in, 71–72
full-text indexing with, 70
graphics not read by, 71–72
hiding content from, 76–77
listing with, 68
META elements added to increase hits with, 74–75
query processor, 71
registration to access sites, 77
text used to increase hits, 74–75
user data gathered through, 72–74

WebCrawler, 68, 76
Web servers reprogrammed to increase hits with, 75
Secrets, Lies and Democracy (Barsamian), 353
semantic tags, 38, 347–348
server logs
access to Web server, logging all, 112–113
alternative methods of tracking information, 117–121
analyzing. *See* log analyzer programs
bytes sent, logging, 112
cached copies of documents, accessing, 114
click-throughs, tracking, 116–121
client machine, logging, 112
content, using information from server logs for refining, 126
cookies, issuing, 115–116, 121–125
date of connection, logging, 112
document, determining number of people accessing specific, 113–115
errors, locating, 126
hidden sites, locating, 126
host name lookup, 126
IP addresses, 115, 126
log analyzer programs. *See* log analyzer programs
marketing and advertising, as information source for, 116–121
non-existent files, logging requests for, 112–113
proxy servers, use of, 114–115
reading, 115
redirects, need for, 113
referer headers, 112, 116
request line sent from browser, logging, 112
reverse DNS lookups, 115
security proxies, distortion of Web server statistics due to, 114–115
status codes, logging, 112
time of connection, logging, 112
user activity, tracking, 112–125
user-agent header, logging, 112
visual thread analysis of, 115–116
server-parsed HTML, 162–163
servers. *See* also Web servers
click-through servers, 117
comment servers, 319–321
CORBA servers. *See* CORBA (Common Object Request Broker Architecture)
database management systems, 215
proxy servers, 114–115
remote servers, 81
virtual servers, 99
server-side programming, 149
CGI scripts. *See* CGI (Common-Gateway Interface) scripting
HTML as. *See* HTML
Informix Web DataBlade. *See* Informix Web DataBlade
server APIs. *See* API (application programming interface)
Shockwave animation, limitations on usefulness of, 141
Siegel, David, 41, 126
signatures, digital, 339
software development, 335
image editor programmer options, 336–337
pricing of software. *See* software pricing
privacy issues, 339
publisher options, 337
renting software, 339
user interface programmer options, 336
software licensing consortium, 337–339
software pricing
publisher options, 337
RDBMS vendors, 203–204
software licensing consortium, 337–339
user options based on, 336
software reliability, history of, 139–140
Solaris, 86–87
source code
AOLserver, source code availability for, 98
log analyzer programs, 127
Netscape Enterprise/FastTrack, source code availability of, 103
Web server programs, source code availability as factor in choice of, 95–96
spam resistance, 327–328
spreadsheets, 174
database editors, spreadsheet-like, 248
relational database management system (RDBMS) compared, 187
Sproull, Bob, 333
SQL (Structured Query Language), 186
abstraction barrier, as, 250
database-backed Web sites, statements for, 176
Data Definition Language (DDL) statements, 188
Data Manipulation Language (DML) statements, 188
DELETE statements, 192
HTML, SQL queries embedded in, 236–237
INSERT statements, 190–191
joins, 191–192
many-to-one relations, 190
ODBC (Open Database Connectivity) used to issue, 251
online tutorials, 197
primary keys, 187–188, 191
reference books for, 197
SELECT statements, 189–190, 193–194
self-joins, 194–197
single quotes used in, 188–189
subqueries, 196–197
Tcl procedures and, 194–197
timestamps, use of, 194–197
UPDATE statements, 192–193
Stallman, Richard, 85
stand-alone log analyzers, 127
Steele, Guy, 141
Stock, Kevin, 177, 233
Structure and Interpretation of Computer Programs (Abelson and Sussman), 135
substrate-based log analyzers, 127
Sussman, Gerry, 340
Sutherland, Ivan, 333
Sybase, 202, 249
Symantec Cafe, 140
Symbolics, 199–200

T

T1 lines, 106, 210
Tcl script
AOLserver, Tcl software for, 97–98
arithmetic capabilities of, 157
HTML files, Tcl functions called from server-parsed, 162–163
mailing lists, 228–229, 256–260

procedures, use of, 154, 157
quotes in, 238
sample function, 232–233
sample programs, 158–160, 228–229
SQL timestamps, use of, 194–197
Teach Yourself Java in 21 Days (Perkins and Lemay), 140
3M Precise Mousing Surface, 141
transaction processing, 25, 183–184
Travels with Samantha, 46, 61, 68
type inference, 138

U

uninterruptible power supply, 89, 93
Universal Resource Locator. *See* URLs
Unix, 85–87
batch processing in, 56
CGI scripting. *See* CGI (Common-Gateway Interface) scripting
Digital ALPHA hardware, 88
Emacs, 85
GCC compiler for, 85
Hewlett-Packard hardware, 88
Java, ability to withstand crashes due to, 140
Linux operating system, 88
Silicon Graphics hardware, 88
Sun hardware, 88
support for, 92
Windows NT compared, 91–93
URLs
inability to register, 235
referer URL, 72–73
Usenet, 279–281
user feedback, 309–310, 319
comment servers, 319–321
general topic questions, 316–318
management of, 316–325
Q&A forum for advice, 316–317
specific questions, 316
user interface design
graphic design compared, 172

V

virtual reality, 333
virtual servers, 99

W

Ward, Steve, 335
Web browsers
content, appropriateness of, 341–342
Java, browser crashing due to, 139
Netscape Navigator. *See* Netscape Navigator
redirects, linking to, 153–155
server logs logging request line sent from, 112
Web client, 215–219
WebCrawler, 68, 76
Web directories, 67, 78
WebObjects, 242
WebReporter, 128
Web server programs. *See* also Web servers
AOLserver. *See* AOLserver
Apache, 99
API for. *See* API (application programming interface)
CGI (common-gateway interface) script. *See* CGI (Common-Gateway Interface) scripting
choice of, factors in, 93
C programs, 94–95
example of use of, 145–146
logs for. *See* server logs
RDBMS connectivity as factor in choice of, 95
shrink-wrapped software, availability of, 96
source code availability as factor in choice of, 95–96
speed as factor in choice of, 97
support as factor in choice of, 95–96
Web servers, 215–219
creation of, example of, 210–212
firewalls, 226–227
HTML as programming language on, 163–166
Informix Universal Server, 200
JPEG files organized on, 61–62
Macintosh machines as, 84
Netscape Enterprise/FastTrack. *See* Netscape Enterprise/FastTrack
options for, 81–82
owner of machine inside someone else's network, 81–82
owner of machine inside someone your own network, 82
personalization of interface. *See* personalization
redirect capability of, 153–155
referer URLs, logging, 72–73
remote servers, 81
reprogramming to increase hits with search engines, 75
software for. *See* Web server programs
Unix machines as. *See* Unix
Uptime used for notification of your server being unreachable, 82
Windows 95 machines as, 84
Windows NT machines as. *See* Windows NT
Web sites
advertising on. *See* marketing and advertising
animation on, limitations on usefulness of, 142
API, creativity of site due to, 161
CGI scripting on. *See* CGI (Common-Gateway Interface) scripting
comments. *See* comment server
content of, examples of, 2–4
creativity of, 161
database-backed. *See* database-backed Web sites
evolution of a site, *310–315*
images on. *See* images
links. *See* links
magnet content, example of lack of, 10
marketing. *See* marketing and advertising
multiple views, presentation of, 4–7
non-collaborative sites, 149
performance engineering on, 161
publishing models for. *See* publishing models
purpose of, 7–10
RDBMS-backed Web sites. *See* RDBMS-backed Web sites
registration to access sites, 77
remote servers, use of, 81
revenue from, categories for generating, 15–21
rewards not financial of creating and maintaining, 27–28
user interaction with, 7–10

- user interface, 39–42
- user needs, criteria to determine if site is meeting, 4

Web Tools Review, 34–35, *118*, 121, 130, 319, 325
WebTV, 342
Windows NT, 89–91
- Hewlett-Packard hardware, 90
- Java, ability to withstand crashes due to, 140
- Netscape Enterprise/FastTrack run on, 102
- support for, 92
- Unix compared, 91–93

WWWis program, 62
wwwstat, 127–128

Y

Yahoo, 78, 149, 325, 327
Yang, Jerry, 78

Z

Zang, Ulla, 265